ARMY LIFE
OF AN
ILLINOIS SOLDIER

Shawnee Classics

A Series of Classic Regional Reprints for the Midwest

Personal Memoirs of John H. Brinton
Civil War Surgeon, 1861–1865
John H. Brinton

"Black Jack"
John A. Logan and Southern Illinois
 in the Civil War Era
James Pickett Jones

The Outlaws of Cave-in-Rock
Otto A. Rothert

A Woman's Story of Pioneer Illinois
Christiana Holmes Tillson
Edited by Milo Milton Quaife

Army Life
of an
Illinois Soldier

Including a Day-by-Day Record
of
Sherman's March to the Sea

Letters and Diary of
Charles W. Wills

Compiled by Mary E. Kellogg
Foreword by John Y. Simon

SOUTHERN ILLINOIS
UNIVERSITY PRESS

CARBONDALE AND EDWARDSVILLE

Foreword by John Y. Simon, copyright
© 1996 by the Board of Trustees,
Southern Illinois University
First published 1906 by Globe Printing Company
Printed in the United States of America

99 98 97   4 3 2

Library of Congress Cataloging-in-Publication Data

Wills, Charles Wright, 1840–1883
     Army life of an Illinois soldier : including a day-by-day record of
Sherman's march to the sea : letters and diary / of Charles W. Wills ; with
a new foreword by John Y. Simon.
     p. cm. — (Shawnee classics)
     1. Wills, Charles Wright, 1840–1883. 2. United States—History—
Civil War, 1861–1865—Personal narratives. 3. Sherman's March to the
Sea—Personal narratives. 4. Illinois—History—Civil War, 1861–1865—
Personal narratives. 5. United States. Army. Illinois Infantry Regiment,
8th (1861) 6. United States. Army. Illinois Infantry Regiment, 103rd
(1862–1865) 7. United States. Army. Illinois Cavalry Regiment, 7th
(1861–1865) I. Title.
    E601.W73   1996
    973.7'81—dc20   95-48898
ISBN 0-8093-2046-0 (pbk. : alk. paper)   CIP

The paper used in this publication meets the minimum requirements of American
National Standard for Information Sciences—Permanence of Paper for Printed
Library Materials, ANSI Z39.48-1984. ∞

CONTENTS

FOREWORD

Nearly every young man who went off to fight in the Civil War wrote home. Letters and diaries, treasured and preserved by family members, exist today in great quantity. Quality is another matter. One Michigan farm boy who wrote, "i don't no wat is a going on," and proved his point repeatedly, eventually attracted a modern scholar willing to explain "wat" to posterity. Books of routine and redundant soldier letters form a thicket that conceals those of value. One truly remarkable and incisive soldier's account, privately published in a small edition in 1906, has become a neglected classic.

Charles Wills of Canton, Fulton County, Illinois, a small town about twenty-five miles southwest of Peoria, enlisted as a private immediately after the Civil War began. He wrote frequently to his sister, Mary Emily Wills, and kept a diary during the campaigns of General William T. Sherman in the last year of the war. Wills had first enlisted in the Eighth Illinois Volunteers, a three months' regiment, then promptly reenlisted for three years. He went to war filled with ingenuous idealism and high spirits, hungry for excitement, and determined to chronicle his grand adventure. Wills's correspondence is that of a naive and high-spirited boy. In early letters he reported that he and his comrades "drink no liquors and keep ourselves as cleanly as possible. . . . Almost all are reading or writing, and I defy anyone to find 75 men without any restraint, paying more attention to the Sabbath. . . . Health generally excellent in our company, because we are all careful." Wills boasted that his company had refused to enlist "roughs."

Little is known of Wills's life before the Civil War. He was the son of Andrew and Eliza Brady Wills, originally from Pennsylvania and related to David Wills of Gettysburg, best remembered as the state agent who created the cemetery after the great battle in July 1863, arranged dedication ceremonies, invited Abraham Lincoln to speak, and served as his host. Andrew and Eliza Wills settled in Canton a few years before their son Charles Wright was born in 1840. Andrew was a clerk, a township assessor, and proprietor of a boarding house. Charles clerked in several stores, including one in Peoria that he left when he enlisted. He also attended the state normal university (now Illinois State University) at Bloomington.[1] Army life, he concluded, "beats clerking."

---

1. U.S. Census, Canton, Fulton Co., Ill., 1840, 1850; Ill. State Census, Canton, Fulton Co., Ill., 1855; U.S. Census, Bloomington, McLean Co., Ill., 1860; *Fulton County Ledger*, 29 Mar. 1883.

This twenty-one-year-old private became a twenty-four-year-old major during a bloody war. His letters and diary provide a chronicle of development from youth to manhood. On January 20, 1862, Colonel William Pitt Kellogg of the Seventh Illinois Cavalry, a friend from Canton, gave Wills a commission as first lieutenant and adjutant of the third battalion of his regiment. Major Jonas Rawalt, commander of that battalion, also came from Fulton County. Wills left the Eighth after nine months with some regret, "but cupidity and ambition" had overwhelmed his good intentions. He thought he might eventually have received a commission in the infantry but now held rank "without so much walking."

The son of a Congregational minister, Colonel Kellogg, born in Vermont in 1830 and educated at the Norwich Military Institute, practiced law in Canton for several years before the Civil War. In 1852, Kellogg first saw Lincoln in a Springfield courtroom, where he made a strong impression with his "tall spare form, his gaunt but intellectual face, his wonderfully piercing eyes, his profuse and careless hair, and somewhat negligent dress."[2] Kellogg headed the Fulton County delegation to the Republican Convention in Bloomington in 1856, where Lincoln delivered his famous "Lost Speech." In 1861, Lincoln rewarded Kellogg for his Republican party activity with an appointment as chief justice of Nebraska Territory. At the request of Governor Richard Yates of Illinois, Kellogg took a leave of absence from his territorial post to recruit the cavalry regiment. As of June 1, 1862, however, he resigned as colonel for reasons of health and returned to Nebraska. Shortly afterward, Wills lost the position of battalion adjutant, a rank abolished by military authority.

By this time, Wills had developed enough taste for rank to return to Fulton County to assist in recruiting a new regiment in which he could serve as a properly commissioned officer. Amos C. Babcock, a former Whig member of the Illinois legislature, who took the lead as presumptive colonel, resigned his commission almost immediately. Babcock preferred to accept the federal position of assessor of internal revenue but soon turned his attention to the cotton trade, using political connections that extended to the White House, where Lincoln complained that little proved "so troublesome to the government as the fierceness with which the profits of trading in cotten are

---

2. "The Recollections of William Pitt Kellogg," ed. Paul M. Angle, *Abraham Lincoln Quarterly* 3 (1945): 320. See John Edmond Gonzales, "William Pitt Kellogg, Reconstruction Governor of Louisiana, 1873–1877," *Louisiana Historical Quarterly* 29 (1946): 394–495; William T. Davidson, "Famous Men I Have Known in the Military Tract," *Transactions of the Illinois State Historical Society for the Year 1908* (Springfield: Illinois State Journal Co., 1909), 157; New Orleans *Times-Picayune*, 11 Aug. 1918.

sought."[3] While Babcock slunk toward wealth, Captain Wills marched with the 103rd Illinois. In June, however, Wills was "gobbled" for staff duty by Richard J. Oglesby, former colonel of the Eighth Illinois, who had since won promotion to major general. Wills chafed at service behind the lines with Oglesby, who still suffered from a wound received at Corinth in October 1862. When the 103rd Illinois joined Ulysses S. Grant's army at Vicksburg, Wills was left behind. When Wills rejoined his regiment in September 1863, the troops were once again on garrison duty. In November, the 103rd participated in the battle of Chattanooga. Of 237 men engaged, 20 were killed and 68 wounded, but two companies, one of them commanded by Wills, were on detached service rounding up horses to mount the regiment.[4] Wills could only "curse my luck to the best of my ability." "I get the blues," he wrote. "Haven't I a brilliant record, Thirty-three months in service and not a battle." In the year ahead, Wills would have more than his fill of battles.

By the time he entered the Georgia campaign, Wills was clearly no longer the callow recruit of three years earlier. He had gone to war solely to preserve the Union; his comments on slaves lacked sympathy, even decency. In June 1863, he recalled that eighteen months earlier, "I didn't like to hear anything of emancipation. Last fall accepted confiscation of Rebel's negroes quietly. In January took to emancipation readily, and now believe in arming the negroes." Like many others, however, Wills saw in the arming of blacks an opportunity for white officers to advance in rank through gaining commissions in the new regiments. Yet the anomalies of slave society disturbed him. In Arkansas he met the son and daughter of a slaveholder, "bright quadroons." The son had been educated in France, the daughter at Oberlin. Wills was particularly impressed by the latter, who spoke vivaciously, played the piano and sang, and served a toddy of peach brandy and honey. Three miles away, the officers visited "two of the regular snuff-dipping, swearing, Southern women, of the low, white-trash family," from whom they took a flock of chickens and a bag of sweet potatoes.

Not unexpectedly, the young bachelor paid close attention to any young woman who crossed his path. While scouting near New Madrid, Missouri, Wills "captured a lot of ginger snaps, and had a good talk with a handsome widow, while the boats were firing on the Michigan cavalry on our left." Wills frequently had a low opinion of the women he met and once speculated that

---

3. Amos C. Babcock to Lincoln, 15 Oct. 1862, Abraham Lincoln Papers, Library of Congress, Washington, D. C.; Babcock to Governor Richard Yates, 1 Dec. 1862, Records of the 103rd Ill. Volunteers, Records of the Adjutant General, Illinois State Archives; Roy P. Basler et al., eds., *The Collected Works of Abraham Lincoln* (New Brunswick, N. J.: Rutgers Univ. Press, 1953–55), 6: 307, 8: 334–35.

4. J. N. Reese, ed., *Report of the Adjutant General of the State of Illinois* (Springfield: Phillips Bros., 1900), 5: 637.

if Confederate gunboats broke past Union vessels and steamed to Illinois, Southern officers would be "sparking our girls as we do theirs now and the worst is, there is no doubt the girls would take to it kindly, for they do here, and I'm satisfied there is no difference in the feminines of the two sections, except that ours do not say 'thar' and 'whar.'" As for the men, Wills believed that Southern bushwhackers "would murder Jesus Christ if they thought he was a Union man." Yet the North contained men just as dangerous, and Wills railed that Lincoln ought to hang copperheads, the popular term for Northern opponents of the war. Wills vowed that, were he provost marshal in Fulton County, he would hang "at least ten men whose names I have." Officers spent much time, he reported, in countering the effect of letters received by their men from "cowardly vipers."[5]

The captain who moved into Georgia with Sherman in spring 1864 was no longer the light-hearted boy from Canton. Battles that had eluded him previously now awaited him in such abundance that he eventually conceded that campaigning "occasionally gets a little *old*." Knowing that opportunities to mail letters would come infrequently, he began to keep a diary, which proved an even more valuable record of his experience. On June 27, 1864, Sherman's men charged strong Confederate positions at Kennesaw Mountain. Wills was filled with exhilaration; revisiting the site in October, he reassessed the charge as the "maddest folly of the campaign." Incessant fighting induced war-weariness. At Griswoldsville, Georgia, in November, he joined in repelling an attack that he later learned had been that of the Georgia militia. After the battle, he discovered that the dead and dying were old men and boys forced to fight by Confederate cavalry. As Sherman moved beyond Atlanta, then marched to the sea at Savannah and turned northward through the Carolinas, war lost much of its appeal. Promoted to major in early 1865, Wills assumed greater responsibility for troops who impressed him with their "endurance, spirit and recklessness." As for their commander, "if Sherman was Mahomet we'd be as devoted Musselmen as ever followed the former prophet."

On June 6, 1865, Mary Emily Wills, five years older than her brother, married her brother's former colonel, William Pitt Kellogg.[6] Near the close of the war, Lincoln had appointed Kellogg collector of the port of New Orleans, a position that enabled him to prosper as a carpetbag politician. After two postwar years in Canton as a collector of soldiers' claims, Wills went to New

---

5. For additional complaint about such letters from another soldier of the 103rd Illinois, see *We Are Sherman's Men: The Civil War Letters of Henry Orendorff*, ed. William M. Anderson (Macomb: Western Illinois Univ. Monograph Series, No. 6, 1986), 34. See also William M. Anderson, "The Fulton County War at Home and in the Field," *Illinois Historical Journal* 85 (1992): 23–36.

6. "William Pitt Kellogg," *National Cyclopædia of American Biography* (New York: James T. White & Co., 1892–1977), 10: 82.

Orleans, where his brother-in-law employed him in the customhouse. Before he left Canton, Wills apparently prepared a condensed history of his regiment for the state adjutant general, his only other known publication—and it appeared anonymously.[7] Kellogg was elected to the U.S. Senate from Louisiana in 1868, then resigned in 1872 to accept the Republican nomination for governor. Both candidates claimed victory, but President Grant never waivered in supporting Kellogg. At the conclusion of his term as governor, he was again elected to the Senate. A wealthy retiree by 1906, with extensive real estate interests in Washington and a sugar plantation in Louisiana, Kellogg resided at the elegant Shoreham Hotel in Washington. Kellogg lived until 1918; when his wife died is not known.

Immediately after taking office in 1869, President Grant appointed a former officer of his staff, Sidney Stockdale, as collector of internal revenue in Louisiana. Stockdale, also from Fulton County and a close friend of Wills, had served as a captain in the 103rd Illinois. Wills found a spot as Stockdale's deputy and later purchased, jointly with his brother-in-law Kellogg, a sugar plantation about ninety miles west of New Orleans.[8] Wills died there in 1883, leaving a widow, the former Katherine McCaulliffe, who lived until 1911, but no children.[9]

Mary Kellogg assumed responsibility for preserving her brother's memory. Wills's diary was first printed in a 1904 book misleadingly titled *Reminiscences of the Civil War from Diaries of Members of the 103d Illinois Volunteer Infantry*.[10] The diary fills 172 of 293 pages of a book in which rosters and lists pad most of the other pages. Perhaps it was the favorable impression that Wills made in that book that induced his sister to compile and publish her own book two years later, embodying both the diary and the letters that Wills had written to her earlier in the war. Wills had a witty style that contrasted sharply with that of both his contemporaries in the field and the seven regimental veterans who compiled their diaries. In assembling this book, Mary Kellogg wisely allowed her brother to speak for himself, rarely intruding a comment of her own, excising from his letters home inevitable expressions of concern for his sister and her welfare but leaving intact the sparkling flow of camp gossip and military speculation.

Arranging to have the letters and diary privately printed, Mary Kellogg did little in the way of editing, except perhaps suppressing family matters.

---

7. C. W. Wills to I. N. Haynie, 20 Mar. 1867, Illinois State Archives. In this letter, Wills acknowledges a request for "a condensed History of our Regiment" by answering, "[I]t will afford me pleasure to comply."

8. New Orleans *Daily Picayune*, 25 Mar. 1883; *Fulton County Ledger*, 29 Mar. 1883.

9. Reese, ed., *Report of the Adjutant General*, 5: 635–40.

10. (Chicago: J. F. Leaming & Co.).

Charles Wills had an older brother, William H., known as "Tip," who lived in Mississippi at the outbreak of war and entered the Confederate army. William's obituary portrayed him as an unwilling conscript even though he was captured and then returned to Confederate service. After the war he was with Charles in New Orleans and on the Jeanerette plantation, but their relations during the war remain unknown.[11]

Concerned about her brother's reputation, Mary Kellogg attempted to perfect his spelling, grammar, and gentility, even though he was a far better writer than she was. In printing his diary of the Atlanta campaign she provided, "Our line of battle checked them and made them run." Wills had written, "Our line-of-battle checked them, and made them run like cusses."[12] When Wills neglected to advance the year in January, his letters were printed out of order: a letter dated January 7, 1862 (pages 52–53) was clearly written one year later, as was a letter of January 21, 1864 (pages 212–13), and a diary entry of March 25, 1864 (page 222). A diary entry of June 16, 1864 (page 256) should bear the date June 6, and an entry of June 17, 1864 (page 280) should be July. Letters dated November 1862 (pages 141–45) appear among those of January 1863. A mysterious and nonexistent Colonel "Raritan" (page 25) is probably Reardon, and a brigade commander transcribed as "McCormick" (page 25) must be McClernand. Since original letters are no longer available, Mary Kellogg's transcriptions will have to suffice.

Editing flaws only slightly diminish the value of these fresh and vibrant impressions. Wills exists as his sister wanted him to be remembered, as an observant and insightful author of letters and diaries that capture the essence of his experience as a soldier. Wills lacked the opportunity, and his sister the inclination, to improve these letters for publication. Fortunately, then, they form a contemporary record of campaigns and battles, thoughts and speculations, complaints and misjudgments, that truly reflect the reality of the Civil War.

John Y. Simon

---

11. *Canton Daily Register*, 18 May 1895.

12. Attributed to William Pitt Kellogg in "The Illinois Scrapbook," *Journal of the Illinois State Historical Society* 23 (1940): 527.

Army Life
of an
Illinois Soldier

INTRODUCTION.

To his surviving comrades of the Fifteenth Army Corps
these letters and diary of their former fellow soldier,
CHARLES W. WILLS, are respectfully dedicated. They do not
profess to be a history of the war; only a chronicle of events
recorded from day to day when the impressions were fresh
and vivid. Some opinions are expressed which time afterwards modified or reversed. Doubts and criticism of the
strategy of the commanding generals reflect the views that
prevailed at the time they were written, and show, as the
writer himself says, how little the actual fighting soldiers
sometimes knew of what was going on around them. Neverthe-
less it is believed that the story of courage, endurance, self-
control and unflinching patriotism herein told, with character-
istic modesty and quaint humor, and the life-like portrayal of
incidents of the great struggle and of the social conditions prevailing in the Border and Seceding States during the contest
will be found of interest and historic value.

CHARLES WRIGHT WILLS was born in Canton, Fulton County,
Illinois, April 17, 1840, of Pennsylvania parentage, and was
educated in the Canton public schools and the State Normal
School at Bloomington, Illinois. On the outbreak of the war,
responding to the first call of President Lincoln for three
months' volunteers, he enlisted in Company E, Eighth Illinois

Infantry, April 26th, 1861, and re-enlisted for three years at the end of his first term of service. Subsequently he was commissioned First Lieutenant and Battalion Adjutant of the Seventh Illinois Cavalry. When by order of the War Department in 1862 all Battalion Adjutants were mustered out of service, he returned to Canton, raised a company in the One Hundred and Third Illinois Infantry, and was elected its Captain. In 1863 Major General Oglesby appointed him upon his staff, but after a brief service as such, he gladly returned to active duty with his regiment, and on the resignation of Major Willison, was unanimously chosen to succeed him, though he was at that time the youngest Captain in the regiment. During the campaign in the Carolinas he was commissioned Lieutenant Colonel, but was never mustered. At the close of the war he settled in Louisiana and engaged in sugar planting. He died on his plantation at Jeannerette, on the banks of Bayou Teche, Louisiana, March 24, 1883, and was buried at Canton, Illinois. His widow now resides in Denver, Colorado.

Washington, D. C., August 8, 1906.

Army Life of an Illinois Soldier.

I.

April 28, 1861 to January 30, 1862. Full private in the 8th Illinois Infantry. Early days of drill, expectancy and enthusiasm. Traitors and spies in camp. Primitive arms and equipment. Rough side of camp life. False alarms of threatened defective attacks. Hospital service. Whipping and hanging of Union men in Missouri and Memphis. First uniforms. Reconnoitering down the Mississippi. River communication with the South cut off. Sleeping on cornstalks, cord wood, gates and rails in the rain. First experience in tents. Scouting in search of a fight. Promoted sergeant. Learning to confiscate and appropriate. Acting sheriff of court martial. Entrenching and bridge guarding. Hunting the elusive Jeff Thompson. "Cramping" live stock on a Rebel plantation. Taking further liberties with Rebel property. Adverse opinion of the Belmont fight. Log houses for winter quarters. Skinned "deer" that ate like pork. Heavy muster of gunboats. A New Year's frolic in camp. Investigating a disloyal regiment. Murder in a pirate's den. Mismanaged river expedition. Commissioned first lieutenant of cavalry and appointed battalion adjutant.

Cairo, April 28, '61.

This is the twilight of our first day here. We started from Peoria last Wednesday at 11 a. m. amid such a scene as I never saw before. Shouting, crying, praying, and shaking

hands were the exercises. Along the whole line from Peoria
to Springfield, from every house we had cheers and waving
of handkerchiefs. Got to Springfield at dark and marched out
to Camp Brick (it is a brickkiln) by moonlight. Our beds
were of hay, scattered on the earthen floor of the dry shed.
We had to sleep very close together, being cramped for room.
Our eatables are bread, bacon, beef, coffee, beans, rice, potatoes and sugar and molasses and pickles.

I had to quit last night because the light wouldn't wait for
me. Well, we stayed at Camp Brick until Thursday 25th in
the p. m., when we were marched over to Camp Yates to form
a regiment. Ten companies of us, numbering from 93 to 125
men in each, were trimmed down to 77 rank and file, each.
This created considerable dissatisfaction and made a deal of
very wicked swearing. Some of the men who were turned
out of our company threatened to shoot our captain, but he
is still living. After we were trimmed to the required number we were sworn in by company and then quartered in
Camp Yates, though we elected our officers first. You will
see by the papers who they are. To be certain I will put them
down: Colonel, Oglesby; Lieutenant Colonel, Rhoads; Major,
Post; Captain, Denison; First Lieutenant, Wetzel; Second
Lieutenant, Probstein. Our quarters are the old cattle stalls.
Eight men are allowed the same room that one cow or jackass
had. I heard Douglas Thursday night and cheered him for the
first time in my life. Saturday night at 9 we started for this
place. Flags were displayed from houses the whole distance,
and the feeling seems as good here as at home. Sixty miles
above here, at the Big Muddy bridge, occurred the only trouble
the boys have had here. A lot of traitors from over the Ohio
river tried to burn the bridge and are still trying to do it. A
company of Chicago Zouaves are posted there with a 6:25 field
piece. They shot at fellows spying around four times Saturday
night. We are more afraid of ague here than of the enemy.
We drink no liquors and keep ourselves as cleanly as possible.
There are 3,000 of us here and we think we can hold it against
15,000. If they cut the levee the river is so low that we will not

be flooded. We have 15 cannons now and will have 15 more to-day. We stop every boat that passes and take off all provisions and ammunition and clothing. The boys are allowed to appropriate what clothing they need from that which is seized. There are now 5,000 men twenty miles below here, at Columbus, Ky., who intended trying to take this spot, but the arrival of our regiment will, it is thought, stop that movement. It is well worth their trouble to take us for we have thousands of dollars worth of their goods here which are seized. You cannot conceive anything like the feeling that possesses our troops here. Although about half of us are green, raw militia, and will need discipline to make us what we should be, yet to a man they all pray for an assault. Kentucky, right across the river, is as strongly for secession as Mississippi can be, and I have no doubt but that we will be attacked the latter part of this week if no more troops come.

Our quarters here are much the same as at Camp Yates. The shed in which our company sleep is entirely open to the south, and very well ventilated otherwise. It is quite warm here though, and we all go in our shirt sleeves even when off duty. The trees are nearly in full leaf and grain is up eight or nine inches.

If any boys go from Canton, they should have a pair of woolen undershirts, ditto drawers, and two flannel overshirts, woolen stockings (feet don't blister as quick in them) and a heavy blanket or pair of light ones. Our company all have a revolver (Colt) and knife each. Mine were given to me by friends in Peoria.

This is a lovely place—a gorgeous hole! It smells just like that bottom below Dorrance's mill, and will breed fever and ague enough to disable all the men in this state. I just now hear the boys saying that we move to-morrow up the river to form a battery to stop a move expected from the Rebels. We can't rely on any of these rumors, though. The boys are shooting at marks all round us with their revolvers. I shoot about as well as any of them.

George Bestor, Jr., sits near me and just now said that he saw a man from Memphis this morning, who said that they were making preparation to come up here and take this Point, relying partly on the disloyal citizens for help. They will have a good time of it.

Cairo, May 5, 1861, Sunday, 11 a. m.

The bells are just ringing for church. I intended going, but it is such hard work getting out of camp that I concluded to postpone it. Anyway, we have service in camp this p. m. This is an awful lazy life we lead here. Lying down on our hay constitutes the principal part of the work. As our routine might be of interest to you, I will give it. At 5 a. m. the reveille is sounded by a drum and fife for each regiment. We arise, fold our blankets in our knapsacks and prepare to march. We then "fall in," in front of our quarters for roll-call; after which we prepare our breakfast and at the "breakfast call" (taps of the drum at 7) we commence eating; and the way we do eat here would astonish you. At 9 a. m. we fall in for company drill. This lasts one hour. Dinner at 12. Squad drill from 1 to 3 and supper at 5:30. At 6 p. m. the whole regiment is called out for parade. This is merely a review by the colonel, and lasts not more than 30 minutes and often but 15. After 8 p. m. singing and loud noises are stopped; at 9:30 the tattoo is beat when all are required to be in quarters, and at three taps at 10 p. m. all lights are put out, and we leave things to the sentries. Our company of 77 men is divided into six messes for eating. Each mess elects a captain, and he is supreme, as far as cooking and eating are concerned. Our company is considered a crack one here and we have had the post of honor assigned us, the right of the regiment, near the colors. Our commanders, I think, are anticipating some work here, though they keep their own counsels very closely. They have spies out in all directions, down as far as Vicksburg. I think that Bradley's detective police of Chicago are on duty in this vicinity. We also have two very fleet steamers on duty here to stop boats that refuse to lay to, and to keep a lookout up and down the Mississippi river. Yesterday, p. m., I noticed considerable bustle at headquarters which are in full view of our quarters, and at dark last night 20 cartridges were distributed to each man, and orders given to reload revolvers and to prepare everything for marching at a minute's notice, and to sleep with our pistols and knives in our belts around us. That's all we know about it though. We were not aroused except by a shot at about 2 this morning. I heard a little while ago that it was a sentinel shooting at some fellow scouting around. The Rebels have a host of spies in town but I think they are nearly all known and watched. The men confidently expect to be ordered south shortly. Nothing would suit them better. I honestly believe that there is not a man in our company that would sell his place for $100. We call the camp Fort Defiance, and after we receive a little more drilling we think we can hold it against almost any number. We have 3,300 men here to-day, but will have one more regiment to-day and expect still more.

We are pretty well supplied with news here; all the dailies are offered for sale in camp, but we are so far out of the way that the news they bring is two days old before we get them. *Transcripts* and *Unions* are sent to us by the office free. I wish you would send me the *Register* once and a while, and put in a literary paper or two, for we have considerable time to read. We have a barrel of ice water every day. Milk, cake and pies are peddled round camp, and I indulge in milk considerably at five cents a pint. Everything is much higher here than above. Potatoes, 50 cents; corn, 60 cents, etc. It has been raining like blue blazes since I commenced this, and the boys are scrambling around looking for dry spots on the hay and trying to avoid the young rivers coming in. Almost all are reading or writing, and I defy anyone to find 75 men without any restraint, paying more respect to the Sabbath. We have not had a sick man in camp. Several of the boys, most all of them in fact, have been a little indisposed from change of diet and water, but we have been careful and are now all right. There are 25, at least, of us writing here, all lying on our backs. I have my paper on a cartridge box on my knees.

Camp Defiance, May 11, '61.

We have been seeing and feeling the roughest side of camp life, ever since my last. Rain in double-headed torrents; lightning that will kill easily at five miles; thundering thunder; and wind from away back. But the mud dries like water on a hot brick, and six hours sun makes our parade ground fit for drill. Afternoon when the sun is out its hot enough to scorch a phœnix; yesterday we drilled from 1 to 3. I was almost crisped, and some of the boys poured a pint of grease out of each boot after we finished. Up to 10 last night when I went to sleep it was still boiling, but at five this morning, when we got up, we shivered in coat, vest and blankets. Bully climate! And then the way that the rain patters down through the roof, now on your neck; move a little and spat it goes, right into your ear, and the more you try to get away from it the more you get, until disgusted, you sit up and see a hundred chaps in the same position. A good deal of laughing, mixed with a few swears follows, and then we wrap our heads in the blankets, straighten out, "let her rip." I never was in better health, have gained four pounds since we started, and feel stronger and more lively than I have for a coon's age. Health generally excellent in our company, because we are all careful. There has not been a fight yet in the whole camp. A man was shot dead last night by one of the guards by accident. We have a fellow in the guardhouse whom we arrested a couple of days since as a spy. He is almost crazy with fear for his future. His wife is here and has seen him. His trial comes off this p. m. We all hope that he will be hung, for he laid forty lashes on the back of a man down south a few weeks since, who is now a volunteer in our camp. The boys would hang him in a minute but for the officers.

The news of the fuss in St. Louis has just reached us. We suppose it will send Missouri kiting out of the Union. General Prentiss has some information (don't know what it is) that makes our officers inspect our arms often and carefully. I know that he expects a devil of a time here shortly, and preparations of all kinds are making for it.

The boys are just now having a big time over a letter in the *Transcript* of the 10th, signed W. K. G. Of course it is a bundle of lies. We have given nine groans and three tiger tails for the writer W. K. G. A man just from Mobile is in camp now. He landed this morning. He took off his shirt and showed a back that bore marks of 30 strokes. They laid him across a wooden bench and beat him with a paling. His back looks harder than any one I ever saw. He says that nine men were hung the day before he left, good citizens, and men whose only crime was loyalty to the United States Government. They would not volunteer under the snake flag. He reports 1,500 men at Memphis, a few at Columbus, only 50 at Mobile, and none worth mentioning at other points. A man has been here this morning from 20 miles up the river in Missouri. He wants arms for four companies of Union men that have formed there, and who are expecting an attack from the secessionists. The Union men have but 20 shotguns now. A boat came up yesterday crowded with passengers. Looked as though she might have a thousand on her. All Northerners.

One of the boys has just come in with a report that there are "to a dead certainty" 5,000 men now at Columbus (20 miles below) who have just arrived this morning. They are after Cairo. The boys are all rumor proof, though, and the above didn't get a comment. One of the boys has just expressed my feelings by saying: "I don't believe anything, only that Cairo is a damned mud hole." I have not stood guard yet a minute. Have been on fatigue duty is the reason. A general order was given last night for every man to bathe at least twice a week. Most of us do it every day. The Ohio is warm enough and I swim every night now. There were over 2,000 of us in at once last night. We had a candy pulling this p. m. There was an extra gallon in to-day's rations, and we boiled it and had a gay time. Our company is, I believe, the orderly one here. We have lots of beer sent us from Peoria, and drink a half barrel a day while it lasts. (Do those two statements tally?)

Sunday, May 12th, 6 p. m.

Several men from Alabama arrived here to-day with their backs beaten blue. We caught another spy last night. The drums rolled last night at 11 and we all turned out in the biggest, dark and deepest mud you ever saw. It was a mistake of the drummer's. Six rockets were let off and he thought that they stood for an attack but they were only signals for steamboats. We thought sure we were attacked, but the boys took it cool as could be, and I think never men felt better over a prospect for a fight. Two hundred troops have landed since I commenced writing this time. Just now the clouds seem to be within 100 yards of the ground. Prospect of a tremendous storm. I am writing standing up in ranks for evening roll call.

May 17, 1861.

Sun and dust. Hot as —— the deuce. Lots of drilling and ditto fun. Suits me to a T. Am going in for three years as quick as I can. All chance for fight is given up here. We are getting sharp. We trade off our extra fodder for pies, milk and good things.

It's too hot to write. I am going to sleep.

Cairo, May 23, 1861.

Lots of men come through here with their backs blue and bloody from beatings; and nine in ten of them got their marks in Memphis. A man from St. Louis was in camp a few days since with one-half of his head shaved, one-half of a heavy beard taken off, two teeth knocked out and his lips all cut with blows from a club. This was done in Memphis the day before I saw him. My health continues excellent. Never felt so well, and think that care is all that is necessary to preserve my health as it is. I can't think that this Illinois climate is mean enough to give a fellow the chills, after it has raised him as well as it has me.

I never enjoyed anything in the world as I do this life, and as for its spoiling me, you'll see if I don't come out a better man than when I went in.

We have commenced fortifying this Point. One company is detailed every day to work on this. It is said that it will cost three million. As for enlisting for three years, I can't, or rather won't say now. 'Tis a sure thing that as long as this war continues I will not be satisfied at home, and if I would there will certainly be no business. There is no use trying to coax me now for I can't tell until my three month's are up. Then, if I feel as now, I shall certainly go in for the war. Our company gets compliments from all the newspaper correspondents.

The whole camp is aching to be ordered to Memphis. Bird's Point is not occupied. We had a company there for one day but withdrew them.

I commenced this about 12 last night in the hospital, but I had so much to do and there were so infernal many bugs that I concluded to postpone it. We do have the richest assortment of bugs here imaginable, from the size of a pin-head up to big black fellows as large as bats. I was sitting up with an old schoolmate from Bloomington, whose company have gone up to Big Muddy and left him to the tender care of our surgeons. The poor devil would die in a week but for the care he gets from a dozen of us here that used to go to school with him. There are about 50 men in our regiment's hospital, and save the few that go up to care for their friends unasked, the poor fellows have no attendance nights. I gave medicine to four beside my friend last night, two of whom are crazy with fever. One of the latter insisted on getting up all the time, and twice he got down stairs while I was attending the others. Not one of our company is there, thank heaven.

Yesterday our company with the whole 7th Regiment were at work on the fortifications. Wheeling dirt and mounting guns was the exercise. The guns we mounted are 36 pounders and weigh three and one-half tons each. Our regiment, except this company, are at the same work to-day. To-morrow the 9th works. General Prentiss paid us a very handsome compliment in saying that our company did more work than any two companies have yet done in the same time. You should see our hands. Mine are covered with blisters. You might as well be making up your mind to the fact that I am not coming home soon. There is but one thing in the way to prevent my going in for the war. That is the talk of cutting off the heads of all lieutenants over 25 years of age, and of all captains over 35. Now under that arrangement all three of our officers will lose their heads, and we know we cannot replace them with as good. This thing, though not certain yet, has created a great deal of excitement in camp, and if it goes into effect will smash our company completely. Our company is the best officered of any in camp. There are no two sides to that proposition.

You'll see that your Canton company will not regret the selection of officers they have made. The companies here with inexperienced officers have worlds of trouble, and five captains and one lieutenant, though good men at home, have resigned at the wish of their companies. Four of these companies tried to get our first lieutenant for captain, but he won't leave us. The thousand men who occupied Bird's Point the other day are most all Germans; many of them "Turners," and a very well drilled regiment. They will get their cannons from St. Louis next week. None of the men expect an attack here, but we know that General Prentiss thinks it at least possible, and from his actions we think he expects it. A family were in camp yesterday who were driven away from a place only 12 miles from here in Missouri, and left a son there with a bullet through his brains. It happened yesterday morning. We have had our uniforms about a week. Gray satinet pants and roundabout, with a very handsome blue cloth cap. Nine brass buttons up the jacket front and grey flannel shirts. We are obliged to wash dirty clothes the day we change and to black our shoes every evening, and polish our buttons for dress parade. Our company is the only one that does this though, and they call us dandies. We have done more work and better drilling though, than any of them, so we don't mind it.

Cairo, June 9, 1861.

I have been over to Bird's Point this morning for the first time. They have thrown up breastworks and dug a deep ditch outside of them, making a pretty strong camp. We don't apprehend a shade of a fuss here but the officers are making as much preparation as if a Waterloo No. 2 were coming. I went to old Bird's house this morning. It is just like the pictures we have seen in Harper's of southern planters' homes. A wide, railed porch extends around two sides of the house from the floor of each story. On the lower porch sat Bird and his family talking with a number of officers and their ladies. Looked very pleasant. Back of the house were the quarters filled with 46 of the ugliest, dirtiest niggers I ever saw, dressed in dirty white cotton. Awful nasty! The soldiers at the point have plenty of shade. We have but one tree on our grounds. The boys took a lot of ammunition from Bird the other day, and also another lot from a nest five miles back in Missouri. It was all given back, however, as private property. Our whole brigade of six regiments had a parade yesterday. We are all uniformed now and I think we made a respectable appearance. The general gave us a special notice. Are the Canton boys going or not? Do they drill? We have been sleeping on hay up to this week, but have thrown it away, and now have but the bare boards. The change has been so gradual from featherbed at home to plank here that I can't think where it troubled me the least. I had a mattress in Peoria, straw in Springfield, and hay here. Our living is now very good. Fresh beef every day, potatoes, rice and beans.

Cairo, June 13, 1861.

I am converted to the belief that Cairo is not such a bad place after all. The record shows that less deaths have occurred here in seven weeks among 3,000 men, than in Villa Ridge (a higher, and much dryer place with abundant shade and spring water), in five weeks among 1,000. There has been but one death here by disease in that time, and that with miserable hospital accommodations. The soldiers lie like the d——l about Cairo. The days are hot of course, but we do nothing now between 8 a. m. and 9 p. m. but cook and eat, so that amounts to not near as much as working all day at home. The mosquitoes and bugs are furious from 6 p. m. to 11, but we are drilling from 7 p. m. to nearly 9, and from that to 11 we save ourselves by smoking, which we all do pretty steadily. The nights after 11 are splendidly cool, so much so that we can cover ourselves entirely in our blankets, which is a block game on the mosquitoes, and sleep like logs. I believe those Camp Mather boys are hard sticks from the accounts we get of their fingers sticking to chickens, vegetables, etc. The citizens here say that the boys have not taken a thing without permission, or insulted a citizen. "Bully for us."

We had a little fun yesterday. At 8 p. m. we (the Peoria and Pekin companies) were ordered to get ready for marching in ten minutes. So ready we got (but had to leave knapsacks, canteens and blankets) and were marched down to the "City of Alton," which had on board a six pounder and one 12 pound howitzer. We cast off, fired a salute of two guns and steamed down the Mississippi. After five miles the colonel (Oglesby) called us together, told us that he was out on a reconoitering expedition, and his information led him to think we should be forced into a little fight before we got back. We were then ordered to load and keep in our places by our guns. At Columbus we saw a secesh flag waving but passed on a couple of miles farther where he expected to find a secesh force. Failed and turned back. At Columbus the flag was still waving and the stores all closed, and quite a crowd collected on the levee, but one gun though, that we could see. The colonel ordered the flag down. They said they wouldn't do it. He said he would do it himself then. They answered, "We'd like to see you try it." We were drawn up then round the cabin deck guards next the shore in two ranks, with guns at "ready," and the captain jumped ashore and hauled down the serpent. We were all sure of a skirmish but missed it. Flag was about 15 x 7, with eight stars and three stripes. I send you some scraps of it. They raised another flag one hour after we left and sent us word to "Come and take it." The ride on the river was the best treat I've had for two years.

Cairo, June 23, 1861.

Camp is very dull now, and we are more closely confined in it than ever. Not a soldier goes out now except in company with a commissioned officer or on a pass from the general. The latter not one in a thousand can get and the former maybe one in five hundred.

We have no drilling now between 8 a. m. and 7 p. m. on account of the heat; so we have plenty of spare time. If I only had some good books! But I can't send for them now for our colonel keeps us about half excited all the time with a prospect of a move. He says we have two chances: First, if General McClellan suffers anything like a serious repulse in Western Virginia, our whole brigade will move out on two hours' notice. Second, if any reliable reports come of Arkansas troops moving into Missouri, we will double quick over the river and leave the Point to some other troops. The last is the most likely chance. A thousand of our boys went off on the "City of Alton" at dark last night. We don't know where to, but 'tis rumored that they went up the Mississippi 25 miles and then marched back into Missouri 30 miles to intercept a train of wagons loaded with provisions going south. The colonel made them a speech; told them they were sure to have a brush and asked them if they would sustain the credit of the 8th. You should have heard them shout! Only two companies went from our regiment under Lieutenant Colonel Rhoads. The Battallion was under Colonel Morgan. The three year question causes more excitement than every thing else now. Nearly our whole company will go. The most worthless fellows are the ones that will go home. I feel as if my place is here. I know I could not content myself at home, and if I could, every young man with no one

2

depending upon him is needed in the army more than anywhere else. I know I have your approval in this resolve, but I would like to have you tell me so. The Americans in our company think some of seceding, filling up from home with American boys and letting the Dutch now in the company paddle their own canoe. I wonder if we could not get a dozen good strong fellows from Canton. We don't want any poorer men than I am, for we are going to make a crack company.

Cairo, July 1, 1861.

Writing letters is getting to be harder work than drilling, and is more dreaded by the boys. Lots of people are visiting the camp now, many of them ladies, but I tell you that they use their fans more than their spy-glasses after a very few looks.

I was up to Mound City yesterday with nine others of our company on a United States boat that has three cannons on her. Mound City is a beautiful little place, and takes it name from a mound about 30 feet in diameter and 10 feet high, on which grow a dozen spindling locusts. I have been about 12 miles up each river from the point here. At that distance the river banks are, say 25 feet high, and slope down to the point, and run into a broad wide sandbar that ends Illinois.

Fishing is a principal amusement or time-killer now. I have fished about four days and caught nary a "minner."

There is no outside influence used to induce a man to re-enlist. Officers tell every man to use his own judgment, and each fellow does his own thinking and—another long dash or words to that effect.

Cairo, July 27, 1861

We number now about 60 and have 25 days in which to fill up to 100. Two hundred and fifty of our regiment of three-months' men have re-enlisted. Two hundred and fifty out of 680, which is considerably better than any eastern regiment that I have seen mentioned. There was not a sick man in our company when we returned, and there is not now. One of the boys just tells me that day before yesterday morning there were but eight in the regiment hospital. Three men from our regiment have died in three and a half months. One of these I know killed himself with imprudence. I have telegraphed to the boys to be in Peoria Wednesday. I have not the least idea that any of them will back out. It does seem real good to be back here again where a fellow can swing himself and lay around loose with sleeves up, collar open, (or shirt off if it suits him better) hair unkempt, face unwashed and everything un-anything. It beats clerking ever so much! We were paid off yesterday. The privates received $56.72 each in gold, silver and copper, which is $24.00 more than we expected.

We are having some more excitement in camp to-day. A rumored attack in prospect on Bird's Point is the subject. We are putting the recruits through in two-forty-style to get them ready. Twenty rounds of cartridges were served to us at noon to-day, and Prentiss' aids are galloping round as if tight. About one quarter of the recruits have their accoutrements on, and some of them scoot up on the levee every ten minutes to look at the Point. We have all kinds of rumors of from 2,000 to 15,000 Rebels within from 6 to 15 miles of us, but if 20 preachers would swear to the truth, there's not one man that has been here three months would believe it. Been fooled too often! Our officers are careful though, and treat every thing from head-quarters as reliable till the contrary is proven.

It is a horrid trip from Peoria to Cairo as the trains run now. We laid over three hours in El Paso, and eleven hours in Centralia; from 11 p. m. till 10 a. m. Awful! and rode down from Centralia in an accommodation freight. The bed was excellent at home, but I think that sleeping on boards rests me better and I know I sleep sounder.

Have worked two hours hard at cleaning up quarters and eating supper since my last period. Supper consisted of coffee, bread and butter, and cold steak pickled in vinegar. Vinegar is a great improvement on cold beef, I wonder you never adopted it. We have a prime lot of boys this time. There are not ten out of the whole company that I would not like to have for associates at home. I don't believe that one of them will ever take quarters in the guard-house.

I think our company will be full in ten days. We have refused lots of roughs here in camp also in Peoria, but three or four little ones have crept in through acquaintances' influence. Those men we have will learn to drill in half less time than any other lot of recruits on the ground, because they have a pride in their appearance and dress, and that has given them a better carriage and command of themselves than rougher customers have.

We will have in a few days nothing but new recruits here except the fractions of regiments that have re-enlisted; the 10th, which calls itself the crack regiment of the post, will all leave for home day after to-morrow. If it does not come back full in 30 days it will be disbanded. This is Prentiss' old regiment.

Tattoo 9 p. m.—They are really expecting an attack on Bird's Point, and we will all be kept close in quarters evenings after sunset till the scare dies away. One of our boys that stood guard at the hospital this morning says the surgeon told him that the sick would be brought from the Point to Cairo to-day. Don't know whether they did it or not.

We were coming on the cars when we heard of the Manassas rout. The boys gave three cheers, for they imagined it would bring us marching orders. I would like very much to hear such orders, but would a devilish sight rather march with men that have had three months' drill than with these new recruits. You can't imagine what a difference there is in one's confidence in a drilled and undrilled company of men. Don't say anything about our expectations of an attack here for there has been a great deal too much said already on going-to-be attacks on this Point

We pay five cents a pint here for milk, and I found a wiggler in a pint this morning. Don't you think they ought to mix clean water with the cow juice?

Sunday, 1 p. m.—I have just woke up from a two hours' sleep that had more dreams than all the sleeping I ever did before. I dreamed everything from being a partner of Adam and Eve in their orchard down to seeing Stephens' iron battery.

Cairo, August 2, 1861.

Hot! You don't know what that word means. I feel that I have always been ignorant of its true meaning till this week, but am posted now, sure. The (supposed-to-be) "never failing cool, delicious breeze" that I have talked about so much, seems to be at "parade rest" now and—I can't do justice to the subject. The health of the camp is much better now than at any time before, since we have been here. There is not a sick man in our company. My health remains gorgeous. We drill now five hours a day, under a sun that cooks eggs in 13 minutes, but we think we feel the heat no more walking than lying around the quarters.

The seceshers this morning took the packet that has been plying between here and Columbus, and have run her off down to Memphis. I thought that Prentiss stopped her sometime since, but this at last closes all communication between the North and South at this point. Our "ossifers" we think are really scared about an attack here, but you could not make the soldiers believe in the like till they see the fight begin. About a thousand of our men were rushed off to Bird's Point to-day to work on intrenchments, and won't they sweat?

My chum heard Colonel Oglesby tell an officer two hours ago that there were 17,000 Rebels within 15 miles of the Point. The scouts reported this body at New Madrid, 40 miles down the Mississippi, two days since. Yesterday 12 men from the Pekin company and 12 from our's with some artillerymen went 30 miles up the Mississippi to collect all the boats we

could find on the Missouri shore. We found three large flats
tied up to trees along the shore which we confiscated. One of
them wasn't very good so we sunk it. The object was to
prevent marauders from visiting Illinois. I had charge of
the men from our company.

Cairo, August 11, '61.

Our Canton boys came down on time, and right glad I am
to have them here. Colonel Ross's 17th Regiment got here
the same day by the river. The boys were sworn into our
company the day after they arrived, and the day following a
lieutenant in the Fulton Blues came over to get them to join
his company. I am glad he was too late. We have all been
over to the Point to visit the Canton boys of the 17th, and
found them looking very well. Will Trites, alone, looks unwell.
A few weeks at home is what he really needs, for he will not
give up work and go on the sick list as he ought to, as long
as he can stand. Billy Stockdale, Chancey Black, George
Shine, Billy Resor and Jesse Beeson are in No. 1 condition.
Their tents are pitched in old Bird's cornfield from which the
corn has just been cut and you can imagine that the stubble is
not equal to feathers to lie upon. They call us boys that live
in barracks in Cairo, Sunday soldiers and Fourth of July
braves; the same names we applied to them when they were
in Camp Mather. The Canton boys in our company get along
finely. They are in the best of spirits and already appear quite
soldierly. They are well satisfied with the company which
now numbers 90 men and will be full this week. We all room
together except John Wallace and Milo Farewell. We are
now drilling about six hours a day, but the greenhorns act as
though they think it fun. We don't suffer from the heat as
much as one would think, and can you believe it the health of
the camp is better now than ever before. We have not in our
company a man on the sick list. Major Smith (our old friend
Marion), says that the 17th have been healthier at Bird's Point
than they ever were before; and so every regiment says that

comes here. If there are any very old people in Canton that want to live 50 or 60 years longer, advise them to come to Cairo. Mosquitoes and fleas are around these times. The whole family are here.

Cairo, August 19, 1861.

The boys are writing to-day for some butter and things from home. The expense by express from Peoria is not worth speaking of and the other boys have things sent them often. We have made up our minds to lying here six weeks longer at least, and conclude that time will pass better with a few home extras to grace our table.

Cairo, September 1, 1861.

We had blankets given us this last week and new accoutrements throughout. If they would only change our guns now we would have nothing but a move to ask for. A uniform was also furnished us last week. It is of excellent all-wool goods, and not so heavy as to be uncomfortable. The color is very fine grey, the pants are fashionably cut and equal to such as would cost six dollars in Peoria. The coats have short skirts and are rather fancifully trimmed with blue. It is much the best uniform I have seen yet, although it costs but $13. We will have a fatigue suit shortly. Yesterday we were mustered for pay. We will get our first month's wages this week "they say." There are wagons and mules here now by the hundreds, and when our tents are ready (they are here now) we will be ready to move. I think there must be near 10,000 men here now. Logan's, Pugh's, Buford's, and another's regiment; Hick's and Raritan's came in last week. The first three belong to McCormick's Brigade. General McClernand is here now. Every one thinks we will move in a very few days. I kind o' feel it in my bones, too, but it is too good to be true, so I'm taking all the bets I can from 10 cents worth of peanuts to a half bushel of apples, I betting that we are here two weeks from now. I've got them any way, for if we move, I hope to be able to borrow apples, etc., from the seceshers to pay my little bills, and if I stay here I'll have some eatables free for consolation. We Canton boys have hired a cook for ourselves and are living much better than I ever did before in camp.

Our cook is a jewel, and by trading off rations keeps us in clover all the time. He sets a better table for us than the Peoria house boarders eat from, honestly. An old schoolmate of mine in our mess furnishes us with milk. He and John Wallace go out every night about 2 or 3 o'clock and—somebody's cow don't milk well next morning. We'll never have such times sojering again, but you can't imagine how we do want to get over into Missouri or Arkansas. We don't have half as easy times as these at home and but for the discipline it wouldn't seem like soldiering. I've been bored like sin the last two weeks drilling new recruits, but I'm glad of it, for it is rather pleasant to me to have something disagreeable when I'm bored feeling good. John Keefer and John Wallace, so far, make as good soldiers as any men in camp, Keef's game leg working against him, too. All our boys are just the men for soldiers. It comes perfectly naturally to Sid. and Sam. Theo. has been in bad health for a week, but I think he is improving now. Fred Norcott is a splendid boy. He and Sam match well. Charley Cooper is acting as post orderly, that is, stays at headquarters of the Post Commandant, preserves order there and carries messages, dispatches, etc., to the different colonels. A good place but very confusing.

I have been visiting Colonel Raritan's and Hick's Camp this p. m. They have no guns yet and their sentinels stand guard with sticks. Looks funny.

We have about 50 prisoners here now. They think they are treated splendidly and say that if any of our boys fall into their hands they will remember it. Several of them are very intelligent-appearing men. One of them is about as big as—a house with a foot like a cooking stove. Charley Maple wrote down to us that he wants to join our company; Keefer wrote him to come. I have to remark once more that the "health of camp is better than ever before," your sarcastic remark not having affected our sanitary condition in the least. You will please make no more impertinent remarks or comments on my letters!

A. H. White was down here last Sabbath, and he and I found Frank Smith in Smith's Artillery. I have been here right by him four months without knowing it and lived. He is a corporal. He, A. H., and I drank some beer, discussed the affairs of the nation and adjourned. Do you remember Enos Lincoln? He is here in the 12th.

We have had some fighting in camp lately. An artillery man stabbed one of the 9th and got knocked, kicked and bayoneted for it. The artillery have sworn to have revenge and every hickory man (the 9th have a fatigue suit of hickory) they see they pounce onto. They have a skirmish every day. One of our company got drunk to-day, got to fighting, was sent to the guardhouse, tried to break out, guard knocked him down with a gun, cut his cheek open, etc. He then got into a fight with four other men in the guard house and of all the bunged eyes and bloody faces they beat the record.

Cairo, September 9, 1861

The refreshments and drygoods from home arrived Saturday. We were at Paducah then and they were taken care of by two or three of the lame and halt, that were not in traveling order and were left behind. We returned this morning and after acknowledging the excellence, profusion, variety, gorgeousness, and confiscarity of your benevolent appropriation to our temporal wants, I will particularize by saying that you needn't worry about your picture, as it is in my possession; that the cakes are both numerous and excellent, that the pickles are prodigious in quantity, beautiful in quality and remarkably acceptable. That the butter and cheese are non ad com valorum. The tobacco and Hostetter, the boys say, are very fine. To Mrs. Dewey and Mrs. Heald we all return thanks and send our kind respects and love. We have sent a share of the eatables to the Canton boys of the 17th, which is again encamped near us; this time on the Kentucky shore. They are hard at work to-day cutting down trees, clearing away for a camp ground. I have seen none of them yet. We had the nicest little trip to Paducah, that ever soldiers had. We have just received orders to get ready to start in five minutes.

Time extended a little. We had 1,500 troops in Paducah, Ky., and received information that they would be attacked Saturday, so Friday night 350 of us were sent up as an advance.—Now we go.

Camp Norfolk, September 12, 1861.

Agreeable to our very short notice we packed our knap-sacks, put three days rations in our haversacks, were carried across the river to Bird's Point in two boats (our whole regiment), and just at dark started out through the woods. 'Twas a confounded, dark, dirty, narrow road, and I was right glad when the word "halt" was given and preparations made for bunking in for the night. The next morning we started again along down the river, the gun-boats, two of them, keeping a couple of miles ahead of us. We started with a couple of pieces of field artillery, but the road got so bad that we had to leave it after about three miles. We advanced about five miles when the gunboats, which were about a mile and one-half ahead of us, opened mouth, and thunder! what a rumpus they did keep up. We could not see them for the thick brush between us and the river, but we thought sure our little fight had come at last. We were drawn up in the front yard of some secesher's deserted house (a fine one), and the colonel with a small party went ahead to reconnoiter. While they were gone we ate our dinners, and made ready for the expected march and fight. But the colonel on his return, scooted us back to our morning's starting place. Whew, but that was a sweating old march. About an hour after we started back, 15 of our cavalry scouts were run in, through the place where we took dinner, by 60 or 70 secesh cavalry. Three or four were wounded and our boys say that they killed several of the Rebels. The gunboats came up in the p. m. reported fighting the "Yankee" and two land batteries, one of which was but three and one half miles below us (and some say but one and one half miles) and had 16 guns. They crippled the dam'd "Yankee" although the latter carries 84's, while ours hadn't but 64's. Our boats were not touched. A deserter came up from Columbus yesterday afternoon and says that our boats killed 200 in the fight. (I believe he is a liar and a spy). We have had it sweet the last day and two nights. Rained like sixty and we have no tents. There is no shelter but a few trees and you know they amount to nothing in heavy rains. It is amusing to see the boys figure at night for dry beds. Every thing, gates, cordwood, rails, cornstalks, weeds and panels of fence and boards are confiscated, and genius is taxed its utmost to make the sleeping as comfortable as possible. Milo Farewell, Hy. Johnson and myself sleep on an armful of cornstalks thrown on a floor of rails. With nothing between us and the clouds. Sid., (Sidney Stockdale) and Theo. each had three sticks of four foot cord wood for a couch, with their feet resting in a mudpuddle. We are further out than any other regiment now. I tell you I like this, and feel like knocking down any man that I hear grumble. None of our boys do that I hear of. We will have our tents here this p. m. though I would rather be without them; they are so much trouble. I know we will have no dirtier time than we have had the last two days, and until it gets cold I would rather not have tents if it is the same all the time. I fell in love with Paducah while I was there, and I think I will settle there when the war is over. I never saw so many pretty women in my life. All fat, smooth-skinned small boned, highbred looking women. They hollered "Hurrah for Jeff" at us, some of them, but that's all right. I could write until to-morrow morning about Paducah, but I must go and confiscate some corn for dinner.

Norfolk, September 16, 1861.

We are still here at Norfolk and now in camp for we don't
know how long. We got tents the day after the date of my last,
and splendid ones they are. They are full 10 feet high and 15
feet across. They each accommodate about 15 men. Since
we have been here we have been out scouting three times. The
first time we were down the river about five miles. That was
the time our gunboats had the fight with the "Yankee" and the
land batteries. Two days afterward a body of the enemy's
cavalry came up almost to our camp, and after dinner we were
sent out to look them up. We were scooting along through a
thick wood when one of our cavalry men came back half scared
out of his wits (we had about 20 of the cavalry ahead acting
as scouts) and reported a whole mess of men just over a rise
of ground ahead of us. Our company was in the van, and the
column came into line on us and our cavalry tried to draw the
enemy back on our position, but Mr. Enemy "drawed" the
other way and again we missed our little fight. Last Saturday
we started out again at noon and went down the river 10 miles
where we thought sure we'd find secesh, but he had again left.
We had 2,000 men this time and 6 pieces of artillery. We had
stopped to rest when a cloud of dust was observed rising on
our side of the river about four miles from us. Some of the
boys had glasses with them and made out the cause to be a body
of cavalry. Our right was marched a few hundred yards to the
front and placed in line of battle with the left at the river bank
and our right extending along an edge of woods and fronting
a cornfield and open pass between it and the river. A splendid
place (for our side) for a fight. Our gunboat then started
down the river, fired at and dispersed one body they saw and
then slipped a few shells into Columbus and returned. We
were within four or five miles of Columbus where there are
(our colonel says) 26,000 troops, and on ground where the
secesh were encamped but lately with 16 pieces of artillery.
We started back at dusk and got home about 10 o'clock; some
of the boys pretty tired. I stand these little trips like a horse
and would rather go every day than lay around camp. Yester-

day (Sunday) the "Yankee" came up and shelled the woods where we were the day before. She tried to throw some shells into our camp but they didn't reach us by a mile and a half. One of our gunboats has to lay here all the time or the "Yankee" would make us skedaddle out of this on double quick. Don't talk about furloughs. They are played out. A dispatch came this last week to Colonel Oglesby that his wife was dying. He went up to Cairo but General McClernand showed him an order from McClellan, vetoing furloughs, no matter for what. So the colonel had to return here. I'd like very much to go home but I'll enjoy it all the more when this business is finished. The 17th is encamped just opposite us on Island No. 1, but we can't get to see them. Our boys are in good spirits. Sid. and Sam and Theo. are now all right. Milo Farewell thinks he has the dumb ague. Fred Norcott is sick in Cairo. Charley Cooper is also sick I have heard. I am all right. My office is sergeant, two grades below private. Our company goes out on picket to-night.

September 17, 1861.

Well, I've slept half of this day and feel sleepy yet. I had a tough time on picket last night. We were divided into four squads and owing to the small number of men we had out (only 50) the corporals had to stand guard as privates; so I had all the stationing of reliefs to do myself and did not get a minute's sleep all night. We were not troubled any by the enemy but the mosquitoes and fleas gave us the devil.

A coon came sliding down the tree Sam Nutt was stationed under, and he thought he was taken sure. The people here say that there are lots of bears and tiger cats killed here every winter. Sam has been to Cairo to-day and says that Keef, Fred Norcott and Cooper are all much better. There is a rumor now that our right is going to Virginia, but I don't believe it. It is too good to be true. Our cook has been sick for several days and we have been just about half living on account of our being too lazy to cook. I don't mean to be disrespectful when I say I was about as glad to see him cooking again this morning, as I would be to see you. He is a splendid nigger, seems to think the world of us boys. He buys a great many little things for us with his own money, which as we are all out, is a good institution. We are to get our pay next week the officers say. My pay is some $18 or $20 a month now. I am entitled to a straight sword now, but as I have to carry a musket also, I'll trade it off for gingerbread if they'll let me, and if they won't I'll lose it sure for I have enough to carry without it. I can hear the tattoo now before the colonel's quarters at the other end of the camp and our boys are singing, "Home Again" as they lie around me in our tent. I thank goodness that none of them get homesick like some do that I know in our right. I do despise these whiners. I expect (I have just this instant heard that they have been fighting in Washington for the last 24 hours. Now I'll finish the sentence I had commenced) to be with those I love in eight months if the expected battle in Washington results favorably for our country, if not, do not look for me for three years. If they whip us again there I want to fight the rest of my life if necessary, and die before we recognize them as anything but Rebels and traitors who must be humbled. I don't believe yet awhile the news but I kind o' feel it all through me that there is a battle more to be recorded and that we are the victors. All that we have heard is that they are fighting. Colonel Turchin's 19th left Cairo last night for the east somewhere. We are rapidly learning to appropriate and confiscate. On our last scout one of our boys rode a stray horse back and another came in with a female jackass and her child. Chickens are very scarce here now and the natives complain that sweet potato hills have turned into holes since we have been here. Our mess have this p. m. confiscated the roof of a man's barn to cover our cook house with.

Norfolk (date torn off.)

The colonel talks some to-night about a forward movement, and two regiments have come across the river from the Kentucky side this evening, the Iowa 2d and 7th. The 17th are still opposite us and I have seen none of them yet. Our cavalry scouts are fighting now more or less every day. Yesterday a party of the Iowa 7th were out hunting bushwhackers when they were attacked by a company of horsemen of whom they killed four. One of our men was shot while returning from a scout. They routed the enemy but came back and reported four of their men missing, but the lost four have all come in to-day. Our men think they finished a couple at least but 'tis questionable. We are all again bored to death with lying still, but patience and we'll get what we want in time. We have the report here to-day that Colonel Mulligan has capitulated to Price, Jackson & Co. at Lexington. This, if true, will certainly retard our movement down the Mississippi. I'm getting perfectly indifferent about Fremont's being superseded or as to who has the command. It seems to me that none of our commanders are doing anything. With at least 75,000 troops at Paducah, Cairo and in Missouri to allow the gallant Mulligan to be forced to surrender is perfectly shameful. It's disheartening to a soldier, I tell you. Let them go on, if this war goes against us 'twill be the fault of our commanders and not of the men, sure. Yesterday information was brought our colonel that a battery was in course of erection on the Kentucky shore six miles below us. We were put on steamboats 2,000 or 2,500 strong and preceded by two gunboats scooted down, when within a mile of the place our regiment was landed and we marched down but of course found no battery.

Norfolk, September 30, 1861.

You think I'm doing pretty well in the number of my letters, don't you? I can afford to for you are the only correspondent I have. You musn't be surprised if you don't get letters from me so regularly after this, for if we start back in the country, as I expect we will, to intercept Price's retreat if Fremont whips him, we may be away from mails and such like for some time. If anything happens to me you will hear it just as quick as the news can be taken to you.

Since my last we have had some more fun here. Our company was out a few miles the other day to capture an old cuss we thought was peddling news from our camp down to Columbus. He had skedaddled though before we got to his house. We gobbled up all the loose plunder we could find lying around, it wasn't much, and marched back. We had a mighty good time on picket a few nights ago. It was confounded cold, bushwhackers or no bushwackers we concluded to have a fire. A couple of the boys volunteered to go back to camp for kettles and coffee, and we found lots of nice roasting ears in the field we were camped in, and a kind of pumpkin that ate very well after a little roast before the fire. Then there were splendid pawpaws, lots of nuts of all kinds which a little fire made ripe, and we sat and cooked and ate all night. I can eat, if necessary, 36 hours without intermission except for an occasional drink, and I drink nearly a half gallon of coffee per day.

Last night the Pekin company in our regiment were on picket and at 3 this morning they were attacked. Ten of them held their ground against 150 half-mounted and half-foot and finally made them scoot. It was a devilish brave thing. The Rebels left one dead and one so badly wounded that he'll die to-night, and carried off two others dead and four badly wounded. A lot more were scratched. But one of our men was wounded, and that a flesh wound in the arm, that will hardly take him off duty. The firing roused us here in the camp and we thought from the noise that the longed fight had come at last for certain. I tell you it was funny when the long roll (we would not get out of bed without the long roll for a thousand cannons these cold nights) to see the boys scramble for shoes and accoutrements. There was some profanity. I have just been to see a poor devil that has blown half of his head off this afternoon to get rid of his troubles. A soldier. Don't know what he suicided for. We are messed off now, 15 in a tent, each tent's inmates cooking and eating by themselves.

Bird's Point, October 2, '61.

Just at noon yesterday orders came to strike tents and in an hour we were under way and have come to a halt in this forsaken hole. It seems that the 8th can't get out of hearing of the Cairo morning and evening gun anyway. Our major says they are talking of chucking us into Cairo and making us garrison it this winter. I'll be tempted to desert if 'tis so. The 22d call us the featherbed regiment now, and if they keep us this way much longer we will be tender as women. It was late and we were tired when we pitched our tents last night and we didn't "ditch round" as usual, trusting to providence for a dry night. But 'twas confidence misplaced and some of the boys found the ground slightly damp under them this morning. It has been raining like the devil all a. m. and the mud is quite salubrious. I find my old Havana schoolmate, Jem Walker, here in the 28th, Ritter's company. Haven't seen Smith yet. The Rebels came right up to Norfolk after we left last night, and about 3 I heard the cavalry called out, and this morning I see the 2d Iowa and 11th Illinois are gone. Suppose they all went down that way. I have disposed of all my surplus baggage and now have two shirts, two pair socks, one blanket, one pair pants, one coat, one pair shoes, one hat, toothbrush and one pocket comb. That's all I'm worth. I can get all the clothing I want of the quartermaster any time. You scout the idea of one's liking such a life as this. I tell you that I never was so well satisfied in my life as I have been since I joined the army. I do really enjoy it all the time, and if our boys here write the truth home they will say the same. Nobody ever heard me grumble a word about soldiering and never will if they don't station us in Cairo.

Bird's Point, October 10, 1861.

I have just finished a dinner of cider, cake, bread, butter, etc. We have just been paid off and of course have to indulge in a few delicacies for awhile. Last Tuesday we were ordered to strike tents and pack for a march. It wasn't much of a

3

march though for we were put on the cars and rolled out to Charleston, 12 miles from here, where we camped on a beautiful little prairie adjoining town. The 11th Illinois, Taylor's artillery and two companies of cavalry and our regiment formed the party. I think we were out looking after that damned Jeff Thompson, who is reported everywhere from Ironton down to New Madrid. I don't believe he has a thousand men, for there seems to be nothing reliable about any of the reports we have of him. The natives up at Charleston told us that Jeff was at Sykestown, 12 miles from there, with 5,000 or 6,000 troops, and our pickets had several little fights with his, or what we supposed to be his, but—well, the generals may know better but we that stay in the ranks think that there is no enemy nearer than Columbus save a few small bands of bushwhackers, who, under the impression that they are upholding principles eternal and doing their country service, gobble up everything sweet or sour, that weighs less than a ton. We came down from Charleston Thursday. We marched about 10 miles of the way through an immense (it seemed so to me) cypress swamp. I think Mrs. Stowes' "Dred" would have enjoyed that swamp hugely. It was rather an interesting piece of scenery for a first view, but I don't think I should enjoy living in sight of it. The 18th, Colonel Lawler, worked six or eight weeks in this swamp repairing bridges the secesh had burnt, and it put half their men on the sick list. We got our pay in treasury notes but they are as good as the gold. Lots of the boys have traded them off for gold "even up." I get $21 this time for two months and five days, our other boys got $14 or $15. I am third sergeant now, our second having been appointed sergeant major. I think I should rather be sergeant, for the field officers make a kind of servant of the sergeant major. I send you a couple of daguerreotypes to let you see what a "skeleton" I have become. Our boys are all very well. The 17th is in a pretty hard condition, nearly half of them sick and as a regiment pretty badly used up. We have been paid twice and they only $10 yet.

Bird's Point, October 18, 1861

We yesterday drew our overcoats, and splendid ones they are. The cloth is light blue and they reach nearly to our feet. They have capes on them that come over a fellow's head nicely nights. The weather is about like you have I expect, but I know we will be very comfortable with the clothing we have in any weather. I wouldn't have the war end before next spring for anything, for I want to try a winter out doors. Every one of the Canton boys is in excellent health and all very well satisfied. The boys are receiving letters almost every day that read "we have heard that so and so is sick," and this morning John Wallace got one that said that Sam Nutt and three others were shot while on guard. You may know that such reports are always lies unless you see it with the names in the papers long before a letter would reach you from here. John Wallace is just one of the best boys in the camp. It would do you good to see how contentedly the boys all take things. There is more life and fun in our tent every night than we ever had at home. Sam and Fred Norcott make more noise and sport in an evening than all Canton can furnish in a week. We love and respect all our officers but one, and he is the best officer we have, but a little too much regular army about him. Our captain is what the girls would call a "dear old fellow," though he does have his own way every time. It seems to be the right way always so we think the world of him. They are just burying some poor fellow. We have had several deaths in the regiment lately. They do not play the prettiest dead marches here. I have been detached from the company for a week acting as sheriff of a court martial. Colonel Marsh, Colonel Logan, Colonel Tuttle of the Iowa 2d, and a couple of captains form the court. I have four men a day to guard the prisoners and two orderlies to send errands for me, so I play big injun strongly. The prisoner murdered a comrade while we were down at Norfolk. Smote him on the head with a club. He is from Company B of our regiment.

That company, besides this case, had a man shot dead the
other day by one of their own company. An accident.
This morning they had a man stabbed, and day before
yesterday they confined one of their men for trying to kill
two others. For all this they are really a good company
of men. We had a review Tuesday this week of 6 regiments, 2 batteries and 400 or 500 cavalry. Very fine. I
suppose you saw an account of the Pekin company of our
regiment killing four or five Rebels that made an attack
on them while they were guarding a bridge. Ten of them
stood their ground against a large party, and held the
ground too. We buried two secesh and they carried off
four. We lost none. The best fight yet was ten miles
below here the other day between 26 of our men and 160
Rebels. You've seen it in the papers. Sam Nutt and John
Wallace stood guard two nights before at the place where
the first fight was. Oh heavens, I hope I can date my
next from somewhere else.

Bird's Point, October 27, 1861.

I haven't written for a full week because I really had nothing to write and in fact I have not now. Although soldiering
is a hugely lazy life, yet these short days we seem to have but
little spare time. We are up nearly an hour before sun up, have
breakfast about sunrise, drill (company) from about 8 to 10.
Cards until dinner time, 12; lounge or read until 2; battalion
drill untill 4:30 or 5, supper, and then dress parade at 4:45;
from candle lighting untill bedtime (taps), 10, we have cards
mixed with singing or some awful noises from Sam Nutt and
Fred Norcott. Those two boys can make more noise than
three threshing machines. Our boys are all in excellent
health and prime spirits. Fred and Sam and Sid are fatter
than the Canton folk ever saw them. There are but four
regiments at the Point now, so we have to work on the en-
trenchments every fourth day two hours or cut down trees
the same length of time. We are clearing away the timber
within 500 yards of the earthworks. It is mostly cottonwood

and very heavy. They stand so thick that if we notch a dozen or so pretty deep and then fell one it will knock three or four down. Lin Coldwell and I are going to get a set of chess to-morrow. That gunboat, "New Era," that the papers blow so much about is of no account as a gunboat. She is laid up at Mound City for a battery. The men on her have told me that she wouldn't half stand before a land battery that amounted to anything. We are beginning to have some frost here, but I don't believe we'd suffer a bit lying in these tents all winter. The sickly season is over now and the health is improving very much. We had 18 on the sick list in our company three weeks ago and now we have but three, and they are only diarrhœa or the like. I tell you I feel as strong as two mules and am improving. I haven't been the least unwell yet. Our boys are perfectly sick for a fight so they can be even with the 17th. We are sure that the 17th doesn't deserve to be named the same day with us for drill or discipline, with all their bragging. They are an awful set of blowhards. Sid., Theo., Ben Rockhold and John Wallace are on picket out of our mess to-night. The picket was fired on last night where they are posted to-night.

Cape Girardeau, November 11, 1861.

We have just arrived here after a week's absence from any sign of civilized life. Saturday the 2d we (our company) went out six or seven miles from the Point to guard a bridge on the Cairo and Fulton Railroad. Sunday we came back to the Point, and found the tents of our regiment all struck and everything prepared for a march. By dark we were all safely stowed on the "Aleck Scott," and also five companies of the 11th Illinois. At 10 p. m. the boat shoved out, but had to tie to all night about 10 miles up the river on account of the fog. Monday at 10 a. m. we landed at Commerce between Cape Girardeau and Cairo and stayed there all night. Up to this time we had not the most distant idea of where we were going, but here we began to guess that we were after Jeff Thompson and company. Tuesday morning we started back into the country and camped for the night on Colonel Hunter's farm, a distance of 18 miles. (I forgot to mention that

the 18th and 22d Illinois with three companies, cavalry and
two pieces artillery joined us before we started from Commerce, making a total of some 2,200 men.)   This Colonel
Hunter is in the Rebel Army When we stopped at his farm
there was a large flock of sheep, at least 40 goats and pigs,
turkey, geese, chickens and ducks without number. After we
had been there a half hour I don't believe there was a living
thing on the farm that did not come with our train. I never
saw a slaughterhouse on as large a scale before. The
next day the boys made an awful uproar on the road, playing
that the sheep, hogs, geese, etc., inside of them were calling
for their comrades. Wednesday night we stopped at Little
Water River and the slaughtering commenced immediately.
All along the road up to this place every horse or mule that
showed himself was gobbled instanter, a bridle cramped, and
some footman made happy. It was hard to tell whether our
force was infantry or cavalry that night. This was too much
for the colonel, so next morning he drew the brigade up in
column of company and gave us fits. He made the men turn
every horse loose; told us that the next man that cramped
anything without permission would be dealt with as severely
as the regulations would allow. That suited me. I never
have been disgusted with soldiering save in those two days, and
I tell you that I did then feel like deserting. When we are
marching through a country as thoroughly secesh as this is,
I think that the men should be allowed fresh meat at the expense of the natives; but there is a proper and soldier-like way
to get it. We can send our foraging party ahead and have
all we want at camp when we halt, but to allow men to
butcher everything they see is moblike. Wednesday night
Jeff's men tried to burn a bridge a short distance from us
and this led to a little brush, but the cavalry only were engaged. Thursday we marched all day and went into camp
at night without seeing a horse. The march was through the
"Black Swamp." The ground was covered with this black
moss four inches deep and so thick that 'tis like a carpet.
That was an awful gloomy road and I was glad enough to

land at a nice clear stream and have orders to pitch tents.
That night not a thing was pressed. The next day we got into
Bloomfield about 9 a. m. and found Jeff gone. For the third
time we pitched tents on one of his deserted camps. I have
just now heard that we started with orders to push on down
to New Madrid, but here the orders were countermanded and
we were started to Cape Girardeau. This Bloomfield is a rank
Rebel hole. The first Rebel company in Missouri was raised
here. It is the county seat of Stoddard or Scott, and a very
fine place. Here the boys got the understanding that we were
to be allowed some liberties and take them they did. They
broke open four or five stores whose owners had left, and helped
themselves. Colonel Dick (Oglesby) thought this was going too
far, so he stopped it and sent a police force around to collect the
stolen (pressed rather) property. I walked around and took
a look at the pile they collected. There were lots of women's
bonnets, girl's hats, mallets, jars of medicine, looking glasses
three feet long, boys' boots, flat irons, a nice side table and
I don't know what wasn't there. It beat anything I ever saw.
The men had no way to carry these things but on their backs,
and what the devil they stole them for is more than I know.
Well, the colonel divided the stuff out again among the men,
but stopped stealing entirely for the future. We have been a
respectable regiment since then. On the march back to the
Cape, the 10th Iowa was ahead of us and they fired several
houses. We (our regiment) saved one of the houses but the
rest burned down. The march back to the Cape was a fast
one but quiet. We arrested some 20 or 30 of Jeff's men but
released them all again. At Bloomfield my tent was pitched
under a tree on which we saw the marks of three ropes to the
ends of which Colonel Lowe attached three men not very long
since. The ropes had cut through the moss on the tree and
the marks will be visible a long time. We also arrested a
number of men that had been concerned in hanging Union
men through the country, At Round Pond an intelligent man
told us that 17 men (Union) had been hung and shot inside
of three days and he saw their bodies in one pile lying in the

woods. We have marched over 100 miles this trip, and we have not seen a mile of prairie. I haven't been 20 feet from a tree for three months. The 17th are going into winter quarters here. Our regiment will certainly be in the next fight at Columbus. We start back to the Point at 3 to-morrow morning.

Bird's Point, November 13, 1861.

Home once more. We all call this home now. Just as we landed last night the Iowa 7th was forming for dress parade. One company had but 11 and another but 15 men; all that came out of the Belmont fight safely. Other companies had half and some three-fourths of their men they started with. General Grant tries to make out that there were about 150 or 175 men lost on our side, but I'll stake my life that we lost not less than 500. I am sure that the 22d Illinois lost not less than 175, the 7th Iowa at least 200, and the other three regiments 150 more. Grant says that he achieved a victory and accomplished the object of his expedition. It may be so (the latter part of it) but almost every one here doubts the story. He says his object was to threaten Columbus, to keep them from sending reinforcements to Price. Well he has threatened them, had a fight, and why they can't send reinforcements now as well as before, is more than I know. I never will believe that it was necessary to sacrifice two as good regiments as there were in the West, to accomplish all that I can see has been done this time. Altogether there were some 6,000 men from here, Cape Girardeau and Ironton, on the expedition that our regiment was on marching by different roads. Grant says now that we were all after Jeff Thompson. I don't believe it. I think the Paducah forces were to take Columbus, Grant was going to swallow Belmont, we were to drive all the guerrillas before us to New Madrid, and then with Paducah forces and Grant's we were to take Madrid and probably go on to Memphis or maybe join Fremont with our Army of say 15,000 men. Well, Grant got whipped at Belmont, and that scared him so that he countermanded all our orders and took all the troops back to their old stations by forced marches. There was some very good fighting done at Belmont by both sides. The 22d Illinois and 7th Iowa did about all the fighting, and sustained much the heaviest loss. The boys are not the least discouraged and they all want to go back and try it again. The whole camp has the Columbus fever, and I don't believe there are 20 men that would take a furlough if they thought an advance would be made on Columbus while they were absent. The enemy there are very well fed, clothed and armed. Arkansas and Tennessee troops with some Mississippians. The retreat was a route, for our men were scattered everywhere. I don't care what the papers say, the men that were in it say that every man took care of himself, and hardly two men of a regiment were together. The men ran because they were scattered and saw that the force against them was overwhelming, but the universal testimony is that there was no panic, nine out of ten of the men came on the boats laughing and joking. They had been fighting six or seven hours, and cannon and musketry couldn't scare them any more. There are hundreds of stories, and good ones, out but I always spoil them by trying to put them on paper.

Bird's Point, November 20, 1861

Part of Pitt's (Col. W. Pitt Kellogg's) cavalry are here. We are glad to see them as it will relieve us of considerable picket duty. But otherwise cavalry are of not much service in this brushy, swampy country. That fox of a Jeff Thompson that we chased down to New Madrid last week, had the impudence to follow us right back and we had hardly got our tents pitched here at the Point before he passed within 12 miles of us to the river above, and captured a steamboat. Report says that there were nearly a dozen officers on the boat, and a paymaster, with money to pay off the Cape Girardeau troops. Jeff is a shrewd one, and the man that captures him will do a big thing. Back in the country where we were, he made the natives believe that he whipped Ross and company at Fredericktown, and killed 400 federals with a loss of only ten of his men. Don't it almost make you sick the way that 17th brag and blow about themselves? That affair at Fredericktown didn't amount to a thing. From the best information I can get, there was not to exceed 50 Rebels killed, and I'm sure not that many. Thompson is stronger to-day than ever. This thing of sending infantry after him is all bosh, although we tried it again yesterday. It failed of course. The boys came back through the rain last night about 10, tired and mad as the deuce. A thousand cavalry may possibly get him some day, but they will be sharp ones, sure. In this fight at Belmont 1,200 of our men at first completely whipped 2,400 of theirs, four regiments, then the whole of ours, 2,600 ran like the devil before and through 5,600 of theirs. These are the true figures.

Bird's Point, Mo., November 24, 1861.

Sabbath morning, 10 o'clock.

I'm in clover. I've got a great big "comfort," weighs a ton, that has been sent to my partner and myself from a young lady in Bloomington. We've tramped so much since I received that pair of blankets from you, and we never know when we start whether we're coming back here again or no, that being unable to carry them I sold them. We have had considerable cold weather. Lots of frost, and for the last two days it has been freezing all the time. We have always slept perfectly warm and getting used to it by degrees.

I never hear anyone complain. Yesterday we made a furnace in our tent that works admirably and now I wouldn't give a snap for any other winter quarters. This furnace is a grand thing. It keeps our tent dry and healthy and is as comfortable to me now as ever our house was. Don't trouble yourself in the least about our underclothing. We all have more than

we want and can get any quantity at any time. Other clothing the same. We commenced building log houses for winter quarters this morning. Theo Thornton and Clem Wallace
of our mess are up the river now cutting logs for them. We
never drill Sundays, but for anything else we have no Sunday.
We have no chaplain in our regiment. Our captain is religious but he is out now doing as much work as any of the
men. We can enjoy ourselves very well here this winter, but
of course we are very much disappointed in not getting into
active service. I think that when our gunboats get here we
will at least be allowed a trial on Columbus, but you know,
and I know, that I don't know anything about it. We have
had two awful rains within a week as the ponds covered with
ice on our parade ground will testify. The first one caught
six of our boys fifteen miles up the river cutting logs for our
huts. It wet them beautifully. In camp for some reason they had
doubled the pickets, strengthened the camp guard and ordered
us to sleep on our arms. I think they were troubled with the
old scare again. About 10:30 while the storm was at its
height heavy firing commenced all at once right in the middle of the camp. What a time there was. Colonel Oglesby got
his signals ready, regiments formed in the rain and the devil
was to pay generally. It turned out that it was a green Iowa
regiment that had just returned from another unsuccessful
chase after Jeff. 'Twas an awful trick and only the greenest
troops would have done it.

Bird's Point, Mo., December 1, 1861.

This, the beginning of winter, is the warmest and altogether
the most pleasant day we have had for several weeks. During
our whole trip to Bloomfield and back we had splendid
weather, but ever since our return it has been at least very
unsplendid. The climax was reached day before yesterday
and capped with several inches of snow. I was up the river
15 miles at the time with a party loading a flatboat with logs
for our huts. We had a sweet time of it and lots of fun. The
mud was from six inches to a foot deep, and by the time we
got the logs to the boat they were coated with mud two in-

ches thick, and before we got a dozen logs on the boat we had a second coat on us, from top to toe of mud. It snowed and rained all the time we worked but I heard no complaint from the men, and in fact I have never seen so much fun anywhere as we had that day. There is any amount of game where we were, the boys said that were out, and they brought to camp several skinned "deer." I tried some of the "venison" but it tasted strangely like hog.

Of course drill is discontinued for the present, and as working on the quarters is almost impossible we sit and lie in the tent and gas and joke and eat and plan devilment. We have a barrel of apples now, lots of pecans and tobacco and not a thing to trouble us. The enemy have quit coming around here and we can stroll six or seven miles without danger if we get past our pickets safely. There was a great deal of firing down at Columbus yesterday and I heard some more this morning. I don't know whether the gunboats are down or not. It may be the Rebels are practicing with their big guns; or maybe they are firing a salute over the fall of Fort Pickens. It will be a great joke if they take that, won't it? I believe myself that they will take it. Two of our new gunboats came down day before yesterday. We will have in all 12 gunboats, 40 flatboats carrying one mortar each and 15 propellers for towing purposes, besides the steamboats for transporting troops. Makes quite a fleet and will fill the river between here and Columbus nearly full. There are not very many troops here now. Only five regiments of cavalry and four or five batteries of artillery. Not over 12,000 in all. We have nearly 1,000 sailors and marines here now and they are such cusses that they have to keep them on a steamboat anchored out in the river. We see by the papers this morning that the fleet has captured another sand bar. A good one on the bar. We are greatly puzzled to know if we really are going down the river this winter. We are preparing winter quarters here for only 12,000 men. Now all these troops they are running into St. Louis cannot be intended for up the Missouri river, for the troops are also returning from there. I don't believe either that they intend to keep them in St.

Louis this winter for they have only quarters provided there for a garrison force, so I guess it must mean down the river, but am sure they won't be ready before six weeks or two months. We have a report here that Governor Yates is raising 60 day men to garrison these points while we "regulars" will be pushed forward. Jem Smith is down here trying to get information of his brother Frank who is a prisoner. There are a good many Rebels deserting now. Our pickets bring them into camp. They are mostly Northern men who pretend they were pressed in and are glad to escape. Frank Smith is in Company A, Captain Smith's company, at Paducah. It was Company B, Captain Taylor's, that was in the Belmont fight. You could see just as well as not why I can't come home if you'll take the trouble to read General Halleck's General Order No. 5 or 6, that says, "Hereafter no furloughs will be granted to enlisted men," etc.

We had a first rate lot of good things from Peoria yesterday. They were sent us for Thanksgiving but were a day late. Chickens, cranberries, cake, etc. The boys say that a Rebel gunboat has just showed his nose around the point and Fort Holt is firing away pretty heavily, but I guess the boat is all in some chap's eye. Hollins is down at Columbus with about a dozen vessels of war. I have just been out to see what the boys said was the pickets coming in on the run, but some say its only a gunboat coming up through woods, so I guess I'll not report a prospect of a fight.

Monday, December 2, 1861.

While I was writing last night there really was a Rebel gunboat came up the river and fired into Fort Holt. Impudent, wasn't it? The Fort replied, and Fort Cairo also shot a couple of shells over our heads toward the rascals, but they fell short. We could see the troops at Fort Holt out under arms for an hour. Taylor's battery went off down the Norfolk road at a slashing pace to try and get a shot at the boat but was too late.

It is very cold this morning and snowing again. We are perfectly comfortable, though.

Bird's Point, Mo., December 11, 1861.

Our cavalry brought in 16 prisoners to-night, about 10 last night; a band of Thompson's men took a couple of boys from our regiment prisoners, out 10 miles from here at the water tank on the railroad. The owner of the house happened to be outside when they surrounded the house and he scooted down here with the news, and by 2 o'clock we had a lot of cavalry and infantry en route for the scene of action. The cavalry started them out of the brush and captured this 16. The Rebels killed one of Colonel Oglesby's men. They did not recover our men but started up and lost another gang that probably has them.

We will be in our quarters next week although we don't need them. It is rather pleasant here now. I took a swim yesterday. 'Twas confounded cold, but I wanted to bathe so I took the river for it. We haven't had a man complaining in the company for a week. We buried one poor fellow last week, but he would have died at home. When I was home last I weighed 142, now I weigh 160. Can you imagine me.

Bird's Point, Mo., December 22, 1861.

This is a dark, dismal, snowy and confoundedly disagreeable Sunday. Cold, sloppy and nasty! We moved into our cabin last night but it is not finished yet, as a crack along the comb of the roof and sundry other airholes abundantly testify. The half snow half rain comes in when and where it pleases, and renders our mud floor comfortable in about the 40th degree. Don't this sound like grumbling, Well, I don't mean it as such, for I am sure the boys are as cheery as I ever saw them, and I wouldn't think of these little things except when writing home, and then the contrast between its cozy comforts and soldiering in cold, wet weather makes itself so disagreeably conspicuous to my spiritual eyes that I can't pass it unnoticed. Love Hamblin came over here last night and is now standing by the fireplace indulging in an ague shake, which if not pleasant is not to my eyes ungraceful.

No more troops have arrived here, and save the whole gunboat fleet being here there are no new signs of the down-river trip we are all waiting so impatiently for.

Bird's Point, December 29, 1861.

Your letter giving us notice of your sending a box came to hand yesterday with express charges inclosed. I shall go over to Cairo to-morrow to get them if they are there. I haven't been to Cairo for a month. All of the 7th cavalry are on this side now and there are about a dozen of them here all the time. Colonel Kellogg will be here next week. One company in that regiment did the first scouting for the 7th this morning. They rode out southwest about 15 miles and brought in 22 prisoners. 'Tis said there are two or three officers among them, but I rather think they are only a lot of swamp farmers. The boys got only three or four guns it is said, and that is not more than the complement of one woodsman in this country. The boys think they have almost taken Columbus. It was not our Canton company. We are at last established in our quarters and thoroughly "fixed up" with all the modern improvements in the housekeeping line, coupled with the luxuries of the ancients and the gorgeous splendor and voluptuousness of the middle ages. We have a chimney whose base is rock, the age of which man cannot tell, whose towering top is constructed of costly pecan wood boughs embalmed in soft Missouri mud cement. We have a roof and floor, beds and door, of material carved or sawed from the lofty pines of Superior's rock-bound shores. Our door latch is artfully contrived from the classic cypress, and curiously works by aid of a string pendant on the outside, and when our string is drawn inside who can enter? We have tables and chairs and shelves without number and a mantle piece, and, crowning glories, we have good big straw sacks, a bootjack and a dutch oven. Government has also furnished a stove for each mess of 15 in our regiment, so we have nothing more to ask for; not a thing. This is just no soldiering at all. Its hard, but its true that we can't find a thing to pick trouble out of. We are to-day more comfortable

than 45 out of 50 people in old Canton. Our building is
warmer than our house at home, our food is brought to us
every third day in such abundance that we can trade off
enough surplus to keep us in potatoes, and often other comforts and luxuries. Within 500 yards of us there is wood
enough for 10,000 for 20 years, and—I can't half do it justice, so I'll quit. I borrowed a horse of the cavalry, Christmas,
slipped past our picket through to the brush and had a long
ride all over the country around Charleston. No adventures
though. General Paine took command here to-day. He is an
old grannie. We are glad he is here though, for we will get
our colonel back by it. You can't imagine what a change the
last month of cool weather has produced in our troops. From
a sick list six weeks ago of nearly 300 in our regiment, with
65 in the hospital, we have come down or up rather, to eight
in hospital, and not over 25 or 30 on the "sick in quarters"
list. It is astonishing! And here these "damphool" "Forward to Richmond" papers are talking about the fearful deci-
mation that winter will make in our ranks. They "don't know
nothing" about soldiering.

January 2, 1862.

We've waited patiently until after New Year for the box
of provisions, and nary box yet. Have given it up for a goner.
We're just as much obliged to you as though we had received
it. We haven't yet eaten all the tomatoes, etc., that came with
the quilts. Partly because we are too lazy to cook them, but
mostly because we don't hanker arter them. Beans, bacon
and potatoes are our special hobbies or favorites rather, and
we are never dissatisfied on our inner man's account when we
have them in abundance and of good quality. Company H
of the 17th, Captain Boyd, was down here on the 30th. All
the boys save Chancy Black and Billy Stockdale were along.
We had a grand time, Nelson's, Boyd's and our boys being
together for the first time in the war. Yesterday, New Year,
the camp enjoyed a general frolic. A hundred or two cavalry boys dressed themselves to represent Thompson's men

and went galloping around camp scattering the footmen and making noise enough to be heard in Columbus. The officers of the 11th Infantry were out making New Year calls in an army wagon with 30 horses to it, preceded by a splendid band. The "boys" got a burlesque on the "ossifers." They hitched 20 mules to a wagon and filled it with a tin pan and stovepipe band, and then followed it in 60-mule wagon around the camp and serenaded all the headquarters.

General Paine said to-day that our regiment and the 11th would move in a week, but I don't believe it.

Bird's Point, January 5, 1862.

We received the box of provisions to-day in very good order considering the length of time they have been knocked about on the route. It came by freight by some mistake or other. The doughnuts were the only articles spoiled. They had moulded. I sent the box over from Cairo but was not here when it was opened, so that aside from one cake labeled from Aunt Nancy, I don't know where a thing comes from. I did recognize your home snaps, too, and thought there was something very familiar in the taste of a mince pie that I ate, but I am too badly used up to-night to be sure of anything, and tell you as I want to how much we are obliged to our good mothers for their thoughtful care for us. I believe every boy in our mess has received socks and mittens from home. One received them by mail from his mother in New York City. At 7 this morning I went over to Cairo with 50 men after forage for our teams. We stood around in the cold, mud and rain for five hours before we got to work, and then the men had all run off but 15 or 18 and we had to roll bales of hay over a way almost impracticable—and all told, it was a mean job and used me up very near totally.

Ame Babcock, Ike McBean, English and Leary have been to see us nearly every day for a week. Colonel Kellogg took supper with us last night. The gunboats were hammering away all day yesterday down the river, and after dinner the general sent our company with four others from our regiment

4

and nearly all of the 1th, with one day's rations, down the
river. We waded about six miles through the mud down the
creek and then came back without knowing what we went for.
There are none of us that are sick, but we don't feel as well
as we did in tents. I wish we hadn't built these cabins.

Holly Springs, Miss., January 7, 1862.

The colonel and I were ordered to report here to give evidence before the "Court of Inquiry," convened to inquire into
the case of the 109th Illinois Infantry reported for disloyalty.
I started from Jackson yesterday but had to lay over at Grand
Junction last night waiting for a train. We got here this
p. m., immediately gave our evidence, and will return to-morrow. Don't know that they will do anything with the 109th,
but am satisfied that to prevent its dishonoring our state it
should be broken up. I heard General Grant say that if the
charges were sustained he would transfer the loyal men to
some of the old regiments, cashier the officers and make the
disloyal men work their time out at Alton. Am staying to-
night at Mr. Barney's. He is a Northern man and thank
God, a loyal one. He built a portion of the M. & C. R. R.
and most of the M. C. R. R.. His wife is also Northern and
loyal. Have been very wealthy, but the war has reduced them.
They both, after seven years in the South, bear me out in the
opinion I expressed in my last, of these Southern people.
They have lost $50,000 worth of negroes by our army, but are
willing to lose the rest for our cause. The army has all
moved back to the M. & C .R. R. line except one division,
Lanman's, which occupies this place. General Grant's
headquarters are yet here. There is the d——st state of affairs in this country now that 'tis possible to think of. Every
house within ten miles of the army is visited about five times
a day by our soldiers, and the guerrillas (both work on the
same principles) and each time visitors divide with the family
the provisions and household goods. There is more stealing
in one day here than the whole United States suffered in a
year before the war. The correspondent of the St. Louis

Democrat is writing on the same table with me for his paper, ever and anon ripping out some tall oaths because he was not at the Vicksburg battle. We heard last night, direct, that the place was taken, but we are not sure of it yet. We have lost immensely at that place but the gain is worth it. Trains are coming through from Memphis now and the army will be on full rations again shortly. The M. & O. R. R. will not be running for ten days yet. There are some eight miles of the latter road almost totally destroyed above Trenton, much of it trestle work. The sick will all leave here to-night and within five days this secesh hole (what there is left of it) will be left to its secesh inhabitants.

Bird's Point, January 10, 1862.

Since daylight yesterday morning we have been all ready with five days' rations and expecting every moment the orders to fall in and commence a march. We were delayed untill 11 a. m. to-day by a fog so dense that boats could not run even from Cairo to this point. All that time we were in the greatest suspense and after everybody had conjectured all their conjectures, we were yet perfectly in the dark in regard to our destination. All the troops here, save enough for guard duty, are going. I believe I'm within bounds when I say that 75,000 different lies have been circulated here in the last 36 hours, and all in regard to the present expedition. Well the suspense is over and we (think we) know that Columbus is our goal.

At 11 a. m. to-day the fog was dispersed by a cold north wind, and immediately two gunboats steamed down the river, giving us the first intimation of our route. They were shortly followed by other gunboats and then by steamers loaded to their utmost capacity with soldiers. All afternoon they have been going down. The last boat that I saw was towing a couple of flats loaded with ambulances, or "soldier-buggies." I think all the troops have gone from Cairo and the boats that carried them will be back and take us at daylight to-morrow noon. I think they are landing them about six miles this side of Columbus, maybe not so far from there. General McClernand is taking his whole stock in the soldier business with him. It's a permanent thing certain. If this really means Columbus, and I don't see how it can be anything else, it has been managed with more secrecy than any expedition, besides, up to this time in war. I never guessed it within the possibilities of a month. These generals, we have three of them here (Grant, Paine and McClernand) may know their business, but we of the ranks don't understand what kind of truck 20,000 men want with the army at Columbus. And 10,000 is, I'm sure, considerably outside of the number that will move from here. There are probably 10,000 more at Paducah, that I think are also going. Well, maybe we'll get the place, hope we will. If we don't it won't be the men's fault, for we do hate that hole. It's funny what an effect this soldiering has on men. I suppose there is no mistake about our being within two days, at farthest, of a great battle, and yet these men don't to any eye show a sign of even a shadow of care or concern. Since I commenced this I don't believe that one of them has given it a thought. To save my neck I can't get up enough excitement to kill a flea or even to warn him. The boys are almost all playing cards. Sam Nutt and my chum Hy thought they didn't get enough supper to-night, so they put about a peck of beans in to boil and have just got them in eating order. I suppose Sam can plant more beans than any other living man of his weight. They have also a lot of pig's feet between them. Little Ame Babcock and Ike McBean are going with us to-morrow. Colonel Kellogg goes with five companies of his regiment. The Canton company does not go. I am not real well now but I wouldn't miss this trip to Columbus to save my life. I've had my heart set on being at that fight a long time and I'm gong if I can walk two miles.

January 13, '62. I wrote this letter and thought I wouldn't send it untill we'd start and save myself a chance of being fooled, but now I'll send it to show how badly I was misled.

Bird's Point, Mo., January 13, 1862.

After all the excitement and promise we have had of a trip into Dixie, we are still here in our cabins, with the prospect of a move further off than ever. The 25,000 troops that are "on their way from St. Louis to Cairo" must have went up in a fog. General Grant must have credit for fooling everybody from the reporters up. He did it beautifully. We all here at this point kept our wagons loaded for two days with five days' rations, expecting to start every hour. The troops have all left Cairo and gone down opposite Norfolk (where we were a month) and camped. It is cold as the devil, and they must suffer a good deal as none of them have ever been out of Cairo before, and hardly know what rough soldiering is. Charley Cooper's company is with them. I believe that the whole object of the expedish is to keep the Columbians from sending reinforcements to the Bowling Green folks. The dispatches about the 25,000 forward movement, etc., all work to the same end. Some "damb'd" hounds shot four of our 7th cavalry boys dead a couple of mornings since. It was regular murder. They were on picket and in the evening they went out some seven miles from camp and got their supper and engaged breakfast in the morning. Just before daylight they started out for breakfast and when within two miles of the place three men that were concealed behind a log by the roadside shot them all dead. Their horses wheeled and trotted back to the infantry picket. The infantry sent word to camp and some cavalry went out and found them all dead. They could find tracks of but three men, and it is supposed that they ran as quick as they fired, for our boys' bodies were not touched. They were only armed with sabers and the 7th refuse to go on any more picket duty untill they are better armed. One of the murdered was Dan Lare, a boy that was in Canton a good while, though I believe he did not belong to Nelson's company. The others lived near Bushnell, their names I do not know. We have the chap they took supper with. The boys all think him guilty and have tried to get him away from the guard to kill him, but unsuccessfully so far.

Last night Nelson's company went up to old Bird's and brought him, his three sons and five other men and all Bird's buck niggers down to camp as prisoners. They also got 10 good guns. His (Bird's) house is four miles from camp. Some of the boys noticed a long ladder leaning against the house and one of them climbed it and got on the housetop. There he found a splendid ship spy glass with which he could count the tents and see every move in both our camp and Cairo and Fort Holt. Old Bird is a perfect old pirate and a greater does not live.

Bird's Point, Mo., January 20, 1862.

It goes confounded good once more to stand on boards, and be able to sit down without wet coming through a fellow's pants. If I write and tell you where we've been, you won't read it, and if I don't write all about it you'll scold, so of the two I'll choose the first and tell you all I know. We got on the steamer "Aleck Scott" last Tuesday morning with five days' rations and started down the river through very heavy floating ice. 'Twas a very cold day and full three inches of snow lay on the ground. We landed at Fort Jefferson and camped for the night. By some mismanagement our tents and equipage failed to come and we had to cook the bacon we had in our haversacks on sticks over the fire, for supper, and sleep out on the snow, without tents to protect us from the wind. That was a sweet old night! Next day we shouldered our knapsacks, blankets all wet by a rain from 2 to 5 in the morning, and awful heavy, and tramped about ten miles in a southeast direction, through Blanville, Ballard County; and camped on Mayville Creek. Again we lay on the snow and frozen ground with feather beds of brush, and at 9 next morning started on the road to Columbus. We went out to Little Meadows which is about eight or nine miles from Columbus, and halted. Taylor's battery was with us and they now unlimbered and planted their guns to cover all of the four or five roads which lead from here to the river. McClernand's brigade of six or seven regi-

ments, and Cook's of two regiments, were in advance of
us with 1,000 cavalry, and I think that we acted here as a
reserve, for them to fall back on if repulsed in a fight.
We waited here two hours and then formed again and
returned to our camp of the previous night. It had turned
warm by this time and the slush was six inches deep on
our backward march. Slept in the mud that night and
remained in camp all next day, during which it rained
every hour. Friday night it rained in a small way all the
time, and in the morning, (if you remember when you have
too many clothes in a tub of water how the water will
"slosh" when you press the clothes) you'll understand
my "condish." I had my blanket spread on some stiff
brush, and Mr. Aqua surrounded brush, and every time
Wills turned, brush would bend and water would slosh
and blanket would leak and upshot was, Wills was damb'd
wet, but too spunky to get up until he'd had his nap.
Saturday we got out of "provish," and at 1 p. m. we struck
tents, and thought we were off for home sure. But
we only marched back a few miles and camped at Elliott's
Mills. Here, by orders from the colonel, we killed two
hogs for the company, and he took what cornmeal we
wanted from the mill, and we supped sumptuously. Here
although the mud was deep we slept finely. There was a
cypress swamp near and the bark can be torn into the
finest shavings. That was just as good as we wanted.
Sunday we started for the river and of all the marches,
that beats! We waded through at least eight streams
from one to two feet deep and five to ten yards wide.
I had shoes, and after wading the first stream, I cut all
the front upper off to let the water out handier. I made
it gay and festive after that. Object of expedish, don't
know, don't care, only know that it did me good. I feel
100 per cent better than I did when I started. Col. Pitt
Kellogg has brought me my commission as 1st lieutenant
in his regiment, and I am adjutant in the 3d batallion,
Major Rawalts. I go to Cape Girardeau the last of this
week.

II.

February 3, 1862 to June 29, 1862. Brisk cavalry service. Collecting the bones of murdered Union men. Some of the horrors of war. Hankering after his old regiment. Fighting Jeff Thompson and the Rebel gunboats. State jealousies among the troops. Capture of New Madrid. Hunting bushwhackers in the swamps. Rebuilding destroyed bridges. Bullies and plunderers. • Good and bad luck. Spectacular artillery and gunboat duel. Embarking down the river. Sent back. Skirmishing in front of Pope's command. Beauregard's return reconnaisance. Halleck's unfathomable waiting policy. Rear-guarding Pope's division. Intruding on a Rebel dinner party. Sufferings of the sick. Encounter with secesh ladies. Lizards, snakes and scorpions for company. Appointed assistant adjutant general of brigade. Evacuation of Corinth. A masterly retreat. Skirmish fights with the retreating Rebels. Dress parade of brigadier generals. Forcible opinions from Rosecrans. Makes acquaintance with snuff-dipping. General Beauregard's "toddy mixer."

Headquarters, 3d Battalion, 7th Illinois Cavalry,

February 3, 1862.

I am pretty sure that we will start on a scout to-morrow that will give us a ride of 150 miles. From the knowledge I have of it believe that we are going to raise the devil before we get back or get raised ourselves. There are only about 300 of us going, but we are all cavalry and are going fast, will make our mark and then return probably at the same gait. We are going pretty close to New Madrid, into a hot place, where a long stay would not be pleasant. I believe there are 300 or 400 men about 70 miles from here guarding commissary

stores. We are going to try and surprise them and destroy
the goods, kill what we can of the secesh "and get out o' that."
It will be my first scout horseback but I'm going if it busts me.
This is one of Colonel Kellogg's ideas and looks more like work
than anything I have tried yet. It's awful rough weather to
start out in but that makes it more favorable for us. Well, I
have got over the hardest part of soldiering, though I doubt if I
enjoy myself as well as I did in the ranks. I never in my
life spent nine months more pleasantly than those I passed in
the "8th." We had some rough times, but good health and good
company made them as pleasant as and often happier than
life in quarters. I disliked very much to leave the boys I had
been with so long and knew so well, but cupidity and ambition
got the better of the just resolves I made never to leave them
untill the war was over. John Wallace, Fred Norcott and my
chum, Hy Johnson, I did hate to leave. They'll get along just
as well though after they have forgotten us. My chances for
a lieutenancy in that company were first rate but I have got
a better thing, and without so much walking. You never saw
a gladder boy than Sam was when he found himself safe out
of the infantry. He couldn't begin to hold his body. I suppose he and Keefer are having very gay times all by themselves. Sidney and I concluded that our best policy was to
stay here and I'm glad I did so, although I would have liked
a visit home more than I can tell. If we can manage it so as
to get off together some time this spring we will do so, but I
have little hopes now of seeing you untill the war is over. The
major (Rawalt), Seavy, Billy Resor and myself mess together.
We have the wife of one of the men cooking for us and are
living as well as I want to, in regular home style. White table-
cloth, white ware and a fork and spoon for every man. Warm
biscuits and excellent coffee every meal. My duties are light
and not many of them. All writing. We live in a house, too.
My health is booming again. That trip brought me out all
right. This is a splendid place to camp in—high, healthy and
beautiful. There are lots of pretty girls here too, that smile
very sweetly on shoulder-strapped soldiers, but well, you un-

derstand me. I have Billy Stockdale, Trites, Chancey, Geo.
Shinn, Jesse B. and the rest of the Canton boys in the 17th
and they are all in excellent health. Chancey will be home in
a few days I think. He is second lieutenant in the Fairview
Company now. Billy Stockdale is sergeant major. Trites is
romantic, enthusiastic and desponding as ever. Major Rawalt
is one of the best officers there is in the service. He and I
will get along splendidly. We are really off in the morning,
and for a 200-mile march. There will be fun before we get
back.

Cape Girardeau, February 9, 1862.

I, like a good boy, wrote you a long letter yesterday, and,
like a careless fellow, lost it. I told you in it how we "300"
of us, left here in the p. m. of last Monday, rode all night and
at daylight made a desperate charge into Bloomfield where
we found and captured nothing. How a little party of 15
of our boys were surprised some eight miles beyond Bloomfield by 80 Rebels and one of them captured, one badly
wounded and another's horse shot and he at last accounts
running in the swamps. How the major got together his
men and went out and captured some 20 of the bushwhackers
and killed five and how he returned to the Cape, etc. You
have read about this riding and marching all night until I
expect you hardly think of its being fatiguing and somewhat
wearing on the human system, etc., but allow me to assure
you that it is. Novice as I am in riding, the cold and fatigue
were so severe on me that I slept like a top horseback, although
I rode with the advance guard all the time and through country the like of which I hope you'll never see. There is a
swamp surrounding every hill and there are hills the whole
way. Damn such a country. We passed, a small scouting
party of us, the bones of seven Union men. They were all
shot at one time. I didn't go with the party to see them. One
of our guards went out with a party of nine of the 17th Infantry boys and captured some 20 secesh and brought in, in
a gunny sack, the bones of five other Union men. I noticed

there were no skulls and asked the guide where they were. He said that "as true as truth the secesh who murdered them had taken the skulls to use for soup bowls." I was talking with a man to-night who had his two sons shot dead in the house by his side last week. A gang of fellows came to the house while he was eating supper and fired through between the logs. He burst open the door and escaped with but one shot in him after he saw that his sons were killed. I can hardly believe that these things are realities, although my eyes and ears bear witness. In my reading I can remember no parallel either in truth or fiction for the state of things we have in this southeastern portion of Missouri. Anyone can have his taste for the marvelous, however strong, glutted by listening to our scouts and the refugees here. I thank God from my heart that dear old Illinois knows nothing of the horrors of this war. The 17th left here yesterday for Fort Henry. The boys were very glad to start. The old 8th was there with the first. I almost wish I had stayed with her. Without bragging or prejudice I am satisfied that the 8th is the best in every respect of the whole 100 regiments I have seen and has the best colonel. Colonel Kellogg is now commanding the post and Sid. is "A. A. A. General," and I am "A Regimental Adjutant." My duties are light, though, and I am in tip-top health. That ride didn't hurt me at all. I can stand riding with the best of them. I suppose that Sam will be with us soon. I hope our regiment will be ordered to Kentucky. I believe I'd rather be shot there than to bushwhack around in Missouri much longer. The major and I will get along capitally. He stands fatigue equal to any of us. He and I took a ride of 30 miles alone through the swamps the other day. Send my watch the first chance you have.

Cape Girardeau, Mo., February 14, 1862.

Sam arrived here to-night and brought me everything I could wish for except my watch. Jem Harper from Company K is home on furlough and we expect him now shortly, also

Benton Spencer. If you could manage to send the watch by one of them I would be much obliged. I cannot well get along without one now. You seem to be very happy about my getting away from the Point. Rather more so than I am myself. If I had stayed there I would have been with a fair chance to fight—to fight soldiers. Here there are no forces to fight but a few hundred bushwhackers that will lie by the roadside in the swamp, and I believe they would murder Jesus Christ if they thought he was a Union man. We failed in doing what we wanted to the last trip, but I believe we'll get even with them yet. I'd hate mightily to get killed by such a pack of murderers, but that isn't my business. If U. B. and father have experienced such trips as we have, I'll bet I beat them in one thing—enjoying them. I always feel better out that way than in camp. The 11th Missouri is still with us and the 17th has gone to Tennessee. The colonel, Ross, picked out 50 or 60 of his most worthless men and put them on the gunboats. There are some hopes that our regiment will be ordered to Kentucky soon or to Wheaton, Mo., for there is a regiment of Missourians here forming that will be sufficient to guard this vicinity. This place if not entirely secession is very strongly southernly righteous. I am getting acquainted with the female population slowly, not very, and one family of three girls tell me they are positively the only unconditional Union women in town. But the others show nothing of the cold shoulder to us. They are all very friendly and sociable. Quite a number of beautiful girls here. The aristocracy here are all Catholic. Funny, isn't it? Frenchy.

Headquarters 7th Illinois Cavalry,

Cape Girardeau, Mo., February 19, 1862.

Aren't things working right now? Do you notice the accounts of the old 8th, and will you say again that I got out of her ranks at the right time? I knew that the 8th would never make her colonel (God bless him!) to blush, or dishonor her friends or herself. I have seen only the St. Louis papers of 18th with very meager dispatches, but enough to know that she had the "post of honor" and plenty of fighting. Two hundred of them with Major Post are prisoners. I'll bet my life Company E is not among them. If the Rebels will keep the major and exchange the men the regiment will gain. If I was in the 8th yet and knew what I do now I wouldn't leave her for any commission there is in this post. I've got a good easy place here and have the good will of everybody around me, but my soul and sympathies are with the 8th, and it makes me sick to think what a fool I was to leave her. I'll be shot if I don't love that regiment more than I do the whole world beside. I never thought of it so much untill I got away. I expect some of our boys of my old mess are killed, but its all right, "military necessity," somebody has to go under. Eight or nine boatloads of prisoners have passed here to-day. They look a little better than our Missouri prisoners but are not uniformed, although comfortably dressed.

Commerce, Mo., February 25, 1862.

We start to-morrow morning for——with from 25,000 to 40,000 men, who are all piled up here in all kinds of shifts. Our regiment takes the advance. At a venture I'll bet we get whaled, by vastly superior forces. Goodnight.

Near New Madrid, Mo., March 6, 1862.

What oceans of fun we are having here. Here goes for all of it to date, and I'll be lucky if I'm able to tell you the finale. We went down to Commerce the 26th of February. Troops were scattered everywhere over the town and vicinity for 15 miles about. Could form no idea of the number there, but it was variously estimated at from 15,-000 to 45,000. On the 28th we started, our regiment in advance, and camped that night at Hunter's farm, the same place we stopped last fall when going to Bloomfield under Oglesby. We reached Hunter's at 2 o'clock p. m., and at 11 the same morning Jeff Thompson had been there waiting for us with six pieces of cannon. He skedaddled, but still kept in the neighboring swamps. The next morning we again started in advance and after a ride of five miles heard firing about the same distance ahead. We let the horses go and in a very short time were within the limits of the muss. We came up with a company of cavalry from Bird's Point standing in line at the end of a lane, about a mile down which we could see Thompson's forces drawn up with his artillery "in battery." He saw us about as quick as we got up, and limbered up in double quick and scooted. Then the fun commenced. We chased him for 15 miles over a splendid straight, wide, level road, which he strewed with blankets, guns, hats, and at last dropped his artillery. A dozen of our boys kept up the chase until within a half mile of New Madrid, where they captured a wagon load of grain and a nigger, and returned at leisure. We caught a captain, 1st. lieutenant and some privates. Next day, the 2d of March, our regiment went down to New Madrid to reconnoiter. A regular colonel went along to draw a map of the country. We went it blind right into the edge of town, where we ran onto a lot of infantry. As fighting wasn't the object, we filed off to the left into a cornfield to get a new view of town. We were going slowly down on the town in line of battle, when a battery opened on us right smartly. We got out of that, but in good order. Only one shell touched us and that burst right under a horse's nose. One piece bruised the horse a little and knocked the rider off, but did not hurt the man at all, and the horse is now fit for duty again. Almost miraculous, wasn't it? There were lots of shell and balls fell around us. On the 3d the whole army got here and we again marched on the burg. The gunboats opened on us and we had to draw back. That day three 64-pound shells burst within 30 yards of me. We have been lying, since then, about two miles from town. They throw a shell over here occasionally but haven't hurt any body yet at this distance. To-day the cavalry have been out again to see if the gunboats have left, (that's all that keeps us from taking the town). The boats were still there and again shelled us, killing one man and a horse in the Michigan 3d. They killed one man on the 3d in the 39th Ohio, and the same shell wounded several others. Yesterday 2,000 or 3,000 men went around New Madrid down the river ten miles to Point Pleasant, but were kept off by the damned gunboats, just like we are here. If two or three of our gunboats could only slip down far enough to see their gunboats (two of them) and steamboats coming and going with their secesh flags flying. They have burned a half dozen houses in town since we came here. Don't know what for. Brigadier General Pope who is in command here has been made a major general. The colonel has just come from his quarters, and reports that Foote will be here with his gunboats day after to-morrow at farthest. We have been scouting all afternoon and I'm blamed tired. I took four men and went it alone. Had a good time but got lost and didn't get back until 8 p. m. Captured a lot of ginger snaps, and had a good talk with a handsome widow, while the boats were firing at the Michigan cavalry on our left. These shells don't scare a fellow half as much as the thoughts of them do. Why you really don't mind it at all. I don't like the idea of those musket balls, but maybe that is also worse than the reality.

Yet near New Madrid, March 12, 1862.

The enemy are separated from us by only a few cornfields, the country is perfectly plain; we can see from our tent door the smoke stacks of their gunboat, and the music of their bands mingles with our own and yet 'tis confounded dull.

I received a letter from you by mail a few days since. The colonel and Sid. and myself take a little ride into the country most every evening for mush and milk and 'tis astonishing what quantities they do eat. We are all in perfect health and good spirits, though since we left Commerce the colonel

and major have complained considerably about the fare, but
'tis better than I'm used to, so I have the advantage of them.
The evacuation of Manassas, Columbus, etc., have caused
considerable anxiety for the outburst of these forces which we
think will be on Buel or maybe further east on our little army
at the Cumberland Gap. The impression here is that the Rebel
army at this place has been greatly reinforced since we arrived here from Kentucky. We number though, full 30,000
(with a brigade that is now advancing to join us) and feel
fully able to attend to all of their forces here. General Pope
told our colonel yesterday that Foote would be here within
48 hours sure with his gunboats, and that's all we ask.

There is a review now being made of all the troops here by
the commanding general. You'd think it quite a spectacle,
wouldn't you, to see 25,000 troops in line; 3,000 of them cavalry and 36 pieces of artillery. I was left in charge of the
camp, and although I have my horse at hand saddled wouldn't
mount him to see them. It's funny how all interest in anything dies away in a person when they have a full view or
chance to view the object. We hear a dozen volleys of musketry every now and then, and although we all know there's
been a little fight, it doesn't interfere with conversation and
nine times out of ten we never hear what caused it. But
go up to the hospital and you'll find a couple of long rows
of cots, each with an occupant, and they can tell you of the
shooting and show a wound that they're prouder of than you
can imagine. They and their regiments that were under fire
love to tell it over and over, but the rest of the army, through
jealousy I believe, never mention it. You'll see a vast deal
of state pride here. The 7th Cavalry don't acknowledge the
Michigander troopers to be more than the equals of Jeff
Thompson's scalawags, and the Michigan boys really seem to
think that the 7th regiment is not equal to one company of
theirs. But I notice the generals here have all taken their
bodyguards from our regiment. The Illinois boys and the
Iowaians coalesce more readily and seem to have more family
feeling between them than at least either of these state's

troops have for those of other states. 'Tis the same in the
Southern army. Arkansas and Missouri troops have a mutual
hatred for each other that has extended to the citizens of
these states. This part of Missouri goes a great deal on old
blood, the best variety I believe is Catholic French, and these
people have a sovereign contempt for the barbarians of the
"Arkansaw," while the Arkansawans accuse the Missourians
of toe-kissing proclivities and cowardice.

New Madrid, "by Jingo," March 14, 1862.
Night before last we received four heavy guns from Cairo,
and two or three of these infantry regiments planted them
during the night within a half mile of the enemy's main fort
and within three-fourths of a mile where their gunboats lay.
The seceshers discovered it at daylight and then the fun commenced. Their gunboats and forts, about 30 or 40 pieces in
all, put in their best licks all day. We had two regiments lying
right in front of our guns to support them against a sortie,
and several other regiments behind ready for a field fight.
The enemy kept in their works though and it was altogether
an artillery fight. Our regiment was in the saddle all the
a. m., but in the p. m. we lay around our quarters as usual
with not a particle more of excitement perceptible than the
quietest day in Cairo showed. In the evening the colonel and
Major Case and myself went out in the country for our
regular little mush and milk, but that hasn't anything to do
with the story. The firing ceased about an hour after sunset
and we turned in for the night with all quiet in camp. About
2 o'clock this morning three Rebel regiments made a little
sortie with the intention of doing some devilment, but they ran
against a field battery of ours that sent them back kiting. This
morning the fort and town were found to be evacuated. I
rode down through what is left of the town, for the Rebels
burned many houses to give their guns a better chance at
the approaches, and cut down nearly all of the shade trees.
There was not an inhabitant left in town, they all moved out
before we came here, and every door was open. The Rebels

5

I think plundered the town after the citizens left; anyway our boys grumbled a good deal about the people's leaving nothing in their houses. They went away very badly scared and in an awful hurry, for there were tables with wine on, and cards and beds that had been used last night and blankets, and they left all their heavy artillery. They must have had all of their light artillery with the horses hitched to it and harnessed, and a lot of horses saddled and tied, for the halters cut with the ties left on the posts, showed that they were in too much of a hurry to untie. They also left all their tents, some 500, standing, most all of them as good as the best of ours, and barracks for several regiments, quarters in all for probably 10,000 men, the generals say, but I don't think they will hold so many. I think we got 40 guns, 24's and larger, besides some field pieces. We also get a big lot of amunition, lots of mules and wagons, and the boys are now fishing out of the river whole boxes of quartermaster's goods—clothing, blankets, etc., that the secesh rolled in as they ran. The general is better satisfied than if he had taken them prisoners. Coming back from the town and fort I rode over the ground where the balls lit thickest yesterday. They had scratched things around considerably—barked trees, knocked fences, busted a house or two, plowed ground like everything, and by the way, knocked six of our men for keeps, and wounded horribly about 15 more. That was all that was done yesterday. 'Tis astonishing that no more of our men were killed but you must recollect that these infantrymen that were supporting our batteries lay in trenches and were all killed while well covered, comparatively. One ball struck square in the trench and relieved one man of two legs and another man of one. I saw one man who had been struck by a falling 25-pound solid shot in the centre of his breast and went down and out at the small of his back. That was a pretty hard sight. While they were firing the hottest our boys would jump on their little dirt piles in front of the rifle pits and trenches and swing their hats and cheer and drop back into their ditches very rapidly. A shell 18 pounds fell about 20 feet in front of the ditches, and a boy of 12 or 14 years jumped out and grabbed it up while the fuse was still burning. A soldier saw it and hollered at him to drop it and scoot, but he hadn't time to get away, so he dropped it and threw himself flat with his feet toward it and almost then it burst, but harmlessly. Well, we've got Madrid and enough to pay us for our trouble. I think that our loss will be covered by 20 killed and 35 or 40 wounded in the whole two weeks. That's a large estimate. What the next move will be have no idea, but some say that we'll cross the river and operate with Grant in a southerly direction of course. I'd rather be in this down-the-river movement than any other part of the army. Have thought so ever since I joined the army. This cavalry business is bully. We have all the running around and fun and little skirmishing without much of the heavy work and tall fighting. The loss of the enemy we don't know but there are about 40 fresh graves at the fort and we found several dead bodies there this morning. Also found a half dozen men that were left by some means.

Near Point Pleasant, Mo., March 18, '62.

You see we are creeping along down the river surely if the motions are a little slow. This is about 12 miles below Madrid and said to be 75 or 80 below Cairo. It is said that the Rebels have between a dozen and 20 steamboats above here, and I think the object in occupying this point and planting artillery here is to make the assurances we have of catching them, doubly sure, for the river is considerably less in width here than where our guns are at and near Madrid. We received orders to march about sunset last night and started at tattoo. 'Twas a beautiful ride. The road lay for nearly the whole distance right along the river bank. 'Twas warm enough without overcoat or gloves and Commander Foote added to the interest of the ride by his sleep-disturbing music up at Island 10. The river makes a horseshoe bend here and Island 10 lays almost directly east of here across the peninsula. The neck is very flat, and we could plainly see the flash of every gun and see the bombs burst in the air when more than 20 or 30 yards from the ground. The roar of the 13 and 16-inch

mortars is truly terrific. There was no difficulty in distinguishing their reports from the cannons. The evidences of an
earthquake having performed in this country are visible when
pointed out. The natives will show you a swamp and say
that was once inhabitable, and then they'll point out a sand
ridge about four feet nearer heaven (the surface of course)
and say that was a swamp. Well, we arrived here at 2 o'clock
last night and moved nearly two miles back from the river to
be out of range of a battery the enemy have planted on the
opposite shore. This two miles, after deducting about 300
yards where the road runs through the little town, was a
swamp of mud and water to the horses' bellies. I noticed our
flag flying on the river bank over an inverted Rebel rag. The
flag staff was in front of a store that had received three cannon shots from the Rebels in their efforts to cut down our
flag. Nearly every house in town has had one or more doses
of heavy iron and several have been burned by shells. General Palmer is five miles below here with his brigade. He
was lucky enough yesterday to disable two Rebel gunboats
out of three that attacked him. I am very anxious to get out
of this country and into Tennessee if possible, or if we have
to stay on this side, enough below the swamps to make it a
little more pleasant. That ride of last night was delicious.
The order was to march without any unnecessary noise, and
after 10:30 (it was 2 when we got here), the boys were all
perfectly quiet, many of them asleep, and I believe I enjoyed
myself better than I ever did before in my life. Can't begin
to tell you precisely why, except there might have been some
air-castle building, but 'twas very pleasant. I hear to-night
that Island 10 was evacuated last night. Think maybe Foote
has his hands full up there, and doubt the evacuation idea
some. Gracious how it rained last night, commenced just
after we got here, with some awful heavy thunder and don't
know how long it lasted. 'Twas raining to kill when I went
to sleep. We had no tents with us and every fellow provided
for himself. I went to bed with a lot of bacon and a barrel
under a tent fly and slept a la log. To-day it has been real

warm. Shirt sleeves and shade were in requisition. Well, I'll write you a little every day until I can send letters.

Twentieth.—To-day 'tis cloudy and we have fire in the tent and I wear my cloak besides. There are no news of any kind to-day. We are on a little piece of dry land here (some of the earthquake's "get up" I suppose) entirely surrounded by swamps of the vilest kind, cane and cypress. We have dug wells all through camp. Find plenty of water at five feet. The Rebel battery across the river has been trying to shell us this morning. They sent some shell plenty far enough but they lit off to the right of our camp. General Plummer rides down along the river bank with his staff every day and the Rebels do their best to send him up. The colonel has just started out with him to give the Rebels another chance. There is considerable cane here and it looks as though the country might grow alligators to almost any extent. 'Tis a grand country for a sporting man. The very paradise of geese and their kindred.

Point Pleasant, Mo., March 24, 1862.

It's only 9 a. m., and didn't get to bed until 2 this morning, so if I do not talk rational you will excuse me. That isn't the excuse either. I rode 50 miles between 9 a. m. yesterday and midnight over roughest road. Two hundred of us were sent out after that d—d Jeff Thompson. We exchanged shots with his pickets 20 miles from here, and chased them four miles farther. The last eight miles was a pike only eight feet wide, thrown up through an immense swamp, and planked. The water came so close to the planks that there was not a place in the whole eight miles where a horse dare step off the plank. The total of all the unusual sights I ever saw wouldn't begin to count one in effect where that road and swamp will ten. There are two good sized rivers running through the swamp but they have to be pointed out to you before you can see them, or rather distinguish them from the rest of the swamp. When we first saw these pickets they were

tearing up a culvert. We hurried up and after each side
fired four or five rounds they ran. No one hurt here, although the distance was not more than 60 yards. Andy
Hulit, my sergeant major and myself were the advance
guard, but I have no carbine, and did not get to shoot,
but this didn't seem to make any difference to them for
they threw buckshot round me quite promiscuously. Well,
we fixed up that bridge and pressed on, but they tore down
so many bridges that we could go but slowly. Just before
the fight I had dropped back a dozen files to get out of
building any more bridges, and when our boys saw the
secesh, they had just finished destroying another. The
horses couldn't cross it, but the boys dismounted and
hurrying across on foot, made them take to the swamp
in water waist deep, where they hid themselves behind
logs, vines and a kind of high grass that grows in bunches
as large as a currant bush. When they had concealed
themselves to their notion, they commenced firing at us,
and of the first four of our boys over the bridge (Andy
Hulit led them), three were down, wounded in a minute.
We then charged (on foot) right into the brush and water,
some of the boys up to their armpits, and made them
scoot. They did not number over 20 but their advantage
was enormous. We dropped two of them certain, and—
I don't think any more. Of four of our men they wounded,
three were Company L boys. The two Cockerel brothers,
Mathew and Royal, and Eugene Greenslit. The other was
from Company A. The Company A boy and Mat Cockerel
died before we got them to camp. Royal has a flesh wound
in the arm, and Greenslit is shot in the foot, both slight
wounds. We drove the Rebels clear off, and captured two
horses, and all their blankets, overcoats etc. About 15
miles out we came to Little River. While the major was
examining the bridge, we saw a half dozen men running
through a swamp on the other side. Over the bridge we
went, and into the mud and water after them. We got
them all. I captured a couple in a thicket. Andy Hulit

came up a few minutes after and we had work to keep a lot of boys from shooting them, while we were taking them back to the river. Well, that was a pretty rough trip and I don't hanker after another like it, although the excitement is rather pleasant too. But being set up for a mark on a road where there is not a sign of a chance to dodge, and having the marksman completely concealed from you, and this other fix of letting them throw shells at you when your carbine won't carry to them, sitting on horseback too, I wish it understood I'm opposed to and protest against, although I never think so until I get back to camp. I don't think that I ever get a bit excited over firing, but I know that I don't look at danger the same when under fire that I do when in quarters. We are all well and I'm getting fat every day. It bores considerably here to think that that one horse Island No. 10 won't come down and surrender like a "gem'men." Some of the officers here think that we'd better be getting out "o' this," but I propose to let Pope work out the salvation of this division. We started from Commerce in General Hamilton's division, were put in General Granger's at Madrid, and are now in General Plummer's. Well, I'm going to do a little sleeping.

Camp near Point Pleasant, Mo., March 26, 1862.

It is, to-day, very much warmer. I'm altogether too hot to be comfortable in my shirt sleeves. Don't know what is to become of us in July if it is so hot in proportion. I shake in my boots at the thought of the mosquitoes, flies, etc., we will have to endure. Vegetation is giving the surroundings a greenish appearance already, and have seen a peach tree in nearly full bloom. Wheat is about three or four inches above ground. Makes a very respectable sod. I think there are more Union people here than in any part of Missouri that I have been in, and fewer widows. Men are nearly all at home and putting in their crops as coolly as though there was no war. Some of our

soldiers impose on the natives pretty badly. You don't
know how thankful you ought to be that you don't live
in the invaded country. Wherever there is an army, for
10 or 15 miles around it there will be hundreds of stragglers. Some out of curiosity, some to see the natives and
talk with them, but the majority to pick up what they can
to eat. There is not a farm house within ten miles of
camp, notwithstanding the positive orders against straggling, that has not, at least, 50 soldier visitors a day, and
they are the poorest soldiers and the meanest men that do
all the straggling, or nearly all. They will go into a house
and beg what they can and then steal what is left. Rough,
dirty, coarse brutes, if they were all shot, our army would
be better off. Most of these fellows are bullies at home,
and that class makes plunderers in war. I've seen enough
of war to know that it isn't the brawling, fighting man at
home that stands the bullet whistle the best. A favorite
game of these chaps, where they are not utterly depraved
(there are a good many of the latter), is for a couple of
them to go in the house and make themselves as interesting as possible while the others clean out the smokehouse,
chicken yard, and the premises generally. The greatest
objection and the only one I have to being in the army,
is the idea of being associated, in the minds of the people
of this country, as well as the home folks, with such brutes.
But I tell you, that I have always acted the gentleman to
the best of my ability since I entered the army, and I don't
believe I'm a whit worse than I was at home. I haven't
drank one-tenth as much liquor as I did in the same length
of time at home, and you know how much that was, and
that I hate the stuff too much to ever taste it unless forced
upon me. The last I touched was with poor George Shinn
just before the 17th left the cape. We drank to "Our next
shake hands, may it be at the end of the war, at home, and
before three months." George was a No. 1 soldier. We
boys all think everything of him. Tell him we all sympathize with him and wish him a speedy recovery, and that

his services may not be needed any more. Seems to me
I write you nearly every day, but haven't had a letter
from home for two or three weeks. Our mail is very ir-
regular though, and I can excuse, but I would like you to
get all of mine and save them, for I would like to look
these over myself when I get home, as I keep no diary.
The day is so warm that our boys are all out bathing in
a little swamp lake near here. The Lord knows some of
them need it. Cleanliness is undoubtedly the best preven-
tive of disease in the army. Hardly any of the boys that
are cleanly suffer from disease. The colonel and Sidney
went to Cairo yesterday. The colonel with dispatches
from General Pope, I believe, and Sid. just because he
could. We buried our two boys yesterday morning that
were killed at Cane Bridge, and I never felt sadder in my
life. I'm sure that knowing I would be killed to-morrow
wouldn't hurt me half as much. These poor fellows have
suffered all the hardships and trials of the private soldier's
life, and are now put under the ground in the dark swamp,
without a friend here, save their comrades, and probably
after the army leaves, a friendly eye will never see their
graves. I sent a package of letters back to a young lady
that one of them was engaged to. Our men have been
living on mush and the other messes, makeable from cornmeal, for a week, without coffee or anything else. Couldn't
get provisions through from Cairo near fast enough, and
Pope gobbled up everything that did come for the troops
at Madrid. Chet. Caswell, a Canton boy, is here now and
cooking for our mess. I can live on fried mush as long
as the next man. The frogs, bugs, blackbirds and sich like,
keep up a perfect bedlam around us the whole time.

Point Pleasant, Mo., March 28, 1862.

There isn't a thing to write only that they keep up the infernal "boom, boom," with their cannons all day and night
long. It's perfectly disgusting the way they waste powder
and iron without killing anyone. They have knocked every

house in town to flinders, and round shot and grape and shell are lying thick on the ground and yet we haven't a man touched. They were having a hot time with their cannon and some musketry firing, too, down at Palmer's last night from 10 p. m. to 2 a. m., but haven't heard yet what was up. I have my own reasons for thinking that they are evacuating Island 10. If they don't do it this week I'll believe that they are waiting for a lot of gunboats to come up from Orleans, and that we'll have the fun of a naval engagement in the vicinity. If there is one within 40 miles of here I'm going to see it if I have to wade a swamp ten feet deep, as I probably will, but see it I'm bound to. Then if the Rebels whale our craft you'll be likely to hear the sound of their cannon before long without leaving home, for there's nothing to prevent their going anywhere after they pass our gunboats. It will be a great joke on Uncle Sam if they do make that riffle. Wonder what would become of the home guards. About the worst feature of the case would be the Southern officers sparking our girls as we do theirs now and the worst yet is, there is no doubt the girls would take to it kindly, for they do here, and I'm satisfied there is no difference in the feminines of the two sections, except that ours do not say "thar" and "whar." I see that it requires a good many "ifs" and "theirs" to arrange a case of this kind, but I assure you that it is not out of the range of possibilities. How'd you like to see a "Captain St. Clair de Monstachir" with C. S. A. on his buttons, making calls in Canton? I'll bet ten to one he could enjoy himself in that burg. Bang! Boom! D——n the cannons! It's awful tiresome. I do hope we'll get them cleaned out of this ere long. I don't understand why it is that our mails are so tardy. We get the Chicago and St. Louis papers two days after publication. I almost think that Pope has ordered our mail to lay over in Cairo until further orders.

Camp, near Point Pleasant, Mo., April 4, 1862.
I received your last letter within three days after it was mailed, and praised Uncle Sam duly therefor. Our regiment

has had a run of bad luck since we've been here. Two men killed on the plank road, two wounded at same place, two killed by falling trees in a storm of night of April 1st, and a dozen wounded, and yesterday one drowned while watering his horse in the swamp, and our horses dying off very fast of horse cholera. The latter is a serious thing in a regiment were the men own the horses themselves. For they (or nearly all of them) cannot buy others. Most of them are still owing for the horses they have. The positions of troops and state of the war generally remains the same here as it has been ever since we took Madrid. Main body of our forces at that place. Five regiments here under Plummer and five seven miles further down the river with Palmer. That is as far down as we can go on this side for the swamps. Between here and Madrid we have batteries every three miles and the Rebels have rather more on the opposite side. Both are right on their respective banks and have their flags fluttering their mutual hatred in each others faces. We can see them very plainly without the aid of a glass. The Rebel gunboats lie just below our lower battery and 'tis rumored to-night that several new ones have arrived from Memphis or New Orleans.

This fuss about "Island 10" I think is all humbug. Don't believe they have attacked it yet. It don't sound like Foote's fighting. Look on the map and see what a nice pen there is between the rivers Tennessee and Mississippi. Don't it look that if Grant and company can whip them out at Corinth, that we'll have all the forces at Memphis and intermediate points to "Island 10" in a bag that they'll have trouble in getting through? If they run it will be into Arkansas, and they can take nothing with them but what their backs will stand under. Seems to me that the plans of the campaign are grand from the glimpses we can get of them and have been planned by at least a Napoleon. Certain it is we are checkmating them at every point that's visible. I firmly believe the summer will see the war ended. But it will also see a host of us upended if we have to fight over such ground as this. It is unpleasantly warm already in the sun. It's 10 p. m. now and plenty warm in my shirt sleeves, with a high wind blowing, too. We had an awful storm here to commence April with. We are camped just in the wood's edge and the wind struck us after crossing a wide open field and knocked trees down all through our camp; killed First Lieutenant Moore, one private, seriously wounded Captain Webster and a dozen men. During the storm I though of our fleet at "Island 10" and it made me almost sick. Don't see how they escaped being blown high and dry out of water.

April 5, 1862.—One of our boys has just returned from Madrid and says he saw our gunboat Cairo there. She slipped by the batteries at "Island No. 10" in the storm last night. Mosquitoes here already.

Headquarters 7th Illinois Cavalry,

In a very fine House,

Point Pleasant, Mo., April 7, 1862.

If this isn't fine your brother is incapable of judging. Cozy brick house, damask curtains, legged bedsteads, splendid tables and chairs, big looking glass, and every-thing just as fine as a peacock's tail. I do wish you could have been with me the last two days. They've been two of the best days of my life. During the storm of Saturday night, the 5th instant, one of the gunboats ran by "Island 10." I heard of it early Sunday morning, and got out a pass for Andy Hulit and myself to look for forage, in-tending, of course, to ride down to the river and watch the gunboat as we knew there'd be fun if she attempted to run below Madrid. We rode up the river about six miles (half way) to a point that extends into the river on our side, and got there just as the boat did. 'Twas the "Carondelet," and indeed she looked like an old friend. The sight of her did me more good than any amount of furloughs could. At this point, I spoke of, we have three batteries within a half-mile, and there were two Rebels' batteries visible right at the water's edge, opposite. We just got there in time to see the ball open. Besides the two secesh batteries visible, they opened from four others masked by the brush and trees, and hitherto unknown to us. Their six, our three, the gunboats, all firing together made by far the grandest thing I ever witnessed. I suppose there were from 30 to 40 guns used, and at least a half thousand shots fired. Andy and I were on a little rise of ground a couple of hundred yards from our main battery and where we could see every shot fired and its effect. There were lots of shots fell around that battery, but none near enough us to be disagreeable. About an hour's fighting silenced the Rebel batteries, and that fun was over. Our boat didn't go over to them at that time, but came into our shore and laid up. She was not struck once, nor was there a man hurt on our side. Andy and I rode out in the country and got our dinners with a friend of mine, and about 3 p. m. started home. We just got back here as the gunboat was preparing to attack the batteries immediately opposite here. She ran down the river on our side, a mile below their guns, and then turning her bow square toward the enemy, started for them and commenced firing. We could see every motion of the Rebel gunners plainly, and they worked like men, until the boat got within about 300 yards of them, when they broke, and I tell you they used their legs to advantage; all but one and he walked away with his arms folded perfectly at ease. There's an immense sight of enjoyment in witnessing such fights as these. Well, I saw another fight this morning, but 'twas too far off for interest, after what I saw yesterday. Two more gunboats came down last night in the rain and darkness past the island. This fight this morning was commenced by the Carondelet, on a five-gun battery, only four miles below and across from Madrid. She called the Louisville to her aid, and then one walked up on the battery from below and the other from above. It is grand to see these gunboats walk into the enemy. They go at them as though they were going right on land, if the Rebels would stay there. (One hour later, 9 p. m.)

Just as I finished the last period, an artillery captain came dashing up through the door, just from Madrid, and wanted to know where the gunboats were. He said that the Rebel floating battery, that has been lying at Island 10, was floating down and the transports were afraid to try and bring her into land, and he wanted to notify the gunboats so they could catch her. We told him they had gone down to Palmer's division, six miles below, and away he went. I've been out waiting to see her pass, but she hasn't arrived yet. He said she was not more than three miles above. All such items help to make soldiering interesting. Our three transports have taken 20,000 troops over into Tennessee since 9:30 this a. m. I call that good work. Colonel Kellogg has gone over with Pope to see the battle, if there is any. These Rebels don't begin to fight a gun equal to our boys, and all the people here say so. I really do not believe they have the "bullet-pluck" that our men show. Our regiment is left here alone in its glory. We're occupying the town, enjoying life, and having all the fun we want. I killed a mosquito to-night, and it brought up such disagreeable thoughts that I couldn't eat supper. If they don't eat my surplus flesh off me, I know I'll fret myself lean as they increase. The colonel got back yesterday. You ought to have seen him look at the eatables last night, and shaking his head with disgust, go back to his tent without touching a bite. The first camp meal after a furlough I suppose isn't particularly delightful. There's no telling whether there'll be a fight to-morrow or not. We'll probably not assist if there is. But after the fight is over and the victory won we'll come in and chase the Rebels until they scatter. The infantry do the heavy, dirty work and get the honor, and we have all the fun and easy times there are going. I'm willing. I'd rather scout and skirmish than anything I know of, and am perfectly willing to let the infants do the heavy fighting, for they only make an artillery target of us when we're brought on battle fields.

There wouldn't be much left of my letters if I'd leave out the war gossip! Forty of the Rebels deserted and came to our gunboats to-day. Sergeant Wells, who while over there is a spy, was taken prisoner the other day, escaped to our gunboats. It saved his neck.

April 10.—The Rebels have run and left Island 10, and our boys have taken some 2,000 of them prisoners below here. They passed up on a boat this morning. We will be paid off to-day or to-morrow.

Camp New Madrid, Mo., April 12, 1862.

I have the extreme happiness to inform you that there is at last a hope of my dating the next letter from Memphis or vicinity. Our regiment has for several days been alone at Point Pleasant and we enjoyed it very much. When we are under a general of an infantry division we are run to death or thereabouts, for whenever anything is to be done the cavalry is sure to be called on. Yesterday we were ordered to report here immediately to General Granger, commanding cavalry division which numbers full 4,000. There are two brigades in this division; Colonel Kellogg commands the 1st brigade and therefore is now a brigadier general. There have been about 25 steamboats arrived here since 4 p. m. yesterday and the army will probably commence embarking to-day. It will take full 60 boats to hold us all. The rain has been falling in torrents ever since we started from the Point yesterday, and you can imagine the time we had pitching tents in a cornfield, and yet we are comfortable now as we can wish. I have faith to believe that they (or anybody else) can't keep me from being comfortable under any circumstances, if my hands are loose and I can walk. I think that Pope's hurry is caused by his fear that Grant and company will reach Memphis before him. We hardly think that the Rebels will make a stand at Pillow, Randolph or Memphis if the news from Corinth is correct. I'm almost afraid to look over the list of dead that fight was made. Sid. says he is sure Billy Stockdale is killed. We received papers of the 10th last night but

are not sure the victory is a complete one yet. I can't think
of the point where the enemy will make another stand if they
are perfectly whipped at Corinth.

I know as many people here as in Fulton, almost, and I
have yet to hear the first insulting speech or word to me.
"What are they going to do with Island No. 10 I wonder;
I am afraid that Commander Foote and his gunboats are a
humbug." Aren't you ashamed of that speech? Damn the
New York *Tribune.* I do believe in McClellan and nearly all
the rest of our leaders. If those Tribunes, big and little, were
where any regiment in this army could get at them they
wouldn't stand fifteen minutes. McClellan knows his business
and we don't know a thing about it. Now old Pope here is
as mean a man as ever lived, curses every man that comes
within a hundred yards of him and nobody knows a thing of
his designs, but we all have the utmost confidence in him.
I've never seen him and wouldn't go in sight of him for a
horse, but he's my man for a' that.

Orders have just arrived for embarking this p. m. Will
be under way down the river to-night. Wish us a pleasant
voyage.

On Steamer Henry Clay, off New Madrid, Mo.,

April 16, 1862.

I finished my last in a great hurry, helped strike and load
our tents and equipage and started for the levee, confident that
we would be off for Memphis, Orleans and intermediate
landings, before the world would gain 12 hours at farthest in
age. That day over 30 steamers arrived, received their loads
of soldiers and departed, all down stream, preceded by six or
eight gunboats and 16 mortarboats. Word came at nightfall
that there were not enough boats for all and the cavalry would
have to wait the morrow and more transports. We lay on
the river banks that night, and the next day all the cavalry got
off except our brigade of two regiments. Another night on
the banks without tents, managed to get transportation for

two battalions, one from each regiment. They started down
yesterday at about 10 a. m. and more boats coming we loaded
two more battalions, but at 9 p. m. a dispatch boat came up
with orders for us to stop loading and await further orders.
The same boat turned back all the cavalry of our brigade
that had started and landed them at Tiptonsville; we are at
6 this p. m. lying around loose on the bank here awaiting
orders. That boat brought up word that our fleet was at
Fort Pillow, and the Rebels were going to make a stand there,
but that nothing had occurred when she left but some gunboats skirmishing. What the devil we are going to do is
more than three men like me can guess. It's awful confounded dull here. Nothing even half interesting. Saw a
cuss, trying to drown himself yesterday, and saw a fellow's leg
taken off last night. These are better than no show at all,
but still there's not much fun about either case. I'm bored
considerably by some of my Canton friends wanting me to
help them get their niggers out of camp. Now, I don't care
a damn for the darkies, and know that they are better off with
their masters 50 times over than with us, but of course you
know I couldn't help to send a runaway nigger back. I'm
blamed if I could. I honestly believe that this army has taken
500 niggers away with them. Many men have lost from 15
to 30 each. The owners were pretty well contented while the
army stayed here, for all the generals assured them that when
we left the negroes would not be allowed to go with us, and
they could easily get them back; but they have found out that
was a "gull" and they are some bitter on us now. There will
be two Indiana regiments left here to guard the country from
Island 10 to Tiptonsville, and if you don't hear of some fun
from this quarter after the army all leaves but them, I'm mistaken. They'll have their hands full if not fuller. We have
not been paid yet but probably will be this week. I tell you I
can spend money faster here than anywhere I ever was in my
life, but of course I don't do it. Am trying to save up for
rainy weather, and the time, if it should come, when I'll have
only one leg to go on or one arm to work with. That Pitts-

6

burg battle was one awful affair, but it don't hurt us any. Grant will whip them the next time completely. Poor John Wallace is gone. He was a much better boy than he had credit for being. We all liked him in the old mess very much. Ike Simonson, of same company, I notice was wounded. He was also in my mess; was from Farmington. There are no rumors in camp to-day. Yesterday it was reported and believed that the Monitor had sunk the Merrimac, that Yorktown was taken, and that another big fight had taken place at Corinth and we held the town. That was very bully but it lacks confirmation. Think it will for sometime yet, but Pope says we'll come out all right through all three of those trials. It's just what's wanted to nip this rebellion up root and all. That's a rather dubious victory up to date, that Pittsburg affair, but guess it's all right.

Headquarters 7th Illinois Cavalry Camp, on Hamburg
and Corinth Road,

May 3, 1862.

I arrived here yesterday in safety. Stayed in Peoria the Monday night that I started, and was in Cairo at 9 p. m. Wednesday. Woke up Thursday morning on a boat at Paducah and devoted the day to admiring the Tennessee river. Stopped long enough at Fort Henry to get a good view of its well pummeled walls, and not-much-to-brag-of defences. The line of ditching without the works was the best I have ever seen, but the parapet, excepting that of the Fort proper, wasn't to be compared to our works at Bird's Point, which are the most inferior of ours that I have seen. The Tennessee runs through a perfect wilderness. There is not a landing on the river up to this point (Hamburg) that can begin with Copperas Creek, and indeed, although I watched closely, I did not see more than three or four points, that of themselves, showed they were boat landings, and those only by the grass being worn off the bank; and I did not see a warehouse on either bank unless,

maybe, one at Savannah, where there are also, say four fine
dwellings. At no other point did I see more than three
houses, and very rarely, even one. Having heard so much
of the richness of Middle Tennessee I cannot help talking
so long of what ought to be, to it, what the Illinois river
would be to us were we without railroads. I reached
Hamburg yesterday afternoon (Friday) and started for
my regiment, which I learned was five miles out on the
Corinth way. I walked out as fast as I could, and reached
there to hear that the army had moved on and were probably two miles ahead and yet going. I laid down and slept
a couple of hours, borrowed a horse, and after six miles
riding found them going into camp. Monstrous hilly
country, this, and save a very few clearings, all heavily
timbered. Pope's army has been reinforced considerably
since we arrived here. Think he has, say 30 odd thousand
men. I think the ball opened just before I commenced
this letter. For two days past we have had one batallion
out about four miles beyond our present camp holding an
important position. They have been within gunshot of the
enemy all the time, but so protected that although they
skirmished a good deal, but one of ours was wounded. In
one little charge our boys made out they killed four and
wounded a number of Rebels that they felt of. Pope's
infantry came up to-day in force and relieved them.
Paine's division was advanced and when not more than
40 yards beyond the post our cavalry held, were opened
on first by musketry and immediately afterwards by artillery. There was very heavy firing for an half hour, but
it has ceased since I commenced this page. Haven't heard
the result. We have orders to move forward to-morrow
morning, but although we are so close to the enemy's position, (not more than three miles) (Infantry, of course, I
mean) don't think our side will commence the attack before Monday morning, when we will see—sure—if they
don't run.

Supper.—Some of our boys have just come in with a lot of overcoats, trinkets, etc., spoils of the afternoon skirmish. They were all Illinois regiments that were engaged. A sergeant has just showed me an overcoat that he stripped off a dead secesh, who with eleven others was lying in one pile. He captured a captain who, after he had thrown down his sword, offered to give him a fist fight. The artillery firing was mostly from Rebel guns at Farmington at a regiment of our boys building a bridge. The Northern Mississippi line runs through our camp. We cannot be far form Iuka Springs, although no one that I've seen ever heard of the place. Report has just come that Mitchell has been driven out of Huntsville, and another that Yorktown and 45,000 prisoners are ours. Don't believe either. Shall write you from Corinth if have luck.

Near Farmington, Miss., May 8, 1862.

I've been within one and a half miles of Corinth to-day. Didn't see anything especially worthy of mention, but had full rations in the way of leaden bullets whistle. Yea, and larger missiles also. For four days past our battalion has been the advanced picket of Pope's army, full five miles in advance of the army. We have been skirmishing the whole time, not five minutes passing without more or less shooting. Our picket line was on one side of a long prairie or clearing, from 300 to 450 yards wide, and theirs on the opposite side. With all the firing, the losses on our side was but one horse up to this morning, and we were congratulating ourselves on getting on so well, when the advance of a large reconnoitering party under General Paine came in sight and we were ordered to lead them. Well, it's all over now, and we've had our Maj. Z. Applington killed, several wounded, and horses hurt by bursting shells. It's all right, I suppose, but damn the general that sent us on a fool's errand. We've a strong old place to take here at Corinth, but guess we'll make the riffle. The major fell while leading a charge along a road. The timber and brush by the roadside were so thick that we could see nothing until our boys received the volley of musketry, of which one ball reached the major's brain. The reconnoitering party returned to camp last night, and this morning the Rebels took their turn. They advanced in considerable force, drove our men back some two miles, captured a couple of pieces of cannon, and filled our hospitals pretty well. Our regiment was not in that fight. The Iowa 2d Cavalry suffered badly, 'tis said, in trying to take a Rebel battery.

Lieutenant Herring was wounded by a drunken soldier of the 4th Regular Cavalry yesterday, and Captain Nelson knocked down by the same man. Herring was shot through the arm. A suspender buckle that the ball glanced from saved his life. It's a little doubtful whether this fight comes off immediately. I think and hope that our folks are going to let them concentrate all their troops here and then make a Waterloo of it. That is, a Waterloo for them, but if they whip us, call out the home-guards and try them again. Weather here almost too warm for comfort in daytime, but deliciously cool after sunset. Apples and peaches are as large as hickory nuts, and blackberries the size of peas. The water is very good. Think will like it as well as Mississippi water after a while. The well water is not as cool though as I have seen it. I have not visited the 8th or 17th yet. They are in a division that forms a reserve (McClernands) and will not fight until the rest of Thomas's (formerly Grant's) division have had a chance. Shall go and see them immediately after the battle if I have luck. My health is perfect yet and am in hopes 'twill remain so. My love to inquiring friends, and do not expect to hear from me regularly as the mail only leaves here semi-occasionally. What a change in climate two day's ride make. Trees all in full leaf, and saw peaches to-day larger than filberts. Summer coats are in demand.

Corinth and Hamburg Road, Miss., May 11, 1862.

You remember that in my last I spoke of a reconnoisance our people made on the 8th inst. On the 9th Beauregard returned it with interest, driving our advance back some two miles and almost scaring this wing of the Eagle. He appeared on our left flank, where I think Pope thought it impossible for him to reach, and drove Paine's division from the front like a drove of sheep. 'Tis said that a charge made by the 2d Iowa Cavalry was the salvation of both of Paine's brigades. The charge, if we hear correctly, was one of the most gallant things of the war. One of our battalions was out yesterday examining our left to see if the Rebels were still there. They found no signs of them, but on their return to camp were fired into by some of General Buford's artillery, and one man killed by a 6-pound solid shot from Company A. There is almost incessant firing along the front but too light and scattering to forbode an immediate fight of itself, although 'twould surprise no one to hear of the dance commencing at any hour. Corinth is a tremendously strong place, very difficult to approach, and holding a force that our officers think much superior to our own. This is kept from the army, though I don't think now that we have more than 80,000 fighting men here. They must have over 100,000, and this conscription act is pouring in reinforcements to them by thousands. But, notwithstanding this, I think the superior discipline of our men will give us a victory when the fight does come. The strongest evidence that I see of Halleck's weakness is his delaying the battle so long We are in distance to strike any day; roads splendid, army in better condition every day than it will be the next day, weather becoming too hot for men to endure much longer, and yet we wait. What for, I don't know, unless 'tis for reinforcements. They say Curtis and Siegel are coming. I hope they'll get here to-night and finish the thing up to-morrow. The weather is taking the vim out of the men remarkably. To-day there is a good stray breeze, and yet a man can hardly get enough of the rarified stuff they call air here to fill his lungs. Plenty of chestnuts in this country. Plenty of hills and plenty of woods but a great scarcity of about everything else. There is no more soil on the earth here than you'll find on any Illinois school house floor, and 'tis a question which would grow the best crops.

The colonel is anxious to have the regiment in the battle when it comes off, while your brother thinks if they can do the work without us he won't be at all angry. I like skirmishing pretty well but am dubious about the fun showing itself so strongly in a battle. I guess I had a dozen shots thrown at me individually on the 8th at from 100 to 450 yards, and I got my return shot nearly every time and some extra ones, but rather think they all got off as well as I did. The carbines are not very correct shooters, and your brother is a ditto, so I have the satisfaction of knowing that I haven't killed anybody yet.

Still in Camp near Corinth, Miss., May 15, 1862.

It seems to me that we are a long time in bringing this "muss a la probable" to a focus. What under the sun our Halleck is waiting for we can't guess. One hour's march will commence the struggle now and you don't know how anxious we are for that little trip. Buell and Thomas have both thrown up long lines of earthworks to fall back behind if repulsed, I suppose. We have nothing of that kind in our division. We have all been under marching orders since morning, and Assistant Secretary of War Scott told the colonel last night that the battle would commence to-day—but he lied. Talk is to-night again that Corinth is evacuated. The main body of our army moved up within three miles to-day. My battalion has been out since daylight this morning, but we have been lying at ease near Pope's headquarters all day waiting for orders. I came back to camp to stay to-night because I had no blanket with me and there was no possibility of any more before morning. Have a sore foot now. My confounded horse fell down with me in a creek the other day, threw me out on the bank in a bunch of blackberry bushes and then

crawled out over me, stepped on my foot in the melee by way
of showing sympathy, I suppose.   It don't hurt my appetite
any and hasn't put me off duty.

                    Near Corinth, Miss., May 19 ,1862.
    Our regiment now is acting as a kind of rear guard for
Pope's division.   The enemy's cavalry in bodies of from 1,000
down have been running around our left flank and threaten-
ing to interfere with our trains.   Every day we send out six
companies to patrol between here and the river and forward.
Yesterday (Sunday) I was out.   We went to Red Sulphur
Springs, one of the most romantic, beautiful places I have ever
seen.   There are about 40 double cottages for families, and
stables, kennels and quarters for the servants, hounds and
horses. The buildings are in good repair, though the place has
not been frequented much for the last three or four years.
White Sulphur Springs are four miles from the Red and
more fashionable.   I am going there to-morrow.   There were
about a dozen real ladies at the springs yesterday, and they
were quite sociable and so interesting that I could not help
staying an hour after the column left We were the first of our
soldiers that the party had seen and they were much surprised that our boys behaved so well.   None of them had
ever been North, and they occupied about all the time I was
with them in asking questions, principally though, about the
conduct of our army.   About a mile before we got to the
springs we passed a house where there were as many as six
young ladies in full dress.   The major sent me to make some
inquiries of the man of the house, and I noticed the party
were in something of a flurry but ascribed it to the presence
of our men.   Of course Sunday was an excuse for the finery
and there being so many together.   After we had advanced a
little way one of our captains took a squad, went ahead and
passed himself for a Rebel officer just from Corinth.   By his
figuring he found out that at this house I have spoken of they
were expecting some Rebel officers and men, 14 in all, from
Corinth to dinner and a visit.   We set a trap for them, but

they heard of us through the citizens and sloped. They came within a mile of us and then their tracks showed they had gone off through the woods and a swamp on a run. We got one of their horses, a beauty, fully equipped. It being a hot day the owner had strapped his coat on his valise and not having time to take it off we got it. A dozen of our boys went back and ate the dinner, but without the company of the ladies who had flown. Our line has now closed to within two and one-half miles around the north and east sides of Corinth. Our men have thrown up breastworks within that distance along nearly the whole line. The cannons play on each other occasionally, say as an average four times a day, a half hour each time. Our line is, I think, nine or ten miles long; am not sure. The Rebels are suffering for rations, not more than half rations having been served for the last ten days. Hundreds are deserting from them. One battalion that was raised in this county, over 500 men, have all deserted but about 90. The commander himself ran off. Of a 100 men that deserted from them probably five come within our lines. The rest all go to their homes. If Porter takes Mobile, and Farragut and Davis get Memphis, I think in ten days afterward there will not be enough Rebels left in Corinth to oppose our regiment. There is no doubt that they have more men now than we have but they lack discipline. Success at the points above named will leave them without any railroad communication whatever or telegraph either. I'm afraid that our gunboats got the worst of that little affair at Pillow the other day. An army is the slowest moving animal. Here we've been over a month making 20 miles. I think I shall run off to McClernand's division this p. m. and see some of the 17th and 8th boys.

Near Corinth, Miss., May 24, 1862.

I returned last night from a two day's scout. Our orders were to scour the country along the Tennessee river to near Eastport and return through Iuka, Burnsville and Glendale. A Michigan colonel commanded the party and skipped Iuka three miles. There were little bands of Rebels in sight nearly all the time we were in that vicinity, so that I could not gallop off to the place alone, and of course the colonel wouldn't let me have men to go with me.

We rode all day yesterday through a steady rain and over roads that were for miles obstructed by felled trees and bridges burned. We came back through Pope's division yesterday. Think he is as about as well fortified as Beauregard can be. 'Tis astonishing how much ditching he has done within a week. Has also cut down enough trees (to make his left unapproachable) to last all of Illinois ten years for firewood. There's no site for a Bull Run here. Confederate scrip goes among the people here freely. If a man refuses to take it they lynch him. Not the citizens but soldiers do the dirty work. The people here all say that the seceded States will have to go back where they started from.

Camp on Corinth Road, Miss., May 27, 1862.

Why don't you write me just a word, if no more? I'm almost uneasy. Not a line from home for a month. We hear that smallpox is raging in Canton, and—I want you to write. They say there is some smallpox in the center and right of the army, but think 'tis like the milk sickness of our Egypt, "a little further on." There's enough sickness of other kinds, so we have no room for grumbling if we can't have that disease. The hospitals at Hamburg make almost a city. I think there can be no more sorrowful sight, real or imaginary, than that camp of the sick.

I don't know the number of patients, somewhere in thousands, all packed in tents as closely as they can lie, and with not one-tenth the care a sick horse would get at home. I suppose the surgeons, stewards and nurses have feelings like men when they first enter the hospitals, but familarity with disease and suffering seem to make them careless and indifferent to a degree that surprises me, and I can't but look upon it as criminal. I suppose nearly half the bad cases are typhoid fever. Yellow fever, cholera and smallpox have never been known here to the citizens. They all say this is a very

healthy country, and I believe it. Our boys are suffering
from the change of climate and water, and as much as anything, the sudden change in temperature. Our regiment is improving in health now rapidly. We have gained about 40
for duty within a week. We had about 250 sick last week.
The 17th has some 300. I found a batch of live
secesh women last Sunday. I rode up to a fine
looking house to get a glass of milk (I suppose I
drink more milk than any six calves in Fulton) and found
eight or ten ladies at dinner, accepted a rather cool invitation
to dine wid' 'em, and did justice to their peas and fodder generally, and was much amused. Think there was more spice
to that dinner than I ever before saw. One black-eyed vixen
opened the ball with "I don't see how you can hold your head
up and look people in the face, engaged in the cause you are."
I told her I thought she had a free way of 'spressing her
opinion. "Yes," says she, "I can't use a gun but I can tongue
lash you, and will every chance." Then they all joined in,
but I found that eating was my best "holt," so they had it
their own way. When I'd finished my dinner, told them "a la
Buell," that I thought their house would make an excellent
hospital, and that we'd probably bring out 80 or a 100 patients
the next day for them to take care of. Scared them like the
devil, all but one, and they all knew so much better places
for the sick. This odd one said she had a way of "putting
arsenic in some people's feed, and she'd do it, too." Told her
we'd give her a commish as chief taster, and put her through
a course of quinine, asafœtida and sich. Said she'd like to see
us dare to try it, she would. They were too much for me,
but I'll never pass that place without calling. I'd give my
shirt to have had Ame Babcock there. Those are the first
outspoken female seceshers I have yet seen.

Deserters say that the Rebels have positively no forage or
provisions in Corinth. That the Memphis and Mobile railways
can barely bring enough daily, scraped from the whole length
of the lines to feed the army. It is reported here that Sherman took possession of the Memphis road west of Corinth

yesterday and has fortified his position. Pope got two or three men killed yesterday. There was about 5,000 of the enemy camped in the woods one and one-half miles in front of his posish, and he drove them back until they were reinforced and made him scoot again. I was out with a scout Sunday and started again last night at dark (Monday) and was out until 9 this a. m. The cause was some small bands raising the d——l on our left. We didn't catch them. We were over to the Tennessee, Sunday, where we could see the sacred soil of Alabama. I like Alabama better than any other Southern State. She's never done the "blowing" the others have and people here say that she's nearer loyal than any other Southern state. They're raising loyal companies here now. There are two full in Savannah.

General Jeff C. Davis' division passed here to-day to join Pope's corps. Davis stopped with us and made quite a visit. General Ash of this division goes forward to-morrow. The 21st and 38th Illinois from Stules division went out yesterday. Eleven regiments in all added to Pope's command in two days; except the last two they were all at Pea Ridge and some at Wilson's Creek. A splendid lot of men but not drilled equal to many regiments of the "Army Miss."

I don't honestly believe that we have with all our reinforcements 100,000 men here; but don't believe the Rebels have 75,000; of course I mean effective men that can be called on the field to fight. We have just received orders to move to front to-morrow.

Near Farmington, Miss., May 28, 1862

We moved up here this morning under the hottest sun and over the dustiest roads, and I then helped the major lay off the camp, and pitched our tents ourselves. Gracious, how hot it was! I worked and sweated and blessed General Pope for ordering us forward on such a day. I'll wager we are the only field and staff that pitch and strike our head quarter's tents without the aid of the men. But I can't bear the idea of making men who are our equals

at home do our work here. Soldiering in the ranks spoils
a man for acting officer "a-la-regular." We're ordered to
have our horses saddled by 3 a. m. to-morrow. There
has been the liveliest kind of cannonading along the whole
lines to-day. Our whole army advanced about a mile. I
think that at almost any point on the line we can throw
shot into their works. Distances vary from one and one-
half miles to two and a quarter or two and one-half. Many
of the generals think that to-morrow there will be a general
fight. They talk a great deal more since the news correspondents have been sent off; and of course anything of
that kind, that a brigadier says, goes the rounds of the
whole camp in real telegraph style. Have heard of a number of killings to-day, and haven't heard a tithe of the
whole. The enemy are beginning to dispute our further
advance right strongly. Many think that Halleck has commenced a regular siege. He has left a line of splendid defences to-day, and if he forms new works on the position
taken up to-day, we will know that we are in for a long
fight, a-la-Yorktown. Two regiments of cavalry went out
this morning to destroy the Ohio & Mobile R. R., 30 miles
south of Corinth. I wish them luck. Many of the Rebel
shot and shell struck within a half mile of the front of our
camp to-day. It looks somewhat like the times at Madrid
and Point Pleasant, but will probably be a little more
interesting before we finally finish it.

May 30, 1862.—We have our horses saddled all the time
since 2:30 yesterday morning. Owing to Colonel Kellogg's
continued illness he was this morning retired from further
command of brigade, and Mizner put in his place. We could
hear the cars running at Corinth all last night, and now
there is a heavy black smoke hanging over the place. Some
think they have evacuated, but 'tis doubtful. Firing all
the time since 3 this morning. Up to this time we (our
regiment) have had but three men killed and nine
wounded here. Have been remarkably fortunate. I gave
up my cot to Major Rawalt and am sleeping on the ground

now, and the confounded lizards are working me into a fever. They are as thick as you ever saw grasshoppers. One of them ran into Allan Heald's shirt bosom yesterday and they say he moved rather sprightly for a few minutes. Lots of snakes here, cottonmouths, copperheads, rattle-snakes, and commoner varmint. There's also a scorpion that looks like a lizard with a green head. They say it is poisonous.

June 4, 1862. No. 10.

We've been living out here a week without any tents until to-night, and General Pope is ripping and swearing because we dared to move them up here without orders. He says we shall not move a thing back. The colonel I am with is a regular army officer and he shows it all over, but I like him very much so far. I won't get to go out on near as many scouts, for will only go when the whole brigade moves.

Camp near Boonville, Miss., June 4, 1862.

Since the evacuation of Corinth we have been pushing after them after a fashion. That is follow them until we catch up with their rear guard and then retreat three-fourths the distance we have advanced. Have been five or six days following them 25 miles. Yesterday we advanced some 10 miles beyond this point, skirmishing with them all the last five miles, and then we all returned to camp here. I think we must have had 40,000 men out yesterday and yet it was only a re-connoisance in force. But what the devil was the use thereof I cannot see, for the day previous some of our cavalry was out farther than we went. Our regiment had the first skirmish with the Rebels after they left Corinth. 'Twas about seven miles out of the town. We had two killed and three wounded. They were of the Decatur Company. Our boys killed five of them. This is the most masterly retreat yet. They have positively left nothing of any value. I don't think they left tents enough for one regiment. They left not one cannon. No arms of any value and very few of any kind. We have only found one wagon since we passed Corinth, although there were a number in the place that they did not need. We haven't taken 50 prisoners, although they have lost hundreds, maybe thousands, by desertion. There is not the least evidence that they yere in haste at any point, and just 20 hours before we entered Corinth we were ordered to saddle our horses and be in perfect readiness for a fight, as it was expected that the enemy would attack us before three hours. At that time they could not have had more than enough men in Corinth to do the required picket duty. They are now, or at least a large body of them, in camp within 12 miles of us, and the story through the army is they are marching on us. Our boys are fairly wild to be on after them But then another rumor from a tolerably reliable source, is we are going to fall back to Corinth and camp until plans are more fully matured. Still another says Pope's army is ordered down the Mississippi river again. I hope the last is not so, for I have a dread of that river in the summer season. I am acting assistant adjutant general for Colonel Mizner, commanding 1st Brigade Corps.

Headquarters 1st Brigade Cavalry Division,

Camp near Boonville, Miss., June 6, 1862.

I am leading an inglorious life now, nothing to do but the brigade writing and ride with the colonel when he goes out on business. The only time I am on the fighting list is when the brigade goes out, and that is very rarely, and only when reconnoisances in force are made, and there is seldom any fighting done then. General Hamilton's whole division marched by our tent to-day and it was a splendid sight; I had thought that I'd never want to see any more troops but his division looked so splendidly, that I really enjoyed the sight of them. I knew that they were only marching into a new camp, but they all had got the idea that they were going into a fight and they were in grand spirits. I never saw the men look as healthy as they do now. One reason is those who were sick have been all left at the river and the weakly ones do not pretend to march in the ranks this hot weather. We are within one hundred yards of General Pope's headquarters and there are continually a lot of brigadiers passing. They nearly always ride on the gallop, and with the aids and escorts all told, say 60 in number to each general, they make quite a dashing appearance. Rosecrans, Buell, Granger, Smith, Sherman, T. W., Plummer, Paine, Hamilton and Pope all rode by at one time to-day.

All the companies we have had out to-day report skirmishing with the enemy We lost two men prisoners, some wounded and several horses. Got some prisoners. The enemy are in some force six miles from here. They are dodging all around us. Rumor says to-day that Buell with his army is going down through Alabama to Montgomery. Pope will move slowly after the enemy through Mississippi, and Thomas will go across to Memphis and down the river to co-operate with Butler in a movement through Southern Mississippi. 'Tis probably the plan of some cuss in the ranks. I wish for one day that you could hear all the camp rumors. They would make a remarkable book.

Rienzi, Tishomingo Co., Miss., June 9, 1862.

Saturday morning the 5th inst. the colonel and myself started for a little pleasure ride as a relaxation from the many cares and troubles people in this profession are incident to. We started for Corinth, as neither of us had yet visited the place, and plodded along through dust in air and heat—words can't tell how oppressive. We stopped at General Rosecrans about 1 p. m. and stayed and dined with him. The general was in his most pleasant mood and I thought him very engaging and winning in his manner. He told a number of amusing stories and 'twas all very pleasant, until somebody happened to mention General Fremont's name. General Granger was also at the table and the two generals commenced and each tried to outdo the other in—yes, reviling the "bumble-bee catcher."

They changed the subject over the wine and General Rose-crans became quite enthusiastic and prophetic in his conviction in regard to the war question, settlement thereof, etc. But I couldn't see any remarkable difference between him and the rest of mankind, and the same remark will apply to all that I know of the other generals here. I remember he said that he considered "slavery a vile blot on the face of the earth," and that unadulterated abolitionism alone was its equal; but I don't claim that the speech showed any remarkable talent. We left him swearing at his A. Q. M. and journeyed on. We luckily met an old acquaintance of the colonel's, a captain in the 1st Regular Infantry, and went with him to his quarters for the night. All the regimental officers quartered together in a very fine house that belongs to a secesh colonel. They were a jolly set of men, and the empty bottles lying around loose when we retired testified strongly thereto. I remember seeing one of them at Point Pleasant, Mo., have a couple of little fights (he commanded a two-gun battery of siege pieces) with a Rebel battery on the opposite shore.

We left Corinth early next morning for Farmington, and as we passed I saw where Major Applington fell. It was as I supposed about one-half mile from Corinth (hardly that) and what I did not know, was within 400 yards of the strongest part of the Rebel fortifications. We lunched at 10 a. m and paid an old lady the modest sum of 50 cents for a piece of cornbread and a glass of buttermilk. She complained bitterly of some of Buell's soldiers killing three of her chickens without paying for them, and just the day before her husband had been to Corinth and received meat, flour, etc., free from the aid society. She had three sons in the Southern Army. At 12 m. we drew rein 25 miles from Corinth at Iuka.

There are a couple of splendid springs in Iuka. One chalybeate, and the other sulphur water, and the town is the neatest I have seen in the country. Snuff-dipping is an universal custom here, and there are only two women in all Iuka that do not practice it. At tea parties, after they have supped, the sticks and snuff are passed round

7

and the dipping commences. Sometimes girls ask their beaux to take a dip with them during a spark. I asked one if it didn't interfere with the old-fashioned habit of kissing. She assured me that it did not in the least, and I marveled. There was only one regiment at Iuka, and they were expecting an attack from the hordes of guerrillas that infest the country all along our front from Memphis to Florence. I stayed at the hotel in town and had just retired (about 11) when crack, crack, two guns went, only about 60 rods from the house. There was a general shaking of the whole building, caused by the sleepers rising en masse and bouncing out on the floors. I thought if there was no fight I wouldn't be fooled, and if there was I couldn't do any good, so I kept cool. 'Twas only a little bushwhacking. A soldier policeman having been shot at from the brush, and he returned the favor by guess. This infantry always thinks the enemy is just out of gunshot of them, and they are three-fourths scared to death all the time. At noon of Monday we left Iuka, rode to Burnsville, a place that I have spoken of in my letters before, as we scouted through it while lying before Corinth. None of our soldiers have camped there yet, and we were the only ones there while we stayed. The colonel took a nap to recover from the heat and fatigue of riding, and I strolled down town to look up some acquaintances I made while scouting. They treated me pretty well, and made me a letter carrier, as many of them had letters to send to their friends who are prisoners. At dark we started for Jacinto, ten miles south, but for so many hills had a splendid ride. 'Twas through the woods, all the way, and over real young mountains. We got to Jacinto at 10 p. m. and concluded to stay all night. I laid down an hour or two, but the fleas were so bad that I got up and stayed up the rest of the night. I walked around the town and stopped at headquarters of the guard and talked with the boys. (They were of Jeff C. Davis's division, of Pea Ridge, Ark., and Siegel.) They all think that Siegel is the only man and hate

Davis like the devil. I waked the colonel at 4 p. m. and we started for home. The road from Jacinto, home, was lined with infantry, the whole left wing of our corps being on it. They had no tents but seemed to be preparing the ground for a camp. We got home in time for a little nap before breakfast, both of which I enjoyed very much. We found the garrison much excited about an attack that was expected every hour. The 2d Brigade of Cavalry had been about eight miles in front doing outpost duty, and having been alarmed by rumors had abandoned their camp and retreated to this place. Their sutler gave up his goods to the boys, preferring they should have them free, rather than the enemy. The next day (yesterday morning) a scout was sent out and found their camp just as they had left it. All of which was considered quite a joke on the 2d Brigade. The enemy may come up here and may whip us out, we are scattered so much, but they will have a riotous time of it. All told we had a very pleasant ride, but if we are gobbled up some of these times when riding around without an escort you must not be surprised. I don't think it just the straight way of doing such business, but Charles can go where the colonel dares to, and my preference is for riding as far from a column as possible on several accounts. The colonel is a very interesting companion on such a trip, full of talk, and he has had six years experience on the frontier. I induced a very young lady with a well cracked piano to favor me with some music at Iuka. She sang "The Bonny Blue Flag That Bears a Single Star." It was as near the music we used to hear in the old Presbyterian church at home as you could think, and that's all that kept me from laughing in her face. We celebrated the capture of Richmond on the 4th, but are now trying to forget that we made such fools of ourselves. Damn the telegraphs. We have awful news from Richmond to-day. It would make me sick to write it. I would rather have the army whipped than McClellan.

Camp near Boonville, Miss., June 13, 1862.

This is the fourth camp that we have had to call as above.
We have lived all around the burg, but to-morrow we leave.
We have just got nicely arranged here after working hard all
day, and now an order comes to move brigade headquarters
back to Rienzi, nearly 10 miles toward Corinth. Bah! how
sick it makes me to write that name. I haven't seen the place
yet, and have no desire to. I feel about once a week as though
a little skirmish would do me good, but I don't see any use
in getting mad because they won't give me a chance to fight.
I couldn't feel any more out of the war at home than I do
here. The enemy have all gone further into Dixie and we're
left the undisputed occupants of this neck. Our headquarters
here are about 25 miles south of Corinth, and we have pickets
at Baldwin, 15 miles south of this. Pope's whole division has
moved back to just this side of Corinth except our brigade,
so here we are, maybe 1,200 effective men, doing outpost duty
nearly 40 miles in advance of the army. Yesterday the colonel,
his A. D. C. and myself rode around our entire picket line, I
mean the part of our brigade that is guarding the M. & O.
R. R. There is only one regiment doing this, and they
are strung out so that our ride was full 40 miles. When we
were within two miles of our camp, coming in, I was galloping along ahead of the colonel, maybe 50 yards ('twas 10
p. m.) and I thought I heard a "halt," but was so sure there
were no pickets there (full a dozen miles inside of our corps'
pickets) that I didn't mind it until bang, went an old musket,
and the bullet zipped considerably over my head. I halted.
They were some infantry pickets whose regiment was close
by in the woods (some two miles). Well, we hadn't the
countersign and they wern't going to let us pass. The colonel
swore, I was awful hungry, and I cussed, the A. D. C. raved,
but the picket sergeant was immovable. At last we coaxed
him to send us in with a guard to his colonel. He sent six
men with us as guard, and the cuss gave orders to shoot us
if we tried to run. The chap that shot was one of the guard,
and he told me that he shot over my head on purpose after

he had halloed "halt" several times. They didn't know there was cavalry outside of them and said they'd shot us sure if they hadn't seen the glimmer of my straps in the moonlight. We got their colonel up, took a toddy with him and—home. Did I ever tell you about my darkey, "Charley"? We got him at Cape Girardeau. He informed our troops where his master and company had hidden some 14 kegs of powder and some arms. His massa found out he had informed and put him in irons four weeks. He escaped and came to us We lost him at Madrid and never knew what had become of him until he turned up here a week since He had been sick in the Cairo hospital. He comes very handy to me when I'm a little lazy, which, though, is only 30 or 40 times a day. He has my boots blacked and clothes brushed when I get up in the morning, is a splendid hand to take care of a horse, and all told a very handy institution. He wants me to promise to take him home with me. If you will have him, I'll do it. He'd be right handy about our house. I have the nicest horse. He is a perfect staver. A little tiresome to ride because so anxious to go fast, but he is so strong and never tires. After that ride yesterday of 40 miles through a broiling sun he danced along at the last as much as when we started. We were coming in from a reconnoisance one night last week and about 10 p. m., dark as Egypt, an artillery wagon crowded me off a causeway and Siegel (my horse) went into the mud to his shoulders and I, over his head, gracefully. He got out and sloped, and I walked into camp. 'Twas only a quarter of a mile. An artillery sergeant caught him and I walked out to the road just in time to see him passing. He dismounted very spryly. Siegel licks my hands just like a dog and he will follow me away from his oats any time. After he got away from me that night he went back again to where we fell and that's where the sergeant got him. He is a large bay and I wouldn't take anything for him. I was riding to-day with the colonel, and as we crossed the M. and O. R. R. I saw a couple of fellows 300 or 400 yards down the road coming towards us, and one of them threw up his hands. I thought he was a de-

serter and waited. They proved to be what I thought. One
was an Alabamian and the other from Arkansas. They had
seen our pickets further out but thought them Confederates
and slipped by them through the brush. I took them to the
colonel, and since then, this p. m., nine more have come in, and
'tis not a very good day for deserters either. These people
here are very tired of war. You would be if this army should
march through Canton, indeed you would. You can't go into
hardly a house here but what they'll ask if you know anything
of "my son," "my brother," or "my husband" that was taken
prisoner at this place or that place, and then the poor creatures
will cry as though their hearts were broken and you begin to
feel queer about your throat, and—I can't stand that at all.
It hurts me under my vest to see these poor women suffering,
for maybe not the fault of those they mourn, but of rich men
and politicians who have by threats and lies induced these
poor devils to leave their families to die of starvation, to fight
for, they can't tell what.

I have just seen a Mobile *Register* of the 5th. It says they
have taken at Richmond 7,000 prisoners, 80 pieces artillery,
wagons, etc., innumerable quartermaster and commissary
stores in vast quantities. That McClellan is driven back 30
miles and his army is surrounded, but a few of them may
escape by James river. Very jocular and highly edifying.
They also claim 15,000 stands small arms captured.

Rienzi, Tishomingo Co., Miss., June 14, '62.

We have located for a somewhat permanent stay, as the
clumsy order said, in the most beautiful little town I have
yet found in Mississippi. We have pitched our tents in a
little grove in the edge of the burgh and are preparing to live.

We have been rioting on plums and blackberries the last
week. Dewberries are about gone. I don't think the plums
are as good as ours. There is already much suffering amongst
the poor here, and God only knows how these people can live
until the new crop of corn is harvested. The wheat is all
cut these ten days, but ten acres of it will hardly keep one

person a year. Cotton is not planted this year to any extent, a tax of $25 per bale being laid on all each man raises over one bale. I told you how we rode out to Baldwin on the 12th; well, this morning the enemy nearly surrounded our picket there and killed or captured a few of them, scattering the rest. They have nearly all got in. There are no troops between here and the picket at Baldwin, 25 miles, and this little body is 12 miles ahead of the main army. 'Tis an outrage to post troops in this manner, and if they all get cut off (the two battalions on picket) it won't surprise me. There are not many slaves here, very few planters work more than 25, though 60 miles further down many have from 300 to 400 each. We don't think these are large bodies that are troubling our outposts, but they will hover around so long as the picket is advanced thus far.

Rienzi, Tishomingo Co., Miss., June 16, 1862.

We are camped here enjoying ourselves grandly. As our brigade is scattered over a line of 50 miles we just pitch our headquarters in the quietest spot we can find independent of the command. There are only two companies now out of the 24 within 8 miles of us, and all we have to do with any of them is to send them orders and receive their communications and forward them. In the heat of the day we read and lounge in our tents, and mornings we go to the creek and bathe and then ride a dozen or so miles to keep our horses exercised. I have a clerk, too, for my copying, etc., so I'm a gentleman. Evenings I visit generally some of the half dozen families within a half mile of us of whom I borrow books and in return furnish them with occasional papers. We have splendid water and my health is perfect. This is the healthiest part of the South.

Rienzi, Tishomingo Co., Miss., June 19, 1862.

This is one of the few days that remind one of Illinois, although there are very few nights that might not remind a Greenlander of his home. I think there has not been a night

yet that I have not slept under three blankets, and there have
been many nights that I would have used a dozen if I had had
them. The natives say that 'tis the Gulf breeze that makes
the air so cool after about 7 or 8 p. m. I wish that it would
get along about eight hours earlier daily; but to-day there are
clouds kiting about so o'erhead that the sun don't amount to
much only for light, and 'tis cool enough to make underclothing comfortable. The colonel, A. D. C. and myself visited the
camp of the 7th Illinois yesterday at Jacinto. We found them
surrounded with a brush parapet, felled trees, etc., ready as
they said for a twelve-hour's fight. They'd been visited by a
scare. There is no enemy within 15 miles of them and hasn't
been. They are camped in the suburbs of a beautiful little
town that fell in among the hills in a very tasty manner (for
a Mississippi town). In one little valley near a fine residence
there are three springs bubbling up in line and within a foot
of each other, which are so independent that each furnishes a
different kind of water. The first pure, cold, soft water without taste, another chalybeate, and the third, strong sulphur.
The waters of the three fall into one little basin and run thence
into a bathhouse twenty steps distant. There is a neat vine
covered arbor over the springs with seats arranged within,
and altogether 'tis a neat little place—good to water Yankee
horses at. There were several gangs of negroes at work in
the corn and cotton fields along the road yesterday, and I
thanked God they were not in Illinois. Candidly, I'd rather see
them and a whole crop of grindstones dumped into the Gulf,
than have so many of them in our State, as there are even here.
Yet, it don't look square to see the women, if they are niggers,
plowing. I have no reason for the last sentence, only it isn't
in my opinion what petticoats were designed for. Talking
about niggers, these headquarters are fully up with anything in that Potomac mob on the colored question. They
got Jeff Davis' coachman. What of it? J. D. isn't anybody
but a broken-backed-politician-of-a-civilian, and of course his
coachman is no better than a white man. But we, we have,
listen, General Beauregard's nigger "toddy mixer," and my

experience fully proves to the satisfaction of your brother that
the general's taste in selecting a toddy artist is fine. He is
a sharp cuss (the nigger). He left them at Tupelo day before
yesterday, p. m., slipped by the pickets while 'twas light without their seeing him, but after dark he was suddenly halted
by their videttes when within ten feet of them. He ran by
them and they fired, but as usual missed. He is really the servant of Colonel Clough, of Memphis, but the colonel is now on
Beauregard's staff, and John (the boy) was selected as drink
mixer for the general-pro tem. He reports that Price started
with the flower of the flock, only some 3,000 posies, to Virginia,
but said posies, like their vegetable brethren, wilt and droop
by the wayside, and unlike them, scoot off through the brush
at every chance, and that is the last of them as far as soldiering is concerned. Hundreds of the dissatisfied Rebels pretended sickness and lay by the roadside until the army passed
and then heeled it for home. All the prisoners and deserters
that we get concur in saying that at least 10,000 have deserted since the evacuation. A couple of very fine-looking young
fellows, Kentuckians, came in this p. m. Their regiment with
two others are the outpost guard between the Rebel Army and
ours. They were in a skirmish the other day at Baldwin,
where two of our companies were surprised and lost six men,
taken prisoners. There were 60 of our boys and they reported
400 Rebels. These deserters say there were only 42 Rebels;
but the next day 700 Rebels came onto 75 of our men and
the chivalry were put to flight in a perfect rout. So it goes.
There was a flag of truce came in last night to our picket.
Brought a dozen packages for Halleck and company, with a
number of letters for Northern friends, all unsealed. Several
of the envelopes were of common brown wrapping paper.
There are a good many things about this advance of an army
that are more interesting than the main army the infants know
of. We cavalry feel as safe here as in Illinois, but General
Ashboth keeps calling on Pope for more men all the time.

What do you think we'll have to eat to-morrow? Answer:
Lamb, roast goose and liver (beef), blackberry pies, plum

pudding, new peas, string beans, onions, beets, fresh apple sauce, etc. That's a fact, and we have a cow that furnishes us milk, too, and a coop full of chickens, maccaroni for our soup, and we get all the beef brains.

Tell Colonel Kellogg that the boys are talking about him yet, like a lot of chickens for their lost "Mar." The 7th has plenty to do now, if I wasn't so tired I'd write you a copy of the orders I sent them to-day.

The enemy keeps annoying our outposts, and rumors come to-day of their being on the way for this place to surprise us. All bosh, I suppose. I hope they are too gentlemanly to disturb us while we are doing as well as we are here. It would be worse than the old lady where I stayed night before last. I went to bed at 12:30, and about 5 she sent a servant up for the sheets to wash. The joke was on our family, but I told her that she had better let me roll over the whole house if she had to wash up after me, for it would improve the health of her family to scrub the premises and them. Fine people here. They've commenced bushwhacking. One of my orderlies was shot through the thigh night before last while carrying some dispatches. "Concilate," "noble people," "high spirited." Oh! Strangulate is the better direction.

Headquarters 1st Brig. Cav. Army of the Miss.,

Rienzi, Miss., June 29, 1862.

What the deuce this army is trying to do, I cannot guess. Buell's corps moved off in an easterly direction two weeks since. Grant's is, I think, between Corinth and Memphis, and the headquarters of Pope is about four miles south of Corinth, while his army is scattered for 75 miles west of here. The left wing, Plummer's and Jeff C. Davis' divisions moved through here yesterday, bound for Holly Springs, 60 miles due west. General Ashboth's reserve division, stationed here, have thrown up quite extensive works, fronting the enemy, who are not in any force, within 75 miles of us. Our cavalry division is doing the outpost duty on a line 40 miles long, running east and

west, and about 20 miles south of Corinth, with videttes out
eight or ten miles further, and scouting parties go 15 miles
below the videttes. We are losing about two men a day
skirmishing. I noticed a statement in the papers that 20,000
new-made graves could be seen between Corinth and the
Tennessees, caused by the swamp miasmas, etc., during our
approaching the enemy. We don't believe that there have been
400 deaths from disease since the battle of Shiloh, and 250
will cover the number of deaths from wounds received since
that fight. You know there have been an immense number of
sick men furloughed, but that was to satisfy the State govern-
nors more than necessity. For instance, John Shriner went
home on sick furlough and you know his condition. There
were thousands of such cases. I think the health of our army
never was better than now. I notice that our Illinois troops
stand this climate very much better than the men from Michigan and Iowa. Do not think we have more than one-third
the sickness in our regiment that the troops from the last
named States have. There is a prospect of our brigade's being
ordered to Ripley this week. I am well satisfied here, but have
no doubt will flourish equally well there. They charge outrageous prices for eatables throughout the country. Half-
grown chickens 25 cents each, eggs 25 cents per dozen, buttermilk 20 cents per quart, etc. We keep a cow for our headquarters, though, that supplies us with milk, and we have six
hens that lay as many eggs every day, and my colored boy
plays sharp and buys new potatoes, peas, beans, etc., for half
what I can, on the strength of his chumming it with colored
folks of the farms. There was a regiment raised in this
country that are now flourishing in Camp Douglas. A lady
played the piano and sang for me last night that has a husband
and brother residing in said camp. Mourning goods are quite
fashionable here, and I see limping around town several that
lost a limb, each, in some of the early battles. There are a
few that I have met who were taken prisoners by our troops,
one of them at Manassas, and paroled. Deserters come in
yet every day. An intelligent man that belonged to an Arkan-

sas regiment came in yesterday. He says that he thinks the main body of the Southern Army started for East Tennessee, via Chattanooga the day after he left them. Breckenridge's brigade has gone to Vicksburg, etc. I would like to send you some of the late orders issued by Rosecrans, if it were not so much trouble to copy them, in relation to police of camp and discipline. He looks after the health of men more than any general I have served under

People here are very indignant about our taking all their provisions away from them, and then appealing to the North to contribute to keep them from starving. There is some truth in the idea, but not much. They certainly do need eatables here, and the North will have to furnish them free or take scrip. Dinner: Blackberry jam, pie and raw berries. Oceans of them here. Day before yesterday the Rebels surprised one of our picket parties and captured 1st and C men, and yesterday they captured another. But Company K (Nelson's) followed them 12 or 15 miles and I think got the prisoners back with one Rebel, several horses and lots of traps. I got a letter from you a few days since relating the affecting parting scene between those spirits who left home, etc., for three months, and the sweet spirits that wept so heart breakingly thereat. I think your ideas were not unsound in regard to the parting scenes, and if you had boxed a few ears and pulled a little hair belonging to the ninnies that so abused the noble art of crying that day, you would have been excusable in my eyes. I must take a nap as quick as my boy comes back to keep the flies away.

11 p. m., 29th.—There is talk among the officers that Buell with 60,000 men is en route for Atlanta, Ga., intending to occupy that city, and thus cut off connection between the eastern and western portions of the Rebel Army. It will be a bold strike and looks safe; but it seems to me, from a glance at the map, that the occupation of Montgomery, Ala. would more effectually accomplish that end, for then there would be no railroad line open to the Rebels (we holding the Memphis and Charleston) while there are two lines running east from

Montgomery, only one of which a force at Atlanta could cover. A deserter came in this evening who says that they are organizing the army at Tupelo, mustering the men as five years' regulars, with promises of furloughs until this war is over. That England and France have decided that the Southern States shall all have a chance at the ballot box, and must, within 60 days, say whether they will cleave to the Government of the United States or be independent; if the latter, those governments will sustain them and thus end the war, and if the former, the war will be ended accordingly. So they are organizing a regular army upon the supposition that they will be an independent confederacy. The above shows they are able to start as huge a lie in their camps as we can in ours. I wouldn't have believed it before.

The colonel, A. D. C. and myself took tea with General Ashboth this evening. He is such a pleasant man. Has a great liking for pets. He has a tremendous large dog, who lays his head on the table right by the general's plate during meal time, and he gets his share at the first table. On the other side of him two little Indian ponies range themselves as quick as he sits down, and he lays biscuits on the corner of the table for them, which they gobble with the greatest relish. He spreads biscuits for one pony with sugar, and with salt for the other. His conversation is divided about equally between his ponies, the dog, and his other guests. The ponies he got in Arkansas, and they are the prettiest little fellows imaginable. The general is one of the most polite and kind men I ever saw. His troops all love him. He carries his right arm in a sling yet from a wound received at Elkhorn.

If you'd multiply all the bugs, say by 10,000, you'd have something near the number that visit me nightly. They are of all sizes less than a door knob, and the shapes and colors are innumerable. When they're bumping against you by candle light, if you were not acclimated, you would swear someone was brickbatting you.

We could overrun the whole West and Southwest as fast as we could travel, with the army we had here, if it were policy. Vicksburg cannot stand two hours when attacked. But it has leaked out at headquarters that we are letting them think they are holding us in check, so that they will keep all their forces in the West until after the big fight at Richmond. I have heard from Captain Nelson that Sammy Nutt distinguished himself in the skirmish yesterday. He captured that prisoner I spoke of. Captain says Sam was the head man in the chase and that no man ever behaved better. Sam's pistol went off accidentally after he had captured the secesh and the bullet came within half an inch of knocking a hole in the Rebel's head. The boys all give Sam a great deal of praise. 'Twas daring of the captain to run his handful of men almost into the enemy's camp, and 25 miles from any support; but if any company can do it, Company K can. Captain Nelson looks well but grumbles at being brought back from the front to where there is nothing to do but rest. His men feel the same way. For my part I don't consider myself in the war here any more than I would be in Canton.

III.

July 14, 1862 to June 4, 1863. Rosecran's orders as to rights of citizens and treatment of slaves. Comments thereon. Guarding a hundred miles of railroad. Still fretting at inaction. Bogus money imposed upon the ignorant. Growing insubordination of the slaves. Near view of the civilizing influences of slavery. About to be mustered out as battalion adjutant offered three other desirable staff positions. Prefers active service in the field; returns home to raise a company. Succeeds and is elected captain of Company G, 103 Illinois Infantry. Returns to the front. Gives a condensation of prevailing rumors. Experience of jayhawking. On provost guard duty. Demoralization of pillage. Rebel raid on Holly Springs. Two cowardly surrenders. Wrongfully arrested. Lonesome night ride. Infantry turned into cavalry in a night. Indignation at home "Copperheads." More wordy skirmishing with secesh ladies. Too many Negro refugees. Desertions frequent. Demoralization caused by "Copperhead" journalism. Dull round of picket duty and camp guard. Devastation caused by the war. On board of survey to assess damages. Two dramatic incidents. Visit to Memphis. Brigade officer once more. Scouting and rebuilding bridges. Pressing horses and mules and confiscating supplies. On court martial duty. A Union heroine scout.

HEADQUARTERS, ARMY OF THE MISSISSIPPI,

July 14, 1862.

General Orders No. 92:

For the information of all in the command, the following explanations are given, in reference to the rights and duties of citizens of the States in which we may be stationed.

1. All citizens of the States claiming the rights, and holding themselves bound to the duties of citizens of the United States are entitled to the same protection of person and property, which we claim for ourselves.

2. We hold citizens to the performance of active duties, only when they receive protection; if left without protection, they are bound only to good will and abstinence from all acts of hostility to the Government.

3. Persons denying that they are citizens of the United States, repudiating the duties of citizens, by words or actions, are entitled to no rights, save those which the laws of war and humanity accord to their characters.

If they claim to belong to a hostile government, they have the rights of belligerents, and can neither justly claim, nor have anything more from the army. If they are found making war, without lawful organization or commission, they are enemies of mankind, and have the rights due to pirates and robbers, which it will be a duty to accord them.

It is not our purpose to admit the slaves of loyal masters within our lines, or use them without compensation, or prevent their recovery, when consistent with the interest of the service.

The slaves of our enemies may come or go wherever they please, provided they do not interfere with the rules and orders of camp and dicipline. They deserve more at our hands than their masters.

By order of General ROSECRANS,

(Signed)   W. L. ELLIOTT,

Brig. Gen'l. and Chief of Staff.

(Official, R. O. Selfridge, *Asst. Adjt. Gen'l.*)

Camp at Rienzi, July 17, 1862.

I think there is more point and policy in that General Order 92 than in any one that has yet been issued in the West, or East either for that matter; but still I do not think it remarkable for perspicuity, and it is neither as strong nor as definite as the army demands. If I know anything of the "laws of war and humanity," the soldiers will bless "92" for one thing, its relieving them from guarding the property of secessionists, and if they don't make sundry potato patches, cabbage gardens and fields of roasting ears that I know of, "hop" 'twill surprise me much. There will be some wondrous sudden conversions to Unionism when these butternuts get the drift of that order. An old pup in this town that drank "Southern Independence or the World in Flames" the other evening, in the presence of several United States officers has Union soldiers guarding his property, to preserve it from the Northern vandals, and he has used language equally insulting, times without number, yet the guard is kept up. I suppose, to conciliate him. General Ashboth visits all the secesh and rides around town with the daughter of the man I've been speaking of, who is more intensely secesh than her father, if that is possible. Maybe I'm jealous of him, for the girl is very handsome, but I don't think a United States general at all excusable in such conduct, though it may be overlooked in a lieutenant. Did you see Beauregard's answer to Halleck? I honestly think there is more truth in that document, than in any other military paper of the kind I have seen. Suppose you have seen Granger's review thereof. You notice he don't touch any of the principal points and shows his whole object in publishing the article, in these four words, "I led the pursuit." I'll swear we haven't taken, in deserters, prisoners and sick, since the evacuation of Corinth, 500 men (although hundreds have doubtless deserted who did not enter our lines.) I know this because we have had the advance all the time, and on the only roads there have been fighting and prisoners, and all the deserters have passed through our hands. There were about 18 cars burned, but the ruins show there was nothing of much value on them. 'Twas not intentional, of course, but Elliott did burn several men in the depot, or else the people of Boonville are liars, to a man. That fight the other day at Boonville amounted to nothing. The enemy's official report of their loss is four killed and ten wounded. There is an awful sight of bombast and lying about army reports. Beat politicians all hollow. We have had very heavy rains for the last 36 hours, and as water can now be procured on the hitherto dry ground between the armies, I expect

8

some cavalry skirmishing, at least, and if the enemy is yet in force at Tupelo, now is the time for them to attack us, for our army is scattered for 300 miles, almost along the Tennessee line, and cannot be concentrated in time to resist a large force. Many of the officers expect a big fight, but your brother don't.

July 19, 1862.

I don't know whether I have any business sending such a document as I enclose, but guess its no difference. Two spies came in to-night and report that there are not more than 15,000 or 20,000 of the enemy left at Tupelo and Saltillo. Bragg took a large force with him and went over in the direction of Chattanooga a few days since. A fortnight, nearer a month, since we had quite a large force stationed at Boonville. One of the men started to go back to Rienzi on business, and had not been heard of since until day before yesterday, when his body was found midway between the two places with four bullet holes through it. It lay some distance from the road, and was discovered by a man of the 2d Brigade while looking for water. He was undoubtedly murdered by some citizen. Day before yesterday Mrs. Pierce, wife of a captain in the 36th Illinois, rode out in an ambulance, escorted by a corporal, to get some fruit in the country. A party of guerrillas gobbled the party up while they were inside of our pickets, and took them to Ripley. They sent Mrs. Pierce back yesterday. She was well treated. I guess there are no hopes of a fight there until autumn. I'm getting tired of doing nothing, although I certainly should be satisfied, having easier times than almost any one in the service.

Halleck left here yesterday for Washington. Trains are running down here from Corinth every day now, so we are only three days behind the dates of papers received, which is better than eight or ten, as heretofore. We have had the most splendid rains for a few days, and the weather is very seasonable in temperature. We are living almost wholly on fruit: apples, pears and blackberries, fresh, and peaches and straw-

berries canned. Don't want for anything, but I still (so un-
reasonable is man) at times, think that I'm not enjoying myself as well as I used to in the 8th. I know I couldn't stay
out of the service while the war continues, but I would like
so well to have peace once more, and be civilized awhile.
There's a good time coming. Don't it come slowly? I write
all the colonel's letters now except those to his wife, and
shouldn't wonder if he'd have me do that next. At first he
used to read them over very closely, but now he often signs
without asking what they are about. To-night he told me was
going to make me inspector general for brigade. Making two
generals out of one lieutenant isn't fair. I'm too lazy and
modest for such a position and think I can coax him to appoint
a chap I have my eye upon.

Headquarters, 1st Brigade Cavalry Division,

Tuscumbia, Ala., July 27, 1862 (Sunday).
We received orders for our brigade to march on the 19th,
and started the 21st. We only made Jacinto that night, when
the colonel and myself stayed with Gen. Jeff. C. Davis, who is
a very approachable, pleasant and perfectly soldier-like man.
There is a strong sprinkling in him, though, of the Regular
Army and West Point. Next day we rejoined the command
and marched 15 miles, camped at Bear Creek, 22 miles west of
this place and just on the Mississippi and Alabama line. Thursday we joined General Morgan's division and that night the
brigade camped within four miles of Tuscumbia, and the
headquarters came on into town. This is a perfect little Eden.
Houses for 2,200 people with only 1,200 living here at present.
We stayed at the hotel Thursday night, and the old negro who
lighted me to my room amused me considerably with his account of General Turchin's proceedings here. Turchin brought
the first federal force across the Tennessee in Alabama, and I
guess he "went it loosely." The old Negro said that he only
had 1,200 men and brought no luggage, knapsacks or anything
else with him, but went away with 300 wagons, and everything

there was in the country worth taking. That his men made
the white women (wouldn't let the colored women) do their
cooking and washing, and that although they only brought one
suit of clothes, they put on a new one every morning and always looked as though they had just stepped from a bandbox.
People here hate General Mitchell's whole command as they
do the d——l, and many of them more. Well, we've settled
once more, and I'll be contented if allowed to stay here for
sometime. We're guarding about 100 miles of railroad from
Iuka to Decatur, and it promises to be pretty rough work. Day
before yesterday a guerilla party swooped down on a station
24 miles east of here where General Thomas had 160 men and
captured all but 20 of them. We are relieving General Thomas'
command from duty here, but the Rebels saved us the trouble
of relieving that party. We sent out a force yesterday of three
companies and the Rebels surprised and killed and captured
20 of them. I have just heard that there has been a fight eight
miles south of here to-day, between our cavalry and the Rebels,
no particulars yet. 'Tis the 3d Michigan that has suffered so
far. The 7th Illinois are out now after the party that surprised
the Michiganders yesterday, but have not heard of them since
they started yesterday p. m. We are quartered in the house
of a right good secesh, and are enjoying his property hugely.
His pigs will be ripe within a week, and we'll guard them after
our style. The old fashion is played out as far as this brigade
is concerned. We take what is necessary and give vouchers,
which say the property will be paid for at the close of the war,
on proof of loyalty. This valley is 60 or 80 miles long, 15
miles wide and the most beautiful country imaginable. It is now
one vast cornfield. The residences in this town are superb, and
the grounds most beautifully ornamented and filled with shrubbery. There is a spring here that throws out 17,000 cubic feet
of water each minute. It supplies the town. General Thomas,
whom we relieved, has gone to Huntsville to join Buell. I
think they are going to Chattanooga then. People are intensely
secesh here, and whine most mournfully when compelled to
take the oath, or even to give their parole of honor not to give

information to the enemy. Our headquarters is a mile from any troops, just for the quiet of the thing. Peaches are just in season now, and there are oceans of them here. Blackberries are still to be found, and we have plenty of apples.

The weather is beautiful, not too warm and still require my double blanket every night, and often cool at that. We have information that Hardee with a force is marching on this place, and it is the most probable rumor that I have heard since the evacuation. Time will tell.

Tuscumbia, Ala., August 3, 1862.

In the last 15 days I have only written you once; partly because I have been so busy, more, because of my laziness. There is but little save rumors that can be of any interest to you from here, and shall not inflict any of them on you, for the newspapers have certainly surfeited everyone's taste for that article. All this blowing and howling we have in the papers of raids everywhere, and overwhelming forces of the enemy confronting us at all points, is, I candidly believe, part of the plan to raise volunteers. It certainly is one grand humbug as far as this field is concerned. Every officer here that knows anything about the condition of the enemy, their positions and numbers, believes that if our army were concentrated and set at the work, we could clear out all the enemy south of this and west of Georgia in a short two months. The soldiers are all anxious to begin, all tired of inaction, all clamoring for the war to be ended by a vigorous campaign, we running our chances of being whipped by the enemy, instead of waiting until next spring, and then being forced by bankruptcy to abandon our work. The way we are scattered in this country now the enemy can take 1,000 or 2,000 of us just any morning they may feel so disposed, and their not doing it lowers them wonderfully in my opinion. There are about 6,000 of us stationed at nine points along 75 miles of railroad, and there is no point that 4,000 men could not reach and attack, and take before assistance could be afforded. But the Rebels don't show any more dash or spirit than we do, so we all rest perfectly easy in our weakness, confiding in their lack of vim, which we gauge by our own. A line drawn through Fulton, Miss., Warrenton, Ala. and thence to Rome, Ga. (at which last place we think the enemy are concentrating) will give you the route over which the enemy are now moving in considerable bodies, while whole brigades of their numerous cavalry pass nearer us, through Newburg, Moulton and Somerville, Ala. 'Twould be so easy for them to detach a division and send it up to this line of road. Buell, with a very respectable force, is near Stephenson in northeastern Alabama moving so slowly that no one can tell in which direction. I wish they'd give Grant the full control of the strings. He would be sure to have somebody whipped, and I'd rather 'twould be us than live much longer in this inactivity. People are most outrageously secesh here, generally, although there are said to be some settlements very Union. I saw two men yesterday who were raising the 1st Union Alabama Regiment. They have two full companies they say, but I'll never believe it until I see the men in blue jackets. This is the most beautiful valley that I ever saw. It lies between the Tennessee river and a spur of the Cumberland mountains, which are craggy and rough, and rocky enough to disgust an Illinoisan after a very short ride over and among them. Howwever, they form a beautiful background for the valley, and are very valuable in their hiding places for the guerrillas who infest them, and sally out every night to maraud, interfere with our management of this railroad and to impress what few able bodied butternuts there are left in their homes. They either cut the wires or tear up a little road track for us every night. We have guards too strong for them at every culvert, bridge and trestle. This country was entirely out of gold and silver until our cotton buyers came in with the army, and every man of money had his little 5-cent, 50-cent, etc., notes of his own for change. Mitchell's men counterfeited some of them and passed thousands of dollars of their bogus on the natives. I send you a couple of samples of what is known here as Mitchell money. The man I got these of had been fooled with over $20 of it.

The boys couldn't get the proper vignette so, as you will observe, they used advertising cuts of cabinet warehouses and restaurants. Many of our men have passed Mustang Liniment advertisements on the people, and anything of the kind is eagerly taken if you tell them it is their money; of course I refer to the poor country people, who, if they can read, don't show their learning. This man with $20, like that which I send you, is a sharp, shrewd-looking hotel keeper. His house is larger than the "Peoria House." General Morgan, who is in command of the infantry here, is a fine man, but lacks vim or something else. He isn't at all positive or energetic. The weather still continues delightful. I have'nt used any linen clothing yet, although I believe there is some in my trunk. We ride down to the Tennessee river every night and bathe, and 'tis so delightful. I don't believe anybody ever had a nicer place than I have, or less reason to be dissatisfied. Well, I do enjoy it; but don't think I'd worry one minute if sent back to my regiment or further back to my old place in the 8th. I believe I have the happy faculty of accommodating myself to cirumstances, and of grumbling at and enjoying everything as it comes. I am still desperately "out" with these secesh, but borrow books from them to while away my spare time. These people, safe in the knowledge of our conciliatory principles, talk their seceshism as boldly as they do in Richmond. Many of our officers have given up all hope of our conquering them and really wish for peace. For myself, I know its a huge thing we have on our hands, but I believe I'd rather see the whole country red with blood, and ruined together than have this 7,000,000 of invalids (these Southerners are nothing else as a people) conquer, or successfully resist the power of the North. I hate them now, as they hate us. I have no idea that we'll ever be one nation, even if we conquer their armies. The feeling is too deep on both sides, for anything but extermination of one or the other of the two parties to cure, and of the two, think the world and civilization will lose the least by losing the South and slavery.

Tuscumbia, Ala., August 7, 1862.

The enemy is reported nearer us than usual to-night, and in considerable force. Have no idea they intend fighting us here though. This has been the hottest day of the summer, and I've been in the sun all day with thick woolen clothes on, wool shirts, too. I started for Decatur about 7 this morning and got back at 5 p. m. All platform cars, no possible chance for shade. I rode on the cowcatcher going out, and on the tender, which was ahead, coming back. We got within ten miles of Decatur when we came to two bridges burned last night, and had to come back. There is not a bridge or culvert on this road as far as our brigade guards it, that has not been burned, at least once, and many of the cattle guards even have been burned. They don't fire on the trains though in this country, which is some little consolation to the traveler. Since we have been guarding the road, some two weeks, they have burned in our district four bridges, one water tank, and two station houses, and torn up rails several times. All this work is done in the night. The tank and stations were of no use to us and the bridges we can build about as fast as they can burn them, tearing down secesh houses to find the timbers ready hewn. There are some grand plantations along the line I have traveled to-day. Thousands of acres in some of them with from 50 to 250 hands, each. The negroes are under no restraint whatever, now. Don't half work, their masters say, About 40 negro women who were clearing a piece of woodland dropped their axes and picks and came out to the road as the train passed. They were by odds the most antic and amusing lot of slaves I have yet seen. So clumsily ludicrous, with their close-curled wool, great white and black eyes, and heavy-ended motions. Some wore sun bonnets, some men's old hats, but most were bareheaded. The negro women all wear handkerchiefs (I think they are), turban fashion, while indoors, and sun bonnets, or go bareheaded, when out. They seem to be all dressed alike, in very ragged, shabby, thick, cotton stuff, which is either white or yellow. I have never seen one of these dresses clean enough to tell which. I have seen but two negroes yet that have marks of severe punishment. They were man and wife, and belong to a planter living 12 miles from here. The man I think is made a cripple for life from blows by a club on his ankles and knees, the woman is badly cut on the arms and shoulders, as with a horsewhip, but she's all right yet. How a man can be fool enough to so abuse such valuable property as this is more than I can understand. You have no idea to what an extent the habit of dipping is carried here. I have, while talking to women who really had in every way the appearance of being ladies, seen them spit tobacco juice, and chew their dipping sticks, perfectly at ease. I don't think it common to do it so openly, but I have seen two ladies, and any number of common women, engaged in the delightful pastime. Colonel Kellogg seems to think that I will be mustered out in a short time. I'll promise you one thing, that if I am, I'll not enlist again until the policy of this war changes, and in actions as well as words, too. J. Pope is disgusting me with him very rapidly. John is a horrid blower of his own horn. If he don't astonish this country, after all of his blowing, the country will astonish him to his entire dissatisfaction before he's many months older. Oh! if Grant will only go to work and get somebody whipped, or if he'd retreat, that would be better than doing nothing, though not as good as advancing.

Tuscumbia, Ala., August 8, 1862.

My pet negro got so lazy and worthless I was compelled to ship him. I'll take back, if you please, everything good that I ever said of free negroes. That Beauregard nigger was such a thief that we had to also set him adrift. He stole our canned fruit, jellies and oysters and sold some of them and gave parties at the cabins in the vicinity. This was barely endurable but he was a splendid, smart fellow and the colonel would have kept him, but he got to stealing the colonel's liquor. That of course, was unpardonable, when the scarcity of the article was considered. In my last I spoke of a ride on the railroad and having to

turn back on account of bridges being burned There were,
maybe, 150 sick soldiers on board, and they concluded to
march to Decatur, only 10 miles. They were attacked
just after we started back, five of them killed and about
100 taken prisoners. There was a woman along and she
was wounded. There were three little fights yesterday
between here and 25 miles east. In all, four killed and 13
wounded. The fight first spoken of was day before yesterday. Orders have been given us to put every woman and
child (imprison the men) across the line that speaks or
acts secesh, and to burn their property, and to destroy all
their crops, cut down corn growing, and burn all the cribs.
That is something like war. 'Tis devilish hard for one like
me to assist in such work, but believe it is necessary to
our course. Having been very busy preparing reports and
writing letters all day, feel deuced little like writing you.
People here treat us the very best kind, although they are
as strong Rebels as live. Bring us peaches and vegetables
every day. I can't hardly think the generals will carry
out the orders as above, for it will have a very demoralizing effect upon the men. I'd hate like the deuce to burn
the houses of some secesh I know here, but at the same
time don't doubt the justice of the thing. One of them has
lent us his own cook, or rather his wife did; and they don't
talk their secessionism to you unless you ask them to.
We are getting a good many recruits from this country.
All poor people, in fact that is the only kind that pretend
to any Unionism here. There are now three full companies
of Alabamians (Union) at Huntsville, and many more
coming in. It is the opinion of the court that this new law,
a copy of which you sent me, will boost me out of the
service. I will make no objection, although would rather
stay in if I thought the war would last 30 or 40 years. Don't
see how the boys can stay at home under the pressure. A
young man here, and a splendid fellow, if he is a Rebel,
showed me four letters from different young ladies urging
him, by ridicule and appeals to his pride to go into the

army. He was in for a short time, and was stationed at
Fort Morgan. Business keeps him out now—crops, etc.
I think will arrange things so that he can leave, if we carry
out orders. 'Twould be quite a change for me to be out
of the army now. I don' know how I would relish it while
the war continues, although am sure could stand it if peace
times would come again.

Tuscumbia, Ala., August 14, 1862.

Things are progressing here swimmingly. Seldom have
more than two bridges burned in the same night, or lose
more than five or six men in one day. Scared a little though,
now. The 7th went down yesterday through Moulton,
where they were encamped but a few days since, and
gained us the information that they had evacuated that
post. People here are considerably scared about the free
and easy way we are gobbling up their little all. We are
raking in about 100 bales of cotton per day and could get
more if we had the transportation. It makes the chivalry
howl, which is glorious music in our ears, and the idea of
considering these confederacies something else than erring
brothers is very refreshing. But I can't talk the thing over
with them with any pleasure, for they all pretend so much
candor and honesty in their intentions, and declare so
cheerfully, and (the women) prettily, that they will do
nothing opposed to our interest, and express so much horror and detestation of guerrillas and marauders of all
kinds, that one can't wish to do them any harm or take
and destroy their property. But the murders of Bob Mc-
Cook, a dozen of men in this command, and hundreds in
the army, all tend to disipate such soft sentiments, for we
are satisfied that citizens do ten-elevenths of such work;
and nothing less than the removal of every citizen beyond
our lines, or to north of the Ohio river, will satisfy us. We
are all rejoicing that "Abe" refuses to accept the negroes
as soldiers. Aside from the immense disaffection it would
create in our army, the South would arm and put in the
field three negroes to our one. Am satisfied she could do

it. The *Tribune* couldn't publish those articles in the army and keep a whole press one day. Hundreds of the officers who are emancipationists, as I am, if the brutes could be shipped out of the country would resign if the *Tribune's* policy were adopted. Within an hour some rebellious cusses have set fire to a pile of some 200 bales of cotton, and the thick white smoke is booming up above the trees in plain sight from where I sit. I think 'tis on the Russellville road, and about eight or nine miles out. Our cavalry were through there yesterday and this morning. How gloriously the people are waking up again in the North. Should think from the papers that the excitement must be higher than ever. A man that don't know when he is well off, or enough to keep a good thing when he has his fingers on it, deserves what? "Nothing!" I believe you are right; yet such is my miserable condition. Not one officer in a thousand in the army has as pleasant a place as your brother, and yet here I am ready to go at the first chance, and into an uncertainty, too. Colonel Mizner has assured me that I suit him, and that if he is made brigadier he will promote me. Where I am going there is no chance for promotion unless Brigadier General Oglesby is appointed major general. Think I will have a better chance to work with Governor Yates, too, and then probably to not more than a captaincy. But I have decided to go, though I am anything but anxious about the matter. Any of the three places are good enough. I see by the papers that a scouting party from Cape Girardeau went through to Madison, Ark. to Helena, or Memphis rather. I wish I were over there.

What delightful breezes we have here. Believe me, it's all gumption about this being a hot climate. These weak kneed, billious-looking citizens, (so because they are too lazy to exercise their bones) puff and pant with their linen clothes, so thin you can see their dirty skins, almost, and we all wear our thick winter clothes, and at that feel the heat less than we ever did North. Such loves of nights, so everything that's nice; and invariably so cool that blankets are necessary after midnight.

Tuscumbia, Ala., August 19, 1862.

'Tis the old, old, story, burning railroad bridges, skirmishing between our scouts and theirs, etc. They opened on a new program by firing into a train, two days since, wounding five men only, though they put 200 shots into the engine and cars. They are burning cotton in very good style. Night before last eight fires were visible from our headquarters, and last night four. They destroyed about $300,000 in the two nights. They're getting scared about their negroes, and are carrying them off to the mountains as fast as possible. The blacks are scrambling in this direction to a very lively tune. Over 100 came in on one road within the last 24 hours. About 50 can be used in a regiment to advantage, but I am thoroughly opposed to receiving any more than we have work for within our lines. You have no idea what a miserable, horrible-looking, degraded set of brutes these plantation hands are. Contempt and disgust only half express one's feelings toward any man that will prate about the civilizing and christianizing influence of slavery. The most savage, copper savage, cannot be below these field hands in any brute quality. Let them keep their negroes though, for we surely don't want our Northern States degraded by them, and they can't do the Southerners any good after we get them driven a few degrees further down. These nigs that come in now, say that their masters were going to put them in the Southern Army as soldiers. I'm sure the Southerners are too smart for that, for a million of them aren't worth 100 whites. General Paine is gobbling up these secesh here and starting them North kiting. How they are shaking in their boots. Paine is going to clean out the country and make it Union if there is nothing but desert left. There are a number of very fine people here, such men as Jacob H. Bass, highly honorable, conscientious, etc., but strong believers in State sovereignty, and because their State has seceded, they are secessionists, and for no other reason. Paine is going to make them walk the plank with the rest. It looks a little hard to me, as they are willing to be paroled, but I'll never say stop when anybody is pounding the secesh.

Tuscumbia, Ala., August 28, 1862.

The order has been issued requiring battalion adjutants to be mustered out of the service, but Colonel Mizner insists on our remaining, and being either assigned to companies or made regimental adjutant commander and quartermaster, which offices this new law provides. General Oglesby wants me very much. I was down to Corinth a few days since and saw him. Told him about this order mustering me out, and he offered to go with me to General Grant and ask for an order excepting me from muster. I knew that the wording of my commission wouldn't allow such an irregularity and had to decline. If I stay with the regiment now, I will not be able to get on Oglesby's staff, as I wish, for in either of the three places which I can get, I could not be detached. But General Oglesby said that he would give me plenty of time to go home and hunt a lieutenancy in the company, and then he would have me assigned to him. I could not get home in less than eight days, and by that time I think would have a difficulty in getting a position, for regiments will be so near organized that new comers will stand a poor chance. Have almost made up my mind to go home and run my chances. I know I am worth more than a lieutenancy, and that in these regiment staff places there is no chance for promotion. Would almost as lief commence again in the ranks. Am sure I would be a captain as quickly.

[He came home and raised a company in the 103d Illinois Infantry, and was elected captain.—Ed.]

Camp Peoria, October 3, 1862.

I suppose this is the commencement of another series of letters from your army correspondent. You can't imagine how kind of old-fashioned good it seems to be in camp again. You know, of course, that my lucky star still rules, and that I have been elected captain. I think I have an excellent company, though I have but few men that I ever knew before. Charley Mattison is my first lieutenant, and John Dorrance, my second. The first lieutenant is able, willing and industrious. Dorrance will make a great deal better officer than you imagine. Think I will manage to visit you before we march, but can't promise. I am confined very closely, and have a great deal of work to do. But thank fortune, I partly understand it.

Camp at Lagrange, West Tennessee, November 7, 1862.

To say that we have been crowded, jammed, put through, hustled, skited, etc., don't half express the divil-of-a-hurry headquarters has shown and is showing us. We left Peoria one week ago last night, crossed the bridge at precisely 6 o'clock p. m. Since that we have traveled one day and one night on the cars, a day resting, beside stacked arms waiting orders, the first quarter of a night pitching tents, then received orders to march with five days' rations at daylight, and the rest of the night spent in preparation therefor, then two days' marching through the awfullest dust you ever saw, so thick we almost had to kick it out of the way to get our foot to the ground, then a day of rest and fat living off secesh pork, etc., and the seventh day a march of 20 miles by our whole brigade, after a little party of Rebel cavalry that couldn't more than eat a hog a day. Pretty good work for a green regiment, wasn't it? It seems real natural to be down in Secessia, the country where a 300-pound porker don't cost any more than a chicken that costs nothing. But some things we have to buy for our mess, and to show you what they cost, I will mention the items of flour and salt. The former is worth 50 cents per pound, and the latter $1 a pound. We wouldn't have to buy them of citizens, but scarcity of transportation obliged our A. C. S. to leave everything but traveling rations, viz.; Bacon, sugar, coffee and crackers. There is a man making boots in town at $45 a pair, and he can't get leather to fill his orders. Fine country. Between here and Bolivar, some 30 miles, I think there is not a house left or rail left unburned, and 'twas all done on our trip down. The fires were all lit by troops that marched ahead of us, and although the smoke and heat were disagreeable enough, yet I think the 103d generally approved of the proceedings. Yet I was glad enough when the colonel, by the general's orders, called us to answer the question, "Do you know that any of your men burned rails, houses, or destroyed any property on the march from Bolivar?" that the 103d had not participated. Major General McPherson, commanding this corps, disapproves of such conduct and will severely punish offenders if caught, which latter item is not at all probable. 'Tis generally understood that the Union Tennessee Cavalry did the work. The 7th Illinois is here with us and all are well that you know.

We have good tents and are otherwise better prepared for soldiering than I ever was before.

We have between 30,000 and 40,000, I suppose, between here and a point eight miles east. Price is supposed to be in the neighborhood of Holly Springs, 30 miles southwest, with 40,000 to 60,000. They say we are waiting for the Memphis troops to join us before we go down and scoop him. We have the half of the old army of the Mississippi here, and part of the army of West Tennessee, nearly all experienced troops.

Camp near the Tallahatchie, seven miles South of

Holly Springs, Miss.,

December 3, 1862.

We received marching orders at Lagrange, Tenn., at 9 o'clock p. m. on the 27th, and moved at 6 a. m. on the 28th, on the Holly Springs road. We marched some five miles and then waited four or five hours for the divisions of Ross and McArthur from Grand Junction, and Quinby and Moscow to file into the road ahead of us. About 4 p. m. we were again set in motion, and at 7 p. m. (moonlight) we turned into the woods, about 10 miles from Lagrange, and bivouacked for the night. Fell in at 7 a. m., 29th, marched nine miles by 2:30 p. m. to Coldwater, a very nice little stream, the water in which is as cold in July as in December. Here we rested until 6:30 p. m. and then marched six miles by moonlight to

Holly Springs, Miss., where we camped for the night.   At
8 a. m., 30th, moved out and arrived at the present camp about
2 p. m.   The last five miles we were cheered by the enlivening
music of artillery firing ahead, pretty lively at times and then
subsiding into an ocasional bellow, bringing the good old
Madrid and Corinth times very distinctly to my mind.   It's
astonishing what an amount of ignorance I am guilty of in regard to the situation of affairs here, but I really haven't inquired of or listened to any of the powers that be on the subject.   I've had my mind set on a fight in the neighborhood,
and if we get that I don't care about details, if not I'll find
out what I can, though 'tis an awful sight of trouble to sift
sense and matter to be credited out of camp rumors, and that
is about the only source a line officer has for getting information.   Believe I'll give you a little list of rumors condensed.
(1) Enemy 50,000 strong fortified on this side of Tallahatchie.   (2) Rebels driven across the river, only rifle pits on this
side.   (3) Sherman has turned their right flank and we've got
them sure.   (4) Enemy only 30,000 strong in tremendous fortifications opposite side of river; bridge burned, will be rebuilt
by midnight, when we'll pitch into them, etc.   (5) Pemberton
wants to fight; Price opposes the idea.   (6) Fortifications
evacuated night of 1st inst., and Sherman pushing the enemy's
right as they retreat   (To back this No. 6 rumor, heavy columns were pushing past us all day yesterday in a driving rain).
(7) Steel and Curtis have pushed across from Helena or
Napoleon and taken possession of Grenada, cutting off the
Rebel line of retreat; Curtis' force 25,000.   (8) Price has
cut through Curtis' force and escaped.   (9) Price attacked
Curtis, was repulsed and is now coming back this way, etc.

There has been cannonading the last three days some four or
six miles ahead, but none to-day.   Squads of prisoners pass
us going to the rear every day.   The country from Lagrange
to this place is very good, clearings much more extensive and
more evidences of wealth than on the Mobile and Ohio road.
We were on picket the 1st inst. some two miles in advance of

9

our camp and had a grand time. This 103d out jayhawks old Jennison himself. The regiment went on picket the last time with one day's rations, and I swear I believe they came in with six days'. My company "found" 150 pounds of flour, a hog, a beef, two and one-half bushels of sweet potatoes, chickens, ducks, milk, honey and apples. The night we stopped at Holly Springs, Company G must have confiscated $300 (the way these people figure) worth of eatables, among which were one barrel of molasses, 300 pounds of sugar, one barrel of flour, four hogs, etc. But I don't allow them to take anything but eatables. I think it right, and can find no arguments for any other side of the question. Holly Springs is a beautiful little town, but not so rich, I think, as Jackson, Tenn., which beats everything for its size, I ever saw. Our army, trains and all, stretched out in marching shape, is, I think, 30 miles long. Believe without Sherman it numbers from 40,000 to 45,000. Anyway we have enough to skin Mississippi. Major General McPherson commands our right wing of two divisions, Logan's and McKean's. Hamilton has the left wing of three divisions, McArthur, Ross and Quinby. Don't know what Sherman has, but he holds a good hand and has some trumps that we know of, particularly Hurlbut and Lanman. I never saw men in as good spirits and so confident as this army now appears. We are splendidly equipped and want nothing. The only drawback is the men's having to carry their knapsacks, but if the fine weather will only continue we'll stand that. We don't use any tents at night when marching, and 'tis no hardship to lie out at night yet. The boys strip to their underclothing, with only two blankets, and never grumble. I can't see why people will stay at home when they can get to soldiering. I think a year of it is worth getting shot for to any man. I believe I used to get a little homesick or girl sick, but my brief furloughs have taught me the vanity and vexation of spirit folks are liable to in the States, and I think I'll hanker thereafter no more. If I can get into the regular army, I'll do it sure.

Provost Marshal's Office, 4th Division, Army of the
Tennessee, near Tallahatchie, Miss.,

December 8, 1862.

Still we tarry by the wayside anxiously awaiting the order
to move forward. We did provide three days' rations once,
but devoured them without leaving camp. Two divisions, Mc-
Kean's and Ross', have left here, while the remainder of the
army has pushed onward. We hear of the advance skirmishing
50 miles in front of us. Think the main force is at Oxford,
about 25 miles from here. We're probably waiting for the
railroad to be repaired so that supplies can be furnished us
when we move. The retreating Rebels destroyed every culvert and bridge as they fell back, and it of course takes time
to rebuild so many. The road is not yet in running order to
Holly Springs, and everything has to be wagoned to the army,
which but a very little rain in this country makes impossible.
We suffered three days of cold, drizzling rain last week which
most effectually blockaded the roads, but the last three days
have been beautifully clear, etc., and travel is again resumed.
We will change camp to-morrow to improve our water facilities, probably moving four or five miles back toward Holly
Springs. One mile northward is harder to travel than 10 in
the opposite direction. My whole company is detached from
the regiment as provost guard. It relieves us from picket duty,
fatigue, etc., gives us officers' quarters in a house (there are
a sofa, two rocking chairs, soft-bottomed chairs, a library,
feather bed, etc., in the room I am now writing in and occupy).
I've soldiered long enough to never refuse these little good
things Providence throws in my way. The detail is permanent, but suppose I can get back to my regiment when I feel
disposed. The 7th Cavalry had a little skirmish in front a
day or two since; Coe, and a number of others were taken
prisoners. Nelson was a prisoner once, I hear, but was re-
taken by his men, or the 2d Illinois Cavalry. Rumor has it

to-day, that our forces have possession of Jackson, Miss., and have captured 3,000 of General Holmes' Army, which was attempting to reinforce Pemberton. Don't think the rumor worth doubting, unless McClernand has got within striking distance. Can't hear a word from his expedition. Wonder what the deuce Banks is going to try to do. Hope we won't fool away his time and the lives of his men in Texas. We've had enough of those coast expeditions. The one under Butler was the only one that paid expenses. Burnside is beaten badly. Will bet that another change of base will be necessary before Richmond is ours. We're out of all patience with that army. We are slow enough in all reason, but they certainly beat us crawling, wonderfully, making slowness the gage. Our men are using this country awfully rough. Such animals as chickens, fences, swine, etc., are entirely unseeable and unfindable within 15 miles of where our camp has been this last week. This alone is not so bad; but if you wink at this amount of license in soldiers, they go farther and insult and almost scare to death women and children, all citizens indiscriminately. Guess that 'tis the intention of the general commanding to reform this matter. Says he is going to hold company officers responsible for the conduct of their men and punish officers, not soldiers, hereafter for outrages committed. I send my boys out as patrols, and whenever they catch a man with poultry or meat of any kind they relieve him thereof, take him under guard to his regimental commander, and Company G eats up the chickens or pork, or potatoes, of course; so you see this provost duty is not so bad as it might be on us. I have also in my charge 35 Rebel prisoners, Louisianians and North Carolinians. Price had three Kentucky regiments, but they have nearly all deserted him, hundreds have taken the oath at different points along our line and gone to their homes. I have an old negro here now that I wish I could send to you to cut the wood and do your errands. He is 63 years old, but is good for twenty years yet.

Provost Marshal's Office, Waterford, Miss.,

December 12, '62.

From captain of the provost guard, I have been changed to provost marshal. I had charge of two companies, doing the guard duty for the provost of our division until yesterday; the division was ordered forward to Oxford, except our regiment, which was left to guard the railroad between this point and the Tallahatchie river. Headquarters being here, Colonel Dickerman appointed me provost and sent my company to guard a bridge one and one-half miles south of this place. My business is to attend to all prisoners, deal with citizens (administer oaths, take paroles, etc.), give all passes for citizens and soldiers leaving, have charge of all soldiers straggling from their regiments, issue permits to sutlers, etc., and overlook the cotton trade. Altogether, quite enough for any one man to attend to. The little advantage of having a comfortable house to live in, etc., is worth something; but I kind o' feel as if I would rather be with my company. Another regiment came in to-night, 12th Indiana, and we may possibly be relieved to-morrow. Shall be glad if we can only get with our division again. General Lanman has again taken command of our division, and although we know nothing against McKean, yet we know so much good of Lanman, that we're much pleased. Eight of our companies are guarding bridges, so we only have two here. Confound this railroad guarding; I'm down on it. 'Tis more dangerous than regular soldiering, harder work, and no shadow of a chance for glory. There's a smart chance of fun in my present business, particularly in the citizens branch thereof. It would have furnished you with amusement enough for a month, could you have heard an old lady talk who visited me to-day. She was a F. F. and blooded, Oh, Lord! We let all come within the lines; but before they can pass out, an oath or parole is required of them. How they squirm! Rebels, though they are, 'tis shocking and enough to make one's blood boil to see the manner in which some of our folks have treated them. Trunks have been knocked to pieces with muskets when the women stood by, offering the keys, bureau drawers· drawn out, the contents turned on the floor, and the drawer thrown through the window, bed clothing and ladies' clothing carried off and all manner of deviltry imaginable perpetrated. Of course the scoundrels who do this kind of work would be severely punished if caught, but the latter is almost impossible. Most of the mischief is done by the advance of the army, though, God knows, the infantry is bad enough. The d—d thieves even steal from the negroes (which is lower business than I ever thought it possible for a white man to be guilty of) and many of them are learning to hate the Yankees as much as our "Southern Brethren" do. The army is becoming awfully depraved. How the civilized home folks will ever be able to live with them after the war, is, I think, something of a question. If we don't degenerate into a nation of thieves, 'twill not be for lack of the example set by a fair sized portion of our army. Do you remember that I used to write that a man would no sooner lose his morality in the army than at home? I now respectfully beg to recall the remark, but I believe the sight of such devilish, pointless wickedness disgusts me, and that your brother's moral principles are strengthened by contact with these ungodly. Instance, in my present position, I know without danger of exposure, I could pocket at least $500 within five days; but for conscience sake and my self-respect, I sit back with my purity, and tumble my keys and comb round in my otherwise empty pockets and feel good. Well, it won't do to brag on such a subject, but my confidence in the honesty of man has waned so much since I entered the army that I can't help saying, there are few that would not, in my position, make a raise. Can't hear anything from the front. Know that part of Sherman's army has returned to Memphis to join the expedition down the Mississippi and that is all. This town only contains a dozen or 20 houses, but they are good ones. Great many here profess to have always been Union, and many are taking the oath willingly. Good joke on them when the guerrillas come in after we leave. Suspect they have most all been Rebels, so I don't pity them as much as I do out-spoken seceshers. I rode out in the country eight miles day before yesterday, and found three convalescent soldiers of Price's army at one place, A lieutenant of the 53d Illinois was with me, so we brought them into camp and put them with the other prisoners. We have now nearly 3,000 soldiers in the hospital at Lagrange and yet the army is very healthy. Don't be much surprised if you hear of us being gobbled up by the guerrillas, for these railroad guards are only baits for them; nothing more.

Provost Marshal's Office, Waterford, Miss.,

December 23, 1862.

Suspect this will be my last from this country. Where the army is going I know not, but the divisions which have been in front are now filing past us, faces northward. The movement commencing at the time of the raid on Holly Springs, gives it the appearance of a retrograde for that reason, but I think that has nothing to do with the matter, for though I have no idea of the future plans of the general commanding, yet have known for some time that it was not the intention to pursue further than Grenada on this line, and that point has been evacuated by the enemy for some days. The raid into Holly Springs was capitally done. The Rebels made a No. 1 haul. Immense stores of clothing, commissaries and ordnance fell into their hands, all of which, however, they were obliged to destroy, save what they could carry away on their horses. About 1,200 or 1,500 officers and soldiers were paroled by them, some 1,000 horses carried off ,and I think not less than $1,000,000 of greenbacks. One-half million worth of cotton was burned, etc.; loss to Government cannot be

less than three or four millions of dollars. Colonel Murphy is
the man who is responsible for the whole thing, and I can
think of no punishment equal to his deserts. 'Twas but nine
miles from us and we of course immediately prepared for a
visit, but were not so honored. These successful raids of the
enemy almost make me sick. If our men would only be on
the alert so that they could make something of a fight, I
wouldn't care a d——n. But to lose a thousand prisoners
without the enemy's having one killed ,makes me disgusted
with the army. I'm allying a little fun with business as opportunities offer. Friday last I got permission of the colonel
to make a little reconnoisance of the country along Tippah
river, and on the Tallahatchie between the mouth of Tippah
and the railroad. I stayed six miles from camp the first night
and went possum hunting. Hunted until 2 o'clock a. m. and
although we treed a good many, couldn't get them. Examined
the country thoroughly next day, made a map of it, found there
were no guerrillas near our camp and then got a shot gun and
hunted. The young fellow I was with and myself, in an hour
killed seven squirrels and a coon. Got back to town at dark,
Saturday night, and found everybody terribly excited about
the Holly Springs affair. They had given me up for a goner.
The regiment laid on their arms and I laid on my featherbed,
for I knew devilish well there was no danger. We've been on
the alert ever since but the enemy has gone. To-day the guerrillas have been seen on all sides of us within a few miles, but
Ross' division has just arrived so there is no chance for a
fight.

Provost Marshal's Office, Waterford, Miss.,

December 30, 1862.

Fifteen days outside the world and still we live. No papers of later date than the 15th inst. have reached us, and 'twill
be at least five days' move before we can hope to see one. In
that time there have been some six or eight fights in this coun-

try all to our disadvantage, and two cowardly surrenders, Holly Springs and Trenton. Pemberton's cavalry under Van Dorn, turned our left, and striking at our line of communication, first surprised and captured Holly Springs, burned everything belonging to our army with the houses containing the stores; then while a portion of the column retreated another portion successively attacked our troops stationed at Coldwater bridge, Middleton, Grand Junction, and outposts near Bolivar, in all of which they were repulsed. About the same time a portion of Bragg's forces crossed the Tennessee river at or near Musch Shoals, Ala., and marched along the south side of the river toward Corinth. General Dodge at Corinth sent out Colonel Sweeny, who met and defeated the enemy, driving him across the river. The enemy then again crossed the river near Savannah, and moving toward Jackson were met by Bob Ingersoll, whom, after something of a fight, 'tis said, they captured with his command. Trenton was then cowardly surrendered by some 250 Tennessee cavalry. Attacks were made on several other posts garrisoned by our troops, in all of which the enemy were repulsed. Altogether there has been a d——l of a time. When Van Dorn had finished his little bonfire at Holly Springs, this army was left with about five day's rations, which we have to make do 15 at least. In order to make up the deficit in commissaries, General Grant ordered that everything eatable that could be found in the country be seized for army use. In the strip of country from Holly Springs to Coffeeville, for, say 15 miles wide, there is not enough left to feed 50 chickens a week. Colonel Dickerman and I visited Holly Springs yesterday and took a little look at the ruins. I suppose the damage to the citizens amounts to nearly as much as the Government's loss. Most of the best and largest houses were burned. General Grant told Colonel Dickerman that our regiment would be sent to Jackson in a few days to guard that place. Well, if we have to go into winter quarters that will suit your brother very much. We will, be nearer home and communication will not be so apt to be broken between us.

January 4, 1863.

There I quit, for we received orders to get ready at once to march to Jackson, Tenn. The colonel ordered me to take charge of the train (wagons) and with my company guard it through by the wagon road, while the other nine companies went through by railroad. The regiment got off that evening, but I was delayed until the 31st, when just as I got my company into line to start a couple of the finest houses in town took fire, and burned down. The colonel commanding the 15th Illinois Infantry, which had just arrived, put me under arrest and stationed a guard around my company, but after an hour's detention, my strong protestations against arrest and my arguments in favor of the honorable acquital of my men of the charges, induced him to allow us to proceed on our way. By Lieutenant Mattison's personal smartness the train was taken from the road in the p. m., while I was ahead selecting camping grounds for the night, and I did not get with it for two days, which I traveled alone. The distance is about 90 miles. The first night I stayed at Holly Springs and slept in the bed which General Pemberton, Van Dorn and Lovell of the Rebel Army, and Hamilton, of ours, in turn occupied. 'Twas in the room they occupied for headquarters. Mrs. Stricklin, the lady of the house, was charming. Her husband is a major in the Rebel Army. I ate my New Year's dinner at Dr. Ellis'. He was not at home, but his lady treated me very politely, and I give her credit for having the noblest face I ever saw on woman. She is a sister of Rebel General Hindman. Stayed at a private house at Lagrange that night (Mrs. Cockes) and heard some delightful music made by a daughter. Saw seven mounted Rebels on the 2d, and felt uneasy traveling alone, but got through safe to Bolivar. Here I caught up with my train which I thought was behind. When we started my men were on foot, when I caught up with them at Bolivar, 38 of them were mounted on horses or mules. Stayed at Medon Station last night, and arrived here at 3 this p. m., all safe. I have to go back to Holly Springs to-morrow to testify against the 109th for disloyalty.

Camp at Lagrange, Tenn., November 17, 1862.

Our whole regiment went on picket Saturday evening. Didn't reach our posts until 9:30 p. m. Had plenty of fresh meat next day (notwithstanding stringent orders), and beautiful weather. Our going on picket saved us a tramp of 22 miles, for which I am duly grateful. They had a scare at Summerville while we we were out; our brigade (except we who were on duty) were started out, nobody hurt, happy to chronicle. Squads of prisoners taken by our cavalry are constantly arriving from the front. Very little skirmishing though, mostly unarmed citizens, etc. There are an immense number of slaves at the different military posts through here and in this vicinity. The officials are using them to good advantage in securing the large crops of cotton to the Government. The camps are overflowing with them, and their music and dancing furnish the boys with amusement unlimited. Don't have half the fun with the natives that I used to, in fact haven't spoken to any since I have been out this time. Guess I'm steadying down some. Like soldiering as well as ever but the novelty's gone, and its more like a regular way of living to me than a spree as it used to be. Don't see any immediate prospect of a move, but a chap can't tell what any symptom means here. I'd bet several times that we're on the point of starting. We have been reviewed twice within four days by Grant, McPherson, McKean, Logan and Pugh.

Camp 103d Illinois Infantry, La Grange, Tenn.,

November 21, 1862.

Every one seems to think that we will start about day-after to-morrow, Monday. We have drawn eight days' rations, and 200 rounds of ammunition has also been drawn for our corps. I don't think we have more than 14,000 in our corps, Logan's and McKean's Divisions, although there are some eight or ten new regiments here that I don't know, where assigned. Report to-day says that Sherman has moved from Memphis on the Holly Springs Pike.

We are having delightful weather. No fires are necessary until dark, and we have had no frosts since our arrival. Hope we will keep ahead of cold weather if compatible with the interests of the service. I "borrowed" some citizens clothes and wrote myself a pass as suttler's clerk, last night, and strolled around the town a couple of hours. There are many fine buildings here, among the rest two very large academies. Many of the Memphian nobility have country seats here, some of them most elegant. Holly Springs, though, is the most important summer rendezvous for the Memphis folk. Our people have left the Springs, and I don't know that we have any troops in advance of this place. I am very comfortable in my quarters. Have plenty of blankets and a good stove. My colored boy, Dave, went into the country 20 miles last night and returned this p. m. with his wife, a delicate looking black woman, neat and much above the ordinary slave. She has been a sewing girl all her life, and I think would be worth something to a family that has much plain sewing to do. I think I will try to send her to Mrs. S. C. Thompson. "Dave" is a first rate cook and waiter, and I'll keep him with me until the war closes (if he don't spoil) and then take him to his woman. How'd you like a good colored woman for your kitchen? This woman mended my pants (I have two pairs) as neatly as any tailor could. Our regiment beats 19 out of 20 of the old ones for discipline, and averages with them for drill. Colonel Dickerman is a star, and Lieutenant Colonel Wright is proving himself much better than we expected. Colonel Oglesby has figured away ahead of anybody I've heard of yet in procuring wagons, tents, etc., for this regiment. Ours is the only regiment I've heard of yet that is allowed to retain the old complement of transportation, equipage and tents. I'm officer of the day and 'tis my duty to make the rounds of the sentinels to-night at 1 or 2 o'clock; but in consideration of—etc., think the formality will be dispensed with.

Camp at Lagrange, Tenn., November 15, 1862.

We're having more of a rest here than we anticipated when we arrived. Suppose that the organizing of the army into divisions and brigades delays us some; and, maybe, the change of commanders in the Potomac army has something to do with it. Or possibly we're waiting for Mc-Clernand to move from Memphis. I don't think our army here (the Corinth and Bolivar forces) is very large, though some estimate it quite strong, as much as 50,000 or 60,000. I think we have about 35,000, maybe less. General Lanman has been relieved from command of our division by General McKean and ordered to Memphis. Am sorry to lose him. He has few equals for skill in handling a division or honor and courage as a soldier. Am much afraid that the rainy season will catch us in the midst of our slow motions, and then good bye all hopes of the war's closing next spring. McPherson and Logan promised in speeches a few days since that we would finish up the business within 40 days; and I believe we can, West of Georgia, if this weather will continue and our commanders will improve it. Don't believe that Price will dare to fight us anywhere, certainly not this side of Jackson. We can't have more than 40 days' of marching weather yet until the rains come, and in that time we ought at least to make 250 miles. The more I think about the matter, the surer I am that we won't do much before next May. Well, I enjoy soldiering and can stand the delay in proportion; but inactivity when a fellow can't see the reason therefor, is provoking to a degree extensive. We made a capital start from Peoria to this place in five days, but the thing hasn't been followed up. Our cavalry has been doing some dashing work here, sums up about 300 prisoners, etc. But the 7th hasn't figured much therein, at least not in reports, although the 7th boys say they did their share. I have seen all my acquaintances in the 7th, and the 8th Infantry is also here. Fred Norcott and Milo are both looking splendidly. Also Ben Rockhold. 'Tis said that General Logan publicly disgraced the 17th to-day for some insult to himself. Never thought much of that 17th and think less now than ever before. They certainly show no signs of discipline that can be seen by the naked eye. The 7th Kansas Cavalry, 'tis said, proposed in writing to General Grant, that if he would give them a certain time, (no other condition), they would capture or kill General Price. I wish he'd do it. They would raise the d—l around the Rebel army, and I believe it practicable at any time for 500 daring men to reach the person of any of our commanders, and why not theirs. They are cutting our baggage down to a very small compass, so that six wagons can haul for ten companies. I'm opposed to it, but Halleck ranks me and I will have to submit. Nobody in this country seems to care a cuss whether McClellan is removed or not. General feeling is that the Potomac Army is only good to draw greenbacks and occupy winter quarters. We're in hopes that Pope will be sent back to us after he finishes hanging those Indians. I don't believe there is a regiment in this army that would not cheer him as its corps commander. Everybody seems to be willing to bet something on Pope. Hurlbut is the most popular man here as a division commander, and I think that Grant could get more votes than any other man for commander of the army, always excepting Rosy. Grant is not so popular among the general officers, as far as I know, but the whole line believe in him, mostly, because he is for going ahead and will fight his men. The Memphis force hasn't moved yet that I can hear of. Everything goes on swimmingly in the 103d. The old regiments try to bore our boys by calling them conscripts and $40 men, but don't succeed well. In a march of 15 miles last week an old regiment, 3d Iowa, tried to run us down but it ended in our marching right through them. Dorrance is an excellent fellow in the field, wouldn't trade him for any other

lieutenant in the regiment. The Democratic victories at
the polls don't excite anyone here. We only wish the
soldiers could vote. Illinois would talk differently if we
could..

Camp 103d Illinois Infantry, Jackson, Tenn.,

January 12, 1863.

Your letters are beginning to come through with more reg-
ularity and on decidedly better time. Have received your date
of December 30, although the last was dated November 16th,
and was the first you wrote after we left Peoria. You bewailed
our being sent south of Cairo, which I think very un-
generous in you. Well, you'll probably be suited in our
present location, which is the only consolation I have in being sent so far rearward. There are some slight hopes though,
that we may be sent to Vicksburg, which will ripen into a
distant probability (nothing more I'm afraid) if the news of
our repulse there be true. We're encamped in the suburbs of
this delightful little town, but so strict are the orders of the
general (Sullivan) that, as far as seeing the town or making
purchases therein are concerned, we might as well be camped
on Pike's Peak. All right, Mr. Sullivan, have your own way.
He is by all odds the most like a soldier of all the garrison
commandants I have been under. Will wager that you will
never hear of his being surprised. The news from Holly
Springs is that the last house in the town was burned night
before last. Pretty rough, but I say, amen. Its pretty well
understood in this army now that burning Rebel property is
not much of a crime. I for one will never engage in it, until
orders are issued making it duty, and then I think I can enjoy
it as much as any of them. If any part of this army is ever
called home to quell those Illinois tories, orders to burn and
destroy will not be necessary. Since I have seen the proceedings of that traitorous legislature, I begin to understand why
these loyal Tennesseans and Alabamians are so much more
bitter against traitors than we are. It would make your blood

run cold to hear the men in this army, without regard to party, curse those traitors. There is a gay time in prospect for those chaps. Don't think I am much out of the way in saying that Merrick, Jem Allen, Dick Richardson, and the editors of the Chicago *Times* would be hung if caught within the lines of many Illinois regiments in this army. There are many officers who, while they doubt our ability to subjugate (that is the question) the South, would take an active part in ending the man who would propose to give the thing up. I come pretty near belonging to that party, though I think that if we can't accomplish the whole end desired, we can confine the Rebels to Virginia (Eastern), the Carolinas, Georgia and Florida. Alabama, I believe, we can hold if we get Mississippi. Boats which left Vicksburg on the 6th inst. reported it taken, but it must be a mistake, as it has not been confirmed. I think it was wicked to put that brave old 8th Missouri and 4th Iowa into the front of the battle, after they had suffered so severely at Donaldson, Shiloh, Farmington, etc., but ever since Shiloh it seems that the old soldiers have had the front all the time. 'Tis reported that when Grant moves again, he will leave all the new regiments as railroad and property guards, and move with the old army. The last night I stayed in Holly Springs, Mrs. Stricklin invited in some young ladies to help entertain the colonel, Lieutenant Nickolet and myself. They beat all the secesh I have seen yet. One of them played all the secesh pieces she knew, and when I asked her to play "John Brown," she swelled up so with wrath, that I was strongly tempted to propose tying my suspenders around her to save hooks and eyes. One of them asked me if I did not think the Southerners the most polite, refined and agreeable people I had ever met. It took me twenty minutes before I could finish blushing for her lack of modesty, and then I was so dead beat that I could only take up the word refined, and tell her how much I admired their beautiful use of language. I instanced, "what do you'uns all come down here to fight we'uns for," "I recon we war thar," which you'll hear from the best of them. That first quotation as they speak it is the funniest sentence imaginable. I got into a row with every one I talked with, but finally, was fool enough to escort one home. Rumor (almost official) says to-night that we go to Memphis to-morrow, or soon, and thence to Vicksburg. Congratulate us on our good luck. This regiment will never be satisfied without a fight. They run in in our pickets once and awhile here, and I believe two were killed (pickets) yesterday, but guess there is no chance for a fight. The 18th Illinois Infantry is being mounted.

Camp 103d Illinois Infantry, Jackson, Tenn.,

January 16, 1862.

It commenced raining early the morning of the 14th and did not cease until about 2 a. m. the 15th, since when it has snowed steadily until within two hours. The snow is some eight inches deep, underneath which is mud immeasurable. The rain the last six or eight hours came through our tent as through a sieve, the snow came in at the top, through the door, and blew under the curtains. Everybody's wearing apparel, blankets, and self absorbed all the damp possible, and besides carried all that would hold on outside. Our stove was in this extremity our comfort and our joy. We kept two loyal Ethiopians busy during the two days, getting wood, and feeding said comforter. Great was the tribulation, and much audible cursing resulted, while the secret history of oaths unuttered, would I'm afraid, fill many volumes, and in all human probability cause, if made public, the appointment of many army chaplains. This is the first winter weather that we have had, and I'll be willing if it proves the last, although there is a half melancholy pleasure in spludging around in this slop and taking the weather as it comes, without its first being made to feel the refining influence of house walls and good warm fires. Our men have become quite soldier-like, and endure without much murmuring the little ills as they come. It shows some of the principles of manhood, you must believe, when men stand this weather in these worthless little wedge tents, without fires and without grumbling. I got four of my men discharged to-day, and want to discharge some

10

six or eight more. When I get my deadheads off my hands
will have some 70 good men left. Rather think now, that we
are stationary here for the winter, but we may possibly be
sent to Vicksburg, than which nothing will suit us better There
are some eight or nine regiments here, two or three of them
cavalry. The enemy is pretty well cleared out of this strip
of country, and if Rosecrans gets down into North Alabama,
opinion seems to be that some of us can be spared from here
for Vicksburg and Port Hudson. Several houses have been
burned here lately. This town will share the fate of Holly
Springs, sure, if the Rebels trouble us here any more. 'Tis
fearfully secesh, and a little fire will, I think, help to purify it.
Isn't it wonderful how with so much fighting everywhere I
have escaped so long? The whole of the 10th Illinois Infantry were with me in luck until the last fight at Murfrees-
boro, and am not certain they participated in that. There are
two regiments here that have endured all of this storm without tents. I suppose the Lord takes care of them fellows, if
it's a fact that he looks after sheared sheep and birds. From
my heart I pity them, though that strikes me as something
like the little boy who, when his mother put him to bed and
covered him with an old door, told her how much he pitied
folks who had no doors to cover themselves with while they
slept. That's a story mother and aunt used to tell me in my
trundle-bed days. Wonder if aunty has forgotten the story
that used to make Tip and me rave. All about how that "great
big prairie wolf bit a wee boy's head off." I almost forgot
that I am out of woollen socks. Have only the pair of socks
that are on my feet. Put them on this morning, and there
were so many holes that I could hardly tell where to put my
feet in. Wish you'd send me three or four pair. Will make
cotton ones do until then. I can send you a nigger baby
if it would be acceptable. They are more "antic" than either a
squirrel or monkey. I have two he niggers, two she's and
three babies, mess property. Think I will either have to drown
the babies, or sell them and the women, whom I endure because their husbands are such good hands. Will you take
one?

Camp Reed, Jackson, Tenn.,

January 22, 1863.

I received your four-volume letter of the 5th, 12th, 13th inst. last night, and return you my sincere thanks for the time and writing material you expended in my behalf. I suppose that you now understand why you did not receive my letters.

You ask me how I like the news from Vicksburg. All right. That was only a little reconnoisance in force, which paid its way by gobbling up Arkansas post. We want to get these seceshers all together at Vicksburg and then close the war in this country. Wait about a month, if you want to hear a call for bombazine, etc. We'll have that little town then, or a very large portion of the loyal people of Illinois will go to make that a very fertile point. By the way, aren't you afraid that Rosecrans will get his hands full if it be true that Longstreet with 13 brigades has arrived at Chattanooga? Guess those Eastern Rebels must know better how to fight than Bragg, Price, Van Dorn, etc., at any rate I'm a little suspicious of that Longstreet and wish that one or two of these divisions here could be sent to oppose. Believe I would rather we would be whipped here than see "Rosy" beaten. There will be somebody awfully hurt though, before that latter item takes place, and Rosecrans himself will never live to read an account of it.

Staff appointments are nicer than the line business, but chance for promotion is not so great nor so honorable in my opinion. Although one does get more credit in reports, and has more influence. Anyway the chances for a captain to be detached on staff duty are very limited, and nearly always matters of outside influence. A first lieutenant's chance on his merits are much better for several reasons. Officers are beginning to resign in a very lively manner in our regiment. Am satisfied that of the original captains, only Sid., Frank Post and myself will be left in two months from now, and I can see that both Sid. and Frank would not object to being let out gently and honorably, especially if they could happen

on a good little fight shortly, and then leave. Poor fellows!
One has a new wife and the other an old girl, each gets five
letters a week and looks a little sicker after each letter than
before. Guess I'll have to get me one of them girls to be in
the fashion, though I haven't yet got over that one's patting
me on the shoulder when I enlisted, telling me what a
fine, brave fellow, etc., I was and then marrying within three
weeks after I'd gone. I'm not very desperate in consequence,
but can't think it was fair. Sid. got back from Cairo to-night
with his men, minus 30, of whom some ten deserted and the
remainder were left sick. Profitable trip. We are on half
rations again for five days, but I managed to secure a 700-
pound beef for my company, so we'll not starve. I report
more men for duty than any other company in the regiment.
Call that doing pretty well when you consider that mine is a
picked company. Major Phelps is here and says we will be
paid off shortly. That means between now and July as I
take it. Am not particular though. Uncle Sam can go to the
d——l with his greenbacks, if he'll only send us to Rosy or
Vicksburg. Weather here has moderated considerably. It is
1 o'clock a. m. now and I am without coat or fire and am comfortable. I never retire before 1 or 2 o'clock any more. Am
ashamed to say what time I get up. We think here that this
place and Corinth will be evacuated ere long Troops are passing through here from Corinth every day, going to Vicksburg.
Every sign says that we will leave here within ten days, but
all signs are unsartin. The moon to-night says a dry month.
Don't I hope she won't fool us. This half-ration business is
only so in name, the full ration has a tremendous margin for
waste and men can grow fat on half rations. I do believe that
they live just as well. When the 1st of January proclamation
was issued a number of our officers became very much excited. Several of them talked strongly of tendering their
resignations in consequence thereof, and one of them really did.
But we were too strong for the d——d compromising lick-
spittles, and to-day you can't hear a whimper against it. The
major and adjutant were strongly opposed to it, but they dare

not say so to-day. All of that excitement at home is working on the army though, and even if it requires bayonets, the good of the army demands that the agitation cease. That is the cause of all the desertions, and they are many that are occurring, and nine-tenths of the discontent and demoralization spring from the same source. A tremendous number have deserted of late and the evil is growing.. Thousands would leave if we could be stationed on the border. Well, the old soldiers are very, very tired of the war. Any number of them would recognize three or four confederacies to get home, and their influence over the new men is boundless. The Confederate rank and file feels the same way. Nineteen-twentieths would vote for the United States or any other man to secure peace, but their officers and citizens control the matter. It don't make any difference what commission you intrust your sanitary stores to for the stealings are all in the hospitals, and these sanitary commissaries all issue to any hospital that is in need.

Camp 103d Illinois Infantry, Jackson, Tenn.,

February 1, 1863.

I'm on duty as "field officer of the day," and have been tramping around in the mud looking to policing, guards, etc., and just now a detail has come for me to go on picket to-morrow. I was only relieved from picket yesterday morning. We are very short of officers, having only 11 for duty in the regiment. All sick. D—n 'em, they ought to resign and let men draw the pay who do the work. I have seven men in the hospital now, one of whom is going to die. Poor fellow, how I do pity him. I never thought as much, even of my sick comrades in the 8th, as I do of my men when they get sick. James Colton is the one's name who is the sickest. He is a real good young man and has a wife. Lives in the west part of the country. Mine is the only company that has no deserters yet, and I don't believe I will have any. Half of these desertions are the

fault of officers. I have been out this evening calling on
a family named Stephens, living near our camp. They are
strongly secesh, but very fine people. No girls in the
family but a splendid looking young wife. I guess that
we are cut out of that Vicksburg fight, though if this
place is evacuated, there is a chance yet. That is the only
one though, for all the troops except our brigade have left
here. Some to Memphis, and I suppose, below. It makes
our duty pretty heavy. Picket every third day, besides
police, foraging, and fatigue and camp guard. But I always enjoy duty better than quiet camp life. I'm afraid
this agitation North is going to play the d—l with the
army. The great body is loyal enough but can't help being
discouraged and, in a degree, disappointed when treason
is preached openly in the North and unrebuked. Confin-
ing a lot of those traitors would have an excellent effect on
the soldiers; but I believe that Lincoln is almost afraid
to try that again. If this regiment is paid off before there
is the change in officers there should be, I'm afraid desertions will be very numerous. I begin to feel some of the
old soldier's prejudice against the "forty-dollar man," but
I do believe we can, if properly officered, make a crack regiment. I tell you, between ourselves, that of the 30 line
officers there are not more than six that are worth their
salt. The others do 100 times more harm than good to the
service. I modestly count myself one of the six, so that
you can judge better what I think they are. I read Dick
Oglesby's speech to-day. The sentiment is all right, but he
can talk much better than that. Suppose he is out of practice. We are a little afraid of the result of the Vicksburg
fight. If we get whipped I'd like to die there, for I believe
if that army is whipped it will be annihilated; and the cause
about lost, which little event I don't care to live to hear.
You can't imagine how careful the commanders are here
of secesh property. Well, if 'tis through the right motive,
I say all right, and I guess it is, but it hurts me anyway.
I can't help hoping that this town will be burned when evac-

uated, for it is the most intensely secession place of all. It first unfurled the Rebel flag in this State, and sticks to its colors nobly. It is rumored that Van Dorn is coming in this direction again. I do hope he will come here, for if we can drive him off, it would hurt the natives so much to see him whipped.

Camp 103d Illinois Infantry, Jackson, Tenn.,

February 7, '63.

There was a dose of medicine administered to the command in this district yesterday that will certainly be productive of good. I already feel that it has indued me with fresh vigor and really made me quite young again. "The sale or introduction of the Chicago *Times* in this district is hereby forbidden until further orders." By order of Brig. Gen'l. J. C. Sullivan. That same d——d old skeesicks has been protecting secesh property here in the strictest manner, and I'd never thought it possible for him to do as good a thing. It will do an immensity of good to the army, and if the President will only suppress the paper and several others of the same stripe, and hang about 200 prominent copperhead scoundrels in the North, we may then hope that the army will once more be something like its former self. Just as true as there is a God, if I was provost marshal in Fulton County, with my company for a guard, I'd hang at least ten men whose names I have. I know I'd be wrong, and would have no right to do so, but the good I'd do the Uuion troops would amply repay me for getting my own neck stretched. You can't imagine how much harm those traitors are doing, not only with their papers, but they are writing letters to the boys which would discourage the most loyal of men, if they failed to demoralize them. I believe that about every enlisted man in our regiment has received one or more of these letters. My boys have shown me a number from their friends, all of which would help to make a man who relied on his friends for his ideas, discontented. I assure you that it is by no means the lightest portion of an officer's

duties now, to counteract the effect of these letters. I know
that I put in a great deal more of my time than I wish to, in
talking patriotism at the boys and doing good, round, solid
cursing at the home cowardly vipers, who are disgracing the
genus, man, by their conduct. I have the satisfaction of knowing that expressing myself on the subject as I have, and Lieutenant Dorrance's talking the same way, have had a good effect
on our men, for not only have we had no deserters, but the
copperhead letters received in our company have been answered as patriots and soldiers should answer them.

Ninth.—Papers of the 6th give me much pleasure. The dashing move of the ram "Queen of the West," the gallant fight
of our soldiers at Corinth, are certainly enough good news for
one day. At noon roll call to-day, I spoke to my men of the
resolutions passed by the officers at Corinth and approved by
the soldiers, and told them that a chance would be offered
them in a few days to vote on similar ones. They received
the latter statement with a cheer that plainly showed their
mind on the subject. I believe that the whole regiment with
a proper action of the officers for a few days, will denounce
copperheadism, even in terms strong enough to suit the Chicago *Tribune*. 'Twill be the officers fault if we don't. If we
were only officered properly throughout there would never
have been a word of dissatisfaction in the regiment. That is
rather a solemn subject. I have advised my men to whip any
enlisted man they hear talking copperheadism, if they are able,
and at all hazards to try it, and if I hear any officer talking it
that I think I can't whale, I'm going to prefer charges against
him. Doing plenty of duty now; on picket every other day.
Last night I had command of a guard at General Hospital No.
1, or rather we guarded it in the day time, relieved at 9 p. m.
and went on again at daylight. I had some friends in the
hospital, steward, warden and clerks, and they made it very
pleasant for me. That is they fed me on sanitary cake, butter, etc., induced me to drink some sanitary wine, beer, etc.,
and also to sleep between sanitary sheets, with my head on a
sanitary pillow, etc., and again this morning to accept a bottle

of sanitary brandy and a couple of bottles of sanitary porter.
All of which I did, knowing that I was sinning. I write you this
that you may feel you are doing your country some good in
forwarding the above articles for the benefit of the soldiers.
You will of course, give these encouraging items to your co-
workers.

Camp 103d Illinois Infantry, Jackson, Tenn.,

February 15, 1863.

It's 11 o'clock now, so I haven't much time to write. We've
been having some trouble in the regiment this week. The
colonel appointed Lieutenant Mattison, captain of Company
"I," vice Medley, resigned, and Lieutenant Dorrance, captain of Company K, to fill the vacancy occasioned by King's
death. The men in both companies swore they wouldn't do
duty under the new officers, and the devil's to pay. The colonel finally relieved them both from their new commands,
doubting his right to enforce obedience until the new officers
had received their commissions, which will probably be some
two or three weeks hence, when the men will undoubtedly have
to submit, even if harsh measures have to be resorted to to
make them. The colonel has appointed Geo. Wilkinson, of
Farmington, and Mr. Wagstaff, who formerly worked in the
Ledger office, for my first and second lieutenants. My company have received them well, and I am well pleased with both
of them so far. I like quiet people. I enclose you some
resolutions which have been submitted to all the troops here
for their adoption. We voted by companies. Company A, I,
and F opposed them strongly, more on account of the spirit
of dissatisfaction and discontent, which is rampant among
them, than because of opposition to the principles they embody.
Colonel D—— seems to allow the trouble in his regiment to
wear upon him. He has not the decision I once gave him
credit for. Wears gloves at the wrong time in handling men.
One more case where my judgment has fooled me during my
army experience. Can't now remember where it was correct.

You certainly have to measure men by different standard in the army from that used at home. Everybody thinks we are going to evacuate here within a month. It looks like it, but can't see why we should. Nearly all the troops are gone. Our regiment and the 50th Indiana have to do all the picket duty. We are on every other day as regularly as clock work. I like it better than lying in camp.· Union citizens say that we will be attacked here the last of this week or first of next, by forces which are now crossing the Tennessee. That's too old, played out, etc. There's never any danger of a fight where I am. One of my boys died the other day, the first I have lost. Typhus fever, following measles, killed him. Was a real good soldier. Geo. Trader by name; lived near Ellisville. I have two more quite dangerously sick, but the general health of the regiment is improving. You don't know how much I love these men I have under me. Not as individuals many of them, but as soldiers, of my company, for whose actions, and in a measure, health, I am responsible. Something, I suppose, like the love of a parent for his children. I never thought I could feel half the interest in the welfare of my brother man as I do now for these men.

Camp 103d Illinois Infantry, Jackson, Tenn.,

February 18, 1863.

The prominent rumor to-day, and one in which there seems to be considerable stock taken, is that Governor Yates has obtained authority from the general government to have several regiments from Grant's army returned to Illinois, as a kind of public police. That is, to repress copperheadism, enforce the collection of the taxes, etc. The sequel is: Colonel Babcock and Colonel Kellogg are now with Grant, bearing dispatches from Governor Yates to the above effect, and figuring to get certain regiments, one of which is the 103d, and that we will be in Springfield within three weeks. All very nice— but—etc. I know that if we are sent up to that copperhead-infested country we will not be used for anything but to guard

Rebel prisoners; and I do pray to be excused from any such "pursuit of happiness." I would love right well to help manufacture loyal men out of some of those Illinois traitors, but am considerably suspicious of the trip. We finally got those resolutions adopted, after a speech from Colonel Dunham, without a dissenting voice, though it was by no means a unanimous vote. Don't think that more than two-thirds voted aye, though don't let any of the democratic friends know anything to the conrary, but that we all voted for it. The regiment is going to the d——l as fast as time will let it; though my company and Sid's. are all right yet, and two more are tolerable. It almost gives me the blues. Don't say a word of the above, but I can't help writing it to you. 'Tis so late and I'm so sleepy that I must adjourn. Was on picket last night in the rain all night.

Camp 103d Illinois Infantry, Jackson, Tenn.,

February 25, 1863.

I guess it's full two weeks since I wrote you last, excepting a half sheet a few days ago. My reason is that it has been raining ever since, and my tent leaks so that (that's rather a larger story than I think you'll swallow, so I'll not spoil paper by finishing it); but, Scotland, how it does rain here. Commences slowly and gently, comes straight down and continues coming for about 24 hours in the same manner. Mercury at about 35 degrees. Then the wind will commence blowing, cool, cooler, cold. Stop the rain, scatter the clouds, and getting warm again will, in a day or so, gather the moisture from the surface, and probably give us one pleasant day, rarely more. It seems to me there has not been a day this winter when the sun shone, and the air was calm, that I needed a fire, and I remember but one day during which the mercury sunk as low as 10 degrees. We had two nice "falls" of snow, but they found they'd lit in the wrong country and evacuated in quick time. It can't snow here to much advantage, but I am sure the rest of the world could learn from this region on the rain question. Canton is a parlor compared to this town. Part of the town is on rolling ground, but the hillside seems even muddier than the valleys. This town is thrice the size of Canton, and has ten times as many costly dwellings, but the side-walks and streets will not compare with yours. The arrangements of gardens is passable and much taste is shown in the distribution of evergreens. One gentleman living between our camp and town has 10,000 pines, hollies, cedars, etc., in the grounds surrounding his house. The grounds comprise may-be fifteen acres. I mean he had 10,000 trees, but the Yankees burned the fences around his paradise, and have in various ways managed to destroy a few thousand evergreens A kind of a parody, you understand, on that Bible story of the devil in Eden. Colonel Kellogg is here to-night, but goes to Memphis to-morrow where he will join Colonel Babcock. They may both be here again within a week, but it is not certain. He says we may be thankful we are not in the Yazoo Swamp or at Vicksburg, but two months heavy picketing here have rendered me unable to see it in that light. Our pickets have been fired on twice during the last two days. Nobody hurt, I believe. We have news to-night of General Dodge, of Corinth, capturing some 200 prisoners and a train of wagons at Tuscumbia, Ala. How I do wish we could be sent into that country again. It's worth all the rest of the South that I have seen.. I have 11 negroes in my company now. They do every particle of the dirty work. Two women among them do the washing for the company. Three babies in the lot, all of which have run barefooted all the winter, and though they have also run at the nose, etc., some, seem to be healthy all the time.

Camp 103d Illinois Infantry, Jackson, Tenn.,

March 5, 1863.

You certainly should not complain of my neglect, in writing no more than once in ten days while we are quartered at such an intolerably stupid place as this, for there really have not been two incidents ocurred worthy of notice, since we pitched our tents on this ground. Never since I first entered the service have I passed two months in which there seems so little

worth remembering Nothing but a dull round of picket,
fatigue, and camp guard; no alarms and no enemy within a
hundred or more miles of us, save "citizen guerrillas," and
they in no force sufficient to scare even a foraging party. In
lieu of something real to talk of and speculate about, I give
you the following items: There seems this morning to be some
movement on foot, though I have not heard a word of the
object which has raised such a commotion in our usually quiet
military circles. I only know that all the mounted men stationed here have this morning started under command of Colonel Mizner, with an ammunition train and small provision
ditto. Also hear that Dodge at Corinth and the command out
at Trenton have set all their cavalry in motion. To make the
case a little stronger I will add that one of Sullivan's aids
galloped into camp half an hour since, and required at short
notice the number of rounds of ammunition on hand. Well,
I expect that Van Dorn or Morgan is on our side of the Tennessee again. It can't be more than that. I'd give a month's
pay to get this regiment into a fight. Don't want it for myself
particularly, but think it would do the regiment a great deal
of good. The feeling is some better among the men, but there
is still much room for improvement. Desertions are not so
numerous, but one slips off occasionally. Colonels Kellogg
and Babcock were both here a few nights ago. Both in
good health, never saw them looking better Don't know that
anything of importance was connected with their visit. My
own health continues prime. I know that I don't fully appreciate the Lord's goodness to me in granting me such continued
excellent health, but I assure you I do feel grateful to the
Power that rules that matter, although I am tolerably regular
in my habits and intemperate in none, yet I know I am very
careless of myself and health in regard to dress, sleeping any
and everywhere, etc. General Sullivan will visit our camp
at 3 o'clock to-day to look into its sanitary conditions, and inspect our policing. The health of the regiment is much improved. Two months more and we will be veterans. Another of

my boys, the second, died in General Hospital at this place yesterday. James Conyers, is his name. Formerly worked for Stipp.

Camp 103d Illinois Infantry, Jackson, Tenn.,

March 7, 1863.

The rumors from Vicksburg in the *Tribune* of the 5th are enough to make one's flesh creep, and more than sufficient to account for my little touch of the blues I do feel to-night as though some awful calamity had befallen our army somewhere. God grant it may not be so! We have another report in camp this evening that is not calculated to enliven me much, viz.; "Lawler and some four companies of the 18th Illinois Infantry have been captured some 30 miles east of town." In my last I spoke of an expedition having started out to look for some of Van Dorn's forces which were reported as being on the Tennessee river, looking for a crossing place. We don't give credence to the story of Lawler's being a prisoner. But if he is, and the Vicksburg rumor be true and we have been repulsed at Charleston, and were whipped at Tullahoma, I wouldn't feel half as badly over it all if our people at home would quit their wicked copperheadism and give us the support and encouragement they should, as I do now when we are worsted in even a cavalry skirmish. For every little defeat we suffer only seems to make them so much bolder, as is shown in every new set of resolutions which reaches us through the *Times* and the *Enquirer*. So that miserable Davidson really published the lie that only one man in my company really voted for the resolutions. Every man in Company G voted for them and with a will, too. I don't have any politics in my company, although there are some companies in the regiment which indulge considerably in discussing questions of State. Above all things I dislike to hear it. I am glad to hear that my men speak well of me in their letters. I think I have had less trouble in my company than most of the officers. Allen Roodcape, the man you sent your letter of the 1st inst. by, got here to-night. Poor fellow, he will never be fit for a soldier. Davidson has gone home again. The 50th Indiana went out yesterday morning to reinforce Lawler, so we will again be on picket every other day. When it is here, once in three days is the rule. I was out on the worst post last night and it rained nearly all night. It thundered and lightened most splendidly. I like to get pretty wet once and a while for a change. It's raining hard now. I go on picket again to-morrow. I'm sleepy, tired, and the rain is coming through my tent so much that I believe I'll get into bed.

Camp 103d Illinois Infantry, Jackson, Tenn.,

March 9, 1863.

We leave here again in the morning for the Grange. Ordered to report there immediately to relieve a regiment, the 6th Iowa, which is going down the river. Am right glad to be again on the way. Can't think that we will stay there long, though I ought by this time to know that I have no business thinking anything about the matter. The Fulton *Democrat* came into our camp to-day, and that correspondence you mentioned in your last has raised quite a stir. The writer is of course denounced as a contemptible liar. My boys this evening got up a little paper which will appear in the *Register* shortly (it goes in the morning by the same person who carries this) and some fifty of them signed it, all there were in camp. My company would riddle that office in a minute if they could get at it. Worked all day yesterday, Sunday, covering and chinking a picket post, and will not get another day's use of it. Have so much to do that I see I will have to stop this letter writing business.

Camp 103d Illinois Infantry, Lagrange, Tenn.,

March 15, 1863.

I have just returned from a walk to and inspection of the cemetery belonging to this nice little town. There, as everywhere, the marks of the "Vandal Yankees" are visible. The fence which formerly enclosed the whole grounds has long since vanished in thin air, after fulfilling its mission, boiling Yankee coffee, and frying Yankee bacon. Many of the enclosures of family grounds have also suffered the same fate, and others are broken down and destroyed. The cemeteries here are full of evergreens, hollies, cedars, and dwarf pines, and rosebushes and flowers of all kinds are arranged in most excellent taste. They pride themselves more on the homes of their dead than on the habitations of the living. I can't help thinking that their dead are the most deserving of our respect, though our soldiers don't waste much respect on either the living or dead chivalries. Many of the graves have ocean shells scattered over them, and on a number were vases in which the friends deposit boquets in the flower season. The vases have suffered some at the hands of the Yankees, and the names of Yanks anxious for notoriety are penciled thickly on the backs of marble grave stones. Quite a variety of flowers can now be found here in bloom. I have on my table some peach blossoms and one apple blossom, the first of the latter I have seen. Some of the early rosebushes are leaved out, and the grass is up enough to make the hillsides look quite springlike. For three or four days we have needed no fire, and my coat now hangs on the forked stick which answers for a hatrack in my tent. We left Jackson the morning of the 11th, all pleased beyond expression, to get away. We were from 8 a. m. until 11 o'clock p. m. coming here, only 55 miles. The engine stalled as many as ten times on up grades, and we would either have to run back to get a fresh start, or wait until a train came along whose engine could help us out. We lay loosely around the depot until daylight and then moved out to our present camp, which is one of the best I have ever seen, a nice, high ridge covered with fine old forest trees. This town has been most shamefully abused since we left here with the Grand Army last December. There are only about three houses which have a vestige of a fence left around them. All the once beautiful evergreens look as though three or four tornadoes had visited them and many of the finest houses have been compelled to pay as tribute to the camp fires, piazzas and weatherboarding. Not a chicken is left to crow or cackle, not a pig to squeal, and only such milch cows as were composed entirely of bone and cuticle. The 7th Cavalry is here, and also the 6th Illinois and 2d Iowa. There is only one other regiment of Infantry, the 46th Ohio. It does the picket duty and we are patroling and guarding the government stores. The duty is rather lighter than it was in Jackson, and more pleasant. We have no ground to complain now, and the paymaster is all we want to make us perfectly happy. Two nights before we left Jackson 23 of our regiment deserted, 17 of whom were out of Company A, one of the Lewistown companies. One was from my company, the first deserter I have had. He was detailed from Company A to my company and was besides the most worthless trifling pup in the army. I am accepting the disgrace of having one of my men desert, decidedly glad to be rid of him. Johnny Wyckoff came down a few days ago and after being in camp a few days came to me and said he had his parents' permission, so I got the colonel to swear him in. We'll make a drummer of him.

I suppose you will have seen in the *Register* before this reaches you the answer my company made to that Davidson's lie in regard to our vote on the resolutions. I did not see the paper until it was ready to send away. I think copperheadism is not worth quite the premium it was a few months since. These notes from the army should have some weight with the gentlemen that run the copper machine. Do you see how the Southern papers cut the scoundrels? That does me much good, though 'tis mortifying to think we have such dirt-catchers in our State.

Well, we are on the right track now, and a few more weeks and we will be steaming down the Mississippi, I think. Our next move will be Memphis, probably, and then, ho! for Vicksburg! That is rare good news from the Yazoo. I hope Ross has done something there. My health is excellent, 155 pounds of ham and crackers, for that is all I've eaten in four months. One hundred and sixty secesh soldiers lie as closely

11

as they can be packed in this cemetery. Little boards with initials cut on them are all the marks their graves have. Our boys all cut on a large board with full name of regiment, and residence, at the head of their graves. I send you some blossoms from the graveyard.

Camp 103d Illinois Infantry, Lagrange, Tenn.,

March 19, 1863.

Nine whole days of the most beautiful sunshiny weather imaginable. Warm as our home June, almost. The boys bathe in the river that runs near our camp. The little birds warble in the trees, the beautiful young ladies walk out to enjoy the gentle spring breezes. Seldom now do we hear those gloomy omens of cold in the head, viz.: sneezes, and nature, grand old mother nature, almost in human tongue proclaims this balmy Southern spring atmosphere, a sure cure for the wheezes. Poetry, my dear, is the soul of—Sis, I'm getting under the influence of this weather, as happy as a clam, and as lazy as I can be, that is when I have nothing to do. I enjoy it intensely. Lieutenant Nick's resignation has been accepted and he will be at home within a few days. I send this by him, probably. I came pretty near having a fight a few days since. I had 40 men out guarding a forage train of some 125 wagons. There was also about 50 cavalry. We stationed the cavalry as pickets while the teams were loading, and 50 guerrillas attacked and drove our cavalry in (only 20 of our boys). We got ready for a muss, but the other thirty of our horsemen charged secesh and scattered them, wounding several and capturing two. 'Twas certainly censurable in our post commander's sending so light a guard with so large a train, which was over a mile long. My men showed the right spirit. That is the nearest to a fight any of the 103d have yet been.

10 p. m.—I want you to be sure and get "Harpers Weekly" of March 14th, and read that army story about the officers captured by pretended guerrillas. It is all true and happened near Waterford, Miss., while we were there. I

know the two women well. Don't fail to get the paper or you'll miss one of the best things of the war. I have just returned from a whist party. Colonel Wright, Dr. Morris and Dr. Shaw, of the 6th Iowa, and no liquor. I don't drink any, and intend to continue my habits in that respect. Very few of our officers drink.

Camp at Lagrange, Tenn., March 29, 1863.

All perfectly quiet except the regular picket firing every night which here exceeds anything I ever before met in my experience. 'Tis singular, too, for we have a large force of cavalry here and I should think the rascals would hardly dare to venture so near them. A few days since three guerrillas came up to one of our cavalry pickets, and while he was examining one of their passes the others watching their chance gobbled him. They at once retreated. The sergeant of the picket heard a little noise on the post and just got there in time to see the secesh disappear. He raised the alarm, and a party followed them on the run for 15 miles, rescued our man, killed three and captured four of the rascals, Yesterday some of Richardson's men displaced a rail on the track ten miles west of this place, and captured a train. They got away with their prisoners, but hadn't time to destroy the cars. 'Tisn't safe to go three miles from camp now, although 100 men can go 40 miles in any direction safely. Do you hear of any deserters returning under the President's proclamation? I hope to the Lord that my black sheep won't come back. A letter came for him to-day, and I opened it. 'Twas from his father advising him to get out of this "Abolishun" war as quickly as he could. His "Pa and Ma" are welcome to him. Generals Sullivan, Denver and Hamilton have all left this country within the last few days, for Vicksburg. General Smith commands our division now. We are now in the 2d Brigade, 1st Division, 16th Army Corps. The colonel of the 6th Iowa is the ranking officer in the brigade but he is now sick, so Colonel Wolcott of the 46th Ohio now runs. Two captains of the 46th Ohio, and myself have been constituted by Smith a "Board of Survey," to appraise damages committed by our army in the property of loyal citizens here. I think he has just done it to get the citizens off his hands. Have no idea that they will ever be allowed anything for their losses. There were three bills, each over $2,500. sent in to us yesterday. I hope the general will allow us to drop the business this week; if he will not, however, we can be kept busy for almost any length of time. By Smith's orders the reveille is sounded now at 4 o'clock a. m. and the men appear with arms and accoutrements, and form line of battle. This is to avoid any bad consequnces which follow a Rebel cavalry dash at daylight, if we should be found in our tents. I think 'tis an excellent policy to be always ready for the enemy, but I declare I dislike this early rising very much.

Camp 103d Illinois Infantry, Lagrange, Tenn.,

March 31, 1863.

I have lost my negro, Bob. The cavalry have been indulging in a pretty rough fight near here, and I am engaged on a "Board of Survey" which will occupy me for some days to come. There is also a good quality of Scotch ale in town, no paper collars, and a great deal of robbing and scoundrelism generally. There is some kind of a scare along the line, and the authorities this morning shipped to Memphis some 600 negroes, to get them out of the way of the trouble. I made my Bob send his wife and children, and the scamp, when it came to the parting, couldn't resist her pleading, and so he joined the party. It is beautiful to see such an exhibition of love and constancy in the brute species. All of these Africans will undoubtedly be sent to Illinois or somewhere else. I declare I don't like to see them introduced into our State, for they increase like rabbits. I believe will eventually outnumber the white race, in any country in which they are planted. This matter of slavery is an awful sin and I'm satisfied debases the governing race, but if we have to keep these negroes in the country, I say keep them as slaves. Take them from secesh and turn them over to Unionists, but don't free them in America. They can't stand it. These negroes don't average the ability of eight-year-old white children in taking care of themselves. There are exceptions of course; arm all the latter and make them fight Rebels. They will probably be fit for freedom after a few years as soldiers. I received the *Register* with the letters from our regiment and Peterson's dressing of the Democrat. 'Tis jolly to throw stones at that paper. You see if they all don't get their fingers burned by that foul-mouthed Davidson. A decent man has no business talking against him, and will always come out behind. I am sure that he would be hung if he would venture within our regimental lines. One of my boys cut a great caper to-day. He is an old Dutchman, and has been aching for a fight ever since we left Peoria. He has told me several times that he had a mind to run off and go down to Vicksburg until the fight is over and then he would come back again. This morning I sent him to Lafayette (near Memphis) as guard for these contrabands. The old fellow went on to Memphis and I expect will be at the Vicksburg battle. I know that he won't leave me for good, though this act makes him liable to punishment as a deserter. He is a funny old dog but an excellent soldier. For goodness sake send me those shirts. All I have sewed together wouldn't more than make one long enough to reach the top of my pants. Any one of them would fly out over my coat collar if I'd stoop down.

About 100 of the 6th Illinois Cavalry were surprised night before last some 20 or 30 miles north of this place. The first notice they had of the enemy was a volley of balls and shot among them as they lay asleep by their bivouac fires, about 12 p. m. Eight were killed and about 25 or 30 wounded by the first fire. The 6th got up and went into the Rebels in a most gallant manner, killing and wounding a number and capturing a major, two captains and some others. The enemy numbered some 400, and had the advantage of a complete surprise and were then badly whipped. The 6th boys deserve infinite credit for their fighting, and their colonel, a rope for his carelessness. He fought like a hero, though. 'Twas Lieutenant Loomis. I don't believe that Napoleon had any better cavalry than this brigade here for fighting. Second Iowa, 6th and 7th Illinois are the regiments, and well handled they'd whip the devil. Just imagine the details of the above fight, and if you can't help thinking that every one of our men engaged was a hero, I'll disown you. I'll tell you a couple of items to show you how the war is being conducted here now. A train was captured a few miles west of here a few days ago, and three prisoners taken, carried off. A lieutenant among them was footsore and unable to keep up; one of the Rebels, for that reason alone, shot him through the head, killing him. The conductor of the train surrendered, but a Rebel after that shot at him three times, when the conductor concluding it was death anyway attempted to escape and succeeded. This morning I saw a crowd across the street and walked over. Some secesh prisoners had been brought in, among them the conductor had discovered the man who tried to kill him. The conductor tried hard to get to kill the scoundrel, but the guard prevented him. I tell you, if any of that stripe of fellows fall into my hands, you'll have a brother who has been concerned in a hanging scrape. I'm as decided on that point as I know how to be. I don't see any prospect of an immediate fight in this country. There is no force except a few hundred guerrillas within 50 miles of us, but General Smith uses every precaution. We are all under arms an hour before daylight, and the picketing is very systematical and good. The pickets are, however, annoyed more or less every night. These citizens are bringing immense bills of damages before our board. Three came in to-day amounting in the aggregate to $50,000, and more I think. To-morrow General Smith closes the lines at this post. No more going in or out by citizens. That is the best thing that has happened before my eyes during the war. The town has been full of citizens every day since we have been here, and of course they are all spies.

Board of Survey Office, Lagrange, Tenn.,

April 6, 1863.

I was in Memphis a few days since. It is quite a lovely town and quite Northern-like in its general appearance. Many of the blocks would pass muster creditably in Chicago, though the numerous fires it has furnished for the edification of the "Vandal Yankees" have somewhat marred its streets. I think the Fair grounds are not excelled even by those at St. Louis, and we certainly have none in Illinois that will compare with them for beauty, location, or in extent. There are some most beautiful country seats on the M. & C. R. R. scattered along within six miles of the city. I saw but one park. 'Tis called Court Square and is very pretty. 'Tis just about the size of our Canton square and filled with forest trees and evergreens. I think as many as fifty squirrels live in the park. They are very tame and playful. The city is full of butternut refugees from North Mississippi and some from Arkansas, but I could find none from the vicinity of Madison. The M. & C. R. R. is almost classical. From Memphis to Decatur, Ala. (that is as much as I've seen of it) you are rarely out of sight of fortifications, and on almost every mile, lay the remains of a burned train of cars. Hardly a bridge, culbert or cattle guard but has been burned from three to ten times and rebuilt as often. Night before last I had just retired (12 o'clock) when an order came to have the regiment in line and ready for action at a moment's notice. We got up, stacked arms on the color line, and—went to bed again. Heard in the morning that 2,500 Rebel cavalry caused the scare. We still continue to guard against daybreak surprises by rising at 4 a. m., and standing at "guard against secesh" until daylight. All of the vigilance I like. I would hate to be surprised and gobbled without having half a chance. Am still on Board of Survey.

Camp 103d Illinois Infantry, Lagrange, Tenn.,

April 14, 1863.

I am brigadier officer of the day again, and of course it is a rainy, muddy, disagreeable day. Visiting the pickets occupied my whole forenoon and I rode through a constant rain. You may consider it an evidence of perverted taste, or maybe demoralization, or possibly of untruthfulness in me, if I say that I enjoy being on duty in the rain, but it is a fact. I don't like to lie in bed, or sit by the fire, and think of floundering about in the mud and being soaked to the skin, but once out of doors, let it rain and wind ever so hard I enjoy it. At my request the general relieved me from that "Board of Survey," and I am again with my company. If I could but get 15 days' exemption from duty, I could finish up the drilling I wish to give them. Since we left Peoria we have been driven so much with duty that drilling has been next to impossible. The health and spirits of the regiment are now excellent. Such a body of soldiers as this now is cannot be considered otherwise than as a credit to even immaculate Fulton County and New Jersey, two Edens without even one snake. That is one point in which the nineteenth century beats Adam's time. Rumors of another move down the Mississippi Central R. R. are flying now. I credit them. Within 20 days we will again be allowed to strike our tents. I'm getting well over my Vicksburg fever and wishing considerably in regard to this land movement. Before I write again the cavalry, some six to ten regiments, will have started on a raid of considerable magnitude. You can see from the way I write that I know nothing of what is in prospect, but from hints dropped feel certain that a move with force will be made from here at once. Anything to end this horrible inactivity. Every newspaper I read raises my disgust ten per cent. I'm sure I'll become a chronic swearer if it lasts this summer through. I suppose that you know by this time whether the Charleston attack is a failure or not. I'm not much interested in that. It will cause no loss of sleep on my part if we fail there, only I'd like to hear of the town being burned. I believe there are more chances for a general to immortalize himself, working southward from this line of road as a base, than in any other part of the field. But where is the general?

Camp 103d Illinois Infantry, Lagrange, Tenn.,

April 24, '63.

We have just returned from the hardest and yet by far the most pleasant scout in which I have up to this time participated. We started from here one week ago to-day, Friday, and my birthday (how old I am getting) on the cars. We were four and a half regiments of infantry, one six-gun battery and no cavalry. At 3 o'clock p. m. we were within seven miles of Holly Springs and found two bridges destroyed. We worked that p. m. and night and finished rebuilding the bridges by daylight the 18th. We had only moved two miles further when we reached another bridge which we found lying around loose in the bed of the stream. The general concluded to abandon the railroad at this point, so we took up the line of march. We passed through Holly Springs at 12 m. I don't believe that I saw a human face in the town. A more complete scene of desolation cannot be imagined. We bivouacked at dark, at Lumpkin's mill, only one mile from Waterford. At 9 p. m. a dreadful wind and rain storm commenced and continued until 1. We were on cleared ground, without tents, and well fixed to take a good large share of both the wind and water. I'm positive that I got my full portion. 'Twas dark as dark could be, but by the lightning flashes, we could see the sticks and brush with which we fed our fire, and then we would feel through the mud in the right direction. Nearly half the time we had to hold our rubber blankets over the fire to keep the rain from pelting it out. After the storm had subsided I laid down on a log with my face to the stars, bracing myself with one foot on each side of my bed. I awoke within an hour to find that a little extra rain on which I had not counted, had wet me to the skin. That ended my sleeping for that night.

Nineteenth.—We went down to Waterford and then turned westward, which course we held until nearly to Chulahoma. When we again turned southward and reached the Tallahatchie river at "Wyatt," where we camped for the night. Our regiment was on picket that night and an awful cold night it was. We marched through deep, yellow mud the 19th nearly all day, but I don't know that I marched any harder for it. Up at 3 o'clock and started at 4, the 20th, and marched 25 miles southwest, along the right bank of the Tallahatchie. Our rations were out by this time and we were living off the "citizens." The quartermaster with a squad of men he had mounted on contraband horses and mules would visit the chivalric planters, take their wagons, load them with their hams, meal and flour, and when we would halt for dinner or supper, issue the chivalries' eatables to us poor miserable Yankees. While the quartermaster attended to these principal items the "boys" would levy on the chickens, etc., including milk and cornbread. Gen. W. S. Smith commanded and the butternuts failed to get much satisfaction from him. The first night out a "citizen" came to him and complained that the soldiers had killed nine of his hogs, and asked what he should do to get his pay. "My dear sir," said the general, "you'll have to go to the boys about this matter, they will arrange it satisfactorily to you, I have no doubt." "Citizen didn't go to the boys though. Another one came to ask pay for his hams. "Your hams, why everything in this Mississippi belongs to these boys, a great mistake, that of your's, sir." The men soon found out what kind of a general they had and whenever a butternut would appear among us they would greet him with a perfect storm of shouts of, "here's your ham, here's your chicken," etc., and often a shower of bones of hams or beef would accompany the salute. On the 20th the general decided to make some cavalry, and on the 21st at night we had nearly 400 men on "pressed" horses and mules. These soldiers would just mount anything that had four legs, from a ram to an elephant, and the falls that some of the wild mules gave the boys would have made any man laugh that had life enough in him to breathe. How the women would beg for a favorite horse! I saw as many as five women wringing their hands and crying around a little cream-colored mare on whose head a soldier was arranging a rope bridle as coolly as though he was only going to lead her to water. You could have heard those women a quarter of a mile begging that cuss of an icicle to leave the pony, and he paid no more attention to them than he would have done to so many little chickens. An officer made the man leave the animal and I think the women took her in the house. I saw two girls, one of them perfectly lovely, begging for a pair of mules and a wagon a quartermaster was taking from their place. They pushed themselves in the way so much that the men could hardly hitch the animals to the wagon. But we had to take that team to haul our provisions. The night of the 20th at 8 o'clock, the general called all the officers up to his quarters and told us that we would have a fight with General Chalmers before breakfast the next morning. He ordered all the fires put out immediately and gave us our instructions for defense in case we should be attacked during the night. After he was through I, with eight other officers, was notified that we should sit at once as a court martial to try the adjutant of the 99th Indiana, for straggling and conduct unbecoming an officer and a gentleman in taking from a house sundry silver spoons, forks, etc. I'll tell you our sentence after it is approved. That kept us until 11 o'clock. At 1 o'clock a. m. we were wakened without bugles or drums, stood under arms, without fires until 3, and then marched northwest. At this point we were only eight or nine miles from Panola, Miss. We marched along through Sardis on the Grenada and Memphis R. R. and northwest about 15 miles to some cross roads, which we reached just 20 minutes after the Rebels had left. 'Twas useless for our infantry to follow their mounted men, so we turned homeward with 75 miles before us. Just look over and see how much sleep I got in the last four nights. We marched through the most delightful country from the time we left Wyatt. I think it will almost compare favorably with Illinois. We saw thousands of acres of wheat headed out which will be ready to harvest by the 15th or 20th of May. Some of the rye was as tall as I am. Peaches as large as filberts and other vegetation in proportion. There seemed to be a plenty of the necessaries of life, but I can assure you that eatables are not so plentiful now as they were before we visited the dear brethren. We reached the railroad at Colliersville last night. That is 26 miles west, making in all some 175 miles in eight days. The guerrillas fired on one column a number of times but hurt no one until yesterday, when they killed two of the 6th Iowa, which regiment was on another road from ours, the latter part of the trip. We took only some 20 prisoners but about 400 horses and mules. They captured about a dozen of stragglers from us and I am sorry to say two from my company, Wilson Gray and Stephen Hudson. The last three days we marched, every time that we would halt ten minutes one-fourth of the men would go to sleep. You should have seen the boys make bread after their crackers gave out; some lived on mush and meal, others baked cornbread in cornshucks, some would mix the dough and roll it on a knotty stick and bake it over the fire. It was altogether lots of fun and I wouldn't have missed the trip for anything.

Camp 103d Illinois Infantry, Lagrange, Tenn.,

May 7, 1863.

Isn't the Grierson "raid" glorious? Two other expeditions started from this point and were gone respectively five and ten days each. Although they made good long marches and took about 40 prisoners and 500 animals, still we forget them in looking after Grierson. We have the Rebels well scared in this country. Five thousand men could sweep everything north of Jackson, if they could only hold it. Papers to-day give us the news on the Rappahannock up to the 4th of May, which includes the route of Siegel's Dutchmen and leaves Hooker in what seems to me a close place. Well, he can at worst but fail. What a consolation. General Oglesby wrote to Hurlbut to detail

me on his staff General Hurlbut referred the letter
through division and brigade headquarters for the letter of
my company and on its return to Hurlbut, General Smith
objected to my being detailed out of his command. He
thought Oglesby might find his staff in his own command.
All right! I would like to have been with Old Dick
though. I'm on a General Court Martial now. Confound
the Court Martials.

Camp 103d Illinois Infantry, Lagrange, Tenn.,

May 13, 1863.

I have been on a General Court Martial for the last
ten days, and we will not, in all probability, adjourn for
some weeks yet. We tried Governor Yates' brother. He
is Adjutant of the 6th Illinois Cavalry. Another little re-
verse on the Rappahannock. All right! My faith is still
large—in the army, but the commanders and citizens can
be improved. We think that Grant is going to beat them
all yet. But his army is more responsible for his good
fortune than himself. Do you notice that one of our
"raids" missed fire? Straight into Georgia, I mean. Grierson's and Stoneman's make up for all the rest though. We
are constantly active here, in fact our troops move so
much that I am unable to keep the run of even our brigade.

Camp 103d Illinois Infantry, Lagrange, Tenn.,

May 21, 1863.

I am still sitting on this Court Martial. We may finish
up this week. Everything is quiet here. To-day three or
four regiments have gone out with seven days' rations. All
mounted. Rumors reach us daily that Grant is in a critical situation; but I can't so see it. He has enough men
to annihilate in a field fight all the Rebels south of this line.
We know that he has captured Jackson, Miss., and has
now turned his attention to Vicksburg.

Camp 103d Illinois Infantry, Lagrange, Tenn.,

May 29, 1863.

'Tis becoming fiendishly warm in this latitude again; but the delightfully cool nights of which I wrote you so much last summer, are also here again, and amply repay one for the feverish days. We have moved our camp from the town to a grove on a hill about midway between Grand Junction and Lagrange It is one of the best defensive positions that I know of. It seems to me much better than Corinth, or Columbus, Ky., or New Madrid. Our negro troops are fortifying it. I suppose that no one anticipates danger from the Confederates, on this line, any more; but I can understand that the stronger we make our line, the less object the secesh will have in visiting us. We are raising a regiment of blacks here. Captain Boynton, who has an Illinois Battery, is to be the colonel. He looks like a good man, but I think that a better could have been selected. I am afraid they are not commissioning the right material for line officers. Two are to be taken from our regiment, and if we have two men who are good for nothing under the sun, I believe them to be the ones. I know that first rate men have applied for these places, and why they give them to such worthless fellows, I can't see. I think poor Sambo should be allowed a fair chance, and that he certainly will never get under worthless officers. I suppose that the regiment organization here numbers some 800 now, and will soon be full. I don't know whether I wrote it to you or not, but a year ago I sincerely thought that if the negro was called into this war as a fighting character, I would get out of it as quickly as I could, honorably. I am by no means an enthusiast over the negro soldiers yet. I would rather fight the war out without arming them. Would rather be a private in a regiment of whites than an officer of negroes; but I don't pretend to set up my voice against what our President says or does; and will cheerfully go down the Mississippi and forage for

mules, horses and negroes and put muskets in the hand's
of the latter. I have no trouble in believing that all these
Rebels should lose every slave they possess; and I experience some pleasure in taking them when ordered to. Captain
Bishop with some 25 men of Companies A and G did a
splendid thing last Thursday night. He surprised Saulstreet and 20 of his gang, about 11:30 p. m., killed three,
wounded and captured five and six sound prisoners, without losing one of our men or getting one scratched. Three
of the wounded guerrillas have since died. Saulstreet himself escaped. Over at Henderson Station on the M. & O.
R. R. lives a Miss Sally Jones who once, when some Rebels
set fire to a bridge near there, watched them from the brush
until they left and then extinguished the fire. She is a
case. Lieutenant Mattison saw her there a few days since.
The day before he saw her she had been out scouring over
the country horseback, dressed in boys' clothes, with her
brother. She often goes out with the soldiers scouting,
and the boys think the world of her. Any of them would
kill a man who would dare insult her. She is, withal, a
good girl. Not educated, but of fine feelings and very
pleasing manners. Memphis paper has just arrived. Not
a word from Vicksburg but a two column list of wounded.
I expect that you have celebrated the capture of that town,
long before this. All right, you ought to enjoy yourselves
a little once in a while. There are now to my certain
knowledge, 20,000 troops on the railroad between Memphis
and Corinth, and there are not 1,000 armed Rebels within
100 miles of any point on the road. Our presence at Vicksburg could not help deciding the day in our favor. It
makes a man who knows nothing about the matter, sick
to think of the way we manage our army. Hold 100,000 in
reserve and fight with 10,000.

Middleton, Tenn., June 4, 1863.
We made another little change yesterday. The regiment is
now guarding the M. C. & R. R. from Grand Junction to

Pocahontas. We are in detachments of two companies each.
H Company is with mine. We marched 23 miles to make this
point yesterday, and arrived at 10 o'clock p. m. We only made
four miles after dark, and the road was so horrible and the
woods so thick we had much difficulty in finding it at all. We
occupy the depot and have strengthened it by a revetment of
fascines, so that we consider ourselves perfectly safe if attacked by even ten times our number of infantry. Artillery
would scoop us. This little town had when the war commenced some 40 houses; now it boasts of not more than 12
or 15, though a number of extra chimneys add so much to the
picturesqueness of the scene, that I can excuse the houses for
"going out." This country has literally been scraped, swept
and scoured. The guerrillas first ran the Union men off, and
then when we came here the Unionists returned, took up arms
and drove out all the secesh families. You can hear of murders being committed in every neighborhood by either one
party or the other. It will take at least 8,000 years for this
people alone to make this country what Illinois is now, on the
average, and at least 1,000 to bring it up to the standard of
poor, God-forsaken Lewistown township. I have never been
so comfortably situated in the army, except when with Colonel
Mizner, as I am now. The boys have rigged up nice bunks
in the depot wareroom, which are dry and comfortable, have
good water, light guard duty, and the citizens bring in to us
their extra vegetables, etc., and trade them for our surplus rations. The boys give one pound of coffee for two dozen eggs,
or two pounds of butter; sell them bacon for 15 cents per
pound, etc. Two very fine elderly ladies pleading for a horse
to-day, told stories of tremendous length about how "Union"
their husbands were prior to their deaths. I'd almost rather
give up my head than have two women of their age begging
of me for anything that way. I have the telegraph room for
myself and have fixed it up nicely. I know well enough that
it is too good to last long and shall resign it without a sigh,
and if ordered to Vicksburg, with a cheer. I fixed up our last

camp as well as I could in hopes that my pains would bring us marching orders, and we got them, but the direction was wrong. This is so much better that it must surely win. Maybe you don't know that there is a superstition (almost) among soldiers that arranging a camp particularly nice and comfortable brings marching orders.

IV.

June 7, 1863 to April 28, 1864. On General Oglesby's staff. Almost reconciled to negro soldiers. Bringing the raiding business home. Back to his regiment at his own request. Sees Vicksburg at last. Story of a rich Rebel planter and his wife. Leading the advance to Chattanooga. Foraging and bee hunting on the way. Quadroon family of a white planter. Mounting infantry on "borrowed" horses. Criticising the war strategy. Sheep stealer as well as horse thief, under orders. Regiment dismounted and back in permanent camp. Discountenancing army deviltry. Veterans unanimously re-enlisting. Roll call of his distinguished commanding officers. Regimental marching races. Ill feeling between the respective army corps. Monotony of inactive camp life.

Headquarters, Left Wing 16th Army Corps,
Lagrange, Tenn.,

June 7, 1863.

We had occupied our very pleasant quarters but two days when an order came for us to pack up for Vicksburg. Received the order at dark and by daylight the next morning we were in Lagrange. General Oglesby had moved his headquarters here and he gobbled me without a moment's warning. The regiment moved on for the doomed city yesterday and left me. Now don't write me any of your "glads," for I'm almost demoralized over the matter. Am uneasy as the d—. The idea of leaving just when I know that the regiment is moving on to a fight doesn't look at all right; but then I'm where I'd rather be than at

any other place in the army, and suppose that other
chances will be offered for fighting. If the general had entirely recovered from his wound, I am sure that we would
leave this railroad guarding business to some one of less
importance in the field, but he is hardly able to stand an
active campaign yet. Sam Caldwell, Major Waite and myself compose the staff now and it is so pleasant. It's
"Sam" "Waite" "Charley" and "general." I have been
east on the railroad to-day looking at the defenses of the
road. 'Twill be completed to Corinth by Wednesday next,
when the road to Jackson and from here to Corinth will
be abandoned. We've had another scare here to-day.
Some 800 Rebels within a few miles of us. One of the cars
on which our regiment was loaded flew the track yesterday, and one man was killed and several hurt. None of
my company, or that you knew.

Lagrange, Tenn., June 19, 1863.

The general and Sam went to Memphis yesterday to
visit General Hurlbut, and the major and I have charge
of the machine. The cavalry under command of Colonel
Mizner went south last Tuesday. They have a good
sized object in view, and if they succeed will be gone
some ten days, though they may possibly be back by
Wednesday next. They will operate between Panola and
Grenada. Another mounted expedition has gone from Corinth to Okolona, a third from Corinth to Pikeville, Ala.,
and a fourth also from Corinth to Jackson, Tenn., which
place has, since we evacuated it, been occupied by some
Rebel cavalry (infantry also reported) from the east of
the Tennessee river. All of this cavalry (of course excepting the Rebel) belongs to General Oglesby's command. You see he has it in motion. Deserters are
constantly coming in from Johnston's army; and if we
can believe their stories, and the information gained from
the corps of spies employed along this line, Grant's rear
is not in as much danger as our southern brethren

would fain have us think. Johnston's army is not in the best condition imaginable; and it is far from being as strong as he would like it. Have no idea that he can march thirty-five thousand men. Grant must have an enormous army. How awful it would be if the yellow fever would visit his camps. I suppose you know that my regiment is at Snyder's Bluff. I think that is on the Yazoo, near Haines. Don't you see some more of my extraordinary fortune in being detached just as the regiment is ordered to where there is a prospect of hard knocks. We were all loaded on the cars ready to move, when Sam came down to the train and took me. The regiment then left immediately. There is a possible chance now of the general's being ordered to Vicksburg; but I've given up all hope of my getting there. We are having a great deal of trouble with the citizens here. A great many secesh citizens ask to be exempted from taking the oath, because they have rendered service to our army. This one gave a quart of buttermilk to a sick soldier, another donated an onion to the hospital, another allowed a sick officer to stay in his house for only $2. per day, etc. A number of the claims really have some point to them, and although 'tis against my theory, I really can't help pitying some of them. We had a sad accident last week near this post. General Hurlbut ordered a small train with a guard of some 60 men to be sent north on the railroad to repair the telegraph line. Twelve miles only from here the train broke through a little bridge over a deep but narrow "swash" and killed five and wounded ten of the party. An examination showed that the bridge had been burned the night before, and afterward the rails had been propped up only strongly enough to keep their places when no weight was upon them. 'Twas a fiendish, cowardly act, but of course committed by men whose business is robbery and murder, and who have no connection with the army.

Jackson, Tenn., June 26, 1863.

Such splendid weather—nice, fresh breezes ruffling the leaves on the trees all the day long—and plenty of rain to keep the dust in order. I was up early this morning and the mocking birds were playing a reveille, from whose sweetness bees might make honey. There are hundreds of these birds living in a grove near our headquarters, and I can't find time and ease enough to enjoy their concerts as I want to.

A flag of truce came to our lines yesterday on the Holly Springs road. The general sent me out to receive it. A lieutenant and eight men, all rough, dirty fellows, made the party. They were not very communicative. They brought a small mail and a trifling communication about prisoners. They belonged to Colonel Morton's 2d Tennessee (Rebel) Cavalry, and were sent by General Ruggles. The general has promised to let me take a flag to Okolona. Don't know when I shall go. I do think that General Oglesby is the very ideal of a chivalric, honorable, gallant, modest, high-spirited, dignified, practical, common-sense, gentleman. Nobody can help loving him. He hates a particle of meanness as much as he does a bushel. If we were only doing something more active I should be perfectly happy. As it is, I think seriously of asking to be sent back to my regiment. The general will not be able for any more field work, and I hardly think it right manly in me to stay back here with a railroad guard, when there is so much to be done in front, and I am so strong and able to bear the field duty. You should hear the general talk. There is such a big rolling river of fun and humor in his conversation. Such a hearty honest laugh; I know his heart is big enough to hold a regiment. I believe he thinks as much of the old 8th as of his family. When he has been speaking of the gallant conduct of the 8th at Donaldson and Shiloh, I have seen his face flush up and it seemed as though his heart jumped up to his throat. I was over to the negro camps yesterday and have seen a good deal of them since I last wrote you. An honest confession is good for the soul. I never thought I would, but I am getting strongly in favor of arming them, and am be-

coming so blind that I can't see why they will not make soldiers. How queer. A year ago last January I didn't like to
hear anything of emancipation. Last fall accepted confiscation
of Rebel's negroes quietly. In January took to emancipation
readily, and now believe in arming the negroes. The only objection I have to it is a matter of pride. I almost begin to
think of applying for a position in a regiment myself. What
would you think of it? We had quite an alarm two or three
nights since. Nobody hurt, but some Tennesseans badly scared.
I guess I will go to Memphis to-morrow to look for a spy who
has been along our line, and whom we think is now in Memphis. Well, I must go and see the provost marshal about dis-
posing of some prisoners. First, I'll tell you what three soldiers did the night we had the alarm here. Colonel Mizner,
with 1,000 of our cavalry, had been on a scout nine days, and
that night we heard that he was within 15 miles of here on
his return. We heard of the enemy about 1 a. m. and immediately sent these three men (volunteers for the purpose) to notify Colonel Mizner and have him march all night. They reached
the little town, Mt. Pleasant, without incident on the way.
There was a lot of guerrillas camped in town that night, and
their guard hailed the boys and fired. Our men, only three,
charged with a yell and scared the whole party out of town.
They couldn't find the colonel and started to return. When
two miles on the way back, at a turn in the road, they met
Mitchell's Rebel company (60 men). Our boys yelled, "here
they are, come on boys," and charged, firing their revolvers.
They brought one man down, and made the next fall back
some 200 yards where they commenced forming line. Our
fellows then took to the woods, got around them and back to
camp at 6:30 a. m.

Lagrange, Tenn., July 1, 1863.

Everything moves quietly here. No more alarms or anything else to "bust" the confounded monotony of garrison life.
A guerrilla was brought in yesterday who has murdered at
least one of our soldiers, and an unarmed one at that. He rests

comfortably now with a nice lot of jewelry on his arms and legs, and a good heavy chain connecting his precious body to his bed, a not very soft plank. He is a worse fellow than we have in Illinois to my knowledge. We have two regiments of negroes here now, great big, stout, hardy fellows, and they really look right well in their uniforms. I heard from old Company "E" of the 8th this morning. They have had two men killed and five wounded before Vicksburg. There are only 15 left now. Wonder where my bones would have been if I had stayed with the boys.

A woman from Holly Springs is up to-day with the statement that Johnston is marching on Memphis, and proposes to have possession thereof within ten days. Good for Joseph! We had a confirmation of the report of the taking of Port Hudson yesterday, but nothing further to-day. It don't go down here without a good deal of forcing.

Isn't it music to hear those Pennsylvania fellers howl? I almost wish that Lee would cut the levee of Lake Ontario, and let the water over that country. Don't tell father and mother. If Lee don't wake them up to a sense of their misery, he isn't the man that Price is. If ever Price reaches Illinois, and he swears he's going to do it some day, you can reckon on seeing a smoke, sure! Don't you folks feel a little blue over Lee's move? Kind o' as though you wish you hadn't gone and done it! Never mind, you'll get used to it. The first raid isn't a sample. Wait until general Rebel somebody, establishes his headquarters in Canton, and you've all taken the oath of allegiance to the Confederacy. Imagine yourself going up to the headquarters with your oath in your hand and tears in your eyes to ask the general to please keep the soldiers from tearing the boards off your house (for bunks), or asking for something to eat out of his commissary department, and then blubber right out and tell him that the soldiers broke open your trunks and took your clothes and what little money you had, and you don't know what in the world you'll do. Many of these people are in this condition, and I hear a hundred of them tell the story every week. Every man in Illinois ought to die on the border rather than allow an invading force to march into our State.

Decatur, Ills., August 26, 1863.

I write for the purpose of informing you that I am recovering from that miserable attack of the jaundice. You can imagine nothing more disagreeable than a visitation thereof. Am enjoying myself first rate. Am sure I will find a letter from you in the office. Haven't been there for five days. Am nearly white once more.

Decatur, Ill., August 31, 1863.

The general stopped me here and insists on keeping me for a time. Major Wait's resignation, which was forwarded the same time the general sent his, has been accepted, and I now being the only member of the staff in the north, he wants me to stay with him, for should he be ordered away for any purpose, he would want some attendance. I would enjoy myself very much but for my biliousness. Appetite poor, miserable, sickish demoralized stomach, and am becoming yellow as saffron. My duties are not very heavy. The general has some very fine riding horses, and I devote some little time to exercising them. Mrs. Miner has very kindly undertaken to introduce me into society here, which, from what I have seen I judge to be very excellent. I went with the general to a union meeting at Charleston, about 100 miles from here, near the crossing of the Terre Haute and Alton and Chicago Branch of the Central. The general made a big speech, and I made a good many small ones. We stopped with Col. Tom Marshall while there. Had a big dance at night in which I participated heavily, staying with them until the very last moment. Train left at 2 a. m. Never will forget that dance in the world.

Decatur, Ill., September 6, 1863.

Girls, fun, etc., have lost their charm, and I've made up my mind to go back to my regiment. Reasons, as follows: Firstly, the general's health as affected by his wound is no better, and I think it doubtful whether he goes back. Second, if he does go to the army again he will be fit for nothing but "Post Duty." Will not be able for the field. Third, I don't like garrison work, and would rather be with my regiment in the field than with him in garrison. Fourth, my expenses are three times as heavy with him as with my regiment; and fifth and lastly, I wouldn't, on any account, miss this fall campaign, and by staying with him I will be apt to. I presented the matter to the general in about that shape and urged him to let me slide immediately. He agreed to do so, telling me that he will not go back unless they force him to.

Vicksburg, September 18, 1863.

Left Cairo last Sabbath and arrived here this (Friday) morning. Am feeling splendidly. Better than for three months. Intended visiting you before going to my regiment, but know you'll excuse me. Address me 4th Division 15th Army Corps.

Camp at Messenger's Ferry, Big Black River, Miss.,

September 22, 1863.

I wrote you a few lines from Vicksburg on the 18th inst. to notify you that I had escaped the perils of navigation (sandbar and guerillas) and of my safe arrival. I had a delightful trip down the river. A splendid boat, gentlemanly officers, not too many passengers, and beautiful weather. Major General Tuttle and wife and Mrs. General Grant were of our number. I think Mrs. Grant a model lady. She has seen not over thirty years, medium size, healthy blonde complexion, brown hair, blue eyes (cross-eyed) and has a pretty hand. She dresses very plainly, and busied herself knitting during nearly the whole trip. Believe her worthy of the general. Vicksburg is a miserable hole and was never anything better. A number of houses have been burned by our artillery firing, but altogether the town has suffered less than any secesh village I have seen at the hands of our forces. But very few buildings escaped being marked by our shot or shell, but such damage is easily repaired in most cases. No business whatever doing in the town, except issuing orders by generals, obeying them by soldiers and the chawing of commissary stores without price by the ragged citizen population. I was of the impression that I saw some rough country in Tishomingo County, Miss., and in the mountains in north Alabama, but after a day's ride in the vicinity of Vicksburg and to our present camp, I find I was mistaken. They call it level here when the surface presents no greater angles than 45 degrees. I found only one officer to a company present here, and the colonel is also on leave. There is a great deal of sickness but the health of the regiment now is improving. We have lost a large number by disease since I left the regiment. Anyone who saw us in Peoria would open wide his eyes at the length of our line now, and think we'd surely passed a dozen battles. The greater part of the material this regiment is made of should never have been sent into the field. The consolation is that these folks would all have to die sometime, and they ought to be glad to get rid of their sickly lives, and get credit as patriots for the sacrifice. We are now in the 2d Brigade 4th Division 15th Army Corps, having been transferred from the 16th Army Corps. We are camped on the bluffs of Black river, which we picket. Our camp is the finest one I ever was in. There are two large magnolias, three white beeches, and a half dozen holly trees around my tent. I think the magnolia the finest looking tree I ever saw. Many of the trees are ornamented with Spanish moss, which, hanging from the branches in long and graceful rolls, adds very much to the beauty of the forest. Another little item I cannot help mentioning is the "chigger," a little red insect much smaller than a pin-head, that buries itself in the skin and stings worse than a mosquito bite. Squirrels skip around in the trees in camp, and coons, owls, etc., make music for us nights. Capt. Gus Smith when on picket several nights, saw a bear (so he swears) and shot at it several times. The enemy's cavalry are maneuvering around on the other side of the river, constantly making it unsafe for our boys to straggle much over there. Sabbath evening we, our brigade, moved out across the river about four miles to meet a party of Rebels, but as usual they were not there. We ate our supper while waiting for them and returned by moonlight, 8 o'oclock p. m. We've had a brigade review and a short brigade drill, and I've eaten a very hearty supper since finishing the last period. I feel perfectly well once more. Much better than I did any day while North. Did I tell you that I had the ague for a week or so before I started South? My continued ill health more than anything else is what started me off for the regiment so suddenly. The general wanted me to stay until after the fair, but I wouldn't have done it for a horse. Altogether, I feel very happy over getting back to my company. The boys profess being very glad to have me with them again, and I assure you that such compliments do me good. I didn't know that I could take as much interest in any strange humans as I feel in these men of my company. While I was in Central Illinois I wished many times that this war was over, and that I could settle in one of the many good points I saw for trade. I know that I could do well selling goods in any of a half dozen towns that I visited there, and even in Decatur. But I know I could not be satisfied out of the army while this war lasts. I am glad to be out of staff duty for several reasons. One of the most important is that it costs all my pay to keep me. I did not make a cent while with the general, and have only two months' pay due me now.

It has been very cold here. Night before last I had six blankets over me, last night five and will use four to-night. 'Twas quite warm this p. m., but the nights are very cold. We will have hot weather yet. There is a great deal of ague here.

Messengers Ferry, Big Black River, Miss.,

September 26, 1863.

Pass in your congratulations. We are under marching orders for Chattanooga. Our whole corps is going. We steam o'er sand-bars to Memphis, and then will probably "foot it," though may go by cars as far as Corinth. From Memphis the march will be some 450 miles. We will pass through my favorite portion of Dixie, the Tennessee valley in North Alabama. We are all much rejoiced at the idea of leaving a country where there is no enemy save mosquitoes and chiggers and ague. We keep up the form of picketing; but I find it decidedly uninteresting to do such duty, knowing that coons and owls will cause all our alarms. Aside from knowing there is no enemy near, the picket duty is delightful here. I have seldom passed a more pleasant night than the one before last. The moon is about full, and our picket line (the post under my charge), about one and a half miles long, runs along the river bank through most beautiful little magnolia and beech groves and open grass plots. But a knowledge that there are guerrillas in the country is necessary to a thorough appreciation of picket duty. We are camped on the Messenger plantation. The owner thereof was very wealthy. Worth $1,000,000.00. Had some 500 negroes, etc. He armed and uniformed a secesh regiment at his own expense, and was, and is yet probably, a Rebel to the core. He fled at the approach of our troops, leaving his wife to manage for him. General Osterhaus called on her and asked her if she desired Federal protection. She said she didn't ask anything of him or any of his crew. The general told her she had just an hour to select and load two wagons with kitchen furniture and start across the river. She moved, was gone about a month, begged permission to return and is now eating government rations, which she is too poor to pay for.

Messengers Ferry, Big Black River, Miss.,

September 26, 1863.

When we assembled at regimental headquarters this p. m., the colonel informed us that our corps was ordered to report to Rosecrans, at Chattanooga, and that we should prepare to move at a moment's notice.

September 27.

We sent our sick, nearly 100 in number, by wagon to the Big Black railroad depot, six miles, where they took the cars for Vicksburg. They will there await our arrival. I have now but 31 men in my company in camp. Ten months ago I marched 72 men from Bolivar, Tenn., to Lagrange. Not one has been lost by the bullet, and to-day a difference of 41 in the duty list. A rumor prevails to-day that Rosecrans has had a severe battle and has been defeated. It is impossible to learn or hear anything in this place until the date alone would make it uninteresting. Blair's division moved into Vicksburg from the depot to-day to embark. Osterhaus' division is already on its way up the river. In the evening, with Captains Bishop and Smith and Lieutenant Johnson, had a rather dull game of "California Seven Up." All kinds of rumors to-day about the fight in northern Georgia. Have no hope of ever hearing the truth of the matter in camp. We are now 12 days behind in papers. The 3d brigade of our division and some cavalry started, with three days rations, on a scout across the river to-day. Suppose the object is to cover our move to Vicksburg, though I don't believe there are 100 armed Rebels this side of the Alabama line. The soldiers of our division have been having some high fun for the last two days. Orders are very strict against firing in camp, but the men found out they could get up some artificial firing by putting green can in the fire. The steam from the sap generating between the joints will make an explosion equal to a gun fired. And they got up some artillery firing by putting canteens half full of water, stopping them tightly and then putting them in the flames. They did this just to bore the officers who are held responsible by the general for all firing. To-night the general has ordered all the officers of the 40th Illinois to patrol the camp the whole night. This, of course, tickles the men hugely, and from their beds in their tents they have been talking over the duties of a sentry for the benefit of their officer's ears. The devilment that soldiers cannot contrive must be unearthly. To-day some of the 6th Iowa filled an oyster can half full of powder, set a slow train to it and planted it in the ground, they then set a cracker box over it and got a negro to dancing on the box A coal was then touched to the train and the "nigger" was blown full 20 feet. He landed, fortunately, without injury, but so badly scared that he was crazy for an hour. In the evening called on Captain Pinney of the 46th Ohio, and spent a very pleasant evening. He says that Vallandigham will poll about ten votes in their regiment; but that his disciples dare not open their mouths to advocate his cause. He says the loyal men would kill them sure if they dared to boast of their allegiance to a traitor.

September 28, 1863.

By the exercise of a little strategy, this morning I caught a chameleon who had ventured out of a hollow tree to gobble some flies for his breakfast. I enveloped him or rather lassoed him with a pocket handkerchief and then slipped him into a bottle. He only showed two of his colors, changing from a very pretty snuff color to a beautiful light green.

Clear Creek, Miss., September 29, p. m.

As we were studying tactics together, preparatory to a battalion drill, our brigade commander at precisely 2:15 p. m., came into the colonel's tent where we were, asked the colonel if he was ready to move immedi-

ately. The colonel replied that he was, and he then told us
to be ready to start at 3 o'clock, and that the regiment first
on the brigade parade ground, ready to move, should have
the advance. In just twenty minutes we had struck tents,
packed knaps, loaded wagons and formed line, everybody in
the best of spirits at the thought of leaving and joining Rosecrans. We beat the other regiments and therefore got the advance, which was quite an object as the dust lays, when it
don't fly, several inches deep. I let my little chameleon (I wish
I could have sent him home) back into the tree before we
started. Cogswell's battery attempted to pass us on the march,
but our two advanced companies fixed bayonets, and by a few
motions stopped the proceeding. Cogswell got very wrathy,
but when Colonel Wright proposed to shoot him if he didn't
cool down, he became calmer and moved to the rear "promptly."
The dust has been awful. Never saw it worse, except in a
march from Bolivar to Lagrange, Tenn., a year ago. We
bivouacked at 9 o'clock p. m., nine miles from camp. I stood
the march splendidly.

September 29th.

Had just got asleep last night when it commenced
raining. I dressed myself (that means put on my
boots) gathered up my oil-cloth and blanket and made for a
bushy-topped tree. I sat down to lean back against the tree and
I think one of the liveliest motions I ever made was getting up
immediately afterward. The tree was a chinquapin, and I had
sat down on a number of the burs, which are much like those
of the chestnut. After quite a search I secured two small
rails, and balancing myself on them I slept soundly until reveille at 2:30 a. m. It has rained all night, but in a small way,
and just enough to make marching pleasant. We made Vicksburg by 7 a. m., the rain falling all the time. In fact, it has
rained steadily up to this hour, 11 p. m. After a deal of hard
work we are on the steamboat Diana, which belongs to the Ma-
rine brigade. The whole division is loaded on 15 steamboats
and we start for Memphis in the morning. I forgot to mention a
queer tree that I noticed at last night's camp. They say it is

the cabbage tree or mock pineapple. The leaves were many of them fully thirty inches long, giving the tree a tropical appearance. Saw some of the 8th Illinois boys. The regiment is not as healthy as it should be.

Steamboat Diana, 70 miles from Vicksburg,

September 30, 1863.

We left Vicksburg in advance of the rest of the fleet at 8 o'clock this a. m. I am officer of the day and have found a good deal to do. Our regiment and the 40th Illinois are both on board and we are somewhat crowded. Gen. W. S. Smith and our division commander reached Vicksburg just before we left. The boat he came down on, the Robert Campbell, was burned about 50 miles above Vicksburg, and from 30 to 60 persons lost. The general and Colonel Hicks, our brigade commander, both escaped by swimming. General Smith says that a number of boats have been burned within two weeks by Rebel incendiaries and agents, the object being, by destroying our transportation, to make it impossible to reinforce Rosecrans from Grant's army. General Smith is not yet with us, and we think he will not follow if we go to Chattanooga, for he was once under Rosecrans, and they had some serious difficulty. If he does retain command of the division we will probably stop at some point on the M. and C. railroad again. We all think a great deal of Smith, but would ten times rather lose him than have to, on his account, again go to guarding railroads. It has rained steadily for the last 48 hours, not very fast, but everything uncovered is thoroughly soaked. My company was first stationed on the berth deck, but when steam was raised it because so hot that I took them up on the hurricane deck where, though they have to stand the rain, it will certainly be better for them than breathing the hot steam.

Griffin's Landing, Miss., October 1, 1863.

Clear as a bell this morning; about 8 a. m. we reached Griffin's landing 125 miles above Vicksburg. Said Griffin has some 2,000 cords of wood ricked on his plantation, some 500 of which we propose to gobble for the use of our transportation. We found here a part of Blair's division which left Vicksburg over a week ago. Found the 55th Illinois, 8th Missouri and 13 regiments among other regiments. They finished wooding and left about 3 p. m.

October 2, 1863.

Our foraging party brought in forty mules, fifty cattle, beef, twenty-one hogs and thirty sheep. They report a beautiful, rich country, and abundance of eatables within five miles of the landing. Went with party of bee hunters in the p. m. They had found the tree in the forenoon. They took two bucketsful of most beautiful white comb. One of my sergeants in an hour to-day found three trees, and by dark had taken the honey from all of them. We are to stay here and haul wood for the whole division (damn).

Griffin's Landing, October 3, 1863.

To-day one of the pilots and engineers induced the colonel and me go with them over to the Arkansas side. We went over in the yawl, and after a walk of three miles came to a most delightful place owned by Worthington. His son and daughter, bright quadroons, did the honors of the house in his absence. They are the best educated persons of color I ever met. The young man was educated in France and the young woman in Oberlin, Ohio. She played the piano quite well and sings beautifully. A negro lady is something of a novelty, and if I did not conduct myself exactly right in her presence, I think I am somewhat excusable, for I could see the others were equally puzzled. She is well informed, sensible and talks with animation, using very pretty language. She furnished us with peach brandy and honey, a gentle mixture of which produced a very nice toddy. We then moved on some three miles further to the Bass plantation, where we found two of the regular snuff-dipping, swearing, Southern women, of the low, white-trash family. Had lots of fun with them. Got a

13

couple of dozen chickens and a bushel of sweet potatoes of them and started back. Our road lay along a lake and at any minute we could get a shot at cranes, geese, ducks or turtles. A drove of wild turkeys also furnished us with a half dozen shots, but with all the expenditure of powder and lead, our consciences are clear of hurting anything. Got back to Worthington's for dinner at 3 p. m., and to the boat at dark. Altogether one of the most pleasant days I have passed in the army.

October 4, 1863.

Have been over to Worthington's again to-day. Sam got out his hounds and started a deer for us. We stationed ourselves in the runway, but although the deer came near us two or three times in his circling, the dogs didn't push him hard enough to make him break for distant cover. The major killed a very large snake and some of the boys got a shot at an alligator. We then left the bayou and went out to old River Lake, where we got some splendid shooting. I killed a water turkey at 500 yards, shooting into a flock. Our guns, the Henry rifle, threw bullets full a mile and one-half. I found that I could do tolerably close shooting, something I never suspicioned before. A neighbor told me that old Worthington sold the mother of his children, and with her five other picaninnies.

Memphis, Tenn., October 10, 1863, 4 p. m.

Have just got here; bored to death. Had to march around three sandbars between Helena and Memphis. Never want to see a steamboat again. Never want to journalize again. We started at 5 in the morning for Corinth and then, maybe, for Rosecrans. I'll be furiously glad to get ashore once more.

Iuka, Miss., October 21, 1863.

We reached here the evening of the 18th inst., and I have been on extra heavy fatigue nearly ever since our arrival.

We worked all night first night loading wagon trains and unloading cars. We were doing the work of another division, but, such is war. The impression is that we will leave here about the 23d. The other divisions have all moved on, taking with them thirty days' rations. We marched all the way from Memphis. Went about 20 miles out of our way to burn a little secesh town of some forty homes—Mount Pleasant. We reached Collinsville the day after Sherman, with about 800 men, had his fight with Chalmers. I stood the march splendidly, and am good for Chattanooga at 25 miles per day. It rained gently three nights on this march, and one night like the devil. We got in that night about 9 o'clock, and by a blunder of our brigade commander bivouacked in a regular dismal swamp. We had just stacked arms when the clouds sprung a leak, and such a leak, the cataract of Niagara is a side show, comparatively. Build a fire! Why, that rain would have quenched a Vesuvius in its palmiest days. I never saw just such a night. The one we spent at Lumpkin's Mill on the 18th of last April, of which I wrote you, was more disagreeable, because colder; but in six hours am sure I never saw so much water drop as in this last rain.

Iuka, Miss., October 26, 1863.

Let your pocket 'kerchief float out on the breeze, halloo a little and throw up your bonnet. It's only a "march at 12 o'clock to-night" but that's good enough. We've been here a week now, drawing clothing and making all kinds of preparations for a "forward," and the blessed word has come at last. I don't believe anybody enjoys anything better than I do marching. I feel as coltish all the time on a move as I used to, when after a long week of those short winter days at school, with just time enough between the school hours and dark to cut the next day's wood (how I did work), Job Walker and I would plunge into those dear old Big Creek woods with our guns or skates, and make such a day of it that I would almost wish all time was cut up into Saturdays. I was on picket last night; full moon, splendid post, right on the old Iuka battle ground, where the fight was the hottest; the old clothes, straps, cartridge boxes and litter always found in such places, the scarred trees, and the mounds a little further up the road, marking the pits where lay the glorious dead, then a half dozen neatly marked single graves, showing the care of some company commander, all tempted me to commit some more poetry. You know I can. But I nobly resisted the temptation. There were no coons or owls. I wished for them. My picketing the last year has almost all been in swamps, and I have learned to love the concerts those inno-cent animals improvise. When I got in this morning found orders to be ready to move at 12 this p. m. We cross the Tennessee river, I suppose, near Eastport. This beats me all hollow. Can't see the point, unless we're moving to check some of Bragg's flanking motions. Any-thing for a move. I put the profile of a fort here the other day under the direction of Sherman's engineer, and the chief told me if I would like it he would have me detailed to assist him. Have had enough of staff duty and excused myself. The men are rapidly becoming more healthy. I have but one person sick now. Dorrance arrived here a few days since, and brought a splendid long letter from you. Have to go to work on some ordnance reports now.

Am half inclined to think that our big march is played out. Rather think now that we will stop at Eastport on the Tennes-see river. Isn't that heavy? Eight miles only and then go to guarding navigation on a river that's a twin sister of Big Creek. Can't tell though, one rumor says that we will go 128 miles beyond the river. These generals are positively getting so sharp that a man can't tell one month ahead what they are going to do.

One of my men who was captured down near Panola, Miss., last April returned to the company for duty yesterday. Some Confederate soldiers captured him and some citizens offered

them $10 to each captor for the privilege of hanging the
d——d Yanks. They couldn't make a bargain. Transferred
five men to the invalid corps yesterday. Jacob J. Nicholson
among them.

Florence, Ala., November 1, 1863.

We struck tents on the 27th ult. at Iuka, Miss., and marched
to Eastport, eight miles, that night. We had in our division
some 200 wagons, all of which with 1,200 horses and mules
were to be crossed in a barge over the Tennessee river. I
received a complimentary detail to superintend the crossing of
the wagons belonging to one brigade. I think I never worked
harder than I did from 7 o'clock that night until 6:30 o'clock
the next day, a. m. It occupied two days and nights crossing
the whole train, but we marched at 3 p. m., the 28th, and
camped that night at Gravelly springs, 15 miles from Eastport. The road ran for some ten miles along the foot of the
river bluff, and the numerous springs sparkling their beautifully clear and fresh jets of limestone water on the road, from
which they rippled in almost countless little streamlets to the
river, although adding much to the wild beauty of the country, made such a disagreable splashy walking for we footmen
that (I speak more particularly for myself) we failed to appreciate it. We bivouacked for the night at about 9 p. m.
The morn of the 29th we started at 8 o'clock, and after ascend-
ing the bluff, marched through a magnificent country to this
place, 15 miles. Some three miles from here at the crossing
of Cypress creek, something like 50 or 60 girls, some of them
rather good looking, had congregated and they seemed much
pleased to see us. All avowed themselves Unionists.

There had been a large cotton mill at this crossing, Comyn
burned it last summer, which had furnished employment for
these women and some 200 more. This is a very pretty little town. Has at present some very pretty women. Two of
the sirens came very near charming me this a. m. Bought
two dozen biscuits of them. Have been out of bread for two
days before, but had plenty of sweet potatoes and apples. Dur-

ing the march on the 29th we heard Blair pounding away with his artillery nearly all day across the river, I should think about a dozen miles west of Tuscumbia. I was down to the bank the morning of the 30th ult. and the Rebels across shot at our boys, watering mules, but without effecting any damage. I saw a white flag come down to the bank and heard that Ewing sent over to see what was wanted, nothing more. There was some musketry fighting yesterday near Tuscumbia, but don't know who it was. We are four and one-half miles from there. Two companies of the 4th Regular Cavalry reached here on the 30th from Chattanooga, bearing dispatches to Sherman. He is at Iuka. All of these movements beat me completely. Can't see the point and doubt if there is one. We have commenced fortifying here. Have seen much better places to fight. We are "fixed up" most too nicely to hope to live here long. I have a stove, a good floor covered with Brussels carpet, plenty of chairs and a china table set under my tent. Eatables are plenty and would offer no objection if ordered to stay here a couple of weeks. Understand that not a farthing's worth of the above was "jayhawked." Got it all on the square. I wish I could send you the mate to a biscuit I just ate. 'Twould disgust the oldest man in the world with the Sunny South. By hemp, but it is cold these nights. Last night there was an inch of white frost. I was nearly frozen. Dorrance swears that Mattison and I were within an ace of killing him in our endeavors to "close up" and keep warm.

Winchester, Tenn., November 11, 1863.

We arrived here at 9 this a. m., our brigade making the distance from Salem, 11 miles, in three hours. That, we call fast walking. I wrote you last from Florence., Ala., on the 1st inst. From there we marched to Rodgersville and thence up the right bank of Elk river to Fayetteville, where we crossed there onto this place. Rumor says that we draw 20 days' rations here. It is three-fourths official, too. It is certain that we leave here in the morning, but nobody knows where for. We could certainly march to Chattanooga in six days, but could go much quicker by the railroad from Decherd station, which is only two miles from here. The wagon road from here to Chattanooga is awful. But one brigade has ever marched it. The mountains commence right here and continue to, the Lord knows where. Our brigade is to be mounted immediately. In the last 60 miles marching we have mounted 800 or nearly half. The citizens along the road very kindly furnished all of stock and equipments. My company was mounted four days ago. Company C is to be mounted next. As fast as the men are mounted they are put out as foragers for more horses, etc. The first day my company was mounted we got 30 horses, and would have done better, but confound me if I could take horses from crying women, although I am satisfied that half of their howling is sham, got up for the occasion. My first day's foraging almost used me up. We had fed our horses and I went to unhitch a mule from the fence to give him in charge of one of the men, and the brute scared and jerked the rail from the fence and started like lightning. The end of the rail struck me on the calves of my legs and elevated my boots five feet. The attraction of gravitation brought me down to the globe and I landed with a great deal of vim on a rock about the size of our parlor floor, and as smooth as a peach stone. The only severe injury either the rock or myself sustained was a very badly sprained wrist. I got that. My left hip and left shoulder were hurt some, but the wrist has pained me so confoundedly that I don't count them. It has pained me so for the last two days and is so tender that I could stand neither the jolting of a horse or wagon. I tried to ride my horse this morning; we were in column and had to strike a trot and that beat me. Think I will be all right for the saddle in a few days, though will have a tender wrist for a good while. Well, our division came through in the advance and our brigade has had the lead most of the time. We have had plenty of forage, but light issues of regular rations probably average. Half Morgan L. Smith's and John E. Smith's divisions are close up to us, will be here to-morrow. Osterhaus and Dodge are behind them. We have five divisions all told, probably 25,000 or 30,000 men. We met here the first troops belonging to the Army of the Cumberland.

Mud Creek Cove, Jackson County, Ala.

December 8, 1863.

I was at Stevenson yesterday and put a letter in the office for you, but with my accustomed shrewdness failed to either stamp or frank it. It graphically described the gallant exploits of the detachment I have the honer to command during the past three weeks, and its loss will be deplored in common with the other heavy losses of this "cruel war." I can now but give you the topics it discussed or elaborated, and leave to your imagination the finishing and stringing together the skeleton. First and foremost, stealing horses; second, defying bravely the tears and entreaties of helpless women, and taking their last measure of meal and rasher of bacon; third, the splendid conduct of our regiment and brigade at the late Mission Ridge fight; fourth, reflections. Do you remember, how, after the evacuation of Corinth one and one-half years ago, Halleck thought the rebellion virtually ended? And how many of the soldiers wrote home that they expected to be mustered out within three months? Then Halleck sent Buell with half of the army toward Chattanooga, Sherman and Hurlburt to Memphis, McClernand and Logan to Jackson, Tennessee; kept some four divisions at Corinth, and with three others opened and guarded 95 miles of railroad east to Decatur. That was what he called letting the army enjoy the rest they had earned by their glorious victory. The whole of the splendid army that had forced the Rebels to leave Corinth, was divided, subdivided and the subdivisions divided until, except Buell's, there was hardly a detachment left strong enough to hold its own against any overgrown band of guerrillas. The result you know. Buell's retreat with his heavy losses of detachments at Munfordsville, etc., our evacuation of the M. & C. R. R.

between Memphis and Corinth, the driving in of our
guards from Decatur to Corinth, and the fight there in
October which we gained only because our side weighed
only one ounce the most; and finally they shut us up in
Memphis, Bolivar, Corinth and Nashville so closely that
foraging parties hardly dared venture ten miles from the
siege guns, and there our army stayed until relieved by
"500,000 more." I don't like to slander so great and noble
a man as Grant, by insinuating that he has any notion
similar to Halleck's, but what I have seen with my naked
eye, and heard from good authority with my uncovered
ears, makes me think he has in his opinion at the Lookout, Mission Ridge, Ringgold fight, bursted the rebellion
to flinders. I know that Sherman with six divisions has
gone to Knoxville. John E. Smith's and Osterhaus' divisions
are at Bridgeport on their way to Huntsville or Decatur.
Some 12 companies of artillery, (nearly enough for a
corps) went to Nashville yesterday, and Hooker with the
11th and 12th Corps, are going back to the Potomac. Does
that sound anything like active forward movements? And
don't it sound exactly like Halleck's disposition of the army
after he got Corinth? I predict that no good will come
from scattering the army in this way, and much harm.
Bragg has fallen back to Dalton, only 25 or 30 miles from
Chattanooga, and 15 less than Beauregard ran from Corinth. The Rebel cavalry are already driving in our foragers at Chattanooga. That's all I have to say about the
matter. Our regiment, brigade and division have gone
with Sherman to Burnside's relief. They are probably at
Knoxville now. All accounts agree that the regiment
behaved splendidly; and Fulton county ought to either
disown her soldiers or quit disgracing them by her d—sh
copperheadism. You didn't have any fears for my safety
when you heard of the fight, did you? Of course you knew
I wouldn't be there. I heard three days before the fight
that it would probably open Sunday or Monday. Tuesday I was out in the Cumberland mountains, near Paint

Rock, some 50 miles from Chattanooga, when suddenly we heard the sound of cannonading. I thought of our regiment being in the fight and my company away, and cursed my luck to the best of my ability. I never expect to be in a battle. Being shot by a guerrilla is as good as I will probably get. It is strange that there was only the one vicinity in which we could hear the firing that day, and 25 miles nearer the scene of action they were unable to hear it. We are meeting with good success hunting horses. We only lack about 200 of having enough to mount the brigade and will have them by the time they get back from Knoxville. My men were never as healthy as now. My old convalescent "stand-bys" now walk into their double rations of fresh meat and corn pone tremendously, and do their share of duty splendidly. For four weeks we have had nothing to eat but corn bread and fresh pork. I am beginning to like it. It positively does taste better every day, and I destroy immense quantities. When reading about the elephant browsing upon the tree tops, did you ever imagine what an awful crashing he would make? That's about like the smash I make among the spareribs and hoecake. I thought that when they set me up as horse thief, that my measure was filled, that earth had nothing left too bitter for me to quaff or "chaw." But last night a draught was put to my lips of which I drank, and lo, I am undone. Can't look an honest man in the face. Fortunately there are no honest men in this command, so I am spared the mortification of turning my eyes. I was sent out to steal sheep. Can't call taking aught from these poor miserable citizen devils here anything but stealing. I made a pretty good haul. They go to the front to-day; I expect for hospital use. Of course we have to take them, but these citizens are on the verge of bankruptcy as far as eating is concerned. Saw Bill and Davis Trites at Bridgeport two days since. All right. Had just got back with their division from Chattanooga. Were both well. Captain Walsh, who was killed, was one of the finest officers in our regiment. I had formed a strong attachment for him, and mourn his loss as a dear friend and splendid fellow. His company, in camp, joins mine on the left and we were more intimate than I was with any other officer in this command.

Bivouac in Mud Creek Cove, near Belle Fonte, Ala.,

December 11, 1863.

Without any earthly cause I am troubled with a small fit of the blues this evening. I can't imagine what brought it on. I am cross, restless and tired. Don't want any company—wouldn't go to see a girl if there were a thousand within a hundred rods. Interesting state for an interesting youth, isn't it. Guess the trouble must be in the fact that I have no trouble. Everything moves too smoothly. No pushing in my family to knock down a looking-glass balanced on a knitting needle. Nothing in my precious life to keep me awake one minute of my sleeping time, and nothing in the future that I now care a scrap for. All of that is certainly enough to make one miserable. I'm convinced that my constitution requires some real misery, or a prospect for the same, in order to keep me properly balanced. If you can furnish me any hints on the subject, that will induce distress, trouble, or care, in a reasonable quantity to settle on my brain, I will be obliged. I have written you so much about soldiering, sister, that I'm thinking the subject must be pretty well exhausted. You must have received as many as 150 letters from me since I entered the army. I have had a host of interesting experiences since I enlisted, but when I am alone, and naturally turn to my little past for company, I always skip the army part and go back to the old home memories. One finds a plenty of opportunities for such self-communing in the service, and if I haven't profited by mine, it is my own fault. Did I ever tell you how I love picket duty? I have always preferred it over all other of our routine duties, yet it

would take a sheet of foolscap to tell you why; and then
nobody could understand me the way I'd write it. So
we'll pass. It seems a long time since I was at home.
What do you think of my eating Christmas dinner with
you? Don't let's think of that at all. I start for Chattanooga in the morning to get my team and things. It is
six weeks since I have had a change of clothes from my
valise. Borrowed a shirt from a woman once and got mine
washed.

Greasy Cove, Jackson Co., Ala., December 19, 1863.

On examination of my pockets this morning, I find a
letter I wrote you a week since. Will mail it this morning
and tell you the late news in another dispatch. You notice
we have again changed our camp, and you'll probably admire the classic names they have given these beautiful
valleys. I was at Stephenson and Bridgeport a few days
since for our camp and garrison equipage, and was just
starting back with it when I heard that our detachment
was ordered to report to the rest of the brigade at their
camp at Athens, Tenn., 40 miles beyond Chattanooga. So
I left my traps and came back to move. We will start as
soon as our parties get in from scouting. The last party
that went out and returned was some 200 strong. Dorrance had 20 men from our detachment. They brought in
a splendid lot of horses, but had to go 75 miles for them.
The guerrillas killed one man of the party, (46th Ohio)
and captured a number, maybe 15. Picked them up one,
two or three at a time. Dorrance was captured and paroled by some of Forrest's men. He was pretty well
treated, but the parole amounts to nothing. They took
nearly all of his money, his arms, spurs, horse, etc. He
was the only one of my men captured. It is confounded
cold lately and I haven't been real dry for three days. We
have to swim creeks to go anywhere, and there is so much
brush and drift in these streams that a horse will always
get tangled and souse a fellow. I swam a horse across

a creek yesterday, and he went over on his hind legs standing straight up. I never saw such a brute. Rumor says we will be dismounted and go with the corps to Mobile. But the most probable story is that we are going into camp at Athens for the winter. Would much rather go to Mobile but think that we can't be spared from here.

Near Larkinsville, Ala., December 29, 1863.

We have had some busy times since my last. Foraging for horses, looking for something to eat, and trying to obey a host of contradictory orders, has kept us in the saddle almost constantly. I believe I wrote you about Dorrance's going over to Elk river, Tenn. for horses and getting captured. When the next scout was ordered out, I was at Bridgeport on business, and Lieutenant Smith went in charge. They were absent a week and when I heard from them, and that they had but seven extras, I started after them and found them 25 miles from camp. That night I got permission from the officer in command to take 20 men and be absent two days. I went over the mountain into Madison county near Huntsville, got 34 good horses and was back on time. I also captured a guerrilla with his horse and traps, and found a lot of clothing which had been taken from Federal soldiers and officers captured by Rebels and concealed in a hovel on the mountain. In the round trip of the last six days, about 150 miles, the boys have destroyed at least 50 shotguns and rifles. To-day, an officer of Ewing's staff is here selecting our best horses, for the use of Sherman, Logan, etc. We think it confoundedly mean, but guess we'll stand it. We have enough horses to mount the brigade, but there is some doubt about that little event taking place. They can't beat me out of being satisfied whatever they do. Would rather remain mounted, but Sherman's will be done. I have turned into the corral fully my proportion of horses, haven't lost a man, and none of my command have been guilty of robbing, plundering, or stealing. That's what the officer of no other detachment here can say, truthfully. I do think I have the best lot of men that ever soldiered together, and there are now 41 for duty. The rest of the brigade is at Scottsboro, only six miles from here, and they will probably go into winter quarters there. Possibly, at Belle Fountain. I am in splendid health and enjoying myself excellently. My wrist is improving slowly, but there is something broken about it. It will, however, answer my purpose if it gets no worse. One ought occasionally to have something of that kind in order to a better appreciation of our many blessings. What wonderful luck I have soldiering, don't I? Now, in our two month's foraging, I haven't lost a man. Only one wounded a little, and one man and Dorrance captured and let go again. In the same time the 15th Michigan have lost about 20. The 46th Ohio have had two killed, the 6th Iowa two killed, and the 40th Illinois two hung and two missing. We have been over all the country they have, and done just as much work, without losing a man. I am hopeful of obtaining some recruits from the Fairview country, but can get along without them.. Have as good as been out of the world for two months. I haven't worn socks since I left Memphis. Too much trouble. Has rained steadily for the four last days. I have ridden from daylight until dark each day. Got dried off to-day for the first time. Swam our horses over three bad creeks. Lieutenant Smith and three men came very near drowning. My mare swam splendidly.

Scottsboro, Ala., January 5, 1864.

Your brother no longer represents the Festive Mamaluke, but has returned from his paradise of fresh pork, cornbread, honey, milk, and horse, to his original heavy infantry exercise, his nix-Grahamite diet of army rations, to that headquarters of red-tapeism, a "permanent camp," in short, to the elysium of the enlisted men, and purgatory of company commanders winter quarters. In short, the powers that be concluded that dismounting us would not render the salvation of the Union impossible, and as the detachment was getting a very hard reputation, and making much trouble for said powers to settle, 'twas decided to unhorse us. It's all over now, the mounting part has "played" and that string will not probably be harped on again for this brigade to dance to. I think that to-day, Sherman, Logan or Ewing would not trust a detachment of this brigade on sorebacked mules if they had only three legs. This little squad of 500 men in the two months they have been mounted have committed more devilment than two divisions of regular cavalry could in five years. Everything you can think of, from shooting negroes, or marrying these simple country women, down to stealing babies' diapers. From taking $2,700.00 in gold, to snatching a brass ring off the finger of the woman who handed a drink of water. From taking the last "old mar" the widow had to carry her grist to mill, to robbing the bed of its cord, for halters, and taking the clothes line and bed-clothing "to boot." I'll venture that before we were dismounted, not a wellrope, tracechain, or piece of cord of any kind strong enough to hold a horse could be found in the districts through which we have foraged. I want you to understand that my command is not responsible for the heavy devilment. I have steadily discountenanced it, and watched my men carefully. I am willing to be responsible for all they did, and will probably have a chance, as I understand a board of inquiry sits on the subject shortly. Some of the officers will, I think, have cause to wish they were never mounted; and to think that "Mission Ridge" would have been preferable to the duty they have been on.

We had been looking for General Ewing out to our bivouac to review us for several days, and I rather saw in the distance that dismount was an order we'd get shortly, and had sent in to our colonel, lieutenant colonel and staff some of my best horses, knowing that if we got dismounted they would be taken by Sherman, Logan or Ewing. Sure enough, on the morning of the New Year's day came an order to form to be review by some heavy staff. The review consisted in their picking out what good horses there were, turning the rest into a corral, and sending us to our regiments on foot. We got here the same day, found the regiment just pitching camp, with the idea that winter quarters or a good long rest, at least, was their portion. Our company already has good comfortable quarters up, and is as well fixed for winter as we care about being. But already we hear it rumored that our division is to move down to Huntsville in a short time, and we have had no orders to prepare winter quarters. All right. It has been pretty cold here although we have had no snow nor ice that could bear a man. A great deal of rain. The regiment is very healthy. Not a dozen men complaining. My wrist is improving slowly. Not worth very much yet. Doctor says 'twill take it a year to get well. That bone at the wrist joint protrudes considerably. All right. The veteran feeling is "terrific" here. Three regiments in our brigade the only ones eligible (that is that have been in two years) have re-enlisted almost to a man. 40th Illinois, 46th Ohio and 6th Iowa. In our division there are seven regiments eligible and all have re-enlisted, and are going home in a few days. It is, I think, the grandest thing of the war. These old soldiers so enthusiastically and unanimously "going-inimously." I guess no one is more astonished at it than the very men who are enlisting. One of the 40th boys told me that "about 15 of us were talking about it and cussing it, until every son of a gun of us concluded to, and did re-enlist." Our regiment hasn't been in long enough to make veterans. Wouldn't you rather have me stay in service until this war ends? I get the blues, though, sometimes, and think of getting out and denying that I ever was in the war. Haven't I a brilliant record, Thirty-three months in service and not a battle.

Clear and cold this morning. I'm very comfortable. Have built me a brick fireplace and chimney, raised my tent two and one-half feet on a broad frame. Made me a good bed with broom sage for soft, and am living high.

I received three recruits yesterday and have at least one more coming. I have more men for duty than any other company. Night before last two Confederate soldiers came into our camp and stole three horses, two of them belonging to our surgeons, and the other to the adjutant. The Rebels crossed the Tennessee river, which is only four miles from here and recrossed safely with their horses. I call that pretty sharp. The horses were only about 30 yards from where I sleep. They might just as well have got me. I feel highly complimented by their prefering the horses to me. We had one-fourth of an inch of snow last night. Gone now. Yesterday three teamsters, belonging to Logan's headquarters while foraging went to pillaging a house. The woman of the house tried to stop them, when one of the fellows struck her on the head with a gun and killed her. This was about three miles from here.

Scottsboro, Ala., January 9, 1864.

We have settled down into fully as monotonous a monotony, as I ever experienced. The powers pretend that the army is tired down and needs rest, so duty is very light, no drills ordered; no scouting and no nothing, but a first-class preparation to have a tremendous sick list in a very short time. You know how we have been moving for the last three months, and that we have hardly suffered a half dozen cases of sickness. Now see, if we lie here four weeks longer, if I don't report you 60 on the sick list. Do you think that I am something of a grumbler? Either having too much travel, or too much lie still. Too much to eat (I guess not) or not enough, etc. I suppose that news here is about as scarce as ice cream on the African desert, and of nearly the same quality. We are camped in the edge of dense woods, about three quarters of a mile from the town, which consists of 20 or 40 rather neat houses, and presents, I think a better appearance than any other town of the size I have seen in the Confederacy. It hasn't been squashmolished like most of its sisters. General Logan's headquarters are here. Our corps

14

is camped along the road from here to Decatur, our whole division being here. Our division commander, is, I expect, the most unpopular officer with his corps that there is in the West. I never knew his match for meanness. See if I can think of all I have been ordered by: Prentiss, Grant, Logan, McClernand, Wallace (W. H. L.), Oglesby, Paine, Pope, Granger, Palmer (———) formerly colonel 11th Missouri., Rosecrans, Morgan, Buford, Sheridan, Hurlbut, Lanman, Hamilton 1st, Hamilton 2d; Sullivan, Lawler, Sooy Smith, Ewing, Corse, Halleck, Sherman, Davis, and at least two more whose names I can't now recall. One of them commanded this division last March, and the other the 4th Division 16th Army Corps, last December, for a few days. I have lots of work on hand writing up my accounts, but this lying still begins to bore me awfully. I thought a few weeks ago that 'twould be very nice to have a tent again, and things somewhat comfortable, but the beauties of the thing don't last long. I'm ready to move now. We have had several pretty cold days, but to-day I have been in my shirt sleeves, without vest, all day, and felt very comfortable, though it didn't thaw very much, and I believe there was ice in our water bucket all day. Expect you are having a gay time this winter at home sleighing, dancing, etc., but I would rather take mine out in the army. If I didn't have any happy Christmas myself, I had the pleasure of smashing the happiness out of a good many secesh Christmases. That's not so. It was not pleasure, but I had to.

Steamer "Cosmopolitan," bound to Beaufort from
Savannah, Ga.,

January 21, 1864.

I was at Beaufort some three days when I received a detail on a "military commission" to sit at headquarters, 4th Division of our corps at Savannah. Reported at Savannah on the 17th and found my commission had finished its business and adjourned, all of which satisfied me. Have been ever since trying to get back to the regiment, but all of the vessels which run on this line have been in use as lighters, transfering the 19th Corps (which now occupies Savannah) from the large steamers which have to stop at the bar up the river. This 19th Corps is a portion of Sheridan's command and helped him win those glorious victories in the valley. They are a fine soldierly-looking body of men, but have already had some difficulty with our troops. As I left the city I saw the wind up of a snug little fight between a portion of the 20th and 19th Corps. Noticed about 40 bloody faces. All this kind of work grows out of corps pride. Fine thing, isn't it, We left the wharf at 2 p. m. yesterday, grounded about 5 p. m., and had to wait for high tide, which came at midnight; then a heavy rain and fog set in and we have made little progress since. Are now, 11 a. m., at anchor, supposed to be near the mouth of Scull Creek waiting for the fog to clear up. I am terribly bored at being away from the regiment so long. I feel lost, out of place and blue. What glorious news from Fort Fisher, and what a horrid story that is about 13 out of the 15 prisoners the Rebels had of our regiment, dying of starvation. One of them, W. G. Dunblazier, was of my company, and a better boy or braver soldier never shouldered a musket. He was captured on the skirmish line at Dallas.

May 27, '64.—Dr. Buck is on board with me just from the North. He is terribly disgusted with the service, and furnishes me some amusement. I believe I take as much pleasure in seeing other people miserable—over small matters—as I do in a good thing for myself.

12 a. m. Have just been badly beaten at cribbage by Colonel Bloomfield, and the boat is under way again, the fog having gone up.

Scottsboro, Ala., February 7, 1864.

This has indeed been a day of rest. More like a home Sabbath, than the Lord's day often seems, here in the "show business." None of my company have been on duty, and as the day has been bright and warm, the men have been nearly

all out in front of the quarters; all looking natty and clean
and healthy, sunning themselves real country-Sunday fashion.
Seems to me that I grow prouder every day of being captain
over these men. If I could only get 30 good, healthy recruits,
I expect I'd have to be "hooped." The boys brought a fiddle
in with them yesterday from our Lebanon march, and as
nearly all of them play, "more or less," it has seen but little
rest to-day. Every man I have present (42) is for duty, and
if there are any soldiers in the army who can outmarch them,
or do duty better, "I want them for Babcockses," as the boys
say. Frank Post was in my tent to-day, and informed me that
in her last letter, Laura told him that some horrible stories
of my cruelty to women and children while in command of
the mounted detachment, were in circulation at home. He
wanted me to trace the author of them, but I respectfully
begged to be excused. The person who told such stuff, falsi-
fies; for I never killed a fly, or stepped on a worm, or kicked
a dog, or threw a stone at a cat, and know I wouldn't treat
a woman or child worse, if they were Rebels. I do take a
little private satisfaction in knowing that I have never said
a word, except respectfully, to any woman in the Confederacy, that I have ever touched a cent's worth of private property for my own use. We, with 600 more of our brigade,
had to take horses and rations from a poor set of people, but
that was no more our fault than the war is. Those pretty
crystals I sent you by Lieutenant Dorrance, are "Iceland
Spar," which is, I believe, the only stone which possesses the
power of double refraction. If you put a thin piece of it over
a black mark on paper, and look closely, you will see two
marks; try this piece which I enclose. I took a lesson in chess
last night, played a couple of games. Don't thing I would
ever make a player. Colonel Dickerman is at present commanding the brigade, and Major Willison the regiment, Lieutenant Colonel Wright being on detached service as a division inspector general. Mattison is in his quartermaster department almost constantly, and Dorrance's absence leaves

me quite alone. Dorrance was in a way, good company. Always in a good humor and talking. Real accommodating, too, if carefully handled.

I went to the nearest house to camp to-day, to beg a little piece of tallow to soften a pair of marching boots. I sat down by a fire, in company with three young women, all cleanly dressed and powdered to death. Their ages were from 18 to 24. Each of them had a quid of tobacco in her cheek about the size of my stone inkstand, and if they didn't make the extract fly worse than I ever saw it in a country grocery, shoot me. These women here have so disgusted me with the use of tobacco that I have determined to abandon it. Well, we are again under orders to march at a moment's notice. Received them about noon to-day, and expect to start in the morning. It is intimated that we go to Chattanooga, first, and then either to Dalton, Knoxville, or garrison Chattanooga, and let its present occupants go. I was much pleased to get the orders, for above all things, do hate a permanent camp. I enjoy the tramping, the mud, the cold, and being tired, and everything mean there is about soldiering, except being hungry. That beats me to a fraction. If I could only go without eating three or four days at a time I would pass as a soldier, but bless me, missing a meal is worse than drawing a tooth. I never tried it as long as I have been in the army, but it seems to me that putting me on quarter rations would be equivalent to putting me in a hospital bed.

Hurrah for the march. No such place for real fun elsewhere. We have our regular races, and tough ones they are, too, sometimes. Each regiment takes its turn in having the advance, one day at a time. Say, to-day we have the lead, then to-morrow we will march behind all the rest, and the next day the regiment which succeeded us in the lead will fall behind us, etc. It is a great deal easier to march in front than in the rear, because in passing defile, or crossing streams on single logs, all of the time that is lost falls, finally, on the rearmost regiment, and after it crosses it sometimes has to double-quick it a mile or more to catch up again. A common time step or 90 to the minute, in front with a brigade of 1,500 over the average of these roads, makes the rear in order to keep up, take more than quick time, or over 112 steps to the minute, during their marching time. So you can imagine our races, though fun to the advance, make the rear work—no laughing matter. The point of the race is for the advance regiment to move so fast that the others will break up, tired out, and straggle. Yesterday the 97th Indiana coming in had the lead and undertook to run us. We had the rear, but by not waiting to cross on logs, but wading through creeks up to our knees or middles kept at their heels for 8 miles without a rest. 'Twas raining all the time and the roads were awful slippery. Our brigade tried hard to run us down at first, but now none of them doubt our ability to march with any regiment. When the men are resting along the road they have a great fashion of making remarks about any strange soldier or citizen who passes. As we were resting on the 5th inst., a bare-footed, sick-looking soldier came hobbling through. One man said, "He's sick, don't say anything to him;" another said, "No, he's shod a little too rough;" another, "Yes, and he interferes;" another, "Keep still he's slipping upon something;" another, "He's showing us how Fanny Elssler went over a looking glass;" another, "Come here and I'll take the pegs out of your shoes," etc. Wouldn't that be interesting to the passerby?

Scottsboro, Ala., March 6, 1864.

By marching 21 miles on the railroad ties we reached "home" yesterday, after an absence of 24 days, in which we traveled 280 miles. Altogether it was a very pleasant trip, although the first 10 nights were almost too cold for outdoor sleeping. I kept a "sort" of a diary of this trip in a memorandum book, and being too lazy to copy, tore out the leaves and mailed to you. You should receive three letters of that kind. One about the "Wills Valley" trip, one of the march from here to Cleveland, and the third of the trip from Cleveland to Dalton and back. The rain was pouring down when we received orders to start home from Chattanooga and it rained almost until night. We marched 16 miles without a rest, and did it in five hours. Did exactly the same thing next day, although it did not rain. This was from Oltewah to Chattanooga. In addition to this march I took a look over the part of Mission Ridge where our regiment fought, and also climbed Lookout mountain. The 103d, the brigade they were with, undoubtedly got the hottest part of the whole Lookout, and Mission Ridge fight. The nature of the ground was such that not a shot was fired by either side until they were within 200 yards of each other, when our men charged. Some of our boys were killed a little to the right of, but on a line with the Rebel guns. The trees and shrubs show marks of extraordinary hot musketry work. I cut a hickory walking stick right where our men commenced the charge. This hickory stood by an oak that I should think was hit by 400 musket and canister balls. It helped me later in the day to climb Lookout Mountain. I think the view from Lookout worth 1,000 miles travel. The high mountains of Western North Carolina, and the Blue Mountains of Virginia are very plainly seen from the summit. There is a summer retreat, some 40 or 50 nice houses with public hall and school on top.

Scottsboro, Ala., March 15, 1864.

I am again on court martial duty, with a prospect of a long siege; but we have an experienced President and a Judge Advocate who promises to be a fast worker; so we may get through quicker than we anticipated. The President, Colonel Heath, 100th Indiana, is a Bob Ingersoll for the world, that is, full of anecdote and fond of malt. 'Tis probably fortunate that at this time none of the latter is to be had in our division. I dislike detached service in any shape, but prefer court martial duty to almost any other. Would much rather be with my company, and if it were not considered so nix military would ask to be

relieved from this. You can't imagine how proud I am
becoming of my company. I have never had an iota of
trouble with them. We certainly work as smoothly as any
company could. We are all in high feather over the prospect of going to Richmond. Everybody wants to start
immediately. If the 15th and 17th corps reach the
Rapidan, we doubt your hearing anything more about
recrossing the Rapidan and taking positions inside the
Washington fortifications. Our corps don't get along well
with these Cumberland and Potomac soldiers. To hear
our men talk to them when passing them or their camps
marching, you'd think the feeling between us and the
Rebels could be no more bitter. We are well off by ourselves, but still we don't feel at home. We're too far from
our old comrades, 13th, 16th and 17th Corps. This feeling
that grows up between regiments, brigades, divisions and
corps is very strong and as strange. The 4th and 14th
Corps Cumberland chaps our men can endure, although
much in the spirit a dog chewing a bone, allows another
to come within ten feet. The 11th and 12th Corps Potomac men, and ours never meet without some very hard
talk. I must do the Yankees the justice to say that our
men, I believe, always commence it, and are the most un-
gentlemanly by great odds. I do honestly think our corps
in one respect composed of the meanest set of men, that
was ever thrown together. That is, while on the march
they make it a point to abuse every man or thing they see.
They always feel "bully," will certainly march further with
less straggling, and make more noise whooping than any
other corps in service, but if a strange soldier or citizen
comes in sight, pity him, and if he's foolish enough to ask a
question, as "what regiment," or "where are you bound for?"
he'll wish himself a mile under ground before he hears all the
answers, and ten to one not a whit of the information he
asked for will be in any of them. We have no pay yet,
and no prospects now, but doing good business borrowing.

Scottsboro, Ala., March 12, 1864.

I have been tremendously demoralized for nearly a month in consequence of a terrible cold I caught by some of my carelessness, I suppose, but am now coming out of it all right. Weather is most beautiful. Not too much duty, excellent camp, remarkably good health, and everything so near right, that almost think a soldier who'd grumble here deserves shooting. Were I disposed to complain am sure I could only find two little topics whereof to speak; one being the fact that 'tis impossible to get anything to eat here excepting regular army rations, not even hams can be had, and the other the long-continued absence of the paymaster. We are hoping that both these matters will be remedied 'ere long, but have been so hoping for months. We have a division purveyor now, who pretends that he will furnish us in good eatables. We have had but a few articles from him, and I'll tell you the prices of those I remember. Can of strawberries, $1.75; cheese, 80 cents a pound; bottle (about one and one-half pints) pickled beets, $1.50. If I could draw the pay of a brigadier general, and then live on half rations, think I might come out even with said purveyor for my caterer.

Everything perfectly stagnant. We did hear day before yesterday some quite rapid artillery firing for an hour or two; it sounded as though it might have been some ten or twelve miles southwest of us. 'Twas reported by scouts a few days ago that the enemy was preparing flatboats at Guntersville to cross the river on, with intent to make a raid up in this direction or toward Huntsville. The 15th Michigan Mounted Infantry was sent down to look after the matter, ran into an ambuscade and lost a dozen or so killed and wounded. That's all I heard of the matter. We were very sorry that the loss was so light, for they are a miserable set. We are going to have a dance here in a few days. Think I'll go. Anything at all to get out of camp. I'm as restless as a tree top after marching so much. You don't know how tame this camp business is. Am afraid I will get the "blues" yet. Hurry up the spring campaign, I say.

Scottsboro, Ala., March 20, 1864.

What under the sun can I tell you that will interest you. That it is intolerably dull, bah! Have just had a long visit from Lieutenant Colonel Wright, now army assistant inspector general of the division, and Lieutenant Van Dyke, A. D. C., to our new commander, General Harrow. The lieutenant is a splendid looking fellow of about 23 years, and has served up to the time of coming into our division with the 2d Corps, Army Potomac. Van Dyke informed me that a despatch from Logan was received by Harrow this a. m., informing him that Forrest was prowling around on the other side of the river with intention of crossing and making a little dash on some part of our line. "Our" railroad from Nashville via Decatur is about completed (will be finished to-morrow) and then we hope to have something to eat once more. This railroad will be all for our corps, or at least we will get the choice of what comes over it. We are at outs with the general to-day. In the field we are not accustomed to having camp guard, considering a strong picket and the regular property alarm guards sufficient. But because two or three men got drunk yesterday, and a gun or two was fired, out comes Harrow in an order and requires a strong camp guard. It may be one of the faults of our discipline, but 'tis a fact that our men would much prefer two days of any other duty, to one of camp guard. Our court gets on slowly. Oh! We had a dance a few nights since. Northern ladies, officers' wives, and a few "Mountain Ewes" (the poetical name given the Jackson county beauties by some genius of a Yankee). We really had a delightful time; and I understand they are to be continued, one every two weeks Anything to keep a man from getting blue. I see Abraham calls for 200,000 more. Keep asking for them Lincoln, that's right, I'm sure there are yet many who can be spared for their country's good in more meanings than one. It's queer that our regiment don't get more recruits. We need them very much, and yet I dread getting them, they are so much trouble

for a year. The 26th and 48th Illinois have respectively
200 and 500 and the officers are bored terribly over them.
There is to my eye, as much difference between the average of recruits and the average of veterans, as there is between
the physique of a tailor and that of a blacksmith. Some
of the veterans who have returned to camp, are sick of
their last bargain with the United States, but the majority
are right glad to get back.

Scottsboro, Ala, March 24, 1864.

Two months and twenty-four days without changing
camp; which is the longest time our tents have covered
one piece of ground since we organized. We have
marched, though, some 35 days during this time, and some such
marching. Whew! I think I never suffered on a march as
I did on the Sand Mountain in DeKalb county. I wore
a thin blouse, and had no overcoat. I'd lie so close to the
fire nights that the clothes on my back would scorch and
my breath would freeze on my whiskers. We had nothing
to keep the freezing dews off us, and it seemed to me
that it went through my clothes and an inch of flesh
before the dew-point would be blunted. One night about
2 o'clock I had a huge pine knot fire and was trying to
warm some half frozen portions of my body, when Captain Smith came over from his bed, as blue as a conscript,
to thaw out. He turned one side and then t'other to the
blaze, time and again but without much progress; finally
he shivered out, "By G—d, Captain, I could wish a tribe
of cannibals no worse luck than to get me for breakfast.
I'm frozen hard enough to break out half their teeth, and
the frost would set the rest aching." Next morning a lot
of us, were standing by a fire nearly all grumbling, when
the major asked me how I passed the night. "Capitally,
slept as sweetly as an infant, little chilly in fore part of
night, but forgot it when sleep came." They looked so
pitifully, doubtfully envious, that I got me laugh enough
to warm me clear through. Captain Smith, Soot and Lieu-

tenant Ansley have been in with me playing old sledge all evening. A storm came up, blew half of my camp house down, and broke up the party. Have just got fixed up again. Those pine knot fires we had on the mountains, made us all look like blacksmiths. Day before yesterday a foot of snow fell. Last night only drifts on the north side of things were left and to-night you have to hunt for a flake. Two shots on the picket line back of our camp. Guess it's some of the 26th or 48th recruits. Out of every dozen or twenty recruits, there's sure to be one who will see men skulking around his picket post, and who will shoot a stump.

Six-thirty a. m. 25th.—Bless me, how it rained and blew last night. Do you remember the storm at Point Pleasant, Mo., April 1, 1862? Never a high wind that I do not think of it. Believe we had two killed, about a dozen disabled and 20 horses killed. No paymaster yet.

Goldsboro, N. C., March 25, 1864.

We were two days coming back here from Bennettsville; and have Sherman's receipt for another campaign and his promise of a little rest. Have a nice camp ground and will enjoy ourselves, I think.

Huntsville, Ala., April 3, 1864.

Thunder, lightning and rain are having a little time by themselves outdoors to-night. No audience, but guards and government mules, but that don't seem to affect the show. We have a right good hotel here, a rather lively party, and have spent a pleasant, highly gaseous evening, Colonel Oglesby, Dr. Morris and Captain Wilkinson of our division. We came down on two days' leave, principally to see the place, but all having more or less business. Found Will Trites this a. m.; dined with him, and this afternoon four of us have been riding. I enjoyed it very much. Had good horses, and 'tis a beautiful town. I think the finest I have seen

South; but nothing near what Decatur, Bloomington, Quincy and a dozen other Illinois towns promise to be when they have half its age. In the cemetery there are as many really fine monuments as there were in the Chicago cemetery in 1859, and should think it not more than half the size of the new Canton graveyard. Our soldiers have been registering their names on the finest of the monuments. It looks so sacrilegious, and fully as ridiculous. They have a beautiful custom here of placing wreaths of flowers and bouquets upon the graves. This p. m. (Sabbath) nearly every grave had one or more such offerings. I attended the Presbyterian church this a. m., and certainly never heard the English language so abused before. The minister was a citizen. Did not by a word allude to the war in sermon or prayers. Most of the ladies wore mourning. Very full attendance of them. All who refused the "oath" here, have been sent across the river. Saw General McPherson at breakfast this morning looking as of old. We were paid four months last Thursday.

Scottsboro, Ala., April 9, 1864.

Don't be alarmed and imagine that I have "photos" on the brain. This is in all probability the last remittance of the article that I shall make you. General Corse, our old brigade commander, we think a great deal of, and would like to have you preserve his picture. The little soldier, Johnny Clem, was a sergeant at the time of the Chickamauga battle, and fought like a hero. His comrades say he killed a Rebel officer of high rank there. For his gallant conduct in that massacre, General Thomas gave him a lieutenancy and position on his staff, where he now is. He is almost a perfect image of one, Willie Blackburn, who was my orderly in the 7th.

The day of jubilee has come at this post; that is, we have, once more, something fit to eat. This is the first day since we've been here that our commissary has furnished us with aught but regular rations. We can wish for nothing now, except "marching orders." My men are in splendid condition. Everyone of them in A1 health and spirits. All the

veterans of the division are back, except the three regiments
of our brigade. The 55th Illinois has at last concluded to
veteran. Two hundred of them will be at home shortly.
They held a new election, left Malmsberg and Chandler out
in the cold, and I understand, a goodly number of their best
officers besides. Men who have not been under good discipli-
narians, will almost invariably, if an election is allowed,
choose good fellows for officers. That is, men who allow
everything to go at loose ends, who have no business whatever with commissions. Captain Milt. Hainey and Captain
Augustine, I understand, are to be colonel and lieutenant
colonel of the 55th. They are said to be good men and officers, and exceptions to the above, but my experience is such
exceptions are rare, and I'd rather time would prove them
than man's words. I believe my company would veteran, almost unanimously, to-day. I am still on court-martial duty,
and having a very easy time. We seldom sit over two hours,
and never more than four hours a day. The most of the
cases are for desertion, and absence without leave, with occasionally a shooting or cutting affair among some drunken
men. The major and several of the other officers are absent at Nashville on a shopping excursion. Captain Wyskoff
is commanding. He has been trying for the last eight months
to resign, but papers come back every time disapproved. It's
hard work now to get out of the army. By a few items I
have seen in the papers, believe the 17th Army Corps is coming up the river. Wish they would be sent here. We need
another corps to move with us on to Rome. Suppose that
Grant thinks he must have the 17th with him at Richmond.
Operations cannot possibly commence here for 25 days yet.
Wish we could move to-morrow. Colonel Wright and I were
out a few miles this p. m. to see a couple of maidens. While
we were enjoying our visit a party of excited citizens (all
liable to the Southern conscription) rush in, and kindly in-
vite us to go down to Fossets' in the bottom, and clean out a
half dozen "guerils" who were there after conscripts. 'Twas
only a half mile through the woods to Fossets' and that was

closer than we wanted to be to such a party (we had no arms). So we told the excited citizens that they and the guerillas could all go to the d——l and we'd go to camp. Within a mile of camp we met a company on the way to look for the Rebels, but I know they might as well look for a religious chaplain in the army as for the Rebels in that swamp. There is hardly a sign of spring here yet. Have certainly never seen vegetation as far advanced North at this season as it is here now. Need a fire every day. The last month has been colder than January was. I met a woman to-day who prides herself on belonging to one of the first families of Virginia and boasts that her grandsire's plantation and George Washington's almost joined, and showed me a negro woman 110 years old, that formerly waited upon George Washington. She claims to be chivalry, par excellence. Her husband is in the Rebel Army. She lives off of the United States Commissary Department, and begs her chewing tobacco of United States soldiers. She's a Rebel, and talks it with her mouth full of Uncle Sam's bread and bacon.

Scottsboro, Ala., April 24, 1864.

Spring is here at last, and summer is almost in sight. The last two days have been fully as warm as I care to see weather in April. There has been a great deal of cold, wet weather here this spring, and vegetable life is unusually backward; but the last few days have effected a great change in the forests. The north side of the mountains still look bare and wintry, the soft maple being the only tree I have noticed "in leaf" on those slopes; but nearly all of the trees and bushes on the southern mountain slopes are in full leaf. In the valleys, the poplars, the beeches, and the black gums are nearly in full spring dress, being far in advance of their comrades—the oaks, chestnuts, hickories and white gum. Of the smaller trees the dogwood leads in assuming a spring costume. Two years ago this date, vegetation was further advanced at the mouth of the Ohio than 'tis here now. Do you remember, I arrived home just about two years ago this time; stayed two and one half days, and then, for Corinth? How easily my three years in the army have made way with themselves. That I have lived something over a thousand days, in a blue uniform seems incredible. Six months sounds much more reasonable. "Black Jack" reviewed our division yesterday. Only eight of the 13 regiments could be present; but 'twas the finest review I ever saw. Logan rode through our camp, and expressed himself much pleased at our way of keeping house. We have a beautiful camp, every part of it cleanly swept every morning. It is also decorated profusely with evergreens from the mountains. I suppose it is unnecessary to tell you what we killed in the deerhunt, I spoke of in my last, as in prospect; but we did have a power of fun. Colonel Young, the citizen who proposed the party to me, is probably some 55 years old; and at heart a Rebel (he is now a member of the Alabama Legislature) but has taken the oath. I noticed a suspicious "auburn" tinge on his nose, and provided myself with a canteen of pure lightning commissary whiskey. The colonel had tasted none of the ardent for a long time, and his thirst was excessive. He became intensely demoralized; and proved the most amusing character of the party. He made us a speech, and committed so many fooleries, that if he had been anything but a Rebel, I would have been ashamed of myself for my part in his fall. Captains Wyckoff and Brown received orders yesterday accepting their tenders of resignation, and have started home. Lieutenant Worley has been detached to the Signal Corps. He is worthy of it. We (the whole corps) received orders this morning to prepare for the field immediately. The order is from McPherson and says: "Not one tent will be taken into the field, only two wagons will be allowed the regiment, one for the officers and one for the cooking utensils of the men." That is coming down pretty low. Three years ago we had 13 wagons to each regiment. Two years ago eight, one year ago 'twas reduced to six, and now to two. What will it be next? Captain Sid. writes that two divisions of our corps will be left on this line of railroad to guard it this summer. I think ours and Morgan L. Smith's will probably be the two; but 'tis hard to tell. I would for my part much rather march; if we do march, I have no doubt our course will be what I have before told you, Larkin's Landing, Lebanon and Rome, Ga. They have made a change in our artillery. Two batteries now accompany each division, and the rest goes into an artillery reserve, a corps organization. You remember that I told you that the 1,500 horses we foraged in this country would be dead loss to the government. Our authorities fed them all winter, and this last week an order came to give them back to the citizens. Remember they have all been paid for. But they are of no account to the army, and 'tis the best thing that can now be done with them.

Scottsboro, Ala., April 18, 1864.

No changes to note in the military situation of our portion of Dixie, but the note of preparation is heard on every side. All making ready for the Spring campaign, which every one prophesies will be the bloodiest one of the war. Johnston is undoubtedly collecting all the Rebel troops in the West, on the Georgia Central R. R. and will have a large force. But ours will be perfectly enormous. Not one of our regiments but is stronger to-day than a year ago, and many divisions number from one-third to three-quarters more than then. Our division when we marched through from Memphis last fall was hardly 4,500 (for duty) strong. Now 'tis 7,000, and growing every day. We have no doubt of our ability to whip Johnston most completely, but if he can raise 70,000 men, and we think he can, of course somebody will stand a remarkably good chance for being hurt in the proceedings. He has crossed a division of infantry, away off on our right, beyond Elk river. 'Tis hard to tell what for. Maybe to cooperate with Forrest. Certainly to forage some, and some think

15

possibly to attract our attention in that direction while he
makes a dash on our lines east of Huntsville. This latter
would, to my idea, be akin to the action of that youth
Harper represents in his "April," standing on his head on
the railroad track, six feet before the locomotive under
way: "Rash." , Twenty-four years old yesterday, and
three years in the service. Celebrated the day by
calling on a good looking "mountain ewe," and dining there-
with. Made arrangements to have a deer and turkey hunt
with her papa and some of his friends, Colonel Cobb,
(formerly of United States Congress) among others. To
give you an idea of the Southern love for titles, I'll name
part of the citizens who help to form our party next Wednesday. Colonel Cobb, Colonel Provinse, Colonel Young,
and Majors Hall and Hust. Every man who owns as many
as two negroes is at least a colonel. None of them rank as
low as captains. Spring is coming very slowly. At least
four weeks behind time. Trees are becoming quite ver-
dant, and many of the flowers are up. I would like to send
you a few haunches of nice venison after my hunt, but
expect, all things considered, 'twould hardly be worth while
to try. Heard to-day of the wedding of one of my most
particularest friends, a young lady of Decatur. Was sensible enough to marry a soldier; but am not certain she got
the right one. Heaven help her.

Scottsboro, Ala., April 28, 1864.
We received marching orders last night, and will probably move to-morrow morning. Supposition is that we go
to Huntsville first, there store our baggage, and then cross
the Tennessee river and open the Spring campaign. I am
much pleased at the prospect of moving once more. Have
never been so well and comfortably situated in the army,
nor was I ever tired of lying still. Lieutenant Miller
R. Q. M. while hunting some mules a few miles from camp,
last Monday was captured by the enemy, and is now on his

way to the "Hotel de Libby" (not) rejoicing. 'Tis something of a joke on Miller. Weather is becoming most uncomfortably warm. Altogether too hot for marching. Boys of our regiment and troops of the whole corps, never started on a march in better spirits. Will write as often as have opportunities. Swarms of flies interfere with my afternoon naps lately.

V.

April 30, 1864 to August 24, 1864. Under marching orders at last.
"Mule Soup" and cabin smashing. Guying a Potomac general
Playing the "cousin" game on the "cits." Operations around Dalton
and Resaca. Sherman's advice and warning. Lively fighting follows. Kilpatrick wounded. Deploying in sight of the Rebel guns
with artillery duel going on overhead. Digging rifle pits fifty
yards from the enemy's lines. Resaca captured. Fight at Adairsville. Planters running off their slaves. General Harrow and his
"Potomac horse." A dead Rebel colonel in a garden of flowers.
Heavy fighting near Dallas. Sustaining a Rebel charge, losing
ten men out of thirty-one. In rifle pits under storm of shot and
shell. Logan's inspiring presence. In charge of brigade skirmish
line. Moving out from under the enemy's guns. Midnight work
in the trenches. Nine days under continuous fire. Pestered by
"chigres" and ants. Storming the Rebel rifle pits and charging a
hill manned by three Rebel regiments, killing 100 and capturing
542. Fighting three little battles in three days, and repulsing two
charges. Battle of Kenesaw Mountain. Fighting around Atlanta
and on the banks of the Chattahoochie. Desperate charge on
Rebel works across a ravine. A repulse and Colonel Wright
wounded. Great suffering from heat. Battle of Atlanta and death
of McPherson. Gruesome incident in the trenches. Summary of
the regiment's record: Battles of Vicksburg, Black River, Jackson, Mission Ridge, Dalton, Resaca, Dallas, New Hope, Big Shanty
Kennesaw Mountain and Atlanta. Seventy-two days under fire;
300 have fallen in defense of the regimental colors.

Scottsboro, Ala., April 30th, '64.

You know we have been under marching orders for several
days. At dress parade this evening orders were read notifying us that the division would move out on the road to Chattanooga at 6 a. m., May 1st.

This is the first intimation of the direction we would take.

It surprises me very much, and I think many others. I was certain we would either cross the Tennessee river at Larkins Ferry or near Decatur and take Dalton in flank or rear, but Sherman didn't see it. I would rather do anything else save one, than march over the road to Chattanooga. That one is to lie still in camp.

When the boys broke ranks after the parade, cries of "mule soup" filled the camp for an hour. That is the name that has been unanimously voted to the conglomeration of dead mules and mud that fills the ditches on the roadside between Stevenson and Chattanooga.

The whole division has been alive all evening; burning cabins has been the fashion. Captains Post, Smith and myself got into a little discussion which ended in our grabbing axes and demolishing each other's cabins.

May 1st, 1864.

Bivouac at Mud Creek. Up at daylight, and off on time, 6 a. m. The camp was full of citizens early, all after our leavings. The way they did snatch for old clothes was far from slow. They actually stole lots of trash right under the noses of the soldier owners. Out "jayhawking" old jayhawk himself. Started off in best of spirits—men cheering right from their hearts. About two miles out on the road, General Harrow and staff passed us. The men not having the fear of "guard house" in their minds, yelled at him, "Bring out your Potomac horse," "Fall back on your straw and fresh butter," "Advance on Washington," etc., all of which counts as quite a serious offense, but he paid no attention to it. You recollect he is from the Potomac Army. The first expression comes from a punishment he inaugurated in our division. He put up a wooden horse in front of his quarters, and mounted on it all the offenders against discipline that he could "gobble." Some waggish fellows wrote out some highly displayed advertisements of the "Potomac horse" and posted them throughout the camp, and finally one night the men took it down and sent it on the cars to·Huntsville, directed to McPherson, with a note tacked on it, telling him to furnish him plenty of straw and use him carefully, as he was Potomac stock and unused to hardships.

We only marched some ten miles to-day and have a splendid camping ground. Have had a wash in a mill race near by.

West bank of Crow Creek, near Stevenson,

May 2d, 1864.

Only about seven miles from last night's camp, but will have to wait until to-morrow to build a bridge. The creek is some 150 feet wide. Our Pioneer Corps will from the rough put a bridge over it in ten hours, that is to be passed over within the next three days by 800 wagons and 100 cannon of our corps. We reached here about 9 this a. m., and were led into a very large field of prairie grass, standing three feet high and as dry as tinder. A stiff breeze was blowing and the first fire started in our regiment set the grass in our front on a perfect rampage. It run down on the 46th Ohio, and such a grabbing of "traps" and scattering was never before seen, but was equaled about half an hour afterwards when a fire set in *our* rear came sweeping down on us. We threw our things out on the bare space in our front and escaped with little loss. My drummer had his coat, cap, drum and a pet squirrel burned, and a number of ponchos and small articles were also sent up in smoke. The days are almost like summer, but the nights are rather cool. The trees are about in full leaf and vermin are becoming altogether too numerous. Every man is a vigilance committee on the wood-tick question. They are worse than guerrillas or gray-backs. On an ordinary good "tick day" we capture about ten *per capita*. They demoralize one tremendously. The boys did some good work fishing in the p. m., catching a number of fine bass, etc.

A surgeon, who I think belongs on some brigade staff, has been stopping at nearly every house visiting, etc., and then rides past us to his place in front. This morning, after a visit he was passing our regiment; as we commenced crossing a little stream his horse got into a hole some four feet deep, stumbled, fell, rolled over, and liked to have finished the doctor. He was under both water and horse. The boys consoled him with a clear 1,000 cheers, groans, and sharp speeches. Anything short of death is a capital joke. I have seen them make sport of a man lying by the roadside in a fit.

Twelve miles east of Bridgeport, May 3, 1864.

Have made about 15 miles to-day. This is the fourth time I have been over the same ground, have ridden over it five times. This is the first time I ever started on a march where real judgment was used in breaking the men in. We always before made from 15 to 25 miles the first day and broke down about one-fourth of our men. This time you see, our first two day's marches were short and the 15 miles to-day seemed to affect no one. I hear from good authority here that Thomas is in Dalton, after some heavy skirmishing. Everything is moving to the front here. A portion of the 12th, or 20th Corps now, is just ahead of us. Morgan L. Smith and Osterhaus are just behind us, but Logan will not be along until relieved by some other troops.

I expect Dodge, with some 6,000 of the 16th Army Corps, is behind us. The 17th Army Corps was coming into Huntsville as we left.

Camp is in an orchard, and apples are as large as hazel nuts and we make sauce of them.

Whiteside, May 4, 1864.

The day's march has been much more pleasant than any of us expected. Most of the dead mules have been buried, and the road much improved, especially through the narrows. We smelled a number of mules, though, after all the improvements. This, Whiteside, is like Bridgeport, a portable town, with canvas covers and clapboard sides.

The boys have been catching some nice fish in a little stream by our camp this evening. Made about 15 miles to-day.

Between Chattanooga and Rossville, May 5, 1864.

It has been a very warm day, and the 16 miles between 8 a. m. and 4 p. m. counts a hard march. The dust in many places has been ankle deep.

We again crossed the point of old Lookout. I think since yesterday morning at least 20 trains loaded with troops have passed us while in sight of the railroad, with from 15 to 20 cars in each train.

We hear to-day that Dalton is not yet ours, but Sherman only waits for his old corps before attacking.

Have sent everything back to Chattanooga to store. It is estimated that we will have over 100,000 men at Dalton day after to-morrow.

Will keep a diary and send every opportunity.

Camp at "Gordon's Mills," Ga., May 6, 1864.

We lay in camp on Chattanooga creek, two and one-fourth miles this side of Chattanooga, until 11 this morning, waiting for the division train to be loaded and turning the bulk of our camp and garrison equipage over to the corps quartermaster to store for us until we return from this campaign.

We have cut our baggage for the regiment to what can be put in three wagons. Of course, we do not expect to find any of our things again that we leave. The 6th Iowa Veterans rejoined us last night. I notice that all these veterans come back dressed in officer's clothing. They have, I expect, been putting on a great many airs up North, but I don't know who has any better right. The last four miles of our march to-day has been through the west edge of the Chickamauga battlefield. I believe the battle commenced near these mills on our right.

It is supposed that we are moving to get in rear of Dalton. No more drumming allowed, so I suppose we are getting in the vicinity of Rebels, and that skirmishing will commence in about two days. The Big Crawfish springs near the mill is only second to the one that supplies Huntsville with water, neither one as large as the Tuscambia spring, but much more

Beautiful. General Harrow had a fuss with our Company A last night. He struck one or two of the men with a club and put the lieutenant (Willison) under arrest. * * * It is impossible to get along with him. We heard last night that Grant had crossed the Rapidan in four places, but don't know where. We know nothing about what is going on here, but feel certain that the Rebels will get a tremendous thrashing if they don't move promptly. Marched 11 miles to-day.

Two miles south of the Gordon's Mills crossing of

the Chickamauga,

May 7, 1864, 12 m.

We started at 8 this morning and made this by 11. We are now waiting for two or more divisions of the 16th Corps to file into the road ahead of us. I think they are coming from Ringold. A circular of McPherson's was read to us this morning before starting, telling us we were about to engage the enemy and giving us some advice about charging, meeting charges, shooting low, and telling us not to quit out lines to carry back wounded, etc., and intimating that he expected our corps to occupy a very warm place in the fight, and to sustain the fighting reputation of the troops of the department of the Tennessee.

The men talk about hoping that the divisions now going ahead will finish the fighting before we get up, but I honestly believe they'd all rather get into a battle than not. It is fun to hear these veterans talk. I guess that about two-thirds of them got married when they were home. Believe it will do much toward steadying them down when they return to their homes. They almost all say that they had furlough enough and were ready to start back when their 30 days were up.

It is hot as the deuce; two of our men were sun struck at Lookout Mountain on the 3rd.

Dust is becoming very troublesome. I am marching in a badly-fitting pair of boots, and one of my feet is badly strained across the instep, pains me a good deal when resting. That and my sprained wrist make me almost a subject for the Invalid Corps, but I intend to carry them both as far as Atlanta, after our "Erring Brethren," if I have no further bad luck. One of my men, when he rolled up his blanket this morning, found he had laid on a snake, and killed him—poor snake!

Near LaFayette, Ga., 12 m., May 7, 1864.

Have just got into camp and washed my face. Four divisions filing into the road ahead of us, delayed us five whole hours, and their trains have made us seven hours marching 8 miles. Somebody says we are 19 miles from Rome. The boys have started a new dodge on the citizens. One of my men told me of playing it last night. When we camped for the night he went to a house and inquiring about the neighbors found out one who had relatives North; and something of the family history. Then he called on this party and represented himself as belonging to the northern branch of the family, got to kiss the young lady *cousins,* had a pleasant time generally, and returned with his haversack full of knicknacks, and the pictures of his cousins, with whom he had promised to correspond. At one house on the road to-day 10 or 12 women had congregated to see the troops pass. An officer stopped at the house just as our regiment came up, and the boys commenced yelling at him, "Come out of that, Yank;" you could have heard them two miles. Never saw a man so mortified. Colonel Wright tells me we are about seven miles from the Rebels at some ridge. We will get into position to-morrow and fight next day—that is, they would, if I were not present. We camped in a "whale" of a sweet potato patch, and the boys have about dug up the seed and gobbled it.

May 8, 1864, 1:30 a. m.

Have about given up the train before daylight, so will curl down and take a cool snooze, minus blankets. Made 11 miles to-day..

Fifteen miles southwest of Dalton, May 8, 1864.

We traveled to-day over a better country than I have seen for five months; the Yanks were never seen here before. All the negroes and stock have been run off. A little shooting commenced in the front to-day, and we passed a deserted signal station and picket post. Saw some Rebels on a mountain south of us just before we went into camp. Dispatch came to Sherman this p. m. that Grant had whipped Lee three successive days. Our fight will come off to-morrow. I entertain no doubt as to the result. They have cut us down to three-quarter rations of bread and one-fourth rations of meat.

Seven miles west of Resaca, 15 miles from Dalton,

May 9, 1864.

Yesterday we traveled southeast, crossing six or seven ridges, one or two of which were quite high. Taylor's was the highest. To-day we have made only about eight miles all the way through a pass in Rocky Face ridge, which is a high mountain. There are four divisions ahead of us. A regiment of Kentucky cavalry (Rebel) slipped in between ours and the division ahead of us, trying to capture a train. The 9th Illinois Infantry had the advance of our division and killed 30 Rebels and took four prisoners, losing only one man killed and their lieutenant colonel slightly wounded. Pretty good. Dodge has got the railroad and broken it, so we hear. The fight seems to be a stand-off until to-morrow. We are in line of battle for the first time on the trip, and the ordnance train is ahead of the baggage. Just saw an officer from the front (your letter of the 3d of April received this minute); he says Dodge is within a mile of Resaca, and driving the enemy, and will have the town by dark. Has not cut the railroad yet. This officer saw a train arrive from Dalton, with some 2,500 Rebel troops aboard. McPherson and Logan are both on the field. Some Rebel prisoners taken to-day say they intend making this a Chickamauga to us. Have a nice camp. There is some little forage here, but it is nothing for the number of troops we have.

Same camp, May 10, 1864.

The 9th Illinois Infantry lost about 30 men, killed, wounded and missing, yesterday. We find the enemy too strong on the railroad to take, but have succeeded in breaking it so no trains can pass. Gerry's division, of the 20th Corps, came up at dark, and the rest of the corps is within supporting distance. Rations were issued to us this evening—one-ninth rations of meat for three days just made a breakfast for the men. More rumors are flying than would fill a ream of foolscap. We had orders this p .m. to march to the front at 2 p. m., but did not go.

Six miles from Resaca, May 11, 1864.

We had a real hurricane last night, and a tremendous rain-storm. We lay right in the woods, and of course thought of the Point Pleasant storm and falling trees, but were too lazy to move, and thanks to a bed of pine boughs, slept good and sound. There is a scare up this morning. We have moved a mile toward the front, and building breast-works is going on with the greatest life. A full 1,000 axes are ringing within hearing. Our division is drawn up in column by brigade and at least another division is in rear of us. The latest rumor is that "the railroad has surrendered with 40,000 depots,"

May 12th.—We are in just such a camp as I was in once near Jacinto, Miss. Hills, hollows and splendid pines. Pine knots can be picked up by the bushel, and the pitch smoke will soon enable us to pass for members of the "Corps d'Afrique." I am perfectly disgusted with this whole business. Everything I have written down I have had from the Division Staff, and that without pumping. I am beginning to believe that there is no enemy anywhere in the vicinity, and that we are nowhere ourselves, and am sure that the generals do not let the staff of our division know anything. The railroad was not cut at daylight this morning, for I heard a train whistle and rattle along it. I do know for certain that we are putting up some huge works here, and that they run from mountain to mountain across this gorge.

Still in Snake Creek Gap, May 13, 1864.

Moved forward a half mile and our regiment built a strong line of log works. We have had a perfect rush of generals along the line to-day: Hooker, Sickles, McPherson, Thomas, Palmer, Sherman and a dozen of smaller fry. The boys crowded around Sherman and he could not help hearing such expressions as "Where's Pap?" "Let's see old Pap," etc., nor could he help laughing, either. The men think more of Sherman than of any general who ever commanded them, but they did not cheer him. I never heard a general cheered in my life, as he rode the lines. Sherman said in hearing of 50 men of our regiment, "Take it easy to-day, for you will have work enough to-morrow. It will be quick done though." Now see what that means.

May 14, 1864.

Reveille at 3 a. m. and an order has just come to leave all our knapsacks and move at 7 a. m. Great hospital preparations are going on in our rear. I think we are going to take the railroad and Resaca. Large reinforcements came last night. Could hear the Rebels running trains all night. Ten-thirty a. m.—Have moved forward about four miles. Saw General Kilpatrick laying in an ambulance by the roadside. He was wounded in the leg this morning in a skirmish. Met a number of men—wounded—moving to the rear, and a dozen or so dead horses, all shot this morning. Quite lively skirmishing is going on now about 200 yards in front of us.

One forty-five p. m.—Moved about 200 yards to the front and brought on brisk firing.

Two thirty-five.—While moving by the flank shell commenced raining down on us very rapidly; half a dozen burst within 25 yards of us. The major's horse was shot and I think he was wounded. In the regiment one gun and one hat was struck in my company. Don't think the major is wounded very badly.

Three thirty p. m.—Corporal Slater of my company just caught a piece of shell the size of a walnut in his haversack.

Four p. m.—Colonel Dickerman has just rejoined the regiment. We would have given him three cheers if it had not been ordered otherwise.

Five p. m.—Have moved forward about a mile and a real battle is now going on in our front. Most of the artillery is farther to the right, and it fairly makes the ground tremble. Every breath smells very powderish. A battery has just opened close to the right of our regiment. I tell you this is interesting. Our regiment is not engaged yet, but we are in sight of the Rebels and their bullets whistle over our heads. The men are all in good spirits.

Eight p. m.—A few minutes after six I was ordered to deploy my company as skirmishers and relieve the 1st Brigade who were in our front. We shot with the Rebels until dark, and have just been relieved. One company of the 12th Indiana who occupied the ground we have just left, lost their captain and 30 men killed and wounded in sight of us. The Rebels are making the axes fly in our front. The skirmish lines are about 200 yards apart. I have had no men wounded to-day. Dorrance returned to the company this evening.

May 14, 1864, Daylight.

We have just been in line and the intention was to charge the Rebel position, but two batteries were discovered in front of us. The skirmishers advanced a little and brought down a heavy fire. A battery is now getting into position in our front, right in front of our company, and when it opens I expect we will have another rain of shell from the Rebels.

Nine thirty-five a. m.—Our battery has opened, but the Rebels cannot reply. Four of their guns are in plain sight of us, but our brigade skirmishers have crawled up so close that not a Rebel dare load one of them. Joke on them! One of my men was struck on the foot while talking to me a few minutes ago. Made a blue spot, but did not break the skin.

Eleven forty-five a. m.—I think our regiment has not had more than six or eight wounded this morning. Very heavy musketry firing is going on on our left. It is the 14th Corps.

Two p. m.—Since 1 p. m. terrific artillery and musketry firing has been going on on our left. The enemy was massing against the 14th A. C. when Thomas attacked them. I think he drove them some distance.

Two thirty p. m.—My company is ordered to be deployed and sent down the hill to support skirmishers. We are in position, very lively firing is going on.

Five p. m.—A splendid artillery duel is going on right over my head. The Rebel battery is just across an open field, not 600 yards, and one of ours is a short 100 yards in my rear. Osterhaus a half mile on our right is playing on the same battery. Thomas is still fighting heavily. He seems to be turning their right or forcing it back. Every time the Rebels fire our skirmishers just more than let them have the bullets. I tell you this is the most exciting show I ever saw. Their battery is right in the edge of the woods, but so masked that we can't see it, or wouldn't let them load. I write under cover of a stump which a dead man of the 26th Indiana shares with me.

Eight p. m.—Just relieved; I lost no men. The fighting on the left was Hooker and Howard, and was very heavy.

May 15, 1864, 1:30 a. m.

At 11 p. m. went again on the skirmish line with Captain Post and superintended the construction of rifle pits for our skirmishers. A good deal of fun between our boys and the Rebels talking only 50 yards apart.

Five thirty a. m.—At 3 a. m. moved and are now supporting Osterhaus, who is going to charge the railroad. Will see fighting this morning.

Nine a. m.—The skirmishers are fighting briskly. Osterhaus' artillery is on both sides and behind us. Sherman has just passed us to the front. When we first came here about daylight the Rebels charged our folks on the hill ahead, but were repulsed without our assistance. McPherson is now passing. Osterhaus gained that hill last night by a charge, losing about 200 men in the operation. From a hill 50 yards from our position I can see the Rebel fort at Resaca and Rebels in abundance. It is not a mile distant.

One thirty p. m.—Our artillery is beginning to open on them. One man was killed and two wounded within 40 yards of the regiment by Rebel sharpshooters.

Seven p. m.—No charge yet to-day, but has been heavy fighting on the left. I have seen, this evening, Rebel trains moving in all directions. We have a good view of all their works.

May 16, 1864, 6 p. m.

The old story—the Rebels evacuated last night. They made two or three big feints of attacking during the night, but are all gone this morning. It is said they have taken up a position some five miles ahead. Prisoners and deserters are coming in. At Resaca we captured eight cannon, not more than 100 prisoners, and some provisions; don't know what we got at Dalton. Some estimate our whole loss up to this time at 2,500 killed and wounded. Everything is getting the road for pursuit. The prisoners say Johnston will make a stand 40 miles south.

Six p. m.—The 16th Corps moved out on the Rome road, and while we are waiting for the 14th Corps to get out of our way word came that the 16th had run against a snag. We were moved out at once at nearly double quick time to help them. Trotted four miles and passed a good many wounded, but we were not needed. We bivouac to-night on the southeast bank of Coosa river. I hear to-night that our loss in the corps is 600 and that no corps has suffered less than ours. Some think the whole will foot over 5,000.

May 17, 1864, 10 a. m.

Our regiment moves in rear of the division to-day and we are still waiting for the trains to pass. We can hear firing in front occasionally, and although we have seen fighting enough to satisfy us for a time, still it's more disagreeable to be away in the rear and hearing, but not knowing what's going on, than to be in the field. I saw several hundred Rebel prisoners yesterday, among then one colonel. The country is much more level this side of the Coosa, but the pine woods spoil it. Our advance, from the faint sound of the artillery firing, must be seven or eight miles ahead. We will make it very warm for Johnston.

Ten p. m.—Have just got into camp, made 12 miles to-day. Heavy firing on our left, which I hear is a division of Howard's Corps.

May 18, 1864.

Our division has had the advance to-day, but no infantry fighting. At noon we get into Adairsville and meet the 4th Army Corps. Saw Generals Howard, Thomas, Sickles and a hundred others. We are camped five miles southwest of town and by the prettiest place I ever saw. The house is excellent, the grounds excel in beauty anything I ever imagined. The occupants have run away. Our cavalry had a sharp fight here this p. m., and on one of the gravel walks in the beautiful garden lies a Rebel colonel, shot in five places. He must have been a noble looking man; looks 50 years old, and has a fine form and features. Think his name is Irwin. I think there must be a hundred varieties of the rose in bloom here and the most splendid specimens of cactus. I do wish you could see it. At Adairsville, night before last, we lost 400 killed and wounded in a skirmish.

16

Nine a. m.—Rapid artillery firing on our left front. We are waiting for Osterhaus and Morgan L. Smith to get out of the way. Our division has the rear to-day. Our cars got into Adairsville yesterday evening and the last Rebel train left in the morning. Firing on the left very heavy.

Kingston, Cass County, Ga., May 19, 1864, 5 p. m.

The artillery has been working all day, but have not heard how much of a fight. That dead Rebel colonel was Iverson, of the Second Georgia Cavalry; we think he was formerly a M. C. of this State, and a secessionist. The citizens here have most all left the towns, but are nearly all at home in the country. The cavalry had sharp fighting in the road we have come over to-day. Many dead horses and a number of fresh graves by the roadside. I wish I was in the cavalry. This plodding along afoot is dry business, compared with horse-back traveling. I hear this morning that Wilder's mounted infantry captured two cannons and 600 Rebels this afternoon. Also that 6,000 prisoners were yesterday started from Dalton for the North.

Kingston, May 20, 1864.

Our cars got here this morning; the whistle woke me. One of the most improbable rumors afloat is that letters will be allowed to go North to-day. I know you are anxious, so will not lose the rumor of a chance. Billy Fox returned to-day. My things are all right at Chattanooga. I'm in excellent health and all right every way. The news from Grant encourages us very much, but if he gets whipped it won't keep us from whaling Johnston. We're now about 50 miles from Atlanta. Will probably take a day or two here to replenish the supply trains, and let the men recruit a little after their twenty-day march; don't know anything about Johnston; it is not thought he will give us a fight near here.

May 21, 1864.

The 23d Army Corps moved South yesterday. I hear that they found the enemy on the south bank of the Etowah river, and that he disputes the crossing. Grant seems to be checked in his "on to Richmond." It seems that Rebel Iverson, whom I saw dead near Adairsville, was a brigadier general and a son of the ex-Congressman. This Kingston has been a gem of a little town, but the Rebels burned most of it when they left. Our railroad men are very enterprising. The cars got here the same night we did, and a dozen or 20 trains are coming per day, all loaded inside with commissary stores and outside with soldiers.

May 22, 1864.

Two regiments of three-year's men who did not "veteran" started home to-day. The loss of the army in this way will not be much. Not more than one or two regiments in any corps refused to veteran. We are drawing 20 days' rations, sending sick back to convalescent camp at Chattanooga, and making all preparations for a hard campaign.

Four miles northwest of Van Wirt, Ga.,

May 23, 1864.

Weather is getting very hot. We have made 21 miles to-day, and the distance, heat and dust have made it by far the hardest march we have had for a year. Excepting about six miles of dense pine woods the country we have passed through has been beautiful, quite rolling, but fertile and well improved. In the midst of the pine woods we stopped to rest at Hollis' Mill, a sweet looking little 17-year old lady here told me she was and always had been Union, and that nearly all the poor folks here are Union. In answer to some questions about the roads and country, she said, "Well, now, I was born and raised right here, and never was anywhere, and never see anybody, and I just don't know anything at all."

I never saw so many stragglers as to-day. For 12 miles no water was to be had; then we came to a spring, a very large one, say 4 or 5 hogsheads a minute. All the officers in the army could not have kept the men in ranks. Saw no cases of sunstroke, but two of my men from heat turned blue with rush of blood to the head, and had to leave the ranks. Some think we are moving on Montgomery, Ala. Our orders say we need not hope for railroad communications for 20 days; I think that Atlanta is our point, although we were 50 miles from there this morning and 60 to-night. The planters in this country own thousands of negroes, and they've run them all off down this road. They are about two days ahead of us, and the poor people say as thick on the road as we are. Have passed several to-day who escaped from their masters.

Four miles southeast of Van Wirt, Ga.,

May 24, 1864.

Short march to-day—because it is a full day's march from here to water. At Van Wirt we turned east on the Atlanta road. Will pass through Dallas to-morrow. My company was rear guard to-day for the brigade. One of my men spilled a kettle of boiling coffee last night, filling his shoe. All the skin on the top of his foot that did not come off with the socks is in horrible blisters. The surgeon said he would have to march, and he has, all day, don't that seem rather hard? You remember how I used to detest fat meat? If I didn't eat a pound of raw pickled pork to-day for dinner, shoot me. Things don't go nearly as well as on the march from Memphis. 'Tis much harder, though we don't make as many miles per day. One reason is the weather is much warmer, and another thing, each division then marched independently, and now all three of them camp together every night. Dorrance is nearly sick to-night. I thought I heard some artillery firing this morning, but guess I was mistaken. The cavalry report they have not found any force of Rebels yesterday or to-day. Small-pox has broken out in the 6th Iowa—some 20 cases.

Pumpkin Vine Creek, near Dallas, Ga.,

May 26, 1864, 8 a. m.

We did not make more than seven or eight miles yesterday, on account of some bad road that troubled the trains very much. We got into camp at dark, just as a thunderstorm broke. We hurried up our arrangements for the night—kicking out a level place on the hillside to sleep—gathering pine boughs to keep the water from washing us away, and spreading our rubbers over rail frames. Everything just finished, was just pulling our stock of bed clothes over me (one rubber coat), when the brigade bugle sounded the "assembly." It was dark as pitch and raining far from gently—no use grumbling—so everybody commenced yelping, singing, or laughing. In ten minutes we were under way, and though we didn't move a mile, every man who didn't tumble half a dozen times would command good wages in a circus. We finally formed line of battle on a bushy hillside, and I dropped down on the wet leaves and slept soundly until 1 o'clock, and woke up wet and half frozen, took up my bed and made for a fire and dried out. Do you remember the case when the Saviour commanded a convalescent to take up his bed and walk? I always pitied that man, carrying a four-post bedstead, feathers, straw and covering and failed to see it, but if he had no more bedding than I had. I can better understand it. Heavy cannonading all the p. m. yesterday. It seemed some five or six miles east; don't understand the way matters are shaping at all. Sherman has such a way of keeping everything to himself. The country between Van Wirt and Dallas is very rough, but little of it under cultivation; along this creek are some nice looking farms. The Rebels were going to make a stand, but didn't.

Two p. m.—We started at 8 this morning, and have not made more than one and one-half miles. Soldiers from the front say that Hardee's Corps fronts us two miles ahead, and that he proposes to fight. I have heard no firing that near this morning, but have heard artillery eight or ten miles east. A number of prisoners have been sent back, who all report Hardee at

Dallas. I think Thomas now joins our left. McPherson last night rode up to some Rebel pickets, who saluted him with a shower of hot lead, fortunately missing him. Osterhaus' commissary drives along a lot of cattle for the division. Last night he got off the road and drove them into a party of secesh, who took commissary, beef and all. Back at Kingston, a big box came to General Harrow with heavy express charges. An ambulance hauled it 20 miles before it caught up with him, and on opening it he found a lot of stones, a horse's tail, and a block of wood with a horses' face pinned on it labeled, "head and tail of your Potomac horse." At Van Wirt before we got there the Rebels had a celebration over Lee's capturing Grant and half of his army. There's a great deal of ague in the regiment. We will have a great deal of sickness after the campaign closes. I have only seen one man at home in Georgia who looked capable of doing duty as a soldier. My health is excellent. This creek runs into the Talladega river.

One mile south of Dallas, 2 p. m.

After a lively skirmishing Jeff C. Davis' division of the 14th Army Corps occupied Dallas at 2 p. m. The Rebels retired stubbornly. We passed Dallas about dark, and are now the front and extreme right of the whole army. I guess fighting is over for the night. Two very lively little fights have occurred before dark. The heavy fighting yesterday was Hooker. He whipped and drove them four miles, taking their wounded.

Near Dallas, Ga., May 27, 1864, 8 a. m.

There has been some very heavy fighting on our left this morning, and everywhere along the line. We have been moving in line since 6 o'clock, supporting skirmishers and the 3d Brigade. Have driven the Rebels about three-quarters of a mile. The 14th Corps must have had a severe fight about 6:30. The bullets have whistled pretty thick this a. m.

Skirmish line, 11 a. m.—Osterhaus and Smith (I think), have just had a big fight on our left. At 8:30 I was ordered

to take Companies E, K, B and G, deploy them and relieve the
3d Brigade skirmishers. Deployed and moved forward over
one-half mile through the very densest brush—couldn't see
six feet, expecting every minute to find the 3d Brigade skirmishers, but they had been drawn in, and we were right into the
Rebels before we saw them. Three of my company were
wounded in an instant and three of K's taken prisoner, but
our boys made the Rebels skedaddle, and all of them got away.
Twenty-one Rebels came up in rear of Captain Smith and
two of his men. Private Benson shot one of them, and Smith
roared out for the rest to surrender, which they did. They
(Rebels) said they would not have been taken if the Georgia
brigade had not fallen back. I think that is doing pretty well
for four companies of our regiment, running a whole brigade.
Firing is very heavy all around us.

Twelve thirty m.—A chunk of Rebel shell lit 15 feet from
me. Lively artillery firing right over head.

Four p. m.—At 2:15, after firing a few shells, the Rebels
set up a yell along our whole front. I knew a charge was
coming. At 2:30 another yell was much nearer. My men
then commenced firing on them, but they came on yelling
pretty well, but not as heartily as I have heard. They came
jumping along through the brush more then, making the
bullets rain among us. I think they could not fly much thicker.
My men did nobly, but they were too many for us, and we had
to fall back. I heard their officers halloo to them, "to yell and
stand steady," and they were right amongst us before we left.
Our line of battle checked them and made them run. I lost
A. Huffard—killed; Seth Williams—died in two hours; Wm.
Gustine—severely wounded; E. Suydam—ditto; S. Hudson—
ditto; H. Stearns—slight wound; J. H. Craig—ditto; F. Cary
—ditto; W. Roberts—ditto; W. G. Dunblazier— captured.

Seven p. m.—I tell you this was exciting. My men all stood
like heroes (save one), and some of them did not fall back
when I wanted them to. The bush was so thick that we could
hardly get through in any kind of line. Gustine and Suydam

were about 20 feet on my left when they were shot, but I couldn't see them. The Rebels were not 15 feet from them. I had 31 men on the line, and nine killed and wounded, and one prisoner, is considerable of a loss. They took six more of Company K prisoners, but three of them got off. I don't think anyone can imagine how exciting such a fracas as that is in thick brush. As quick as our line started the Rebels running, I went back on the ground, and found a lot of dead and wounded Rebels. Every prisoner of the 20th Georgia had whiskey in his canteen, and all said they had all issued to them that they wanted. I never say such a dirty, greasy, set of mortals. They have had no rest since they left Dalton. On account of my skirmishers losing so heavily, we have been relieved from the line, and are now in rifle pits, and are supporting those who relieved us.

May 28, 1864, 9 a. m.

Still in rifle pits. We have been treated to a terrific storm of shells, spherical case, and solid shot. The batteries are in plain sight of each other, and the gunners call it a thousand yards between them. I don't think either battery does very fine work, but they make it more than interesting for us. A conical shell from a 12 pound gun passed through a log and struck a Company C man on the leg, only bruising him. Two solid shot fell in my company works, but hurt no one. Seven p. m.—Talk about fighting, etc., we've seen it this p. m. sure, of all the interesting and exciting times on record this must take the palm. At about 3:45 p. m., a heavy column of Rebels rose from a brush with a yell the devil ought to copyright, broke for and took three guns of the 1st Iowa Battery which were in front of the works (they never should have been placed there); the 6th Iowa boys, without orders, charged the Rebels, retook the battery and drove them back. They came down on our whole line, both ours and the 16th A. C., and for two hours attempted to drive us out. We repulsed them at every point without serious loss to us, but I believe they are at least 3,000 men short. In our brigade Colonel Dickerman, Lieutenant Colonel 6th Iowa commanding, and Major Gilsey, commanding 46th Ohio, are wounded. Besides these I don't think our brigade lost over 80. It was a grand thing. I did not lose a man and only three companies of our regiment lost any. When the musketry was playing the hottest, Logan came dashing up along our line, waved his hat and told the boys to "give them hell, boys." You should have heard them cheer him. It is Hardee's Corps fighting us, and he promised his men a "Chickamauga," but it turned out a "Bull Run" on their part. It is the same corps our regiment fought at Mission Ridge. Our line is very thin along here, but guess we can save it now. I heard a 40th boy get off an oddity this evening, he said: "If they come again, I am going to yell if there's any danger of their taking us, 'Worlds by Nation Right into line Wheel!' and if that don't scare them, I propose going."

May 29, 1864, 4 p. m.

Have been in the rifle pits all day. We're now expecting a charge from the Rebels, that is, our division commander is. I think they will lose an immense sight of men if they attempt it. News to-day of Davis moving his capital to Columbia, S. C., and of Grant driving Lee across the Savannah River.

Monday, May 30, 1864.

At dark last night I was put in charge of our brigade skirmish line of four companies; by 9:30 I had everything arranged to our notion. About that time the musketry commenced fire on our left and continued for a half hour; it was very heavy. Some three or four pieces of artillery also opened on our side. That thing was repeated eight times during the night, the last fight being just before daylight. When I was down on the right of the line I could hear the Rebels talking about the fight and saying it was a mighty hard one, and "I wonder whether our

men or the Yanks are getting the best of it." These night
fights are very grand. I understand this fighting occurred
between Hooker and the "Johnnies." Attacks were made
by each side, repulses easy. I guess from what little I hear
there was a good deal more shooting than hitting on both
sides. I think it was the intention for us to move to the
left last night, but so much fighting prevented it. I don't
know when I have been so used up as this morning, and
the whole command is not far from the same condition,
but a few hours' sleep made me all right again this morning. The Rebels are much more tired than we; they have
had no rest since leaving Dalton. One of their wounded,
a captain, told me that one of their surgeons told him their
loss since leaving Dalton in killed and wounded would
amount to 25,000. That's pretty strong, the third of it or
10,000 I could believe. I was relieved at dark to-day from
skirmishing duty.

May 31, 1864.

Generals Sherman, McPherson, Logan and Barry visited
our position yesterday. Sherman looks very well. Logan
smiled and bowed in return to my salute as though he
recognized me. During the fight of the 28th I was standing, when he was riding along our lines on the inside of the
rifle pits (with a hatful of ammunition), just over my men.
He stopped by me and said: "It's all right, damn it, isn't
it?" I returned: "It's all right, General." The Rebels
were quite busy last night running troops and artillery
along our front both ways. Some think they planted a
number of guns opposite us. I hear some of the officers
talking as though a fight was expected to-day. Their
sharpshooters are making it quite warm here this morning;
several men have been struck, but none hurt seriously.

Seven p. m.—The Rebels have just finished throwing 126
shells at us, only 19 of which bursted. We expected they
would follow it with a charge, but they hardly will attempt

it this late. I think we have lost none to-day in the regiment. Their shell hurt no one. Logan was slightly wounded in the arm yesterday. Colonel Dickerman died this morning.

Five miles west of Acworth,

June 1, 1864.

At daylight this morning we left our position on the right and moved over here, six or seven miles, and relieved Hooker's 20th Corps, which moved around to the left. It was ticklish business moving out from under at least 30 of the enemy's guns, and we did it *very quietly*. They did not suspect it. We are now within 90 yards of the Rebel works, and the shooting is very lively. Only one of our regiment wounded to-day. I would much rather be here than where we were, for there they shot at us square from three sides, and here they can but from one front. This is dense woods and the ground between our works nearly level. There are two lines of works here, 30 yards apart; we occupy the rear works to-day, but will relieve the 6th Iowa to-morrow and take the front. This is the ground that Hooker had his big fight on on the 25th of May. He lost some 2,000 men killed and wounded. The woods are all torn up with canister, shell and shot, and bloody shoes, clothing and accoutrements are thick.

June 2, 1864.

The 40th Illinois returned to-day, and I was right glad to see them back. We have lost no men to-day. The 17th Army Corps is beginning to come in. We advanced our works last night, commencing a new line in front of our regiment. The Rebels didn't fire at us once, though they might as well killed some one as not. Colonel Wright and ten men picked out the ground and then I took a detail and went to work. By daylight we had enough of rifle pit to cover 50 men and had the men in it. I tell you it waked them up when our boys opened upon them. This is getting on the Vicksburg order. The troops are in splendid spirits and everything is going on as well as could be wished. I think this thing will be brought to a focus in a few days.

June 3, 1864.

Relieved the 6th Iowa at 6:30 this a. m. The Rebels shoot pretty close. Killed Orderly Sergeant of Company I, (VanSycle), and wounded three men in our regiment to-day. This makes 50 in killed, wounded and prisoners, or one in every six.

June 4, 1864.

We have had a good deal of fun to-day. The firing has been brisker than usual on account of our advancing our works. We got up a mock charge this afternoon, which came pretty near scaring the Rebel skirmishers out of their boots and made a good deal of fun for us. Our regiment is on fatigue duty. We are working within 80 yards of the Rebel works. They cut a Company C man's finger off when he raised his pick to-day. Another of our men was shot in the face. I, with my company, work from 12 to-night until three in the morning.

June 5, 1864.

The Rebels run last night. Everything gone this morning slick and clean. Our regiment was the first in their works. I was over their works to-day and find three lines, two of them very strong. A number of dead men, lay beween their lines and ours, which neither side could bury. They were killed during Hooker's fight of May 25th.

Well, I expect another heat like this at the Chattahochie river and when we get them out of there, as we are bound to do, ho! for easy times!

My health continues excellent, and I hope it will until this campaign is over. I am making up for some of my easy times soldiering. The Rebels were awful dirty and the smell in their camps dreadful.

We got some 25 prisoners in front of our division. I think one more big stand will wind the thing up. They made no noise whatever in getting away. I was from 12 to 3 o'clock in the night working within 75 yards of them and did not hear them at all. At one place their works ran through a graveyard, and they had torn down all the palings inclosing graves, to make beds for themselves, and unnecessarily destroyed everything of beauty around. I am sure we would not have done so in our own country, and *I* would not anywhere. I don't give these Rebels half the credit for humanity or any of the qualities civilized beings should possess, that I used to. I estimate loss of our army here at 7,000—killed, wounded and missing. It may be more. Heavy reinforcements are arriving though, and the strength of the army is much greater than at any time heretofore. Spirits excellent. I could tell some awful stories of dead men, but forbear. We moved at 9 a. m. about four and one-half miles toward the railroad and have gone into camp for the night.

This is the first day since May 26th that I have been out of the range of Rebel guns, and hardly an hour of that time that the bullets have not been whistling and thumping around. I tell you it is a strain on a man's nerves, but like everything else that hurts, one feels better when he gets over it.

June 6, 1864.

I will try and send you this to-day. Our postmaster never calls for letters, though we could send them if he would. I will try hereafter to send oftener, though you must not feel anxious about me. I will take the best care I can of myself (and do my whole duty). I yet think that to be connected with such a campaign as this is well worth risking one's life for. It occasionally gets a little *old,* but so does everything in this life, and altogether I don't know but that it wears as well as any of life's pleasures. Do you remember when I

was at home how little I knew about good eatables? Here
it is a great advantage to me. For five weeks we have been
living on "hard tack," pickled pork and coffee, varied by not
half a dozen meals of beef, not even beans or rice. Nearly
every one grumbles, but I have as yet felt no loss of appetite,
and hardly the desire for a change.

Nearly all the prisoners we capture say they are done fighting and shamefully say, many of them, that if exchanged and
put back in the ranks they will shirk rather than fight. It
would mortify me very much if I thought any of our men
that they captured would talk so. It seems to me that the
Confederacy is only held together by its officers exercising at
least the power of a Czar, and that should we leave it to itself
it would crumble. Well, I am calculating that this campaign
will end about the 15th of July, in Atlanta. I cannot hope
for a leave of absence again until my time is out, unless I
resign, and if active campaigning continues, as some think it
will, until the war is over, of course I will have no chance to
do the latter. Cousin James is near me here, and I expect
to see him soon.

Passed Charlie Maple on the road yesterday; also saw Cleg-
get Birney. He is a splendid looking boy. *They say* the 7th
Cavalry will soon be here; also the 8th Illinois. I will try to
write you every week hereafter.

One mile South of Ackworth, June 16, 1864.

We moved through town and arrived here this p. m. Ackworth is a nice little town. All the *"ton"* have moved south.

We will lay here two days, and then for Atlanta again. I
was out of provisions all day yesterday, and when I got a
supply last night filled up to suffocation, but feel splendidly
to-day. They credit a prisoner with saying that Sherman will
never go to hell, for he'll flank the devil and make heaven in
spite of all the guards. The army is in glorious spirits. I
hope the next time to date from Atlanta, but can hardly hope
that for three weeks yet.

Same place, June 7, 1864.

Our brigade has to-day been on a reconnoisance, supporting Girard's (formerly Kilpatrick's) Cavalry Division.

We started the Johnnies not more than a mile from here, and skirmished with them, driving them to the Kenesaw range of mountains, about five miles. Our brigade lost nothing. Wilder's mounted infantry did the skirmishing and had some eight to ten wounded. Four dead Rebels fell into our hands. Cousin James called on me yesterday. I am much pleased with him. He is a No. 1 soldier, I know. He has run some pretty close risks this campaign, but who would not for the sake of taking part in it? I shall always think it abundantly worth risking one's life for. To-morrow night we can tell whether the enemy intends fighting us at this place or not. They left on the field to-day a dozen or twenty real lances. They are the first I ever saw in the service. The staff is eight or nine feet long with a pointed head of ten inches in length. They were a right plucky set of Johnnies.

Our battery burst a shell over the edge of a piece of woods and I saw some 20 Rebels scatter like a lot of scared rats.

Near Big Shanty, Ga., June 10, 1864.

Army moved this a. m. Found the enemy again at this place, and have been in line of battle a dozen times, more or less. Our brigade is in reserve for the rest of the division. This is the Kenesaw Mountain; from the top of one peak the Rebels could see probably 25,000 Yanks. Some ladies were there in sight observing us. We are to-night in a dense wood some three-quarters of a mile southwest of the main road. The enemy does not seem to be close in our immediate front, but there is considerable firing about a brigade to our right. General Sherman's staff say that a general fight is not expected here. A. J. Smith is starting for Mobile from Vicksburg. That's glorious. We to-day heard of the nomination at Baltimore of Lincoln and Johnson. Very glad that Lincoln is renominated, but it don't make any excitement in the army. The unanimity of the convention does us more good than anything else. I received a letter from Gen. "Dick" (Oglesby) last night. He is much pleased with his nomination and has no doubt of his success. Neither have I. If we had the privilege the whole Illinois army would vote for him.

We are having a good deal of rain, say about 6 hard showers a day. The roads are badly cut up. The hour or two hours sun between showers makes the men all right. The Rebels have no oilcloths and must be troubled with so much rain.

June 11, 1864.

Colonel Wright and I rode out to the front to-day. The Johnnies are about one and one-half miles from us, and occupying what looks like a very strong position. Rumor says that Sherman has said that he can force them to leave here any moment, but will wait for supplies and the roads to dry up. The cars got to Big Shanty about noon to-day, and indulged in a long and hilarious shriek. The Rebel locomotive about two miles further down the road answered with a yell of defiance.

I *hear* to-day that the 23d Corps took 2,000 prisoners and two cannon. I guess its yes. Rosencrans is actually coming, *they say*. I don't think we need him. Sherman moves very cautiously, and everybody feels the utmost confidence in him. I saw him yesterday—seems to me he is getting fleshy. He don't look as though he had anything more important than a 40-acre farm to attend to.

It has rained almost all day. You musn't expect me to write anything but military now, for it is about all we think of.

June 12, 1864.

It commenced raining before daylight, and has not ceased an instant all day. We are lucky in the roads where it can't get very muddy, but so much rain is confoundedly disagreeable. The only source of consolation is the knowledge that the Rebels fare much worse than we do. They have neither tents nor oilcloths. For once our corps is in reserve. The 16th and 17th united their lines in front of us this morning. The 17th A. C. especially is using ammunition with a looseness. They are just getting their hands in. The rain is real cold. If it were not for hearing the musketry and artillery firing we wouldn't know there was an enemy within 50 miles. This is said to be the Georgia gold country. I could just pick up some beautiful specimens of quartz and a flinty stone (maybe quartz also) in which the isinglass shines, and in some places I have picked off sheets two inches square. No forage here. Four deserters came in to-day.

They say that Johnston had an order read to his troops that Wheeler had cut the railroad in our rear, and destroyed our supply trains. The troops all cheered it heartily, but hardly had they got their mouths shut when our locomotives came whistling into Big Shanty, one mile from their lines. The deserters say it disgusted them so much they concluded they'd quit and go home. I wish Sherman would attack them now, for we would be sure to get what trains and artillery they have here.

June 13, 1864.

The rain continued until 5 p. m. Everything and everybody thoroughly soaked. Our division moved about one-half mile to the left this p. m. Strategy! We moved out into an open ploughed field. You can imagine the amount of comfort one could enjoy so situated, after two days' constant rain, and the water still coming down in sheets.

The field is trodden into a bed of mortar. No one has ventured a guess of the depth of the mud. It is cold enough for fires and overcoats. My finger nails are as blue as if I had the ague. There is one consolation to be drawn from the cold, it stops the "chigres" from biting us. I would rather have a bushel of fleas and a million of mosquitoes on me than a pint of "chigres,"—don't know the orthography—They are a little bit of a red thing,—just an atom bigger than nothing; they burrow into the skin and

17

cause an itching that beats the regular "camp" all hollow. Some of the men have scars from "chigre" bites that they received at Big Black last summer, and will carry them across the Styx. The ants here also have an affinity for human flesh and are continually reconnoitering us. I kill about 200,000 per day. Also knock some 600 worms off of me. Great country this for small vermin. I pick enough entomological specimens off me every day to start a museum. I do manage to keep clear of greybacks, though.

Every time I commence talking about chigres I feel short of language. I am satisfied of one thing, if my finger nails don't wear out, there'll be no flesh left on my bones by autumn. The case stands finger nails vs. chigres, and skin is the sufferer. Notwithstanding rain, cold or chigres, we are in excellent spirits. Sherman don't tell us anything (in orders) good or bad, but every man feels that we have "a goodly thing" and is content to work and wait. I never heard less complaining, or saw troops in better spirits. If we get to Atlanta in a week all right; if it takes us two months you won't hear this army grumble. We know that "Pap" is running the machine and our confidence in him is unbounded.

We have so far had abundance of rations, but if it comes down to half, we will again say "all right." Our army is stronger to-day than it ever was in numbers and efficiency. I am sure that there is not a demoralized company in the command. There has been considerable shooting along the front to-day, and the lines have been advanced some, but we are nearly a mile back, and being constantly ready to move. I have not been out, and don't know much about the exact situation. Its something new for our division to be in reserve. Time passes much more quickly in the front. The general opinion is that we are gradually working to the left, and will cross the Chattahoochie about east or northeast of Marietta. We are now 26 miles from Atlanta by railroad and something nearer by pike.

June 14, 1864.

Four officers and 28 men deserted from the Rebels last night. The Rebel captain told one of my corporals that in their brigade there is an organization the members of which avow it their purpose to desert the first opportunity. These men are satisfied the game is up with them, and give it as their reason for deserting. They say the whole brigade will come as opportunity offers. Lively artillery firing in front of us this morning. We hear that Grant has pushed Lee to his fortifications at Richmond. Suppose the report will be, Grant will cut his communications south and west and Lee will evacuate. I see the papers have us across the Chattahoochie, away south of the railroad. Of course that is a poor article of gas from our sensational correspondent in the far rear.

It looks to me as if the Rebels have a very strong position in front of us now, but I may be mistaken. We have been quietly laying in camp all day. I must credit Georgia with one pleasant June day, that is not too warm. There has been the usual amount of firing to-day, though few hurt.

June 15, 1864.

This has been a star day, and a better feeling lot of men that compose our brigade will be hard to find, for to-night any way. The morning was occupied in cleaning guns, etc. At 11 o'clock the assembly was sounded, and we moved one and one-half miles, which brought us on the left of the whole army. By 1 p. m. we had our line formed running from right to left, 103d Illinois, 6th Iowa, 46th Ohio, 40th Illinois, with the 97th Indiana deployed as skirmishers. We were in about the center of an open lot of plantations, facing a densely-wooded hill of maybe 300 acres. It was a plumb one-third of a mile to it and already the enemy's sharpshooters were reaching our men from it.

One of Company K's men was shot here, and one of H's. At precisely 1 p. m. we started, the men having been notified that they would have to get to that woods as quickly as possible. The Rebels opened pretty lively. Right in front of where I am now writing is a house. On the porch I see 11 children, not over nine years old. All belong to one woman. Haven't seen her, but from what I have seen in this country, wouldn't dispute the man who would tell me she was only 20 years old. This is a great stock country. As we started, the boys raised a cheer that was a cheer, and we went down on them regular storm fashion. A hundred yards before we got to the hill we ran into a strong line of rifle pits swarming with Johnnies. They caved and commenced begging. The pit I came to had about 20 in it. They were scared until some of them were blue, and if you ever heard begging for life it was then. Somebody yelled out "Let's take the hill," and we left the prisoners and broke. At the foot of the hill we came to a muddy rapid stream, from 10 to 15 feet wide and no crossing, so we plunged in. I got wet to my middle, and many did to their breasts.

The banks were steep and slippery and muddy. Though we all expected a serious fight on the hill, up we went every man for himself, and through to an open field, over which some 200 straggling sandy looking Johnnies were trying to get away, which most of them accomplished, as we were too tired to continue the pursuit fast enough to overtake them. However, the boys shot a lot of them. Well, they call it a gallant thing. We took 542 prisoners, and killed and wounded I suppose 100.

The whole loss in our brigade is not 10 killed and 50 wounded. I only had one man wounded in my company, Corp. E. D. Slater. There were three killed and nine wounded in the regiment.

There were three regiments of Rebels—the 31st, 40th and 54th Alabama. They ought to have killed and wounded at least 500 of us, but we scared them out of it. They shot too high all the time. Osterhaus also had a hard fight to-day, was successful in taking a line of rifle pits. Thomas drove them a mile.

June 16, 1864.

We moved back a mile last night, being relieved by the 17th Corps. Taking it easy again to-day. There has been a lively artillery fight right in front of us to-day. Tell * * * if any of the 31st or 40th Alabama officers report at Johnston's Island, to give them my compliments. One captain offered me his sword, but I hadn't time to stop. We wanted that hill, then.

Near Big Shanty, Ga., June 17, 1864.

Has rained steadily all day, wetting everybody, but "drying up" all shooting. A very disagreeable day. I saw 83 Rebels come in to-day, about one-half of whom were deserters and the rest figured to get captured.

June 18, 1864.

It rained steadily until 4 p. m. and had hardly ceased a minute when our guns opened and the skirmish lines joined issue. General Harrow and Colonel Wright rode out to the left some 200 yards from the regiment and narrowly escaped a trip over the river, a shell bursting right under the nose of the general's horse.

June 19, 1864.

This is the 50th day of the campaign. Our brigade has been under musketry fire 12 days, artillery about 30. We have as a brigade fought three nice little battles, in as many days, repulsing two charges, and making one which was a perfect success. We have captured all told about 650 prisoners, and I think 1,000 a very low estimate of the number we have killed and wounded. I think Cheatham's and Bates' Rebel divisions will say the same. We have thus cleared ourselves with a loss to us of nearly 300, or fully one-fifth of the command. The other nine days we were on the skirmish line, in the rifle pits or front line.

This morning an order was read to pursue the enemy immediately and in ten minutes the "assembly" was sounded. The enemy had fallen back on his flanks, and maybe was intending to evacuate, for our right had swung around him further than I, if in his place, would consider healthy. But he had not yet left the Twin Mountains. The line now runs from right to left by Corps 23d, 20th, 4th, 14th, 15th, 16th, 17th. The 14th Corps lost heavily to-day, but drove the Rebels four miles. The 23d Corps was still going at last accounts. The artillery firing to-day was beautiful. Our division advanced about one-half mile only. The Twin Mountains are right in front of us, and I have seen the Rebels shooting from six batteries on the crest and sides. Our batteries on a line 600 yards in front answer them promptly.

Only one shell has burst near us, and that 100 yards to our right.

The 55th had one killed and two wounded just in front of us, by shells. All parts of the line advanced from one to five miles to-day, the right swinging forward farthest, a-la-gate. Osterhaus' headquarters are 30 yards to our right. A solid shot from the mountain went through one of his tents yesterday. It has rained hard all day, but nobody minds it a particle. The general feeling is that the Rebels have fallen back to their main position, although they have abandoned ground that we would have held one against five. I can't hear that any line of battle has been engaged to-day, but the force on the advance skirmish lines was probably doubled at least. You would not smile at the idea of sleeping on the ground allotted to us to-night. Mud from six to eight inches deep.

Same place, front of Twin Mountains,

June 20, 1864, 11 a. m.

Rebels still on the mountain, a good deal of our artillery, a little of theirs, and not much musketry this morning. Wheeler is in our rear, but we don't care for that. I do hope, though, that Forrest will not be allowed to come over here. We are all well and feeling fine, but wishing very much to see the level country beyond these mountains. In a "Commercial" of the 15th I see the Rebel loss in the charge of Bates' (Rebel) division on the 27th of May was 72 killed and 350 wounded, and 56 missing. That charge was made almost altogether on our brigade, and my skirmish line did three-fourths of the damage. The 40th Alabama we captured the other day inquired for the 8th Illinois. They fought each other at Vicksburg and got well acquainted in the rifle pits. McPherson and Logan have just gone down to the front and there is talk of a fight to-day, but it is hard telling when one will have to go in. Can't tell until the order to "commence" firing is heard. Wagstaff will be home in a few days. I would like to date my next from a new place, but Sherman and Johnston will decide that matter.

This is becoming tedious. Johnston has no regard for one's feelings. We are all exceedingly anxious to see what is the other side of these mountains, but this abominable Johnston has no idea of letting us take a look until he is forced to. He is a good-natured fellow in some respects, too, for here we have our "flies" stretched, and our camp fires and our wagons around us in good range of his guns and not a shot does he give us. You understand that we are in reserve. Our front line is along the foot of the mountain, and we lay back about a mile. But it is all open between us and the front, and we sit in the shade, and (as we have this p. m.) see 20 Rebel guns firing on our men. Why they don't make us get out of this is beyond me to tell. Hundreds of wagons and ambulances are parked around us, and right by us is parked the reserve artillery of our corps, all in plain view of the Rebels on the mountains, but not a gun is fired at us. Yesterday they dropped one shell a hundred yards to our right and quit, as much as to say: "We could stir you Yanks if we wanted to, but it is all right."

I don't know how this looks to outsiders, but it seems to me as the coolest thing of the campaign, pitching tents right under the enemy's guns, without a particle of cover. Being under artillery fire in a fight or while supporting a battery is all right, and if we were in rifle pits or behind the crest of a hill 'twould be ditto, but moving right out and pitching tents under the noses of Rebel 32-pounders beats *me* and I guess it beats *them*. We all feel a pride in the thing and I'd see the the Johnnies to the devil before I'd dodge the biggest cannon ball they've got there. The artillery this p. m. has been the heaviest I have heard this campaign.

June 21, 1864.

No variation to report to-day. Heavy rain yesterday and to-day. Some 350 prisoners were sent in from the right yesterday, and about 80 more that I know of to-day. Figure that we have taken about 3,000 prisoners at this place. Since the army went into position here the right has advanced about six miles, the center two miles, and the left three and one-half to four miles. The musketry from dark last night until 11 p. m. was very busy in front of the 4th Corps, though it may have been only a heavy skirmish line. I hear to-day that the 4th Corps took a strong Rebel position last night while that firing was going on and held it.

June 22, 1864.

Our Adjutant Wagstaff is out of the service and the recommendation for Frank Lermond to receive the appointment has gone on to Governor Yates. Frank is well worthy of the place and has earned it. We flatter ourselves that no regiment has less skulkers than ours in battle, and we have through the corps, a name that Fulton need not fear will disgrace her. We have all day been ready at a moment's notice to support the 4th Corps. Saw Chandler yesterday. He is on M. L. Smith's staff. I wish a little party of Cantonians could be here to-night to see the artillery firing. Our view of the Rebel guns is excellent. With glasses we can see them load. The artillerists

say our field glasses are not so good. Many are prophesy-
ing that the Johnnies will vamoose during the "stilly
night." Much as I want to, can't see it. Looks like too
good a thing.

June 23, 1864, 9 a. m.

The Rebels opened furiously from the mountain last
night about 12. Here they are firing at a division of
the 14th who had advanced and were fortifying. No harm
done. I failed to wake up. It is reported this morning
that Ewell's Corps has arrived to reinforce Johnston.
Don't think it will make him strong enough to assume the
offensive, if true, and don't believe it any way. Artillery
commenced again half an hour since, and goes on slowly.
Rebels haven't gone, surely.

Front of Kenesaw Mountain, June 26, 1864.

Nothing worth mentioning has occurred since my last.
The usual amount of artillery and musketry have kept
us sure of the enemy's still holding his position. I have
sent you, piecemeal, a journal of every day since May 1st,
excepting the last four days, which were stupid. It promises to be interesting enough now. We received orders
yesterday p. m. to be ready to move at dark, and were all
glad enough. When we are in the face of the enemy I
believe one is better contented in the front line than anywhere else, though, like every other good thing, it becomes
old. At 7 p. m. we moved out and it took us until 2 a. m.
to march three miles. We relieved Jeff C. Davis' division,
which moved farther to the right. It is right at the foot
of the west one of the twin mountains. The Johnnies
shot into our ranks with impunity. They have to-day
killed one and wounded three of our brigade that I know
of, and more in the 1st Brigade. Dr. Morris' brother is the
only man struck in our regiment; he is not hurt much.

June 27, 1864, daylight.

The battle comes off to-day. It will be opened on the flanks at 6 a. m. We do not commence until 8 a. m. Our brigade and one from each of the other two divisions of the corps are selected to charge the mountain. The 17th A. C. will try the left hand mountain. If we are successful with a loss of only half our number in this mountain charging, I will think our loss more than repaid. I believe we are going to thoroughly whip Johnston to-day, and if we fail I do not care to live to see it.

June 28, 1864.

The attack was not general; it was made by our brigade and M. L. Smith's Division. We lost nearly one-third of the brigade. Our regiment's loss is 17 killed and 40 wounded. My company had five killed and four wounded. Colonel Wright was shot quite badly in the leg, and Lieutenants Montgomery, Branson and Bailey were killed. In my company Corporals Whittaker, Myers, and Private Sam McIntyre, Art. Myers, and Jacob Maxwell, were killed Sergeant Breed, Privates Bishop, Frank Breed and James Williamson were wounded. We held all the ground we took (under our fire), but had to leave a few of our dead until dark.

On the p. m. of the 26th Colonel Wright told me that General McPherson and Colonel Walcutt (our brigade commander) had been out through the day examining the ground in front, and that it was in contemplation to carry the southwest spur of the mountain by a charge, and further, that it was not impossible that our brigade would be in as usual. This was kept quiet in the command. About 8 p. m. I was at Colonel Wright's headquarters with several of the officers and we were talking the matter over, when an order came for the colonel to report at brigade headquarters. I believe every one present instantly concluded that we were to fight, and knowing the country before us to be about on a par with Lookout

Mountain you can imagine we did not particularly enjoy the prospect. The colonel returned in about an hour. We had all, I believe, fallen asleep. He woke us and said: "Have your men get their breakfasts by daylight; at 6 a. m. the fight will begin on the right, and at 8 a. m. our brigade will, with one from the 1st and 2d divisions, charge a spur of the mountain." I turned away and after notifying my orderly sergeant to have the men up on time, I turned in. Thought the matter over a little while and after pretty fully concluding "good-bye, vain world," went to sleep. Before daylight in the morning we were in line, and moving a few hundred yards to the rear of our works, and stacked arms in a grove, which would hide us from the observation of the Rebels on the mountain. You know from where we have been for a few days, we could see them plainly. Cannonading commenced on the right at 6 a. m. and at 7:30 we moved a half or three quarters of a mile along our lines to the right, after piling our knapsacks and haversacks. A canteen of water was the only extra baggage any one carried. The Rebels caught sight of us as we commenced moving, and opened a battery on us It had the effect to accelerate our movements considerably. Right in front of a Division of the 4th Corps we halted, and rapidly formed our line. While forming the line Corporal Myers of my company was killed by a bullet within six feet of me, and one of Company K's men wounded. I don't know how many more. The ground to be gone over was covered with a dense undergrowth of oak and vines of all kinds binding the dead and live timber and bush together, and making an almost impenetrable abatis. To keep a line in such a place was out of the question. Our skirmishers were sharply engaged from the start, and men commenced falling in the main line; at the same time some 50 of the Rebel skirmish line were captured, and many of them killed. A Rebel lieutenant and five men lay dead, all nearly touching each other.

I understand that they had been summoned to surrender, and were shot either for refusing or before negotiations were completed. Not a man in our regiment knew where the Rebel works were when we started, and I think the most of them found them as I did. I had with my company got within, I think, 60 yards of the Rebel works, and was moving parallel with them. The balls were whistling thick around us, but I could see no enemy ahead.

I did not even think of them being on our flank, until one of the boys said: "Look there, Captain, may I shoot?" I looked to the right, and just across a narrow and deep ravine were the Rebel works, while a confused mass of greybacks were crowding up the ravine. These latter, I suppose, were from their skirmish line, which was very heavy, and trying to escape us. The Rebels in the works were firing vigorously and have no excuse for not annihilating our three left companies K, G and B. The right of the regiment had seen them before and already started for them. I shouted "forward" to my men and we ran down across the ravine, and about one-third the way up the hill on which their works were and then lay down. There was little protection from their fire, though, and if they had done their duty, not a man of us would have got out alive. Our men fired rapidly and kept them well down in their works. It would have been madness to have attempted carrying their works then, for our regiment had not a particle of support, and we were so scattered that we only presented the appearance of a very thin skirmish line. If we had been supported by only one line, I have no doubt but that we would have taken their line of works. Colonel Wright was wounded a few minutes after we got into the hollow, and Frank Lermond came to me and told me I would have to take command of the regiment. I went down to the center and the order was heard to retire. I communicated it to the left and saw nearly all the men out, and then fell back.

I could not find the regiment when I came out, but collected about 30 of our men on the left of the 6th Iowa, and after a while Colonel Wright and Captain Post brought the regiment to where we were, when we formed a brigade line and threw up works within 200 yards of the enemy's, where we remained until 9 p. m., when we returned to the position we occupied in the morning. About 12 of our dead were left in the ravine under the fire of the enemy's guns. But we have as many of their dead as they have of ours. Lieutenant Colonel Barnhill of the 40th Illinois, and Captain Augustine of the 55th Illinois were killed and left on the field. My loss is five killed and four wounded. Two of my dead, Corporal Whittaker and Artemus Myers, were left on the field. Loss in the regiment is 17 killed, 40 wounded. In the brigade 245 killed and wounded. It was a rough affair, but we were not whipped. The prettiest artillery fight I ever saw was over our heads in the evening, about 10 guns on each side.

June 29, 1864.

There was a night charge made by the Rebels on our right last night. They got beautifully "scooped." We have been laying quiet all day. Lots of artillery, though but few shots come near us.

June 30, 1864, 8 a. m.

There was a terrific fight on our right, commencing at 2 this morning and lasting until 3. I have not yet heard what it was.

Some deserters passed us this morning. I have lost just half the men I left Scottsboro with just two months ago, but what I have left, are every man ready to help. We have a good deal more than "cleared" ourselves. I had my canteen strap cut off by a bullet and a spent glancing ball struck my ankle.

July 1, 1864.

This campaign is coming down to a question of muscle and nerve. It is the 62d day for us, over 50 of which we have passed under fire. I don't know anything more exhausting. One consolation is that the Rebels are a good deal worse off than we are. They have lost more men in battle, their deserters count by thousands, and their sick far exceed ours. We'll wear them out yet. Our army has been reinforced by fully as many as we have lost in action, so that our loss will not exceed our sick. You notice in the papers acounts of Hooker's charging "Lost Mountain," taking a large number of prisoners, and the names of officers. You see they are all from the 31st and 40th Alabama. It is also credited to Blair's 17th Corps. Our brigade took all those officers on the 15th of June. I wrote you an account of it then. It hurts us some to see it credited to other troops, but such is the fortune of war, and soldiers who do not keep a reporter must expect it. Colonel Wright starts for home to-day.

July 2, 1864.

We have been taking it easy since the charge. Our shells keep the Rebels stirred up all the time. Sham attacks are also got up twice or three times a day, which must annoy them very much.

July 3, 1864.

Rebels all gone this morning. Our boys were on the mountains at daylight. Hundreds of deserters have come in. Osterhaus moved around the left of the mountain to Marietta, all the rest of the army went to the right of it. We are about one-half a mile from town; have not been in. All who have, say it is the prettiest place we have seen South. Some artillery firing has been heard this p. m. five or six miles south, and there are rumors that an advance has captured a large number of prisoners, but nothing reliable.

July 4, 1864.

I count it the hardest Fourth I have seen in the service.
About 8 a. m. we moved out, passed through Marietta, which
is by far the prettiest town I have seen South (about the size
of Canton), and continued south nearly all the way along
our line of works. Marched about 11 miles. Not more than
one-third of the men stacked arms when we halted for the
night; fell out along the roads. I have seen more than 1,000
prisoners and deserters.

July 5, 1864.

Can hear no firing this p. m. It seems the Rebels have got
across the Chattahoochie. We are about 12 miles from Atlanta. The river will probably trouble us some, but we all
think "Pap" will make it before August 1st. Johnston don't
dare give us anything like a fair fight. We are all in splendid
spirits and the boys have made the woods ring with their
Fourth of July cheers, tired as they are. We have lost no
men since the charge of the 27th. I have an Atlanta paper,
giving an acount of that fight. They say we were all drunk
with whisky and fought more like devils than men.

p. m.

We have continued our march about four or five miles to-
day. Osterhaus and M. L. Smith are ahead of us ,and I
think we are on the right of the army again. The 4th Division, 17th Army Corps is engaged one-half mile ahead of us
or rather are shooting a little with their big guns. I climbed
a tree a half hour ago, and what do you think?—saw
Atlanta, and saw it plainly, too. I suppose it is ten miles distant, not more than 12. The country looks about as level as
a floor, excepting one-half mountain, to the left of the city,
some miles. We seem to be on the last ridge that amounts to
anything. We are, I suppose, two and one-half miles from the
river at this point, though we hold it farther to the right.
Very large columns of smoke were rolling up from different
parts of the city. I suppose they were the explosions of foun-

dries, machine shops, etc. Dense clouds of dust can be seen at several points across the river; suppose it means trains or troops moving.

Have seen but few wounded going back to-day. We are laying along some very good rifle pits, occasionally embrasured for artillery, which the 17th Army Corps took this morning. They were not very stoutly defended, though, and the artillery had been moved back. With some pretty lively skirmishing the line has been advanced this evening. Not much loss on our side; saw some one-half dozen ambulance loads only.

July 6, 1864.

I went down to our front this evening. Our advanced artillery is yet some 1,200 yards from the Rebels, but there is nothing but an open field between, and it looks quite close. The Johnnies have thrown up a nice fort, embrasured for nine guns. They have not fired a shot to-day. The captain of our advanced artillery told me the Rebels have 20 Parrott guns in the fort, and excellent gunners.

We moved this evening one mile to the left and relieved a portion of the 20th Corps, which went on further to the left.

We started on this campaign with 10 field officers in our brigade and now have but two left. Three killed, three wounded and two left back sick. I hear the Rebel works here are the last this side of the river, and but few hundred yards from it.

July 7, 1864.

The shooting still continues in our front, but hear no Rebel artillery. The water here is excellent, and everybody seems to get a few blackberries. We also stew grapes and green apples, and everything that ever was eaten by anti-cannibals. There is so much confounded fighting to be attended to that we can't forage any, and though fresh beef is furnished to the men regularly there is some scurvy. I have seen several black-mouthed, loose-toothed fellows, hankering after pickles.

Teamsters and hangers-on who stay in the rear get potatoes, etc., quite regularly. I do not believe the Johnnies intend fighting again very strongly this side of the river. Our scouts say that between the river and Atlanta the works run line after line as thickly as they can be put in. *Per contra,* two women who came from Atlanta on the 6th say that after we get across the river we will have no fighting, that Johnston is sending his troops to Savannah, Charleston, Mobile and Richmond, except enough to fight us at different river crossings. Our scouts also say that the Rebels are deserting almost by thousands, and going around our flanks to their homes in Tennessee, Kentucky, etc. I have not been in a house in Georgia, but several citizens I have met in camp said they had heard many soldiers say they would never cross the river with Johnston since the charge of the 27th.

Harrow has kept our brigade in reserve, and I think he will continue to do so unless a general battle is fought. We have suffered more heavily than any other two brigades in the army, and when we started we were one of the smallest. I am willing to see some of the others go in a while, though I want to help if Johnston will stand a fair fight in open ground. The chigres are becoming terrific. They are as large as the blunt end of a No. 12 and as red as blood. They will crawl through any cloth and bite worse than a flea, and poison the flesh very badly. They affect some more than others. I get along with them *comparatively* well, that is, I don't scratch more than half the time. Many of the boys anoint their bodies with bacon rinds, which the chigres can't go. Salt-water bathing also bars chigres, but salt is too scarce to use on human meat. Some of the boys bathing now in a little creek in front of me; look like what I expect "Sut Lovegood's" father did after plowing through that hornet's nest. All done by chigres. I believe I pick off my neck and clothes 30 varieties of measuring worm every day. Our brigade quartermaster yesterday found, under his saddle in his tent, a rattlesnake, with six rattles and a button.

18

This is the 68th day of the campaign. We hope to end it
by August 1st, though if we can end the war by continuing
this until January 1st, '65, I am in. Reinforcements are coming in every day, and I don't suppose we are any weaker than
when we left Chattanooga. The Rebels undoubtedly are, besides the natural demoralization due to falling back so much
must be awful. My health is excellent. Remember me to all
the wounded boys of the 103d you see.

Nine miles from Atlanta, two and one-half miles south-

west of railroad crossing,

July 9, 1864.

On the evening of the 7th, just dark, a Rebel battery in a
fort which our guns had been bursting shells over all day,
suddenly opened with eight 20-pound Parrotts, and for one-
half an hour did some of the most rapid work I ever heard.
They first paid their attention to our batteries, then demol-
ished some half-dozen wagons and 20 mules for the 4th Division of the 17th Army Corps half a mile to our right, and
then began scattering their compliments along our line,
wherever I suppose they had detected our presence by smoke
or noise. They kept getting closer and closer to us, and finally,
a shell burst in front of our regiment. The next one went 50
yards past us and dropped into the 40th Illinois. Neither of
them did any damage, and no more came so close. An hour
afterward we fell in, and moving a mile to the left and one-
half a mile to the front, occupied a ridge which we fortified by
daylight, so they might shell and be hanged.

The Rebel skirmishers heard us moving as we came over,
and threw more than a thousand bullets at us, but it was so
pitchy dark that fortunately they did us no damage. From
our colors we can see the fort that fired so the night of the
7th. They are about three-fourths of a mile distant. There
have not been any bullets or shells passed over us since we got
our works up, though the skirmish line at the foot of the hill,
has a lively time. We have it very easy. I was on the 8th in

charge of a line of skirmishers on the left of our brigade.
The Rebels were seemingly quite peaceable, so much so, that
I thought I'd walk over to some blackberry bushes 50 yards in
front of our right.

I got about half way out when they sent about a dozen bullets at me. I retired in good order, considering. In the p. m.
of the 7th, the skirmishers in front of a brigade of the 20th
Corps, and the Rebel line, left their guns, and went out and
were together nearly all the afternoon; 13 of the Rebels agreed
to come into our line after dark. At the time appointed, heavy
firing commenced on the Rebel side, and our boys, fearing
foul play, poured in a few volleys. Through the heaviest of
the fire two of the Rebels came running in. They said that
the 13 started, and that the Rebels opened on them. The rest
were probably killed. One of my men has just returned from
visiting his brother in the 20th Corps. It is reported there that
the 23d Corps crossed the river this p. m. without losing a
man. The heavy firing this evening was our folks knocking
down some block houses at the railroad bridge. The 4th
Corps to-night lays right along the river bank.

July 10, 1864, a. m.

The Rebels evacuated last night, and our flags are on their
works and our skirmishers at the river. A number of Johnnies were left on this side. I believe they have every time left
on Saturday night or Sunday. Their works here are the best
I have seen. Three lines and block houses ad libitum. P. m.—
Every Rebel is across the river, and our 23d and 16th Corps
are also over, away up to the left. It is intimated though that
they will only hold their position a few days. We are expecting orders to join them.

July 12, 1864.

We lay quietly in the shade all day the 11th, save those who
had ambition enough to go fishing, berrying or swimming.
The other bank of the Chattahoochie opposite us is yet lined
with Rebel sharp-shooters, but there is a fine creek from which

the boys get some fine fish. I saw an eel two feet long which came from it. Our boys never have made any bargain with the Johnnies to quit picket firing, even for an hour, but other corps and divisions often do. It would almost break the heart of one of our boys to see a Rebel without getting a shot at him. On the 12th, at 5 p. m., the "General" and "Assembly" sounded almost together, and we were under way in a twinkling. We understand we are going back to Marietta, and then over the river where the 23d Corps crossed it. We stopped here (about seven miles from Marietta), at 11 p. m., and had reveille at 3 this morning. Stoneman, with at least 10,000 cavalry, recrossed the river on the night of the 10th on a grand raid between Atlanta and Montgomery. We had a real amusing scene last night. About 12 o'clock we were nearly all asleep, when a mule came charging at full speed right through our regiment. In an instant every man was on his feet, and all who knew what was up, were swinging blankets and shouting whoa! The most of us did not know whether a cavalry charge was on us or the devil. Many of the men caught up their guns, and "treed," and altogether it was most ludicrous. Our regiment now marches 190 guns and 7 officers. I have 20 guns, all I started with, except what I have lost in battle. Just half.

July 13, 1864.

We passed through Marietta this morning at 9; rested in a cool, nice, woody place from 11 to 2, and made this place in the cool of the evening. We marched about 14 miles to-day. I would rather be in a fight than endure such a day's march, and I think fighting lacks very much as deserving to rank as amusement.

I saw a number of cases of congestion of the brain, and a few had real sun stroke. Saw one poor fellow in a grave-yard between two little picketed graves, who I made sure was gasping his last. Some heartless fellow made a remark as we passed about his luck in getting sun struck so near good bury-

ing facilities. After one heat of only three miles the regiment
had all fallen out but about 50 men, and we had more than any
other in the brigade. If we had been given one hour more in
rests, we would not have lost a man.

July 14, 1864.

Another hot day. We marched down to the river at Roswell
and crossed it, and have gone into camp on the bank a mile
above town.

This Roswell is a beautiful little town, such splendid trees
all through it. Our cavalry four or five days ago destroyed
some very large factories here. Judging from the ruins, they
were more extensive than anything of the kind I ever before
saw. About 1,000 women were employed in them; 700 of
them were taken by our folks and sent to Marietta; I don't
know what for. Can't hear of any enemy here.

July 15, 1864.

This is a glorious place. The current in the river is very
swift, and it is the nicest stream to bathe in imaginable. I've
a mind to stay here and have my meals brought to me. Expect we will catch some nice fish after they get over being
scared at having so many Yanks bobbing around with them.
It is too hot to write, and altogether too hot to enjoy good
health, except in swimming. We are all glad to hear of those
raids into Pennsylvania and Maryland. Go in Imboden and
Early.

July 16, 1864, 76th of the Campaign.

I can hear no firing to-day, but we are so far from the
right or center that we could hear nothing less than a
13-inch mortar. I will tell you all I know of the situation
just to let you know how little a soldier knows of what is going
on. In papers of this date you will see twice as much. The
17th Army Corps lies on the right bank of the river, and to
the right of the army, six miles below the railroad crossing,
skirmishing with the enemy on the opposite side. Next

comes the 20th, 14th and 4th on the same side, the 4th lying across the railroad four miles, further up the 23d crossed the river, but probably only holds a position, as we do. Then the 16th Corps joins the left of the 23d, and the 15th last, both on the left bank. Not being perfect in heavy strategy, I can't exactly see the point, but no doubt Sherman does. I suppose the 4th, 14th and 20th Corps will cross near the railroad bridge, and be the first to occupy Atlanta. If we can't get to give Johnston a sound thrashing, I don't care about marching another step until fall. Health of the regiment still good, but we are expecting sickness soon. We have had a terrific thunderstorm, killed five men and wounded eight in the 18th Missouri, and killed a teamster and some mules. I never saw but one or two more severe ones.

June 17, 1864.

After erecting some good works at Roswell (the best we have yet built), capable of holding at least 25,000 men, we were provided with three days' rations and cartridges "ad libitum," for another of what an Augusta paper calls "Sherman leap-frog-like advance." Our corps is the extreme left of the army. We moved out this morning, our brigade in advance of our division, and Osterhaus and Smith's Divisions following on the Decatur road. Did I tell you in my last among the "locals," that these Roswell factories have been turning out 35,000 yards per day of jeans, etc., for the Confederate Army, that there is the greatest abundance of blackberries and whortleberries here, that one of the 48th Illinois was drowned in the Chattahoochie while bathing, and that of several hundred factory girls I have seen, hardly one who is passably handsome? Some fine fat ones, and a few neat feet, but they are not "clipper built," and lack "get up" and "figure heads."

We moved six miles without meeting a Rebel, and then only a squadron of cavalry that lacked a devilish sight of being "chivalry," for they more than ran without just

cause. We only went two miles farther and then bivouacked. Our brigade was thrown half a mile in front and
across the road. We put up a rail barricade across the
road and a temporary rail-work along our front, and then
abandoned ourselves to the longings of our breadbaskets,
and desisted not until every man was in himself a miniature
blackberry patch. The boys brought me pint after pint
of great black fellows they had picked in the shade of dense
woods or on a steep bank, and I assure you they dis-
appeared without an exception. This road, the last 10
days, has been filled with refugee citizens running from
the Yankees. An old gentleman in whose yard the reserve
pickets have stacked their arms, told me that all the men
of his acquaintance over 45 years old are, and always have
been, Unionists, and are to-day ready and willing to give
up slavery for our cause. I have been a deluded believer
in the hoax of fine "Georgia plantations," but I assure you
I am now thoroughly convalescent. I haven't seen five
farm houses equal to Mrs. James—, and only one that
showed evidences of taste. That was where I saw the
Rebel General Iverson dead among the flowers. The country is all hilly, and the soil, where there is any, is only fit
for turnips. The timber is all scrub oak and pine, and
some more viney bushes peculiar to the climate.

I notice some of the white moss hanging from the trees,
like that there was so much of at Black river. The 16th
Corps is on our right moving on a parallel road, and the
23d joins them. I don't know whether our other corps
have crossed yet or not.

Near Stone Mountain, July 18, 1864.

Osterhaus (or his division, for I hear that he resigned
and yesterday started for the North, en route for Mexico,
where he formerly resided, and that he intends entering
the Mexican Army to fight "Johnny Crapeau") was ahead
to-day, and only lost a dozen or 50 men. Our brigade has
been train guard, and we did not get into camp until 11

p. m. This night marching hurts us more than the hottest day marching. We camp to-night near Stone Mountain, and the depot of the same name 16 miles from Atlanta. It is evident to me that the Army of the Tennessee is doing the "flanking them out" this time. The 1st Division cut the railroad effectually. A train came from the East while they were at it, but discovering the smoke, reversed the engine and escaped. The 17th Corps I hear is close behind us protecting the commissary trains and forming our rear guard.

Decatur, Ga., July 19, 1864.

To-night we are in Decatur, six miles from Atlanta. The Rebels were yet in Atlanta this morning, for they ran a train to this burg this morning, but they may now be gone. Our line of battle crosses the railroad nearly at right angles, facing Atlanta. I think the 23d Corps has swung around in front of us, and the 16th Corps is now on our left. Our cavalry had some fighting after 1 p. m. today. A citizen says there was nearly 4,500 Rebel cavalry here. A small portion of our mounted forces made a half-charge on the Johnnies just this side of town, and the Rebels stampeded. They knew we had a large force, and, of course, could not tell just what number was coming on them. They broke down every fence in town and ran over everything but the houses in their mad panic to get away. Our men, as usual, all stopped in town to flank the onions, potatoes, chickens and sundries, in which they were busily engaged when the Rebels, who had rallied and got a battery in position, opened right lively. Our men drove them away, and then all hands went to foraging again. To-morrow night, I think, will give us Atlanta, or there will be a fair start for a new graveyard near the town. I hear no fighting on the right. We have passed over the same miserable looking country to-day. I caught a small scorpion to-day, also a reddish brown bug not quite as large as a thrush, and as savage as a mad rat. Wish I could preserve some of these bugs and things; I know you'd like 'em

July 20, 1864.

Assembly has just sounded. In a few hours we will know if it is to be a fight. Frank says we are detailed for train guard. If the army marches right into Atlanta, I'll think it d—d mean, but if there is a fight will not feel so badly, unless we can get a big battle out of Johnston. I want to help in that. We have moved up near the town the army has gone on. Can hear heavy guns occasionally, sounds about three miles away, half the distance to the city.

This little town is quite an old place. About half the citizens are still here. I saw a couple of right pretty girls. Some Confederate prisoners tell me that Johnston is gone to Richmond, and that Hood is commanding and intends to fight us at Atlanta.

The wheat and oats raised this year in this part of Georgia, if it had all been saved, would not more than have fed the citizens. Full one-half the cornfields will not turn out anything.

July 23, 1864.

The fight came off the 22d, and a glorious one it was for us. Lieutenant Blair of our regiment was killed, also Charles Buck, of Company F, and John Smith of my company. There were seven wounded only. Our brigade gets credit for 400 prisoners. They took us in rear and every other way, but the repulse was awful. Everybody is wishing that they may repeat the attack. Generals McPherson and Force are killed. (Force, was not killed.) Our regiment gets credit for its part, though we were very fortunate in losing so few. Our skirmish line is within one mile of the town.

July 25, 1864.

We moved up to the rear of the corps on the 21, and had just got comfortably fixed for the night when orders came that we should report back to the brigade on the front line. Just as we started a heavy rain set in, and continued while we marched one and one-half miles to the left, where we stacked arms in rear of a line of work occupied by the 6th Iowa. The Rebel line lay in plain sight, just across an open field, and the bullets made us keep pretty close.

At sunset we were ordered to extend, or rather build a line of works to hold our regiment, between the 6th Iowa and 40th Illinois. We had fairly commenced, and the boys were scattered everywhere, bringing rails, logs, etc., when the Johnnie's bugle sounded "forward," and the Rebels raised a yell and fired a couple of volleys into us. There was a lively rush for our guns, but we saw through it in a minute, and in three minutes were at work again. Only two men were hurt in the regiment, one from Company C, and Wm. Nicholson of my company had the small bone of his leg broken just above the ankle. We got our works in shape about daylight, and about 8 a. m. I heard a cheer from our skirmishers, and saw the Rebel skirmishers run right over their works like deer. Our line followed them and took possession of their works, and no Rebel or works being in sight, and our boys knowing they were only two miles from Atlanta, thought sure they had the town, and all started on the "double quick" for it, yelling, "potatoes" or "tobacco," or what he particularly hankered for. They got along swimmingly until within about three-quarters of a mile from town, when they ran against a strong line of works and were brought up standing, by a volley therefrom. They deployed immediately, and by the time their officers got up had a good line established, and were whacking away at the fort apparently as well satisfied as if they had got their tobaco.

McPherson had an idea that all was not right, for our line was allowed to advance no further than the one the Rebels had left, and we were set to work changing its front. At dinner when we were about leaving "the table," Captain Smith mentioned hearing some heavy skirmishing in our rear as we came to our meal. That was the first any of us knew of the battle. In a few minutes we all heard it plainly, and from our works could see exactly in our rear a body of grey coats, advance

from a wood and the battle opened, although we did not know
what troops of ours were engaged. Have since heard it was
a portion of the 16th Corps who were moving out to extend
the line. Their being just in that position was a piece of luck,
as it saved the trains of the Army of the Tennessee, and, perhaps, the whole army. I should think they fought an hour
before the battle swung around toward us. During the battle,
our regiment changed position three times, facing east, west
and south. We helped repulse four charges, took 115
prisoners, and helped take 400 more. Also ran the enemy out
of a line of works they had taken from our 3d brigade, and
the best of it is, we lost only ten men. I cannot for my life
see how we escaped so well. General Blair is reported to have
said that the Army of the Tennessee is eternally disgraced
for going outside of all precedent, in refusing to be whipped
when attacked in flank and rear, as well as in front. Hood
confines his strategy to maneuvering troops for battle, and
pretends to be emphatically a "fighting cock." He attacked
Thomas on the 20th and 21st, away on the right, and on the
22d walked into us. He got his comb badly cut, and if I
am any prophet at all, will not attempt another fight soon.
Sherman estimates the enemy's loss in the three days' fighting at 12,000. Our loss in the same time is less than 3,500. I
am surprised that we have not attacked them in return before
this, but am far from anxious to charge their works. Although
I do know that if we charge with two lines as good as our
brigade, and don't go too fast, we can take any ordinary works.
The prisoners we got the other day were run down. When
our regiment drove the Rebels out of the works of the
3d brigade, a man shot through the thigh, asked me for water
as I passed him. I asked him if the Rebels robbed him, he
said, no, but they killed a man in the ditch with a spade right
in front of him. I looked where he pointed and found a 97th
Indiana boy with his thigh broken by a pistol shot, and three
cuts in his face by a spade. He was not dead, he knew me,
and reached out his hand smiling. He said an officer rode up
with some footmen and told him to surrender, when he shot

the officer and ran his bayonet through one of the men. Another shot him, and the man he bayoneted used the spade on him. McPherson was killed early in the fight. The Rebels had his body a few minutes, but the 16th Corps charged and retook it. Altogether, it was the prettiest fight I ever saw.

The Rebel plan of attack was excellent, and if their assaulting columns had charged simultaneously, there is no telling what might have been the upshot. As it was, part of 17th Corps changed position in their breastworks three times, that is, repulsed an assault from one side, and being attacked from the rear, jumped over and fought them the other way. I was up to where the 20th and 31st Illinois fought. The dead Rebels lay about as thick on one side of the works as the other, and right up to them. Two more fights like this, and there will be no more Rebel army here. We lost about 600 prisoners, and took 2,000.

Garrard's cavalry division went out to Covington on the Augusta road. Am just going on picket.

One and three-quarter miles southwest of Atlanta,

July 29, 1864.

On the evening of the 26th, Adj. Frank Lermond sent me word that the Army of the Tennessee was going to evacuate its position, the movement to commence at 12 p. m. When the lines are so close together the skirmish line is a ticklish place.

The parties can tell by hearing artillery move, etc., nearly what is going on, and in evacuation generally make a dash for the skirmish line or rear guard. At nearly every position Johnston has fortified we caught his skirmish line when he evacuated. Luckily our line got off about 4 a. m. on the 27th though they shelled us right lively.

That day our three corps moved along in the rear of the 23d, 4th, 14th and 20th, the intention being, I think, to extend the line to the right, if possible, to the Montgomery and Atlanta railroad and thus destroy another line of communication. We have thoroughly destroyed 50 miles of the Augusta and Atlanta railroad. The 16th Corps formed its line on the right of the 14th, and the 17th joined on the 16th, and on the morning of the 28th, we moved out to extend the line still further. At 12 m. we had just got into position and thrown a few rails along our line, when Hood's Rebel corps came down on Morgan L's and our divisions like an avalanche. Our two divisions did about all the fighting, and it lasted until 5 p. m.

We whipped them awfully. Their dead they left almost in line of battle along our entire front of two divisions.

It was the toughest fight of the campaign, but not a foot of our line gave way, and our loss is not one-twentieth of theirs. The rails saved us. I am tired of seeing such butchery but if they will charge us that way once a day for a week, this corps will end the war in this section.

Our loss in the regiment was 17 out of 150 we had in the fight, and the brigade loss will not exceed 100. I never saw so many Rebels dead. We are in excellent spirits, and propose to take Atlanta whenever Sherman wants it.

August 1, 1864.

Since the glorious battle of the 28th, everything has been quiet in our immediate front, though the heavy artillery firing continues to the left. I think it is between the 14th and 20th Corps and some Rebel forts. Prisoners say that our shells have hurt the city very much. We all think that the last battle is by far the most brilliant of the campaign. Our officials' reports show that we buried 1,000 Rebels in front of our and M. L. Smith's divisions.

In fact, our two divisions and two regiments of Osterhaus' did all the fighting. Our total loss was less than 550, the Rebels 8,000. In the last 12 days they must have lost 25,000 men. Our loss in the same time will not reach 4,500. There is no shadow of gas in this, as you would know if you could see an unsuccessful charge on works.

The enemy is reported as moving to our right in heavy force.

August 5, 1864.

After the fight of the 28th July, we advanced on the 30th, 31st and April 1st, when we came to a strong line of Rebel rifle pits, densely populated, and their main works about 400 yards behind the pits.

On the 2d details from each brigade in the corps were ordered to drive the Rebels out of said pits. It was done, our division capturing 78 prisoners. The Rebels tried to retake them, but failed, of course, leaving with our boys, among other dead, a colonel and a major. Only one company (K), of our regiment was in the fight; it had two men wounded. I was on picket there the next day; 'twas a lively place, but I lost no men. Some of the men fired over 100 rounds. The 23d and 14th Corps have swung around on our right, the object being to throw our line across the Macon railroad. We have heard that Stoneman was captured with 400 men at Macon. Kilpatrick started on a raid yesterday. Stoneman burned a Rebel wagon train of 600 wagons, and sabered the mules. Cruel, but right. The 14th Corps yesterday gobbled 700 prisoners. There are a few Rebel riflemen who keep the bullets whistling around us here; they killed a Company E man 20 yards to the right on the 4th. Health of the regiment never better, and that is the best index of the morale.

August 8, 1864.

Never was army better cared for than this. No part of it has been on short rations during the campaign. Extra issues of dessicated potatoes, mixed vegetables, etc., have bundled the advance guard of General Scurvy neck and heels outside the pickets. Extraordinary dreams of green corn, blackberries, new potatoes, etc., have done very much towards keeping up the health and morale of the army, and as much towards reconciling us to this summer sun, that ripens said goodies.

We draw supplies of clothing monthly as regularly as when in garrison, and a ragged soldier is a scarcity. At least 30 days' rations are safely stored in our rear, making us entirely unmindful of railroad raids, for, if necessary, we could build the whole road in that time. The heat has not troubled us much, save during a few days' marching.

We have had hardly three days without a rain for a month. We have done a great amount of work since our last battle, have constructed nine lines of works, and it will take at least two more' before we get the position that I think Howard wants. We keep those poor Johnnies in a stew all the time. Our artillery is any amount better than theirs, and it plays on them from morning until night. Nothing worries troops so much, though compared with musketry it is almost harmless. I guess their ammunition is short, for they don't fire one shot to our 40. I think we'll like Howard first rate. If he is as good as McPherson, he'll do.

Four divisions are on their way to reenforce us. I don't think we need them, but the more, the merrier.

August 10, 1864.

Our "color" that has floated over the 103d for nearly two years has become much worn and torn. One shell and bullets innumerable have passed through it. It is entitled to be inscribed with the following battles: Vicksburg, Black River, Jackson, Miss., Mission Ridge, Dalton, Resaca, Dallas, New Hope, Big Shanty, Kenesaw Mountain, Atlanta. It has been under the enemy's fire 72 days on this campaign. Nearly 300 of the regiment have fallen under it.

August 11, 1864.

We have lost 35 men since Colonel Wright left us. There has been a tall artillery fight this p. m. right here, but as usual no one hurt.

August 20, 1864.

During the last few days cavalry has been operating on the right against the enemy's communications. We have been making demonstrations, as they call it, or diversions in favor of the cavalries; that is, one, two or three times a day we raise a yell along our corps line, and open on the enemy with cannon and muskets. This, aside from scaring them a little (and it is getting most too old to do even that), does but trifling damage, for at the opening yell they all "hunt their holes," in army slang, take position in their works. Everybody is satisfied the Johnnies here are only waiting for dark nights to evacuate.

August 24, 1864.

The Johnnies in our front are either tired out or short of ammunition or inclination, or else, like the quiet swine, "studying devilment." Certain it is, that they shoot but little lately.

Five Rebel batteries which have thrown shell into our division line did not on the 20th or 21st fire a shot, on the 22d but two shots, and in response to a more than usually vigorous cannonading on our part yesterday returned not more than a dozen shots. These Rebels just opposite are a very glum set. Won't say a single word, though the lines are at one point at least, not more than 20 yards apart. Whenever I have seen the line so close, our men invariably get the advantage, and keep the Rebels down. We go on the skirmish line every fourth day, but with ordinary care there is little danger.   .

The 4th, 20th and 16th Corps are preparing to start for the right. The raids in our rear—on the railroad amount to nothing. We have at least 60 days' rations accumulated, and could rebuild the entire road in that time.

VI.

August 29, 1864 to February 13, 1865. Wondering what the Chicago Convention will do. Covering an evacuation. Marching with muffled
guns under Silent "Pap" Sherman. Tearing up railraod tracks by
hand. Fighting near Jonesboro. Charging a South Carolina
brigade, capturing and holding the rifle pits they were digging.
Captain Post wounded. Repulsing sorties. Bringing off the
pickets. Sherman announces occupation of Atlanta. Congratulatory orders by Howard, Logan and Harrow. Destruction of Atlanta. Guarding the neutral ground. On the march again. Sample "grapevine" dispatches. Camp humor. Osterhaus loses
his temper. Tragic fate of ten stragglers; swift revenge.
Rubber pancakes. "Grabbing" for foraged meat. Three witches.
Marching through Georgia. Destroying our own "cracker line"
and preparing to live on the country. Successful and abundant
foraging. Battle of Griswoldville. Old men and little boys among
the Rebel dead. Howard's congratulatory order. Marching
through lonely pine forests with cheers. Hampered by contrabands. Gentle Milly Drake and her slave. Unanimously chosen
major, vice Willison, resigned. By sea to Beaufort, S. C. Why
Buford's bridge was found abandoned. Using up a small town
to build bridges. Burning and destroying railroads and twisting
red hot rails. Wading a swamp to flank the Rebels. Rear guard
of the corps.

August 29, 1864.

I would much like to know what the Chicago Convention
is doing to-day. We hear there is a possibility they may
nominate Sherman. How we wish they would. He would
hardly accept the nomination from such a party, but I would

19

cheerfully live under Copperhead rule if they would give us such as Sherman.   Sherman believes with Logan, "that if we can't subdue these Rebels and the rebellion, the next best thing we can do is to all go to hell together."

We have already thrown our army so far to the right that our communications are not safe, but yet we can't quite reach the Montgomery or Macon railroads.   It is determined to leave the 20th Corps at Vinings to guard the railroad bridge, and I think to move all the rest to the right.   The army has just moved its length by the right flank.   Looks easy and simple enough, but it took three days and nights of the hardest work of the campaign.   The whole line lay in sight, and musket range of the enemy, not only our skirmishers, but our main line, and half a dozen men could, at any point, by showing themselves above the works, have drawn the enemy's fire.   A gun, a caisson, or a wagon could hardly move without being shelled.   On the night of the 25th, the 20th Corps moved back to the river to guard the railroad bridge seven miles from Atlanta; and the 4th moved toward the right.

Night of the 26th the 15th, 16th and 17th moved back on different roads toward the right.   The wheels of the artillery were muffled and most of them moved off very quietly.   One gun in our division was not muffled, and its rattling brought on a sharp fire, but I only heard of two men being hurt.   Our regiment was deployed on the line our brigade occupied, and remained four hours after everything else had left.   At 2:30 a. m. we were ordered to withdraw *very quietly*.   We had fired very little for two hours, and moved out so quietly that, though our lines were only 25 yards apart in one place, the Rebels did not suspect our exit.   We moved back three-quarters of a mile and waited an hour, I think, for some 17th Corps skirmishers. We could hear the Johnnies popping away at our old position, and occasionally they would open quite sharply as though angry at not receiving their regular replies.   When we were fully two miles away they threw two shells into our deserted works. We did not lose a man, but I give you my word, this covering an evacuation is a delicate, dangerous, and far-from-pleasant duty. There was a Johnnie in the "pit" nearest us that got off a good thing the other day. A newsboy came along in the ditch, crying, "Heer's your Cincinnati, Louisville and Nashville papers." Crack! Crack!! went two Rebel guns, and a Johnnie holloed "There is your Atlanta *"Appeal!"* We caught up with the brigade just at daylight, it was raining, but our watch, the hard march, the wear and tear of such duty, made some sleep a necessity, so we tumbled down in the rank smelling weeds, and I was sleeping equal to Rip Van Winkle in half a minute. In half an hour we were awakened, took breakfast and marched a couple of miles to where the train was. Here somebody got Rebel on the brain, and we were run out a mile to investigate. We stopped in a nice, fine grove, and I didn't want to hear any more about the Rebels, but went to sleep instanter. That sleep did me a world of good. I woke about 4 p. m., and found the whole regiment with scarce a half-dozen exceptions, sound asleep. Finally the rear of the train started and we followed. At just midnight we came up to the train corral and laid down for the remnant of the night. At 6 a. m., we left the train and rejoined the division. At dark we camped on the Montgomery and Atlanta railroad, where the mile post says 15 miles to Atlanta. The march has been through a miserable rough country.

We have now been more than half-way around Atlanta, and I have not yet seen a country house that would more than compare favorably with the Coleman Mansion, or a farm that would in any respect vie with the stumpiest of Squire Shipley's stump quarter, or the most barren and scraggiest of Copperas creek barren or brakes. At 12 p. m. they aroused our regiment to tear up railroad track. In one and one-quarter hours we utterly destroyed rails and ties for twice the length of our regiment.

We, by main strength with our hands, turned the track upside down, pried the ties off, stacked them, piled the rails across and fired the piles. Used no tools whatever. On the 29th the 16th Corps moved down and destroyed the railroad to Fairburn. On the 30th the army started for Macon railroad,

Kilpatrick's cavalry in advance. He did splendidly. Had hard skirmishing all the day. Took at least a dozen barricades, and went about as fast as we wanted to. He saved the Flint river bridge, and our corps crossed it, and by 12 p. m., were in good position with works within one-half mile of Jonesboro and the railroad.

Darkness kept us from taking the road that night. The enemy had a strong line of pickets all around us and we built our works under their fire. At daylight the 31st, we found the Rebels in plain sight in front of our regiment. I never saw them so thick. Our regiment is on the extreme right of the division.

Near Jonesboro, August 31, 1864.

We were afraid we would have no battle this month, but our fears were disappointed in a very summary manner this p. m. Hardee, in command of his own and Hood's old corps, attacked the Army of the Tennessee again, the weight of the assault being on our corps. The second division, M. L. Smith's, had the hardest of the fighting. The position our regiment held was unluckily too strong. They did not dare attack us. But we had a splendid view of the fight, both on our right and left.

Six Johnnie lines of battle debouched from the woods on our left, and swept right across our front on open ground, within long musket range, say 600 or 700 yards. This was 2:30 p. m. They were coming over to attack the 16th Corps. A five-gun battery on the right of our regiment and two guns on our left opened on them with spherical case, and threw some canister. They had hardly fired two shots when a Rebel 10-pound Parrott opened on them in front, and a Napoleon battery on our left flank. The Rebels shot admirably and you may imagine our regiment was in a pretty warm position, though our works and traverses made the danger but little.

In ten minutes from the time we first saw the Rebels they struck the 16th Corps, and after a right heavy fight of near an hour they came back flying. Our boys, though not near enough to do much effective shooting, put in 40 or 50 rounds apiece, just to keep our hands in. About the same time they struck Morgan L. they struck our first brigade and the left of our brigade. Our division repulsed them easily and Morgan L. slaughtered them awfully, but he had a hard fight. They charged up close to the left of our regiment, but owing to the direction of our lines not where we could fight them. Our brigade took one colonel, one major, three captains, one lieutenant and 30 men prisoners. The 2d division took several hundred. I can't guess what their loss is, though it is not as heavy as on the 22d or 28th of July, for they did not fight nearly as well. Besides losing a host of men in this campaign, the Rebel Army has lost a large meaure of *vim,* which counts a good deal in soldiering. Our loss in this fight is comparatively nothing. Say 30 men in our brigade; we have four or five scratched in our regiment, but only one much hurt. A spent 12-pound solid shot *rolled on him.*

Kilpatrick started for the railroad south this morning. He has had a big fight with Cleyburn's division, but don't know much about it.

During our fight to-day Schofield and Stanley, 23d and 4th, took the railroad and are destroying it. Hood, with Polk's old corps, are above him and cut off from Hardee.

September 1st, '64.

A real autumn morning. We were aroused at 3 a. m. and the air was then almost crisp. A breath of cold air is a luxury we can appreciate. A fresh, cool breeze is now stirring and I can almost hear the leaves falling. It is a real yellow fall and does me more good than aught else could, except a letter from home. Haven't had one from you for ten days. A prisoner says that yesterday's fight was rougher on them than the 28th of July fight. He said their brigade came up in front of our men, and though they did not stay more than long enough to take one look, when they got back under cover they were 500 men short. They afterwards charged again, and he said he doubted whether any of them got off alive and sound.

This is the 124th day of the campaign, exactly 90 of which we have been under fire. Have also moved 340 miles, though the direct road would be much less. The boys say we just finished the summer campaign in time to commence the fall ditto. I guess the movement surprised Hood. Prisoners all say they understood it to be a raiding party. 'Tis a rather mighty one.

The country between these two railroads is rather better than any we have seen before in Georgia, but I never saw any in Illinois half as poor. Hardly any of the land has been under cultivation since the war commenced. A little sickly corn and a few patches of sorghum and millet are about all the farming evidence I have seen.

Northern Alabama and a few counties in Mississippi are the only passable parts of the Confederacy that I have seen. Mrs. Lee Henty's grand plantations, with their "hospitable mansions, whose broad verandas, supported by graceful pillars," etc., are principally "bosh," at least as far as northern Georgia is concerned. The health of the regiment is excellent, the men being, if anything, healthier than the officers. The lieutenant colonel and major, though both with us, are not yet reported for duty. Captain Boyd, Lieutenants Fox, A. & J. Smith are quite unwell.

Captains Post, Vorhees, Smith and myself have at different times been all the officers fit for duty. I believe I am the only one who has never been off duty during the campaign, though Post, Smith, Vorhees and Dorrance have lost but a few days each, Smith, I believe only one. I don't believe these Rebels can be in very good spirits. I am afraid I'd be a little blue if we'd been whipped as often as they have this campaign. Most of the prisoners are great "peace" men, but they all say that their leaders will never give up as long as they can raise a brigade to fight. Every pup of them has hopes that the Chicago Convention will do *something* for them, they hardly know what. I heard one of the boys say he wished that the Convention could be induced to charge us in these works. There's talk of our going home to vote.

About 2 p. m. a signal officer in a tree reported that he could see our troops moving in line down the railroad toward us. It was the 23d and 4th Corps. The 14th which held the left of our line, about the same time commenced to swing its left around, and by 4 p. m. a battle opened. The 14th broke the enemy's line before the 23d got up, and alone rolled the Rebels up in fine style. By dark the 14th had captured from 12 to 20 pieces of artillery and a large number of prisoners. Three hours more of daylight and Hardee would have had no corps left, for the 4th and 23d were swinging further to the left, and would have been in his rear in less than two hours, when our whole line would have closed in on them.

Six miles south of Jonesboro, September 2, 1864.

At daylight our skirmish line moved forward and found the Rebels gone. When our boys reached the railroad a train of cars was just loading some wounded; the boys made for it, but it outran them. They left a number of their wounded, and when the 14th broke them on the 1st, we captured several hospitals, in one of which were several officers. I saw in a hole by a hospital two legs and three arms. One can't help pitying these Rebel soldiers. They have been whipped here until they have lost all spirit. They don't fight with any spirit when they are attacked and it's more like a butchery than a battle. Our brigade in advance we started after them. The 100th Indiana and 6th Iowa were deployed as skirmishers, and met the Rebel line almost as soon as they started forward. They drove them finely for four miles, when our skirmishers reported that they had run the Rebel army into fortifications.

The country here is quite open, the fields being from half to a mile or more wide, bordered by a narrow strip of wood. The 46th Ohio and our regiment were now deployed to relieve the skirmishers, and take a close look at the enemy's position. They were shooting at us from some rail fences within range, and a mile away, over the fields, we could see them digging; seemed to be constructing a line of pits. We pushed forward under a heavy skirmish fire, and took from a S. C. Brigade the line of pits we saw them making, and went on a little way until we drew a fire from their main works, when we retired to the pits we had taken and prepared to hold them. Found tools in them. This was 3 p. m. About dark the Rebels made three little sorties, but only in light force. We easily repulsed them. Captain Post was wounded in the right breast. Loss in the regiment is seven wounded, raising the loss in the regiment to 178. The 103d and 46th Ohio captured 19 prisoners and killed and wounded at least 25.

September 3, 1864.

Rebels still here. Congratulatory order from Sherman commences, "Slocum occupied Atlanta yesterday at 11 a. m." We can see nothing of our position here. I don't know where the 23d and 14th are. Our line here is very crooked, but generally faces southeast. Commencing at our right our line runs 17th, 15th, 16th and 4th. Kilpatrick is on our right or in the enemy's rear. Can't hear a word of Hood's or Polk's old corps or the militia. Hardee is in our front, and they are the only Rebel troops I know aught of. Cheatham's Division faces us, and a S. C. Brigade is opposite our brigade. Captain Wilkinson was wounded in the arm to-day.

September 4, 1864.

Received a half official notification to-day that the campaign and fighting are over. Orders to clean up arms came also, and the boys, showing their contempt of the enemy's power to do harm, took their guns all to pieces and set to polishing the should-be bright parts, right in view of the enemy's pickets.

September 5, 1864.

News of the capture of Fort Morgan. Orders to march at 8 p. m. I was detailed to bring off the pickets, which was accomplished without trouble. Rebels did not know when we left, as we heard them shooting after we got back in our old works at Jonesboro. The whole army moved into the works we built the 30th. I, with my pickets, got back just before day.

September 6, 1864.

Lay quiet all day. Some Rebel cavalry followed us up and fired a few shots into our regiment's works from the old Rebel fort, but Osterhaus swung his pickets around and gobbled 25 of them, and the rest troubled us no more.

September 7, 1864.

At 7 a. m. moved out on our return, and camped for the night on the left bank of Flint river, six miles south of Eastpoint. The Rebels had fortified to this place, and I don't know how much farther south. As soon as Hood found out that Sherman was attempting to turn his left, he commenced extending his lines down the railroad. He had built six miles of new works when we reached Jonesboro the night of the 30th of August. His line was too long for his troops, so he sent two corps to oppose us, and the 23d and 4th moved into the vacant space in his line right over his works.

Near Eastpoint, September 8, 1864.

We are again in camp for a rest; don't know for how long. What do you think now of the confidence I have so often expressed to you in Sherman and his army? I have every hour of the campaign felt that a failure in it was impossible.

The following complimentary orders were issued, as dated immediately after our going into camp at Eastpoint:

HEADQUARTERS DEP'T. AND ARMY OF THE TENNESSEE,

Eastpoint, Ga., September 9, 1864.

GENERAL FIELD ORDERS,
     No. 16

It is with pride, gratification, and a sense of Divine favor that I congratulate this noble army upon the successful termination of the campaign.

Your officers claim for you a wonderful record—for example, a march of four hundred (400) miles, thirteen (13) distinct engagements, four thousand (4,000) prisoners, and twenty (20) stands of colors captured, and three thousand (3,000) of the enemy's dead buried in your front.

Your movements upon the enemy's flank have been bold and successful; first upon Resaca, second upon Dallas, third upon Kenesaw, fourth upon Nickajack, fifth via Rosewell, upon the Augusta railroad, sixth upon "Ezra Church" to the south-west of Atlanta, and seventh upon Jonesboro and the Macon railroad. Atlanta was evacuated while you were fighting at Jonesboro. The country may never know with what patience, labor and exposure, you have tugged away at every natural and artificial obstacle that an enterprising and confident enemy could interpose.

The terrific battles you have fought may never be realized or credited, still a glad acclaim is already greeting you from the government and people, in view of the results you have helped to gain, and I believe a sense of the magnitude of the achievements of the last hundred days will not abate but increase with time and history.

Our rejoicing is tempered, as it always must be, by the soldier's sorrow at the loss of his companions-in-arms. On every hillside, in every valley throughout your long and circuitous route, from Dalton to Jonesboro, you have buried them.

Your trusted and beloved commander fell in your midst; his name, the name of McPHERSON, carries with it a peculiar feeling of sorrow. I trust the impress of his character is upon you all to incite you to generous actions and noble deeds.

To mourning friends, and to all the disabled in battle, you extend a soldier's sympathy.

My first intimate acquaintance with you dates from the 28th of July. I never beheld fiercer assaults than the enemy then made, and I never saw troops more steady and self-possessed in action than your divisions which were then engaged.

I have learned that for cheerfulness, obedience, rapidity of movement, and confidence in battle, the Army of the Tennessee is not to be surpassed, and it shall be my study that your fair record shall continue, and my purpose to assist you to move steadily forward and float the old Flag in every proud city of the rebellion.

(Signed)   O. O. Howard,
Major General.

(official)
        Sam'l L. Taggart,
            Ass't. Adj't. Gen'l.

HEADQUARTERS FIFTEENTH ARMY CORPS,

EASTPOINT, GA., September 11, 1864.

Officers and Soldiers of the Fifteenth Army Corps:

You have borne your part in the accomplishment of the object of this campaign, a part well and faithfully done.

On the 1st day of May, 1864, from Huntsville, Ala., and its vicinity, you commenced the march. The marches and labors performed by you during this campaign will hardly find a parallel in the history of war. The proud name heretofore acquired by the 15th Corps for soldierly bearing and daring deeds remains untarnished—its lustre undimmed. During the campaign you constituted the main portion of the flanking column of the whole army. Your first move against the enemy was around the right of the army at Resaca, where, by your gallantry, the enemy were driven from the hills and his works on the main road from Vilanaw to Resaca. On the retreat of the enemy, you moved on the right flank of the army by a circuitous route to Adairsville, in the same manner from there to Kingston and Dallas, where, on the 28th day of May, you met the veteran corps of HARDEE, and in a severe and bloody contest you hurled him back, killing and wounding over two thousand, besides capturing a large number of prisoners. You then moved around to the left of the army, by way of Acworth, to Kenesaw Mountain, where again you met the enemy, driving him from three lines of works, capturing over three hundred prisoners. During your stay in front of Kenesaw Mountain, on the 27th of June, you made one of the most daring, bold and heroic charges of the war, against the almost impregnable position of the enemy on Little Kenesaw. You were then moved, by way of Marietta, to Nickajack Creek, on the right of the army, thence back to the extreme left by way of Marietta and Roswell, to the Augusta railroad, near Stone Mountain, a distance of fifty miles, and after effectually destroying the railroad at this point, you moved by way of Decatur to the immediate front of the Rebel stronghold, Atlanta. Here, on the 22d day of July, you again performed your duty nobly, "as patriots and soldiers" in one of the most severe and sanguinary conflicts of the campaign. With hardly time to recover your almost exhausted energies, you were moved again around to the right of the army, only to encounter the same troops against whom you had so recently contended, and the battle of the 28th of July, at Ezra Chapel, will long be remembered by the officers and soldiers of this command. On that day it was that the 15th Corps almost unaided and alone, for four hours con-

tested the field against the Corps of HARDEE and LEE.. You
drove them discomfited from the field causing them to leave
their dead and many of their wounded in your hands. The
many noble and gallant deeds performed by you on that day
will be remembered among the proudest acts of our nation's
history. After pressing the enemy closely for several days,
you again moved to the right of the army, to the West Point
railroad, near Fairburn—after completely destroying the road
for some distance, you marched to Jonesboro, driving the
enemy before you from Pond creek, a distance of ten miles.
At this point you again met the enemy, composed of LEE's
and HARDEE's Corps, on the 31st of August, and punished
them severely, driving them in confusion from the field, with
their dead and many wounded and prisoners left in your hands.
Here again by your skill and true courage you kept sacred the
reputation you have so long maintained, viz.: "The 15th
Corps never meets the enemy but to strike and defeat him."
On the 1st of September, the 14th Corps attacked HARDEE,
you at once opened fire on him, and by your co-operation his
defeat became a rout. HOOD, hearing the news, blew up his
ammunition trains, retreated, and Atlanta was ours.

You have marched during the campaign, in your windings,
the distance of four hundred miles, have put *"hors-du-combat"*
more of the enemy than your corps numbers, have captured
twelve stands of colors, 2,450 prisoners and 210 deserters.

The course of your march is marked by the graves of patri-
otic heroes who have fallen by your side; but at the same time
it is more plainly marked by the blood of traitors who have
defied the constitution and laws, insulted and trampled under
foot the glorious flag of our country.

We deeply sympathize with the friends of those of our com-
rades-in-arms who have fallen; our sorrows are only appeased
by the knowledge that they fell as brave men, battling for the
preservation and perpetuation of one of the best governments
of earth. "Peace be to their ashes."

You now rest for a short time from your labors; during the
respite prepare for future action. Let your country see at all
times by your conduct that you love the cause you have es-
poused; that you have no sympathy with any who would by
word or deed assist vile traitors in dismembering our mighty
Republic or trailing in the dust the emblem of our national
greatness and glory. You are the defenders of a government
that has blessed you heretofore with peace, happiness and pros-
perity. Its perpetuity depends upon your heroism, faithfulness
and devotion.

When the time shall come to go forward again, let us go with the determination to save our nation from threatened wreck and hopeless ruin, not forgetting the appeal from widows and orphans that is borne to us upon every breeze to avenge the loss of their loved ones who have fallen in defense of their country. Be patient, obedient and earnest, and the day is not far distant when you can return to your homes with the proud consolation that you have assisted in causing the old banner to again wave from every mountain's top and over every town and hamlet of our once happy land, and hear the shouts of triumph ascend from a grateful people, proclaiming that once more we have one flag and one country.

John A. Logan,
Major General Commanding.

Headquarters 4th Division, 15th A. C.
Eastpoint, Ga., September 13, 1864.

Officers and Soldiers:

The commander-in-chief, the department commander, and corps officer have each expressed to you their approbation of your conduct during the campaign just closed. They have spoken in general terms to the army, the department and corps.

It is my privilege to address your immediate organization. Your department commander announces the capture of four thousand (4,000) prisoners by the Army of the Tennessee. You have taken one-third of that number. This army has taken from the enemy twenty (20) battleflags; eight of these were wrested from him by your prowess.

Your lists of killed and wounded in battle are larger by one-half than any other division in the Army of the Tennessee.

You have destroyed as many of the enemy as any similar organization in the entire army.

You have never been defeated in this or any other campaign.

Your record is therefore spotless, and you should be and doubtless are proud of it. Your friends at home and the comtry at large will some day understand and appreciate your conduct.

Had your lamented department commander been spared, his familiarity with your history, and identification with yourselves, would have commanded for you more complete justice. Your corps commander is not now, nor has he ever been, slow to acknowledge your merits, but he is powerless to do more.

Your organization will probably soon be changed, and the stranger to you will reap the reward of your devotion and self-sacrifice. The just reward, always so highly prized by the true soldier, may not be yours, but the consciousness of duty well performed will remain with you forever. You will sustain your high reputation by doing battle, as heretofore, for your country, and not for men. Do so cheerfully. My connection with you as your division commander may possibly soon be severed. Support any future officer as you have supported me, and success must attend your efforts. I ask from you the same kind of remembrance I shall ever give to each true soldier of this command.

(Signed)   WILLIAM HARROW,
Brigadier General U. S. Vols.

EXPLANATORY NOTE.

[The Army of the Tennessee remained at, or near, East Point, until October 4th. When General Sherman decided to destroy Atlanta, he gave the inhabitants their choice as to where they would go, either north, south, or remain, and take their chances in the ruined city. Prisoners captured during the campaign were also exchanged, and a detail of some 70 or 80 men from the regiment, commanded by Captain Wills, and a like command from the 100th Indiana, was given the duty of guarding the "neutral ground" at a place called Rough and Ready, some eight or ten miles south of Atlanta. This duty being performed, the detail rejoined the regiment, having been so occupied about ten days. The 4th Division was here broken up, and the "old 2d Brigade" was transferred to the 1st Division, commanded by Gen. C. R. Wood.]

The diary is now resumed.

October 4, 1864.

We have been expecting to move for several days. The Rebels have crossed the Chattanooga and are moving on our rear, *a la* Jonesboro. If half the force they took over get back I'll be much disappointed. We yesterday sent our extra baggage to Atlanta to store, and at 11 last night orders came to march at 5 a. m. to-day. We will be off in a few minutes now. Marietta is in our route direction.

Six miles south of Marietta, October 5, 1864.

Had an awful day's march yesterday, full 20 miles and the road very muddy and slippery. County peculiarly Georgian, the like of which, I hope, is to be found nowhere else in Uncle Sam's domain. When we started the "spring or grapevine" dispatch said that Hardee's headquarters were in Marietta, and that he was living very high on sanitary stores, of which there is enough to feed an army for a time. We crossed the river on pontoons near the railroad bridge, a very fine work, considering it was built inside of a week.

We then heard that Marietta was not in Hardee's possession, but that lively skirmishing was going on along the lines, and that Hardee's army was before the place. About three miles from the river we met a wagon train just from Marietta; part of the guards had not heard that any Rebels were near the town. Others said that Hood's army was just the other side of Kenesaw, about two miles north of Marietta. Finally a cavalry man said part of our (guard's) cavalry occupied Kenesaw, from the top of which *he* had seen the Rebel army occupying an old line of works of ours just this side of Big Shanty. I just thought I would give you a sample of the "grape cuttings" that accompany a march. A body of Rebels is evidently above Marietta, on the railroad; how strong I don't know, and it is none of my business. "Pap" knows all about it. He never tells us anything. He has not issued a "battle order" during the whole campaign and hardly a congratulatory. If the Rebels are there in force, there will be a battle. It can have but one result, and cannot fail to be a disastrous one for them. We have at least 50 days' full rations and I think 90, so the breaking of the railroad cannot affect us. Six p. m.—We took all kinds of roundabout roads to-day, and marched eight miles to make not over four. I have been really sick all day, but hope it will be over by morning. The Johnnies have left Big Shanty, moving north on the railroad, tearing it up as they travel. Go it, Rebels!

October 6, 1864, 12 m.

Rained all last night, and has just suspended for a few minutes, I expect. Kept dry, thanks to our rubber blankets. Drew five days' rations this morning, full of everything except beans; plenty of beef, though. We only drew one-quarter of a pound per man for the whole five days. Part of our railroad bridge across the Chattahoochie washed away a few days ago. It will be finished again to-day. There was some fighting up near Allatoona Pass yesterday, in which, rumor says, our folks were worsted. The Rebels are moving up the road in that direction. They will have to leave there or wait and fight us. I hear that Kilpatrick burned 200 or 300 of their wagons yesterday. We'll warm those fellows if they will only wait for us somewhere. We are under orders to start at a moment's notice. Mud is not over a foot deep and everything else is lovely in proportion. I was confoundedly sick all day yesterday, could not eat any supper, but about 9 p. m. the boys brought some beans about half cooked, and the notion taking me I ate a couple of quarts thereof. Have felt splendidly ever since. Our pickets that we left at Eastpoint have just got in. The division field officer of the day who had charge of them misunderstood his instructions and marched to the river at Sandtown, 15 miles below where we crossed. The Rebels fired into them and I suppose captured half a dozen stragglers.

October 7, 1864.

The Rebels have left the railroad after being whipped by General Corse at Allatoona Pass. The 14th Corps drove them out to Lost Mountain yesterday. No hard fighting. They tore up not more than eight miles of railroad, which will be rebuilt in a very few days.

Deserters report the whole Rebel Army here, but that the ten days' rations they started with have run out. Other deserters say that their army has started for Nashville, Huntsville, or hell; that they are satisfied they can't make either of the first named places, and would rather go to Sherman than the last named. It is wonderful what confidence this army has in Sherman. Every man seems to think the idea of these Rebels being able to do us any permanent harm is perfectly preposterous, and all are in the best of spirits. I can't help thinking that the Rebels must have all cleared out of this vicinity, or else we'd be going for them. Our stock is in too bad condition to follow them far over the, at present, horrible roads. A man rode along on a poor old bone-rack of a horse a while ago. Some wag commenced, "caw," "caw," "caw." The whole camp took it up and for five minutes you would have thought that 10,000 crows were holding a jubilee. Let some one start a squirrel or rabbit and 500 men will be after it in a minute. Old soldiers are just a lot of men with school-boy spirits.

Officers don't draw meat like the men. I have just had two meals of beef (and no other meat) in the last ten days. All our officers are the same way. It is mostly our own fault.

On picket four miles south of Marietta, October 8th.

We occupy the old Johnny skirmish pits. It was outrageously cold last night. I elected myself fireman and did not neglect my duties. I have men from every regiment in the brigade (seven). There are an abundance of chestnuts here, and at every post the boys have worked pretty steadily all day roasting and eating. All sit on their knapsacks before the fire, every fellow with a stick to take out the nuts. It is right interesting to hear the men talk. Nearly all have been in the service three years or over, and almost every battlefield in the West has been seen by some of the brigade. We move. The Rebels have crossed the Etawah.

20

Two miles north of Kenesaw Mountain,

October 9, 1864.

About 5 o'clock last night, just when we should have been relieved, we heard the "General" sounded through the camp, and in half an hour more the "Assembly." The corps started toward Marietta, and in another half hour we assembled, and in charge of the division officer of the day followed as rear guard of the train.

At 12 p. m., after a cold, tiresome march, the train corraled, and we built fires and turned in beside them for the balance of the night, right at the northeast base of Kenesaw Mountain. This a. m. found the brigade two miles further north. The Rebel Army was here three days ago and tore up the railroad all along here. They are now near Van Wirt. If they go north across the Etawah, we will probably follow. Their present position menances the whole line of road from Rome to the Chattahoochie crossing.

Near Kenesaw Mountain, October 10, 1864.

Was on the ground we charged on the 27th of June, and also on top of Kenesaw to-day. Very fine view, but nothing like equal to that from Lookout. The signal station here communicates direct with Atlanta, Allatoona and Roswell.

I picked up some black oak acorns to-day from a tree that shades the graves of 12 or 15 of our soldiers, mostly from our regiment, who fell on the 27th. They were buried where they fell. That charge was the maddest folly of the campaign.

Allatoona Pass, October 11, 1864.

Our corps moved at the setting of the sun, and continued moving until we were all confoundedly tired. I never saw the men so noisy, funny, or in any way or every way feeling half so good. After we had marched about eight miles, one of Howard's staff came back along the line and informed us that Sherman had just notified Howard that Richmond is ours. Everybody believed it, but nobody cheered. They were saving the yells for the confirmation. We camped at 1 a. m. with orders for reveille at 4 and march at 5 a. m.

Three miles south of Kingston, October 12, 1864.

Started at daylight this morning. The Rebels were then at Rome. Stopped here at 5 p. m. It is understood that the Rebel Army has moved southwest into Alabama.

Passed through the best country to-day that we have seen in Georgia. We are camped on what has been a splendid plantation (equal to anything on Copperas creek), and on the only clover field, I think, in Georgia. This is about the only ground on which I have seen the Jamestown weed, plantain, or clover. We are very scare of forage, and the officers turned their horses out on the clover to graze. The Northern stock enjoyed it exceedingly, but the Southern horses did not know enough to eat it. They nosed around among the rich bundles of clover to pick out the weeds and hard wild grass, the latter not near as good as our poorest prairie grass.

Three miles from Rome, Ga., October 13, 1864.

Started at 8 this morning and landed here at dark. Heard 40 or 50 cannon shots in vicinity of Rome during the day's march. The country to-day is fair for Georgia, but not equal to that between Cartersville and Kingston. While we were resting to-day, Osterhaus (at present commanding our corps) rode by our regiment and a few scamps hollowed "sowbelly, sowbelly." You know the men have been living on army beef for a month, and it is not desirable fare; still they were only in fun, and I noticed the general smile, but some puppy finally cried out "kraut," and another echoed it with "kraut by the barrel." The general wheeled his horse and rode up to us, his face white with passion. "Vat regiment ish dis?" No one answered. He rode up near me and again asked, "Vat regiment ish dis?" I told him. "Vy don't you kit up?" I arose and again answered him respectfully, "The 103d Illinois, sir." "Vare ish your colonel?" "At the right of the regiment, sir." He rode up to Wright and gave him the devil. I have not been so mortified for a long time. We all think a great deal of Osterhaus, and just coming into his division were all desirous that his first impressions of our regiment should be favorable.

As it is, two or three insulting puppies have given us a name
with him that I have no doubt will cause us trouble for a long
time. Yelping "sauer kraut" at a German is a poor way to
gain his favor.

(A duplicate of dates.) October 12, 1864.

Last night while our train was passing through Cass-
ville, a town four miles south of Kingston, an ambulance
gave out and the driver unhitched and concluded to stay
all night. That was some three miles from where we
stayed. Nine stragglers also laid down beside the ambulance for the night. The 17th Corps came through there
to-day and found the driver dead, with a bayonet thrust
through him, and the traps of the nine men laying around.
The horses and nine men are missing. I heard to-night
that the bodies of the nine men had been found altogether.
Our men burned the town. I expect we will lie here to-
morrow, and if Hood's army is in this vicinity go for it
next day. Nobody thinks he will dare to fight us. We
have parts of five corps here.

(Duplicated also.) October 13, 1864.

The men drew full rations of bacon to-day. There has
been some fighting nine miles down the north side of the
Coosa river to-day. Our corps moves back on the Kingston road at "retreat." Don't know where to.

Received two letters from you to-day, also papers, for
which am very thankful. Have had a good rest to-day.
Everybody is in glorious spirits. Kilpatrick started west to-
day with 50 days' rations of salt. I wish I was with him.

Three miles southwest of Adairsville, October 14th.

We marched at sunset last evening and halted not until
3 this a. m. Marched miserably slow the first five miles
through a deep gorge, but about 1 o'clock got straightened
out on the Rome and Calhoun road, a good one, and then
got along nicely. In the fighting at Rome yesterday, our

folks whipped them and took some artillery. We got to bed at 3:15, and reveille sounded at 5 and we marched at 6:30. Not much sleep after marching 20 miles, was it. We had no crackers this morning, and before I got up my imagination was reveling in the prospect of a breakfast on parched corn, but at the festive board the cook surprised us with a mess of pancakes. They looked like plates cut out of a rubber blanket, and tasted accordingly. One member of the mess said they just came up to his ideal of a poet's dream. Another, that they only lacked one thing, and that was the stamp, "Goodyear's Patent." The Surgeon advised us to use them sparingly, for, said he, "If they mass against any part of your interior lines the consequences will be dire." But we were hard up for breadstuffs, and closed with the dreadful stuff manfully. Twelve m.—Have stopped for dinner.

The Rebel army was, or part of it, at Resaca yesterday, about nine miles from here.

Calhoun, Ga., October 15, 1864.

Stayed here last night. Reveille at 3 a. m., but our brigade brings up the rear of the corps to-day, and we won't get off until after daylight.

Resaca, October 15, 1864, 10 a. m.

We are waiting here for rations. The 4th and 14th Corps are ahead, and for the last half hour we have heard very heavy skirmishing toward "Snake Creek Gap," just about where we heard the first fighting of the campaign, a little over five months ago. There is enough to interest me in the prospect for the next three days. Snake Creek Gap, 10 p. m. We have the whole gap.

North end Snake Creek Gap, October 16, 1864.

After a tedious march got here at 11 p. m. The Rebels about six hours ahead of us had blockaded the road in good style. They did some half a day's work, with hundreds of men, and delayed us about—ten minutes.

On summit of Taylor's Ridge, Shipp's Gap, p. m.

Our division has the advance to-day. The Rebels drove very well, until we got here, when, having a very good position, they resisted us with some vim. A few men of the 1st brigade, finally climbed the hill, flanked and routed them. Our loss, seven wounded. We got 35 prisoners and killed and wounded a dozen or so.

October 17, 1864.

I incline to think that the raid and pursuit are both over, though we wish that Sherman would follow them until they get the punishment they deserve for their impudence. They tore up some 20 miles of railroad, killed and wounded not over 750 for us, and captured about 1,100. Their loss in wounded and killed, whom we have buried, is 1,900; prisoners, that I know of, 600; besides a lot of deserters who have come in. Eight hundred of the prisoners captured by them were negroes, who could not have been taken but for the cowardice of their Colonel, Johnson.

The tearing up of the railroad amounts to nothing. We have not had our rations cut down an ounce in anything.

The man that run that raid ought to be ashamed of himself, and I'll venture he is.

In Snake Creek Gap, but for General Stanley's laziness, we would have got enough prisoners to make Hood howl. He rested his corps three hours, just as he did when entrusted with a critical piece of work at Jonesboro.

We have been having a gay time this morning. It is cold enough to make us sit close to the fire, and the negroes keep us in chestnuts.

La Fayette, October 18, 1864.

Our brigade was marching through Cane Creek Valley yesterday until 4 p. m., when we struck out for this place five miles, which we made in one and one-half hours. Nice little town almost surrounded with half-mountains. There has been a pair of cavalry fights here, the fruits whereof can be seen in an addition to the cemetery, near which we are bivouacked, some 25 Rebel graves, and half as many Yankees. Divers fair creatures can be seen here, chiefly Rebels; I have thought though, to-day, much Union. We are now bound for Rome.

Near Summerville, October 19, 1864.

Reached this place yesterday. The cavalry advance had some sharp skirmishing, and brought back some two or three prisoners. We are drawing full rations, besides preying off the country, all kinds of meat, apples, potatoes, and I believe the men find a little of everything known to be eatable. Entering houses is prohibited under penalty of death, but some scoundrels manage to pillage many houses. Foraging is also *half* prohibited, but I am satisfied that our general officers do not object to our taking meat, etc., if houses are not entered. Ten p. m.—Have stopped here to draw rations. The 23d and 4th Corps have already moved forward on the old Alabama road. That looks as though we were intending to follow the Rebels. We "liners" have no idea where they are. One rumor is that they are moving northwest, intending to cross the Tennessee river, south or southwest of Huntsville. Another that they are moving to their new base at or near Blue Mountain, on the road from here to Talladega, Ala. If we are going to follow them, I look for a long campaign. But for one thing, we would rather go into a campaign immediately than into camp. That is, the men have not been paid off for ten months, and many families are undoubtedly suffering in consequence. Our money is waiting for us, and we will get it whenever the Johnnies will let us stop long enough for the paymasters to catch up. Don't you people ever think of us as being without rations. We sometimes wish the Rebels would cut our communications entirely, so that we could live wholly off the country. The Rebels only take corn and meat, and we fatten on what they are not allowed to touch.

Alpine, Chatuga Valley, October 20, 1864.

Got here at dark last night, eight miles from Summerville. We seemed to be headed southwest. I have the sorest feet I have enjoyed for two years. Do you notice how accurately I miss it in every prediction I venture? I am a fair sample of the ignorance "Pap" keeps this army of his movements. He has shown his ability to keep us from divining his purposes, but he or any other general cannot keep us from guessing. Fine country here, for Georgia. An officer and 20 men are detailed daily for foragers.

They start ahead in the morning, and shoot hogs, sheep, gather sweet potatoes, apples, etc., and bring all out to the roadside. The hogs and sheep are cut into pieces of about 20 or 25 pounds. When the regiment comes along every man makes a grab as he passes at the pile, throws his chunk over his shoulder, and all without breaking ranks. You can imagine the appearance a battalion would make at nightfall.

Gaylesville, Ala., October 21, 1864.

Marched about 18 miles yesterday down a very fine valley, between Lookout Mountain and Taylor's Ridge, crossed the latter after dark through a pass that beat all for blackness and stones, to tumble over, that I ever saw. Got a very large mail yesterday, but only one letter from you. We move again this morning, but don't know when. Can send a letter back from here, first chance we have had this month. I guess we have halted here to wait the building of a bridge over the Coosa. The Rebels burned it yesterday.

What we are going for nobody knows. I saw Sherman yesterday as we passed through Gaylesville. He was talking with Jeff. C. Davis. He always has a cigar hanging from the corner of his mouth. It is always about half-gone, but I never saw it lighted. He is certainly the most peculiar-looking man I ever saw. At one house we passed this morning we saw three of the ugliest-looking women imaginable. They sat on the porch step, side by side, hoopless, unkempt and unwashed. I'll swear that man never before witnessed three such frights together. All three were singing a Rebel song. I knew they were trying to sing, but although close to them, could not distinguish a word. Some of the men recognized the tune as belonging to a tune called the "Rebel Soldier." The men were so completely surprised and thunderstruck by the show that they had not a word to say. It tickles us to see that you home folks are uneasy about us because Hood has got into our rear. I tell you that I have not seen a man uneasy for a minute, on that subject, and that Hood has to run like a hound to get away from us. If Hood's army was to-day, twice as strong as it is, we would be too many for him.

October 22, 1864.

I was foraging to-day for the regiment with about 20 men. Got plenty of hogs and potatoes. Sweet potatoes are about the size of ordinary pumpkins and most delicious.

October 23, 1864.

A day of rest and washing. The cavalry was out some dozen miles southwest, and report the enemy intrenched and in force.

Eight miles southeast of last night's camp,

October 24, 1864.

With five brigades of our corps started at 3:30 p. m. to look after Rebels reported. Came through a little hamlet called Blue Pond from a little lake in the neighborhood of a dirty mud color. Plenty of milk and honey.

Nine miles northwest of Gadsden, Ala.,

October 25, 1864.

Found the Rebels about noon to-day in position behind a rail work, running across from Lookout Mountain to Coosa river. It was only Wheeler's cavalry, and we blew them out easily. We formed to charge them, but they wouldn't wait. We followed until we were satisfied there was no infantry behind them, and then settled for the night, and sent out foragers. There was some miserable artillery firing by both sides. Not a dozen men were hurt; only one in our brigade, 100th Indiana.

At Little River again, October 26, 1864.

Got back on the 25th, and have been laying quiet. Our foragers have been skirmishing a good deal with the enemies' scouts, but few casualties however.

Cedar Bluff, Ala., October 27, 1864.

Waiting here for the 17th Army Corps to get across the Coosa. It is a beautiful little river, not as wide as the Illinois, but has a deeper channel. We are starting on the road to Talladega; don't even know whether we are starting on a campaign or not. Hood is reported across the Tennessee. We understand that Sherman has men enough to attend to him, and that Sherman intends to use us to Christianize this country. Many think we are now on the way to Montgomery or Selma. River here about 120 yards wide. About a thousand head of our cattle swam across, some of them swam over and back two or three times, and many of the thin ones drowned, for which we were grateful to the drovers as it saved us some very hard chewing.

Camp in piney woods, five miles South of Cedar Bluffs,

October 29, 1864.

Such a march over pine ridges and through swamps; Egyptian darkness would take a back seat in comparison with this night. It just happened to strike the men as funny, and they kept up a roar of cheering the whole distance.

Near Cave Springs, Ga., 26 miles south of Rome,

October 31, 1864, 1 a. m.

We think we are going to Rome. Had an extremely disagreeable march yesterday of only 12 miles, over pine and scrub oak ridges. A swamp in every valley. Camped before dark for almost the first time of the trip. This is the 27th day since we broke camp at Eastpoint. Everybody is all right. Compliments to Colonel Wright, if he is at home, and tell him immense rumors are afloat of a Montgomery campaign. Had an immense supper of fresh pork and sweet potatoes.

Cedar Town, Ga., November 1, 1864.

Abomination of abominations, train guard to-day. It is the most disagreeable duty we are subject to on the march. I escaped the afternoon duty by being sent out foraging. Got all the men would carry, and disgusted a rich citizen considerably, also saw a nice, rosy-faced girl, whose teeth and fiingernails would spoil a meal for any one of ordinary constitution. One man in our brigade wounded, 40th Illinois, in a little skirmish to-day.

Van Wirt, Ga., November 2, 1864.

It has rained steadily all day. Moved 12 miles. I have an excellent pair of shoes. A good deal of water got into them to-day, but it all ran out. Camp to-night on a high pine ridge. Pine knot fires come in first rate. That 40th boy that was wounded last night was captured with three more of our men by 30 Rebels and taken eight or ten miles, then formed in line and ordered to about face and fired upon; two fell dead and the other two ran away.

Five miles northwest of Villa Rica, Ga.,

Novembebr 3, 1864, 6 p. m.

Forty-eight hours' rain without a stop and a good prospect for as much more. We left Van Wirt and Dallas to the left, and by 16 miles hard marching have got near enough over this barren ridge, I think, to find a few marks of civilization. Rumor says we are going to Atlanta to relieve the 20th Corps, and will then be paid. Passed to-day a one-horse wagon, a large ox in the shafts and four women in the wagon dressed for a party.

Powder Springs, November 4, 1864, 6 p. m.

Cold rain to-day. Made 15 miles. Country only fit for (?) Come through a long line of fine works the Rebels put up after they took up our railroad at Acworth. This about the last day of pork and potatoes; to-morrow will bring us to a country we have worn out.

Vinings Station, November 5, 1864.

Our brigade rear guard all day. Foragers could not find a thing. Traveled through a perfect labyrinth of breastworks. Rebel or Yankee grave every 100 yards. One month ago we passed here confident of overtaking Hood, but he was too swift for us, and after 300 miles travel we are back at the starting point. Altogether it has been the most pleasant campaign of my soldiering. The officers of the regiment have all messed together, and we have had all the good living and fun we wanted. I was under the civilizing influence of a white woman's society to-day for five minutes, and in consequence feel duly amiable.

November 6, 1864.

Rain all day. We are preparing for a huge campaign, and are all right glad of it; 50 days' rations is the word. Don't know when we start. Montgomery or Augusta are probably the points. We are going to shake up the bones of the rebellion. I would not miss this campaign for anything.

November 12, 1864.

The Rubicon is passed, the die is cast, and all that sort of thing. We to-day severed our own cracker line. At 11 a. m. ours and the 17th Corps were let loose on the railroad, the men worked with a will and before dark the 12 miles of track between here and Marietta were destroyed. The ties were piled and burned and the rails, after being heated red hot in the middle were looped around trees or telegraph poles. Old destruction himself could not have done the work better. The

way the Rebels destroyed our road on their raid was not even
a fair parody on our style.   The 20th Corps is at it between
Atlanta and the river, and the 14th and 23d north of Marietta.
We have orders to-night to move at 7 a. m.

White Hall, two miles west of Atlanta,

November 13, 1864.

We made 15 miles to-day very easily.   Coming through
Atlanta the smoke almost blinded us.   I believe everything of
any importance there is on fire.   Understand that all the large
buildings are to be burned.   Tremendous smoke also rising
over the site of Marietta.   It is said that we will lie here two
or three days.   We are only one-half mile from where we did
our hard fighting "before Atlanta."

November 14, 1864.

Troops are coming in to-day on all the roads.   'Tis said
that we will be ready to move to-morrow.   So be it.   The
cracker line is cut now and we don't want to lie still eating
up our precious rations.   I was again over the old position we
occupied before Atlanta.   I would like to be your guide over
that ground some day.   Tremendous fires in Atlanta to-day.

Near Jonesboro, November 15, 1864.

The grand expeditionary force has commenced moving.   Our
regiment has the honor of leading our corps in the first day's
march.   Made about 18 miles to-day, the first ten of which
the two or three companies of cavalry who led us had quite
lively skirmishing.

At one point the Rebels took advantage of an old line of
works and made quite a stubborn resistance, but our regiment,
though we were deployed and advanced as skirmishers, did not
get a shot the whole day.   Just as we turned off the road to
bivouac the Rebels opened a piece of artillery on us, but fired
only a few shots and hurt no one.   Item: Saw a lovely girl to-

day. Item: Had on the Union to-day. Item: Had my first drink of milk since the 26th of December, '63. Item: Have an oppossum which "Rueben" is to cook for my breakfast. Heavy cannonading west of us.

McDonough, November 16, 1864, 11 p. m.

Made 14 miles to-day through a really fine country. Only saw one house though, that looked like living. Forage is no name for the good things our foragers find here. I notify you that I had eggs for supper. There was some lively cannonading toward Lovejoy this morning, but it has been quiet ever since. Think the "Militia" has discovered that this party "sizes their pile," and have "fled to the mountain." Our whole corps are on the road to-day. The advance got into camp five miles ahead, at noon. We got here one hour ago, and our division camps six miles back. The roads are excellent and we travel right along. We all voted this morning that opossum meat was good enough for white folks. I liked it very much.

Near Jackson, Ga., November 17, 1864, 12 a. m.

Have just had our coffee. Marched some 17 miles to-day. Begin to see where the "rich planters" come in. This is probably the most gigantic pleasure excursion ever planned. It already beats everything I ever saw soldiering, and promises to prove much richer yet. I wish Sherman would burn the commissary trains, we have no use for what they carry, and the train only bothers us. It is most ludicrous to see the actions of the negro women as we pass. They seem to be half crazy with joy, and when a band strikes up they go stark mad. Our men are clear discouraged with foraging, they can't carry half the hogs and potatoes they find right along the road. The men detailed for that purpose are finding lots of horses and mules. The 6th Iowa are plumb crazy on the horse question.

———— Springs, 40 miles from Macon,

November 18, 1864.

We got here at noon but will wait until to-morrow, I understand, for the 3d and 4th Divisions to lay a pontoon bridge across the Ocmulgee river. This has been a summer resort of some note. From 800 to 1,000 people congregate here. The spring is a little stream of water not larger than your finger, which runs from the rock at the rate of a gallon a minute. It is sulphur water with some other ingredient that gives it a very disagreeable ordor. This is quite a romantic place. Foraged some peach brandy, which was *destroyed*.

Near Hillsboro, November 19, 1864.

Have been foraging to-day. Crossed the Ocmulgee at Ocmulgee Mills, on pontoons. This river is much like the Chattahoochie, but not so broad. I am lost from the division to-night and camped near the 2d Division. By the kindness of Mrs. Elizabeth Celia Pye, I occupy a feather bed to-night. It is the first house I have been in for the last three months. She understood from the Rebels that we burned all houses and she took all her things out and hid them in the woods. The foragers found them and brought them in to her. Had an excellent supper with the boys. This is a level, fine country, and has been well cultivated.

Near Clinton, November 20, 1864.

Struck out foraging before daylight this morning. Almost any house on the road to-day would furnish pork and potatoes enough for a brigade. I got to the regiment about 8 p. m. last night. They say our brigade marched until 3 a. m., and the reveille sounded before the men got through supper. We passed over the scene of Stoneman's fighting and surrender last August. Some of our men found two of our dead soldiers unburied, which don't speak well for the Rebels, and is charged against them. I think there is less pillaging this trip than I ever saw before.

Near Macon, Ga., November 21, 1864.

This makes seven days from Atlanta, 114 miles by the roads we have marched. I think that time for an army like ours, over bad roads, too, for at least four days, is unprecedented.

Our cavalry had a little skirmish at Macon last evening and were driven back. I heard some cannonading, but don't think it amounted to much. There was a little skirmish about the rear of our division at 4 this p. m., but beside racing and maybe capturing some half-dozen of our foragers, it amounted to nothing. Our left occupied Milledgeville. Governor Brown is here at Macon, also Beauregard, and they have scraped together some ten or a dozen *things* to defend the town with. I don't think from looks at present, that "Pap" is going to try the town, but can't tell. We have thrown up a little rail barricade this evening, which looks as if we were intending to destroy the Macon and Savannah railroad, on which rests the right of our brigade. We are afraid at this writing that Sheaff Herr was captured to-day. He was foraging where that little skirmish took place this p. m., and Rebels were seen after, and within 75 yards of him. It has rained steadily all day and for the last 60 hours, but has turned cold and is now clear.

Near Griswoldville, November 22, 1864.

Has been a gay day for our brigade. The other two brigades of our division went to work on the railroad this morning, and we on a reconnoisance toward Macon. Found Rebel cavalry at once. My Companies A and B, were thrown out as skirmishers. Forty of us drove at least 400 Rebel cavalry at least four miles, and kept them a mile ahead of the brigade. I think we killed and wounded at least 20 of them. We finally charged them out of a rail barricade and thoroughly stampeded them. It was the richest thing I ever saw. We got highly complimented on the way we drove them. Griswoldville was the point we started for, and having reached it we lay there an hour or so, and were then ordered back to the brigade. We found it in line along an open field, building a rail barricade along the front. We had a nice open field without even a fence on it, full 600 yards wide in our front. We were getting dinner, not dreaming of a fight, when lively musketry opened on the picket line, and in a minute more our pickets came in flying. A fine line of Johnnies pushed out of the woods after them, and then started for us. We commenced throwing up logs in our front and did not fire a shot until they were within 250 yards of us, by which time our works would protect us from musketry. We all felt that we had a sure thing, and had there been but one line of Rebels, we would have let them come up close to us. But, by the time the first line had got within 250 yards of us, three other lines had emerged from the woods, and they had run two batteries out on the field further to our right which opened on us. Our artillery returned the fire, but was silenced almost immediately. We then let loose on them with our muskets, and if we did not interest them, it is queer. One after another their lines crumbled to pieces, and they took the run to save themselves. There was a ravine 50 yards in front of us, and as the Rebels did not dare to run back over that field, they broke for the ravine. It was awful the way we slaughtered those men. Once in the ravine most of them escaped by following it up, the willows and canes screening them. We let a skirmish line into the ravine, which gobbled some 50 prisoners, a number of Africans among them. It was a most complete repulse, and when the numbers alone are considered, a glorious thing for us. Only our little brigade of say 1,100 muskets were engaged on our side and no support was nearer than four miles (and then but one brigade), while the Rebels had four brigades and two regiments, about 6,000 men. But the four brigades were "Militia." We estimate their loss at 1,000, and I do not think it an overestimate. Ours is 14 killed and 42 wounded in the whole

21

brigade; four killed and seven wounded in the regiment; two in my company; 25 out of 30 Rebel bullets went 20 feet over our heads. Not one of ours went higher than their heads. Gen. C. C. Wolcutt was wounded much as Colonel Wright was, but more severely. No officers in our regiment were wounded. Two Rebel generals were either killed or wounded—General George, who formerly commanded in north Mississippi, and General Hall or Call. I was never so affected at the sight of wounded and dead before.

Old grey-haired and weakly-looking men and little boys, not over 15 years old, lay dead or writhing in pain. I did pity those boys, they almost all who could talk, said the Rebel cavalry gathered them up and forced them in.

We took all inside our skirmish line that could bear moving, to our hospital, and covered the rest with the blankets of the dead. I hope we will never have to shoot at such men again. They knew nothing at all about fighting, and I think their officers knew as little, or else, certainly knew nothing about our being there. About dark we moved back to this place, two miles from the battle field. The Johnnies drew off before we did, I think.

Near Gordon, November 23, 1864.

Came here to-day, about eight miles, find the Army of the Tennessee all here. Have heard nothing of the Rebels to-day; saw ice one and one-half inches thick that formed last night. Wore my overcoat all day. The left wing is either at Milledgeville or gone on east. A branch road runs up to the Capitol from the Macon and Savannah railroad, leaving it at Gordon. It is now all destroyed. This road is very easily destroyed. The iron is laid on stringers, which are only fastened to the ties with wooden pins. We have yet done nothing at it, but boys who have, say they pry up one stringer with the iron on it, roll it over to the other half of the track, lay some rails on, and fire it. The iron being firmly fastened to the stringer, expanding under the heat destroys it completely. The country here is quite rolling, not quite as rich as the Indian Spring country, but there is yet plenty of forage. The woods are mostly pine, and we are all most anxious to get where we will have some other fuel. The smoke of pine wood is so disagreeable.

Irwinton, November 24, 1864.

Made 12 miles to-day over a rolling but well settled country. This is a nice little 700 county town. I hear that the troops that were at Macon are passing us on our right. Suppose they want to get in our front to annoy us again. They had better keep out of our way. Had another romantic meeting to-day with a Miss Howell. Spent the evening at her house. A charming girl, very accomplished. Admire her very much. Understand to-day that "Pap's" headquarters are at Howell Cobb's house in Milledgville. Some of the men saw a Macon paper of the 21st inst. It gave the proceedings of a citizen's meeting. In resolutions they declared that Sherman's army must be stopped in its mad career and pledged themselves to turn out *en masse* and harrass us all day and night. In fact, to give us no rest at all. The operations of the next day show how they commenced their good work. Have not heard anything of them since.

Near Ball's Ferry, Oconee River,

November 25, 1864.

Got off at daylight; made some eight miles, formed in a line in a field. "Halt!" "Cover!" "Front!" "Stack arms!" Now men get rails and fix for the night. So we think we have plenty of time and make our motions accordingly. We had just got our things fairly unpacked when the "General" sounded. Fifteen minutes afterward the assembly, and we were again on the march. All right. This miserable pine smoke again to-night. Saw the 17th Corps to-day for the first time on the trip. They tried to cross the river at the railroad bridge, but the Johnnies would not let them, and they had to come down to our road. I think we are to-night half way on our journey. The boys had a great time last night in Irwinton. The citizens had buried a great many things to keep them from the "vandals" and the boys soon found it out. Hundreds of them were armed with sharpened sticks probing the earth, "prospecting." They found a little of everything, and I guess they took it all to the owners, eatables and drinkables. We fell in at retreat, and had general order No 26 read to us for I guess the 20th time. It declares that "any soldier or army follower who shall be convicted of the crime of arson or robbery, or who shall be caught pillaging, shall be shot, and gives officers and non-commissioned ditto the right to shoot pillagers in the act." There have been 20 to 30 booms of artillery at the ferry this evening. Think it was the 2d Division. They'll be smart Rebels who keep that division from laying their pontoons.

Eight miles east of Oconee River, three miles south of M. & S. R. R.

November 26, 1864, 12 p. m.

Howard wrote Osterhaus a letter congratulating him on the success in the Griswoldville fight, and had it published to us to-day.

HEADQUARTERS DEPT. AND ARMY OF THE TENNESSEE.,

GORDON, GA., November 23d, 1864.

Mayor General Osterhaus, Com'dg. 15th Corps:
General:

I take sincere pleasure in congratulating the Brigade of General Walcutt, of General Wood's Division of the 15th Corps, on its complete sucess in the action of yesterday.

Officers from other commands who were looking on say that there never was a better brigade of soldiers.

I am exceedingly sorry that any of our brave men should fall, and for the suffering of the wounded, the thanks of the army are doubly due to them.

I tender my sympathy through you to the brave and excellent commander of the brigade, Brigadier General Walcutt.

It is hoped that his wound will not disable him.

Very respectfully,

Your obedient servant,

(Signed)   O. O. HOWARD,

Major General.

P. S. The loss of the enemy is estimated from 1,500 to 2,000 killed, wounded, and prisoners.   O. O. H., M. G.

We lay in camp until 4 p. m., when we started, and after three miles of miserable pine swamp we crossed the Oconee on pontoons. It was dark, but I noticed that the current was rapid and the water looked deep.

I counted 80 steps on the bridge and ten boats under it. I am sure that I to-day saw palm-leaf fan material growing. It is a most singular looking plant. The country this side of the river to our camp is quite level and four-fifths cultivated. All the woods pine, and soil all sand.

Riddlesville, November 27, 1864.

Was foraging this morning and supplied the regiment with staples within a mile of camp. Took the road as train guard at 1 a. m. Have had a tedious march over sandy roads and through pine woods for 11 miles. It is too dark to see the town. Have heard no "music" to-day. We crossed the head waters of the Ohoopee river to-day. Saw a magnolia tree by the road. The first I have seen in Georgia.

Old Indian Battle Ground, near Drummond,

November 28, 1864.

Made a dozen miles to-day through the thickest pine woods I ever saw. There is no white or yellow pine here;

it is all pitch. I think the division has been lost nearly all day. We have followed old Indian trails four-fifths of the time.

The foragers have found a large number of horses and mules in the swamps to-day. Plenty of forage. Sergeant Penney, of my company, died in the ambulance to-day. He was taken sick in the ranks at 8 p. m., 26th, of lung fever. He has never been right healthy, but when well was always an excellent soldier. Lieutenant Dorrance swallowed his false teeth a few nights ago, and complains that they don't agree with him.

I hear that Wheeler jumped the 20th Corps yesterday and that they salivated him considerably. We caught a couple of his men to-day, on our road, stragglers. We pick up a good many stray Rebels along the road, but they are not half guarded and I think get away nearly as fast as captured.

Ten miles south of Sevastopol,

November 29, 1864.

All day in an awful pine forest, hardly broken by fence or clearing. I never saw such a lonesome place. Not a bird, not a sign of animal life, but the shrill notes of the tree frog. Not a twig of undergrowth, and no vegetable life but just grass and pitch pine. The country is very level and a sand bed. The pine trees are so thick on the ground that in some places we passed to-day the sight was walled in by pine trunks within 600 yards for nearly the whole circle. Just at dusk we passed a small farm, where I saw growing, for the first time, the West India sugar cane. One of the boys killed the prettiest snake I ever saw. It was red, yellow and black. Our hospital steward put it in liquor. We made about 11 miles to-day.

Eight miles east of Summerville,

November 30, 1864.

Passed through the above named town this morning. All pine woods again to-day. Stopped at the first house I came to this morning and asked the resident, an ash-colored negress, something about the country. She said she'd had the chills and fever so long she didn't know anything, but "over dar was a house whar de folks had some sense." Captain Smith and I walked over to the house she pointed to and found a fine old German, very anxious to know if we intended to burn his house. After he cooled down a little he grew much Union. He said he had been ordered to join the army one, two, three, twenty times, but had told them he would rather be shot than take up arms against the United States. The 12th Indiana band struck up as we passed his house, and the music touched the old fellow's heart. The tears rolled down his face and he blubbered out, "That is the first music I have heard for four years; it makes me think of home. D—n this Georgia pine wood." He said that sugar is the staple here in peace times. The foragers brought in loads of it this evening.

Cushingville Station, east bank of Ogeechee river,

December 1, 1864.

Ten miles to-day. Had just finished the last line when (the officers are talking over the rumors of the day) I heard Captain Smith say, "Our folks captured one Rebel ram." I asked him where, and he pointed out an old he sheep, one of the men had just brought in. Our regiment is the only part of our corps this side of the river. We are guarding the prisoners who are repairing the bridge. The Rebels had destroyed one section of it. The 17th Corps crossed near the railroad bridge, but are ten miles behind us to-night. This river is about 60 yards wide here, and we have sounded it in several places and found it from 12 to 15 feet deep. It has no abrupt banks here, but runs river, lake, swamp, to dry land. I find here again what I thought was palm-leaf fan material, on the Oconee river. It turns out to be swamp palmetto. The palmetto tree also grows near here. Twelve p. m.—Have been out with 25 men burning railroad. I did not do much of it, for it is the 17th Corps' work. Two of Howard's scouts came to us while we were at work. Said they had just left Millen, and left 150 Rebels there. Millen is four miles from here and is the junction of the Savannah and Augusta railroad. One of our men captured eight mules and two horses to-day. The trees along the river are covered with Spanish moss, like we saw so much of at Black River, Miss. The men shake their heads when they see it and say, "Here's your ager." We are only guarding this bridge until the 17th Corps gets here. Our corps are going down the other side of the river. An immense number of "contrabands" now follow us, most of them able-bodied men, who intend going into the army. We have not heard a Rebel gun since the 22d of last month. They don't trouble our march a particle.

West bank of Ogeechee River, eight miles

south of Millen,

December 2, 1864.

Recrossed the river this morning and, joining the brigade, made some eight miles to-day. We are ahead of the rest of the army or could have made more. Pine country, almost uninhabited. Saw to-day my favorite tree—the magnolia. Have seen but few of them in Georgia. In a swamp we passed through to-day a darkey pointed out to us some lemon trees. Saw in the same swamp some yellow pine. Nearly all the pine this side of the Oconee has been the "pitch" variety.

South bank of Scull Creek,

December 3, 1864.

We have laid here all day, being our first rest since leaving Atlanta. Had to wait for the 17th Corps and "left wing" to catch up. We laid a pontoon across the river this morning, and two of our brigade went over to tear up railroad The 17th Corps came up and relieved them about 2 p. m.

Colonel Catterson (our brigade commander) told me today that a dispatch from Bragg to ————— had been intercepted yesterday, that stated that he was moving on us from Savannah, with 10,000 infantry and Dick Taylor's Cavalry. See if he don't "come to grief." Two of our divisions are moving 12 miles to our right—the 2d and 3d—the 4th is with us.

Kilpatrick has gone for the Millen and Augusta railroad. If he hurts it much he'll do more than cavalry usually do.

December 4, 1864.

Got on the road before day-light and made 16 miles easily by 3:30 p. m. Good road, many fine places, and excellent forage, from 75 to 500 bushels of sweet potatoes on a farm. Heard cannonading for two hours this morning. Think it must have been in the vicinity of the 20th Corps. Quite a variety of forest trees to-day among the pines, but all of a stunted growth. Saw a very curious cactus by the roadside.

Almost all of the people from this section have sloped. I think I have not seen more than 12 white male citizens since we left Atlanta, at their homes. Am fully persuaded that Grant's "cradle and grave" idea is correct.

Thirty-six miles from Savannah,

December 5, 1864.

Corse had the road to-day, but Wood side-tracked, took "catch roads" and got into camp, making 16 miles as soon as Corse. Rather poor country, farms small, and much pine. Negroes swarmed to us to-day. I saw one squad of 30 or 40 turned back. Sherman's order is not to let any more go with us than we can use and feed. A nice yellow girl came to our regiment about an hour after dark. She is the property of Milly Drake, who lives 30 miles back. The girl showed our men where Milly hid her horses and mules, in return for which, after the column passed, gentle Milly took half a rail and like to wore the wench out. Broke her arm and bruised her shamefully. That was all the reason that the girl had for running away.

Eden Ferry, Ogeechee river,

December 6, 1864.

We lay in camp until 1 p. m. when we suddenly pulled out and made this point, and had works up by dark. There was a good wagon bridge over the river at this point, which the Rebels partially destroyed. But a portion of our 3d Brigade, which had the advance, got across on the remains and stirred up a little skirmish. Killed four Rebels without any loss to us.

Our 2d Division got across three miles below. The 3d, I guess is with them. Hear nothing of the other corps. In the swamps to-day I saw more of the "barren lemon tree." We were talking over last night what this army had cost the Confederacy since the 4th of October last, when we started from Eastpoint after Hood. We all agree that the following estimate is not too high in any particular: 100,000 hogs, 20,000 head of cattle, 15,000 horses and mules, 500,000 bushels of corn, 100,000 of sweet potatoes. We are driving with us many thousand of the cattle. The destruction of railroad property has been complete whenever within our reach. I can learn nothing of the prospect of a fight at Savannah, or whether we are going there. All think, though, that we will see tide-water this week. People here say they often hear the firing both at Savannah and Charleston.

Wright's Bridge, Ogeechee River,

December 7, 1864.

We have not moved to-day. Sergt. N. Breed, of my company, who was shot through the right lung in the battle of November 22d, died to-day. He has been hauled in an ambulance ever since and improved all the time until the last two days. We were all sure that he would get well. There was no better soldier in the army. Every one liked him. Hear a little cannonading this p. m. a few miles down the river. Lieutenant Dorrance's servant captured a beautiful coal black squirrel, with white nose and white ear tips. He is larger than any fox squirrel I ever saw.

Five miles from James' Point, Canoochie River,

December 8, 1864.

Another "Shermanism." Our 3d and 4th Divisions crossed the Ogeechee river yesterday at Eden. We all supposed that we would follow, this morning, but here we are after 18 miles hard marching. The 2d Division is ahead of us and part of it at the river. Heard a few cannon shots there a few minutes ago. We are after the railroad that runs from Savannah to Thomasville. Kilpatrick crossed the Savannah river yesterday, into South Carolina. Miserable country to-day. The last ten days have been quite warm. One perspires freely lying in the shade during some of the warmest hours.

Same place, December 9, 1864.

The division lay in camp all day. Our regiment marched 12 miles on a reconnoisance, toward the Canoochie river, southwest.. Found nothing, but some good foraging. Cannonading at four or five different points, on our left and front. Citizens say the most distant is at Charleston, Savannah and Fort McAlister. It is said that Corse's Division (4th), of our corps, had a fight east of the

Ogeechee to-day and were victorious, taking 50 prisoners and one gun. Part of our 2d Division crossed at James' Point to-day, and burned the Gulf railroad bridge and four miles of trestle-work west of the Ogeechee. They found very large rice plantations, which are flooded with tide-water. I guess Fort McAlister cannot be reached by infantry on account of the country around it overflowing. The men say that Kilpatrick has gone around Savannah and "cut the coast." Big raid!

Before Savannah, December 10, 1864.

Crossed the Ogeechee near the mouth of the Canoochie, then a canal, and then up the tow path toward the city. All the other divisions of our corps are ahead of us. An awful country to get through, all lakes and swamps. We are now five miles from Savannah. Have just got our works up and got our suppers. Hear some skirmishing on our right, should think a mile from us. Commenced raining at dark and continued. Made 20 miles to-day.

Before Savannah, December 11, 1864, 8 a. m.

Corse's Division is just on our right. He woke me up this morning by firing a volley of eight 12-pounders, in real old Atlanta fashion. He was answered by three Rebel guns planted on the defenses of Savannah, across a field and swamp from us. We are in good range of them. Nine p. m.—Found this morning that the Rebels have a big swamp and lake between their position and ours. It is impossible to get at them there. Our corps was ordered to swing to the right. The Rebel battery had fair view and close range on any road we could take, so we had to wait until night, when ours and the 3d Division passed them without any trouble. We are now on a main road, straight and wide enough for three wagons, which we think leads to Pulaski. This is a country of awful swamps, with level flats, between which are rice fields, and most of them have three feet of water on them. Many think we are not going to make an effort for Savannah at present, but will open communication with the coast. It is as much as we can do to find dry land enough to camp on. We are not caring a cent what "Pap" does. It is quite cold again; to-night promises to be the coldest night of the winter.

Before Savannah, December 15, 1864.

First mail goes in 15 minutes. Our 2d Division charged and took Fort McAlister, at sunset, the 13th—19 guns and 300 prisoners; lost 92 men killed and wounded. We will have Savannah, sure.

Before Savannah, December 19, 1864.

We have only been here a couple of days, but to-night we are to make and occupy a line within 700 yards of the Rebels.

Green Square, Savannah, Camp 103d Illinois "Provost Guards."

December 22, 1864.

We have just by a hair's breadth missed what would have been a most unpleasant fight. We lay on the west side of the Ogeechee, with the enemy on the opposite shore, strongly fortified. We had crawled through the mud and established a line of rifle pits within 125 yards of them; 150 portable bridges had been built in our division and I believe everything was in readiness for hot work the next day, the 20th. The morning of the 21st finds the enemy gone across the river into South Carolina. The next day we moved into town and our regiment and the 40th from our brigade are put on provost duty.

Green Square, Savannah, Ga.

January 9, 1865.

Thinking we for once in the service had a chance to enjoy quiet life, two of our number were sent to Hilton Head for a full supply of men's apparel for the outer man, and of refreshments substantial and fancy for the inner.

They returned to-day just in time to receive marching orders. The men's clothing was packed in valises, and all the eatables sold to parties who remain here, save one barrel of Irish potatoes. We leave to-morrow morning. Major Willison's resignation was accepted to-day, and this evening the officers unanimously agreed to recommend me to fill the vacancy. There was not a hint towards any one else. I take it as a high compliment. I am the youngest captain in the regiment, and this recommendation made by men whom I have campaigned with for two and a half years, and not one of whom has been accused of failing to do his duty in the service, makes me feel a little proud. I will value the recommendation more than the commission, if I get it.

Thunderbolt, Ga., January 10, '65.

We joined the brigade in the suburbs of the city, and took the shell road to this place, only four miles by land, but 18 by water. There are some fine works here, erected by the Rebels to guard the water approach to the city. I send you a little chip of a palmetto log in a Rebel work here.

On board the steamer Crescent, Atlantic Ocean,

January 12, 1865.

We are steaming on that rolling deep we've heard so much of, and which I have already seen and felt enough of. There is but little air stirring and the water is quite smooth, but so near the shore there is always a ground swell, which is to me somewhat demoralizing. We are out of sight of land and just before dark we saw a school of porpoise which looked just like a drove of hogs in the water. Some of the men wanted to go foraging when they saw them. This makes me quite dizzy, but I would not miss it on any account. I saw the full moon rise from the water about 6:30 p. m.

Beaufort, S. C., January 13, 1865.

Retired about 11 p. m. and woke up here this morning. A very handsome, small town, about the size of Canton, but more fine dwellings. All have been confiscated and sold to the negroes and white Union men. Find the 17th A. C. here, but about ready to move out to drive the Rebels away from the ferry, where we will lay our pontoons to the main land. The 14th and 20th will move by land and join us on the main land somewhere. I can hardly imagine what our next move will be, but mostly think we will tear up the railroads through the Carolinas and take Charleston and Wilmington during the spring campaign. The health of the command is perfect, and all are in most soldierly spirits. Thinking nothing impossible if Sherman goes with us, and go he will.

Near Beaufort, S. C., January 26, 1865.

We have had heavy rains and now very cold weather without being in the least prepared for it. We move to-morrow at 7 a. m. for the main land and forage.

All tents are to be left behind "until they can be forwarded by water." That seems to point to a short and sharp campaign, and we all think Charleston is the objective point.

Near Pocataligo, S. C., January 27, 1865.

Moved out at 7 a. m. this morning, crossed Broad river on pontoons, and are about four miles on the main land towards Charleston. Can't tell our position, but here the Rebels hold all the crossings on the opposite side of the river six miles ahead and so far as reconnoitered, with fortifications and artillery.

The 17th Corps lay to our left extending across the C. & S. R. R. We made about 13 miles to-day. Saw some fine plantations on the road, nothing but chimneys in them, though. It feels good and homelike once more to be out loose. The boys all feel it and they act more like school-

boys, having a holiday, than the veterans they are.
Wouldn't it be a joke if we were to get badly whipped
over this river? I believe it would do us good. We are
too conceited. The river ahead is the Combahee, and we
are 43 miles from Charleston on the C. & Beaufort road.

Six miles south of Combahee River,

January 28, 1865, 6 p. m.

The campaign commences Monday. It is yet cold;
about an inch of ice forms every night, and sleeping out
without tents is not a fair sample of paradise. I am in
excellent health and we are all anxious to be en route.

Combahee River, Charleston and Beaufort road,

January 29, 1865.

We have had some rich sport to-day. Our regiment and
the 40th are out here on a little reconnoisance, and making
a demonstration pretending to be building a bridge on the
river, etc. A party of Rebels saluted our skirmishers when
they got to the river bank with a volley, but the boys soon
drove them off, with no loss to us (or the Rebels either).
We lay around a couple of hours shooting at marks, etc.,
when a party of the Rebels attempted to reoccupy their pits.
We saw them coming for a full mile and they had hardly
got within the very longest range before the 40th sent
them back flying. Later in the p. m. half a dozen Johnnies
arose from the mud and weeds and though they were
across the river, surrendered to us. They are really deserters, though they say not. Had a great time getting
them over the river. Four board and log rafts were made,
launched, and put off after them. Two of them were
wrecked against the bridge benches, and the other two
succeeded in bringing over three Johnnies; we left the
other three there. I certainly would not have risked myself on one of those rafts for 500 prisoners or 5,000 deserters. General Hazen of our corps has been made a

full major general. The other division commanders only by
brevet, and they feel a little sore over it. To-day one of
General Wood's aids saw a turkey buzzard, and pointed it
out to the general, saying, "there is a turkey." Old Woods
looked at it and answered, "I think that is a turkey by
brevet."

McPhersonsville, S. C., January 30, 1865.
We returned from Combahee river last night and at 10
p. m. received orders to move at 6 a. m. Came through
Pocataligo and have made 14 miles to-day. Quite a place,
but there is not even a clearing. Say 50 ordinary dwellings dropped down in the pine woods, and you have it.
Not a citizen, white or black, here.

January 31, 1865.
Lay still all day. This place was a country summer
resort. I was in a house to-day; the walls were rough
boards white-washed, the floors were very rough, and I
think had never been carpeted, yet the room was filled
with mahogany furniture of the best quality, had a fine
piano, splendid plate mirror, and a fine library. About 20
sets of buck horns were nailed to the walls in lines. Hear
that the 17th Corps has crossed the Combahee. We hear
that strict orders against burning and all foraging is to
be done even *more* regularly than before.

Hickory Hill, S. C., February 1, 1865.
Fifteen miles to-day and had an excellent supper of
South Carolina ham, honey and sweet potatoes. Found a
good deal of road blockaded to-day, but the pioneers removed the obstructions so rapidly that the train did not
have to halt once. The Rebels disputed our advance a
little, killed a cavalryman and wounded another for us,
but did not stop the column a moment. Sherman rode at
the rear of our regiment all day and was quite sociable with
some of the men. Don't think any of the officers noticed
him. Miserable pine land country, but some quite large
plantations.

22

February 2, 1865.

The advance started at daylight, but we are the rear guard of the corps and will not get off before 4 p. m. We have no idea of our destination, but are now traveling the Augusta road.

The country is very level, but every mile or so there is a little swale or depression of but a few feet, and before a hundred wagons pass over it thorough corduroying is necessary. The foragers had sharp fighting for what they got to-day. We had two captured, Billy Haller and a 40th boy. Our boys captured several and killed three. Only made six miles.

Baren's Mills, S. C., February 3, 1865.

Fifteen miles to-day. The 17th is having some pretty lively firing on our right. At a house I stopped at to-day a "cit" told me we were 95 miles from Charleston, 65 from Augusta, and 33 from Branchville. That is as near as I can tell you where we are. We expect to reach Buford's bridge on the Salkehatchie, to-morrow. The Rebels have fortified there, I hear. Our brigade has the advance, and fun to-morrow, if there is any. It has rained since 12 last night.

Buford's Bridge, north side Salkehatchie River,

February 4, 1865.

Most unaccountably, to me, the Rebels evacuated an impregnable position (if there is such a thing), and our brigade was saved thereby from making some more history, for which I am grateful. A straight pike or causeway three quarters of a mile long and in which there are 24 bridges, was our only chance of crossing. They had strong embrasured works, but left an hour before our adance reached their fortifications. We got a lot of good horses and more good forage than I ever before saw brought in. I am sure that we have either a nice ham or shoulder for every two men in the regiment, and I think, more. A

Company B boy got a good strong horse which he let me have. People here say that the Rebels have all gone to Branchville. Colonel Catterson told Sherman (he was in our camp some time to-night) that a negro reported that the Rebels had all gone to Branchville. "Pap" replied, "They can go to Branchville and be d——d." We infer from that, that *we don't* go there. He also said to Catterson, who was superintending the bridge building, "Build them strong, Catterson, build them strong; the whole army may have to pass over them, and the 'Army of the Cumberland' is a very *heavy army,* sir." Besides the little slur on the 14th and 20th, that gave us an idea of the whereabouts of the left wing.

I just now heard what made the Rebels evacuate this. Mowers' Division of the 17th formed line and marched across this stream and swamp eight miles below at River Bridge. They waded through three miles of water and then took the Rebel works with a loss to us of only 12 killed and 72 wounded. I think that beats anything I ever heard of in the show line. There was a town of 20 or 25 houses here, but we have used it up in building bridges.

Twelve miles south of Johnston's Summit, Augusta and
Branchville Railroad,

February 5, 1865.

They call the stations on this road "turnouts." Negroes are swarming into our camps. I never heard a negro use the word "buckra" until last night. One of the 97th Indiana was killed this morning while foraging close to camp. Our men killed two and captured four Johnnies, all dressed in our clothing. Only moved four miles to-day, and will probably lay here a few days as Sherman told Wood we were four days ahead of time, he having counted it would take that long to effect a crossing at Buford's bridge.

Little Salkehatchie River,

February 6, 1865, 2 p. m.

Yesterday was quite warm, but my overcoat is useful again to-day. General Kilpatrick caught up with us last night, also General Williams with five brigades of the 20th A. C. So instead of waiting several days Sherman said he'd chance them for the railroad with what troops there are up. We took the road this morning. Stopped here for the 3d Division to clear the swamp of some Johnnies, which I think they have about effected.

Five p. m.—Miserable swamp, but the 3d Division only lost two men in crossing. There must have been a division of Wheeler's here by the signs.

Bamber's Station, A. & C. R. R.

February 7, 1865.

Our regiment led the corps to-day. The 17th Corps strikes the railroad at Midway, three miles to our right, and the 20th to the left five miles. We are 14 miles northwest of Branchville. The enemy are on the opposite bank of the Edisto, two miles from us. There is a great "peace" excitement among the citizens here. This day's work cuts off all railroad communication between Georgia and the eastern part of the Confederacy. I saw another new thing (to me) in the destruction of railroads. After the iron has been heated by the burning ties, by a simple contrivance, four men twist each rail twice around. They put a clamp on each end of the rail, and put a lever in the clamp perpendicularly, and two men at each end of the lever, will put the neatest twist imaginable in the heated part of the rail. I never saw so much destruction of property before. Orders are as strict as ever, but our men understand they are in South Carolina and are making good their old threats. Very few houses escape burning, as almost everybody has run away from before us, you may imagine there is not much left in our track. Where a family remains at home they save their house, but lose their stock, and eatables. Wheeler's Cavalry is about all we have yet found in our front and they keep afar off. The citizens fear them fully as much as they do us. A lady said to-day that she would as lief have us come as Wheeler's men; she could see no difference. Wheeler's men say, "Go in, South Carolina!" and the Yankees say the same thing. We got 50 bales of cotton here, which I suppose will be burned. Struck the railroad at 9:30 a. m.

Bamberg, S. C., February 9, 1865.

We were to go to Cannon's bridge on the Edisto four miles, but heard the bridge was burned, so we did not go. I think we will go up the river towards Augusta. Late Confederate papers say that Thomas has started south towards Montgomery, leaving Hood behind him. Many of the officers have strong hopes of something resulting from the peace movement. Can't say that I have.

Near Grahams. C. & A. R. R.

February 9, 1865.

Rear guard on our road to-day. Made about a dozen miles, very disagreeable march. Snowed a little in the morning and terribly cold all day. Got into camp at 7:30 p. m. This is a pine, sand country, with some very good plantations, but all look neglected. The people who remain at home seem an ignorant, forlorn set who don't care for their "rights" or anything else. I think the militia they have brought out to oppose us must suffer, this weather, being unused to the business and unprovided with rubbers, etc. Poor devils!

February 10, 1865.

Had no "general" this morning (our signal for getting up), so when the "assembly" sounded we climbed from our blankets to our saddles and went off on a railroad burning expedition. Our brigade by noon had completely destroyed two and one-half miles. The 17th and our 3d Division crossed the South Edisto to-day, four miles from here. We will cross to-morrow, I hear. Also hear that S. D. Lee's Corps of Hood's Army is at Augusta. We whipped them July 28, '64, and can do it again. I think the whole army is here now. We have 15-day half rations yet. Wonder where it will take us.

Seven miles west of Orangeburg, S. C.,

February 11, 1865.

Made 18 miles to-day. Crossed South Edisto river in rear of the corps. The river here is about 40 yards wide, with a swift current, water very clear. First 10 miles to-day was through pretty good country, the last eight miles mostly pine forest with more rolling ground than I have seen since we left the Oconee river in Georgia. Received my commission as major to-day, also two letters from you dated November 3d and January 4th. I ask pardon for thinking that you did not write regularly. The fault must be in the mails. All kinds of rumors afloat to-night of peace, war, and I don't know what all. We came near being burned up last night, the fire crept along through the pine leaves and burned my vest, partly, and ruined my jacket, and almost spoiled my overcoat, all of which were under my head. Also burned the colonel's pillow. The flames bursting up woke us, and I expect our first motion would have amused a very solemn man.

Shilling's Bridge, left bank North Edisto River,

February 12, 1865.

Started at 7 a. m., moved one-half mile and laid still two hours waiting for Hazen and Smith to straighten out ahead of us. I thought I'd tell you how we had been bored to-day, fooling along the road from 7 a. m. until 3 o'clock in the night, making five miles, but it disgusts me to think of it. Crossing the river is what delayed us. The Rebels held Hazen there four or five hours and shot a few men for him, but he run the 48th Illinois through some swamps on their flank, crossed and got some prisoners. They are from Hood's army and just got here yesterday. This North Edisto is about like the other branch. The 17th Corps crossed below our right, and the 20th on our left. Can't hear anything of the 14th or Kilpatrick. It is freezing now and has been very cold all day, yet to get clear water for dinner hundreds of the men waded out to the middle of the pond (muddy on the border) over their knees in water. They think nothing of it. It was the 2d Brigade 2d Division that waded the swamp and the river to flank the Rebels from the crossing. A large number of foragers waded with them just for devilment. It was from middle to arm-pit deep and I suppose they waded at least a mile. They got 54 prisoners, and the rest threw down guns, knapsacks and everything that impeded their flight. The flanking party did not lose a man. The men of this army surprise me every day with their endurance, spirit and recklessness.

Twenty-four miles southeast of Columbia, S. C.,

February 13, 1865.

Made 18 miles to-day. Rear guard for the corps in the morning, but the 2d and 3d Divisions took a right hand road and in the p. m. the 4th Division also went to the right. We followed a cow path to camp. Passed through two large turpentine camps. The boys fired most all the trees and nearly burned us up. The smoke made the road very disagreeable. There is not much destruction of property since Logan's last order. Hear of no skirmishing. The chivalry give us very little trouble, never stop but at rivers. Foragers get a good many animals. Provisions plenty. Hear nothing of the left wing, or Kilpatrick.

VII.

February 14, 1865 to May 19, 1865. Adopting a badge for the 15th
Army Corps. Its origin. Fighting Wheeler's Kentucky Brigade.
Shelled in bivouac. Crossing the river on pontoons. Mayor of
Columbia surrenders the city. Marching through Main street to
the Capitol, greeted by citizens and negroes wild with joy. Troops
get drunk. Two-thirds of the city burned. Restoring order. On
provost duty stopping progress of the flames. Last to leave the
city, followed by fifty white families and innumerable negroes.
Straggling fights. Shooting prisoners in retaliation for murdering
foragers. Resume of miles marched. More foragers murdered.
Sherman issues retaliatory orders. Sacrilegious stealing. Hungry
for the first time. The country denuded for 15 miles around.
Cheraw captured and burned. Exploding concealed ammunition
magazines. Foraging stopped and army rations resumed. Crossing
into North Carolina. Forager fights and outrages at Fayetteville.
Corduroy roads covering quicksand. Fighting near Goldsboro,
N. C. On picket duty. North Carolina clay eaters. Lee's surrender disbelieved. Reviewed by Sherman in Raleigh, N. C. Truce
between Sherman and Johnston. News of Lincoln's assassination.
Army crazy for vengence. Johnston's surrender. Shocked at
Sherman's terms. Out of Carolina into Virginia. Graphic scenes
and incidents. Meets army of Potomac. Reviewed by Howard,
Logan and Hartsuff in Petersburg. In view of Richmond but
frobidden to enter. In camp at Alexandria, Va. Participates in
the Grand Review, in Washington, D. C., May 24, 1865. Finale.

EXPLANATORY NOTE.

Until this time the 15th Army Corps had never had a Corps
Badge, though the other corps commanders had long tried to
induce General Logan to adopt one. Yielding at last to their
solicitations he issued the following order:

HEADQUARTERS FIFTEENTH ARMY CORPS,

BAKER'S PLANTATION, S. C., February 14, 1865.

GENERAL ORDERS,

No. 10.

I....The following is announced as the badge of this Corps: A miniature Cartridge-box, black, one-eighth of an inch thick, fifteen-sixteenths of an inch wide, and thirteen-sixteenths of an inch deep, set transversely on a field of cloth or metal, one and five-eights of an inch square; above the cartridge-box plate will be stamped or worked in a curve the motto: "Forty Rounds." The field on which the cartridge-box is set will be *Red* for the 1st Division, *White* for the 2d Division, *Blue* for the 3d Division, and *Yellow* for the 4th Division. For the Headquarters of the Corps the field will be parti-colored of Red, White, Blue and Yellow.

II....The badge will invariably be won upon the hat or cap.

III....It is expected that this badge will be worn constantly by every officer and soldier in the corps. If any Corps in the army has a right to take pride in its badge, surely that has which looks back through the long and glorious line of Wilson's Creek, Henry, Donelson, Shiloh, Russel House, Corinth, Iuka, Town Creek, Chickasaw Bayou, Arkansas Post, Champion Hills, Big Black, Snyder's Bluff, Vicksburg, Jackson, Cherokee Station, Lookout Mountain, Missionary Ridge, Ringold, Knoxville, Resaca, Kingston, Dallas, New Hope Church, Big Shanty, Kenesaw Mountain, Nickojack, Decatur, the 22d and 28th of July, before Atlanta, Jonesboro, Lovejoy, Altoona Pass, Griswoldville, Fort McAlister, and scores of minor struggles; the Corps which had its birth under Grant and Sherman in the darker days of our struggle; the Corps which will keep on struggling until the death of rebellion.

BY COMMAND OF MAJOR GENERAL JOHN A. LOGAN:

MAX WOODHULL,

Assistant Adjutant General.

The adoption of the cartridge box as the distinguishing badge of the 15th Corps is said to have originated in this way: Before the battle of Missionary Ridge a soldier in the 11th Army Corps asked an Irish soldier of the 15th Corps what the badge of his corps was.

"And phwat is that badge thing?" he asked.

Being told and having no badge to show in reply, he answered, slapping his cartridge box: "It's that, wid 40 rounds!"

DIARY CONTINUED.

Nearing Columbia, S. C., February 14, 1865.

Good road to-day. Fine rolling country. Sand with pine wood and scrub oak. Saw the wagoners use their locks to-day for the first time since we crossed the Oconee, in Georgia. Logan's escort got after some Johnnie foragers to-day and captured four wagons and 50 or 60 horses and mules. The Rebels are shooting from the other side of the river and there was a lot in front of us when we stopped here. Lee is said to be in front with 40,000 men. It seems to be the opinion that we will have a fight. Can probably tell better to-morrow night. Rain all p. m., and still quite cold. Wear overcoats all the time.

Three miles from Columbia, February 15th.

A rather lively day. We started the Johnnies right by our camp. Our brigade in advance of the corps and army. The 40th Illinois was deployed as skirmishers, and drove them four miles rapidly, losing only five men. Our regiment then relieved them. They opened artillery on us and fought stubbornly. It was the Kentucky brigade of Wheeler's "Critter Co." We drove them from a splendid position and heavy line of works with the assistance of three companies of our 3d brigade, 4th Iowa and —th Ohio. They killed F. M. Cary, of my company and took my orderly Sergt. T. S. Brown's right arm off. Wounded three other men in the regiment, Henry H. Orendorff, Joe Parkinson and Stewart, of company F. It is said we go for the city to-morrow.

February 16, 1865, 7 a. m.

The Johnnies shelled our bivouac all night, but hurt no one, but induced us to extinguish our fires, and killed one of the 48th Illinois. We could hear their cars whistling all night. They had large fires near town. We can see the steeples of the city plainly this morning. Many think the Rebels have left. If not I look for a hard battle to-day. There is no firing this morning yet, and our skirmish line is advancing. I can see it a mile ahead of us. Can see the State House now, and a large portion of the city. We can shell it from here.

Nine a. m.—The enemy opened the three guns on us again that he used last night, but the skirmish line deployed along the river silenced them.

Ten a. m.—The sun has shown himself, dispelled the fog, and we find we have an excellent view of the city. From our position it looks much like Peoria from the left bank of the river. The Congaree here is larger than the Illinois. Our batteries have got in position well down on the river bank, and some of them are bursting shell over the city. Our division moves down to take a closer view in a few minutes. The skirmishers are shooting quite lively across the river. You know our muskets carry up well at 800 yards. 'Tis a beautiful morning and view.

Twelve m.—The 2d Division leading, we pushed for the Rebel works at 9. Johnnies had mostly retired across the river. Our pontoon train running by a Rebel battery made some fun. They were furiously shelled and stood quite a heavy fire of musketry. Casualties, one mule killed, and the seat torn out of a small darkey's pants. We now lay on the river side opposite the town. A number of our guns are

practicing on the State House and other prominent buildings, and the Rebels are not answering a shot, though we
can see a number of cavalry riding through the town.
Hazen is laying the pontoons above the junction of the
Saluda and Broad rivers where we will cross. Yesterday
when the 40th Illinois charged the Rebels out of one of
their numerous barricades a "Forty" boy and a Johnnie had a
real scuffling fight . Forty downed the Rebel and choked him
until he surrendered. Some 26th boys captured a Rebel
colonel after we crossed the Congaree creek. He was
quite drunk and rode up to the boys who were straggling
ahead of the skirmish line, and asked them what they
were waiting for, and why they did not come along.

8 p. m.—Crossed the Saluda, since dark, and stay here
for the night on the bank of Broad river.

Columbia, S. C., February 17th.
The 3d brigade of our division marched all night and
worked all night before they could get a cable across the
river to string the pontoons, and the bridge was not completed until 10 a. m. There was lively skirmishing all
the time. Our division crossed first. The 3d brigade captured 30 Rebels near the crossing. The Mayor came out
and surrendered the town to Colonel Stone, commanding
our 3d brigade. The division marched through Main
street to the Capitol. We were never so well received by
citizens before, and the negroes seemed crazy with joy.
We halted in the street a few minutes, and the boys
loaded themselves with what they wanted. Whiskey and
wine flowed like water, and the whole division is now
drunk. This gobbling of things so, disgusts me much.
I think the city should be burned, but would like to see it
done decently.

February 18, 1865.
Two-thirds of the city burned last night. The colonel
and I got up last night and rode through the streets until
3. At 4 this morning the 40th Illinois cleared the streets

with bayonets and order again reigned. Our regiment is on Provost duty, and I have just been through the streets (8:30 p. m.) and it is as quiet as Sunday night in Canton.

February 19, 1865.

Another block of the city burned to-day. Our regiment was out and stopped the fire from spreading further. Have seen the men work better on other occasions. In destroying some captured ammunition to-day the 63d Illinois, by an explosion, lost three killed and 20 wounded. We captured about 20 cannon here. I noticed one complete battery of fine Blakely guns.

Sixteen miles northeast of Columbia,

February 20, 1865.

The Provost Guards were the last to leave town. Fifty families of Columbians accompany us; have no idea how many negroes. Hard day's march.

Pleasant Hill, S. C., February 21, 1865.

Fifteen miles to-day. Yesterday we traveled the Camden road. To-day we turned northwest. Poor country, quite rolling. Pine, scrub oak and sand.

Page's Ferry, Wateree River, February 22, 1865.

It seems to be certain that we have Charleston. Made about ten miles to-day. Our regiment and the 6th Iowa were sent down to an old ferry to make a demonstration. Found no enemy. The 2d and 3d are already across and we cross in the morning and take the advance. We now have eight days' rations which are to last 30—wish they'd burn them all to get rid of the wagons.

Flat Rock P. O., February 23, 1865.

Fifteen miles. Traveled east or northeast. Very rough, hilly country, hills rock topped. No enemy. Passed through a village called "Liberty Hill," some elegant houses. Forage plenty. No news and don't know anything.

West's Cross Roads, 13 miles northeast of
Camden, S. C.,

February 24, 1865.

Made 14 miles a little south of east. We passed about a mile south of Gates' old battle ground. A dozen foragers of the 99th Indiana were captured to-day, but our foragers caught more Rebels than that, besides 50 wagons and 200 horses and mules belonging to refugees. Stringent orders from Howard, Logan and Wood about stealing. It has rained for 24 hours. No enemy in front to-day. Got out of the clay hills again on sand—pine flats.

February 25, 1865.

Have not moved to-day. Rebels captured 15 men of the 29 Missouri to-day. Our foragers have been straggling for seven or eight miles in every direction; three of our regiment captured a refugee camp of seven men, ten guns, two revolvers, some pistols and 25 mules. Ordered to keep men well in hand this p. m., as Rebel cavalry is demonstrating on our front and flanks. I think it must be at a respectful distance. Rumor says Longstreet is somewhere around. Think we are waiting for the left of the army to get up with us. Our foragers have been to Camden, 13 miles; pretty tall straggling. Others have been out southeast 11 miles, and saw our 2d and 4th divisions moving on a big road, side by side, going east. Nobody can yet decide what our destination is. It is reported to-day that 13 of our 2d division foragers were found by the roadside dead, with a card marked "Fate of foragers;" also four of the 3d division killed. Gen. J. E. Smith, commanding, shot four of his prisoners in retaliation. Colonel Catterson says as we were marching to this camp to-day he had pointed out to him the tree under which Baron DeKalb died at the battle of Camden. Have had 48 hours of rain with a prospect of continuance.

Fullersville, S. C., Sunday, February 26, 1865.

Sixty hours of rain terminated at daylight this morning, but it has not hurt the sandy roads a particle. We made 11 miles in four and one quarter hours, and are now waiting for a bridge to be completed over this creek, "Lynch's." We think now we are on the road to Wilmington. The map shows a good deal of railroad to be destroyed on the way, but I think we will get through by the 15th of March. Expect "you uns" are getting anxious about "we uns" again. This is, I think, a much longer thing than the Savannah campaign. Our 4th division took 103 prisoners here last night and our 2d took 200 more to-day. They are State Line Troops and muchly demoralized. It is a fact about that murdering yesterday. Sherman is out in a big retaliation order to-day. Wilmington is reported ours. Thunder and lightning last evening. Hear that the rain has raised the creek until it is three-quarters of a mile wide, and we won't get across to-morrow. I think I'll put down our principal campaigns:

1st. Dec., 1862, The Tallahatchie River Campaign .... 120 miles.

2nd. April, 1863, The Panola, Miss., 9 day's march .... 180 miles.

3rd. July, 1863, Jackson, Miss., Campaign... 100 miles.

4th. Oct. & Nov., '63, Memphis to Chattanooga, and in

5th. Dec. to Maryville, Tenn., and back to Scottsboro, Ala........................... 800 miles.

6th. Jan., '64, Wills Valley Campaign....... 100 miles.

7th. Feb. & March, '64, Dalton, Ga., Campaign .... 300 miles.

8th. May until Sept., Atlanta Campaign..... 400 miles.

9th. Oct., 1864, Atlanta to Gadsden, Ala., and return .... 300 miles.

10th. Nov. & Dec., Atlanta to Savannah.... 300 miles.

Jan., Feb. & March, '65, The Carolina Campaign .... 400 miles.

Total ....3,000 miles.

A captain and seven men who went foraging yesterday are still missing, supposed to be captured or killed. And 20 men of the 97th Indiana who went out this morning are reported all killed by a 46th Ohio man, who was wounded and left for dead by the Rebels. He says the 97th boys paid for themselves in dead Rebels before they were overpowered. Our corps has now 500 prisoners, three times as many as we have lost.

Tillersville, February 27, 1865.

We have half a mile of bridging to build before we can get across this Lynch's creek, the rains have swollen it so much. Our 6th Iowa foragers we thought captured are all right. They got across this creek before the freshet and it cut them off. The 97th Indiana men are gone up. All of the 20 killed or captured but 3; 11 dead Rebels were found on their little battle field, so the report comes from General Corse, I understand. The Rebels are losing, I should think, about 3 or 4 men to our one, but they are showing more manhood than those who opposed our march in Georgia. It isn't the "militia," for the 360 prisoners our corps have taken within four days surrendered without firing a shot. *They* were S. C. *chivalry,* proper. The men who are most active on their side, I think, belong to Butler's or Hampton's command from the Potomac. They are cavalry and don't amount to anything as far as infantry is concerned, but only think they venture a little closer than Wheeler does. (You are expected to emit a sarcastic ha! ha!! and remark: "They don't know Sherman's army as well as Wheeler does.") They say we can't cross here until the water falls, and as there is an excellent prospect for more rain, we are thinking of building cabins in which to pass the rainy season. All our wounded are doing excellently. The surgeons say that the wounded do much better being transported in ambulances than in stationary hospitals. They escape the foul air is the main reason.

February 28, 1865.

High water still keeps us here. We will probably get off to-morrow. It is thought we will cross the Great Peedee at Cheraw; there is so much swamp lower down that might trouble us.

A thousand rumors afloat to-day. The citizens have it that Grant has whipped Lee since the Hatcher Run affair. It rained some last night and is now—8 p. m.—sprinkling again. If it rains hard to-night we will have to give up crossing here and go higher up. The 17th is across. The left wing is reported near Charlotte, N. C., but don't know that it is so. We have heard that Davis' commissioners have returned to Washington.

We are having a time sure. They say now that we will not get across to-morrow. I heard some outrageous jokes to-day about a Golden Christ which was stolen by some of our thieves in Columbia, and in an inspection on the 26th it was found in a department headquarter's wagon. They are too wicked to tell. This army has done some awful stealing. Inspectors pounce down on the trains every day or two now and search them. Everything imaginable is found in the wagons. The stuff is given to citizens or destroyed. Our last winter campaign ends to-day. Only five and one-half months more to serve.

Left Bank Lynch's Creek, March 1, 1865.

We have finally got across this deuced creek. It has delayed us fully four days, more than any three rivers did before. Our division train is yet to cross and may not get over in 24 hours. We are getting hungry for the first time, having foraged the country *out* for 15 miles around. The 4th division started to-day on the Cheraw road. Prisoners taken to-day report that Wilmington was being evacuated when Schofield with the 23d Corps, dropped in and took the town and a brigade of prisoners. I wish he'd organize an expedition and bring us some late papers. Everybody is speculating on a big time with the enemy crossing the Great Pedee, but I don't believe they will trouble us as much as this confounded creek has.

23

New Market, S. C., March 2, 1865.

A disagreeable, half drizzle, half sprinkle, all last night and to-day. Our brigade in advance and made 10 miles. Poor country, but pretty well settled. Many of the men have had no breadstuffs for three days. They drew two days of hard-bread February 18th, and have foraged everything else we have had since. Don't know when we draw again. Still have our 8 days of "tack" in the wagons. We will get plenty of forage again to-morrow. Can hear nothing of the enemy. We left Darlington 20 miles on our right to-day and will probably strike the Peedee near Society Hill.

Five miles south of Cheraw, S. C., March 3, 1865.

General Wood says we have made 24 miles to-day. Our whole corps on one road and hardly a check all day. This is Thompson's Creek, and the Rebels under Hardee thoroughly fortified it. Logan's orders are to carry the works to-morrow, but as usual the Rebels have left. The 17th A. C. took Cheraw this p. m. without a fight, getting 27 pieces of field artillery, 3,000 stands of small arms, besides a great deal of forage.

There were only two or three small farms on the road to-day. Poorest country I have seen yet. An intelligent prisoner captured to-day says that Kilpatrick has taken Charlotte, N. C., and that Lee is evacuating Richmond. Saw the sun to-day; had almost forgotten there was such a luminary.

Cheraw, S. C., March 4, 1865.

We were from 8 a. m. until 4 p. m. on this little five miles. The 17th have their pontoons down and have a division across. Hear that the enemy is fortified a short distance back from the river. Can hear no firing. Our foragers took Society Hill last night.

This is a very pretty place, about the size of Canton.

The river, Great Peedee, is navigable for boats drawing five feet. The left wing is at Chesterfield 12 miles above. There is an immense amount of cotton here. Noticed guards on it, and some think it is to be sent down the river. A thousand mounted men are to start from here to-morrow (from our corps, and it is said the same number from each corps) for —somewhere—rumor says, to release 8,000 of our prisoners at Florence. Our wounded men are all doing splendidly.

March 5, 1865.

The 17th and all our corps, except our division, have crossed the river. We follow in the morning. The enemy did not attempt to oppose us. The boys say that an intercepted dispatch from Hampton to General Butler reads: "Do not attempt to delay Sherman's march by destroying bridges, or any other means. For God's sake let him get out of the country as quickly as possible." Were I one of the S. C. chivalry I'd be in favor of turning out en masse and building up roads for him.

We will get out of S. C. to-morrow. I have not been in a house in the State occupied by a citizen. Everything in Cheraw of any value to the enemy, including cotton and business houses, is going up in smoke. Hear to-day that Schofield is in Goldsboro or Fayetteville, N. C.

General Wood says we have 120 miles yet to make. You may give the credit of Wilmington, Charleston and Georgetown to whom you please, *we* know Sherman deserves it. We hear that that miserable Foster is claiming the glory over *his* capture of Charleston. We are yet pretty short of breadstuffs, but have plenty of meat. Sherman has been heard to say that this army can live on fresh meat alone for 30 days. I'd like to see it tried on him. We think to-day that Goldsboro is our resting place. You must understand that we don't know anything at all about anything. Our foragers all went across the river this morning and got plenty of flour, meal and meat. They were out 11 miles and saw a few Rebels. The Rebels left seven cannon on the other side of the river, and burned a very large amount of commissary and ordnance stores.

Five miles northeast of Cheraw, S. C.,

March 6, 1865.

Crossed the Peedee this morning. Just after we passed through the town a 12th Indiana boy seeing some powder scattered on the ground threw a coal on it. It communicated with a concealed ammunition magazine and made a fine explosion, killed and wounded 20 or 30 men in our division, stampeded a lot of horses and burned some citizens. There have been half a dozen of such explosions. Good country here, foragers get plenty, and also pick up many Rebel deserters and stragglers. Our foragers yesterday found two of Kilpatrick's men and five Rebel lieutenants all drunk and put them under guard.

Goodwin's Mills, 16 miles northwest of Cheraw,

March 7, 1865.

About 11 miles to-day and in camp at noon. The 14th and 20th had come down and cross at Cheraw. We are waiting on them. That expedition to Florence was a failure. Our men got the town but were driven out before they destroyed a thing. I am inclined to think the officers did not do their whole duty. They should have succeeded or lost more blood. Our loss amounted to nothing. One of the best foraging days of the whole trip. Our foragers to-day captured some negroes and horses. The negroes say they were running them over here to get away from General "Schofield's company." We are about on the State line now, and will leave S. C. to-morrow. I think she has her "rights" now. I don't hate her any more.

Five miles north of Laurenburg, N. C., Laurel Hill,

March 8, 1865.

One   hundred   and   twelve   miles   of   steady   rain, and   the   best   country   since   we   left   Central   Georgia. Looks   real   Northern   like.   Small   farms   and   nice white,   tidy   dwellings.   Wheat   fields   look   very   well.   In the cornfields rows are five feet apart, and one stalk the size of a candle, in a hill. But at every house there were from 200 to 1,000 bushels of corn and an abundance of fodder. Sherman said yesterday that our campaign is over, and to-day Howard issued an order that all foraging for provisions shall cease, there being enough rations in the wagons to last us through. I dreamed last night of being at home on leave and seeing you all, and starting back to the army again. Only 90 miles yet to mail.

Four miles south of Montpelier, N. C.,

March 9, 1865.

Rained nearly all last night and poured down all day. Our regiment had the advance of the division, but we followed J. E. Smith. He is the poorest traveler in the army. We had to corduroy all the road after him. Only made four miles. I never saw such a country. There seems to be a thin crust over a vast bed of quicksand. I saw wagons yesterday and to-day moving along not cutting more than two inches, all at once go down to the hub, and some to the wagon boxes. I was riding to-night on apparently high ground in the woods and three times the ground gave way just like rotten ice, and let my horse in belly deep. We have worked hard to-day.

Randallsville, N. C., March 10, 1865, 12 p. m.

Ten miles to-day, most of which we had to corduroy. Our regiment in rear of the division and corps. Crossed the Lumber river about 4 p. m. Fine country. We had reveille at 3 this morning, and the rear of train with our 1st brigade did not get in until an hour later. They had a hard time. Hope we'll get the advance to-morrow. This Lumber river is a spoon river, with a third of a mile of swamp on each side thereof. Hear to-night that Grant has taken Petersburg, and believe it to be—bosh. Blair, with the 17th A. C., is close to Fayetteville, but it is said he has orders to lie still and let the left wing enter the town.

Davis Bridge, Rockfish Creek, March 11, 1865.

Ten miles to-day, full seven of which had to be corduroyed. The worst road I ever saw. The 17th corps occupied Fayetteville to-day. The foragers took the place. It is as large as Columbia and has a large arsenal. Heard of two or three men being captured by the Rebels yesterday and a couple to-day. They also made a little dash on our rear to-day on the 3d division without accomplishing anything. I do wish you could see the crowd of negroes following us. Some say 2,000 with our division. I think fully 1,000.

Fayetteville, N. C., March 12, 1865.

We are camped a couple of miles from town. Marched about 13 miles to-day. Had to put down pontoons at both branches of Rockfish creek. At the town of Rockfish, the 17th A. C. burned a factory, throwing about 150 women out of employment. One of our gunboats came up to this place to-day with dispatches for Sherman. It went back before our division got in and took a lot of mail.

The 14th A. C. is garrisoning this place, but the 17th got in first. The 97th Indiana boys, who were captured back at Lynch's Creek, all got away from the enemy and back to us to-day, five of them. Sherman said yesterday that the campaign ends only with the war. Hear that Hampton whipped Kilpatrick splendidly. Don't think that is any credit to him. Also hear that Bragg whipped Schofield at Kingston, that Thomas has Lynchburg, and 30,000 other rumors. In the last 23 days the commissary has issued only two and one half days' of bread. I lost my sword to-day. Left it where we stopped for dinner. We have lost so much sleep of late that at every halt half the command is asleep in a minute. I lay down and told them not to wake me for dinner nor until the regiment moved. The regiment had started when Frank woke me, and I got on my horse too stupid to think of anything. Did not miss my sword for five miles, when I went back for it, but no use. Foragers for the last week have been

counting on rich spoils in the town, and many of them
have not reported to their regiments within six or eight
days, camping every night with the extreme advance. The
day before the place was taken, five men who were 15 miles
ahead of the column ventured into town. They were gobbled and one of them killed. Next morning 100 foragers
hovered around town until the column was within about
six miles, when the foragers deployed as skirmishers, and
went for the town.

There were about 1,000 Rebel cavalry herein who fell
back before our boys skirmishing lively, clear through the
town, when they suddenly charged our fellows and scooped
them. Our loss in killed, wounded and captured is 25 or
30. They killed several after they captured them, and one
they hung up by the heels and cut his throat. Our boys
retreated about a mile from town, and went in again in
more solid order. They were too scattered the first time.
They were successful and routed Johnny, who left six dead
in the streets.

March 14, 1865.
It is supposed we will be here two or three days, to get
some shoes up the river.

Left bank, Cape Fear River, Opposite Fayetteville,

March 15, 1865.
Everything valuable to the Rebels has been destroyed,
and we are about ready to push on to Goldsboro. Fayetteville is about a 3,000 town, nearly all on one street. There
was a very fine United States Arsenal burned here, some 20
good buildings, all of which are "gone up." The rest of the
town is old as the hills. We lay on the river bank expecting to cross all last night, and finally reached the bivouac
three quarters of a mile from the river just as the troops
on this side were sounding the reveille. This is the 21st
river we have pontooned since leaving Scottsboro, May

1st, '64. It is more like the Tennessee than any other stream we have crossed. We send from here all the negroes and white refugees who have been following us, also a large train to Wilmington for supplies. The number of negroes is estimated at 15,000. Nearly all the population of this town will go inside our lines. It has rained all day and seems abominably gloomy. Makes me wish for letters from home. Last night while we were standing around fires by the river, some scoundrel went up to a negro not 75 yards from us, and with one whack of a bowie knife, cut the contraband's head one third off, killing him.

At Goldsboro, we are promised a short rest. If it were not that the wagons are so nearly worn out that they must be thoroughly repaired, I don't believe we would get it. Well, time passes more swiftly in campaigning than in camp. Most of the army are moved out.

Two miles from left bank of Black River, N. C.,

March 16, 1865.

About 14 miles to-day. About a dozen swamps, as many showers, three hard rains, and an awfully rough march. The men waded, I should think altogether, one-half mile of water from ankle to waist deep. They went through every swamp yelling like Indians. Rained all yesterday and last night. I saw peach and thorn blossoms, some wintergreen and arbor vitae growing wild. Two days like this would demoralize a citizen much. We drew three days' hard bread to-day to last five. In the 26 preceding our division drew besides sugar and coffee, only two and one-half days' of hard bread. Very poor country to-day. The boats brought us some late papers.

The latest account of Sheridan capturing Early. Don't believe it. Saw *Herald's* account of the inauguration. The writer should be shot. Of half a dozen boats that come to Fayetteville, only two brought cargoes, and both of them oats. Ridiculous, 40,000 pair of shoes would have been sensible. Many of the men are barefoot. Sherman and Hampton are having a spicy correspondence on murdering foragers. Think Hampton is a little ahead at this date. Have only seen the first letter on each side. There is talk of a fight at Goldsboro. I do hope this army will get two weeks in camp before it battles. It is a little too loose now for heavy, steady work. General Wood says that Sheridan with four divisions of cavalry is coming through to join us.

Beaman's Cross Roads, March 17, 1865.

About 12 miles, more than half of which had to be corduroyed. Roads awful. If a wagon pulls off the corduroy, it drops to the hub. There are two or three inches of black sand on the surface covering quicksand unfathomable. No one need tell me that bad roads will stop an army. The 20th corps had sharp little affair yesterday. Hear their loss is over 400. Everyone is expecting a fight before we reach Goldsboro. The whole corps is camped together to-night Our division has been in rear of the corps two days and has not had a fight in the advance since we left Columbia. I believe I have not heard a hostile shot for 27 days. Howard is here to-night. Whole corps is on this road.

Four miles north from Smithfield's, N. C.,

March 18, 1865.

Fifteen miles, good roads, men only waded in swamps. Whole corps in camp before dark. Well settled country and oceans of forage. Our foragers and the 7th Illinois "mounted thieves" had a nice little fight to-day. Came near scaring Wade Hampton's chivalry out of their boots; four dead Yanks, and 11 Rebels is said to be the result. Our fellows run them off to the left of our road into the 14th and 20, who hurried their march a little. We are 27 miles from Goldsboro and 18 from Faisons on the railroad, which point we will probably make to-morrow and possibly get our mail. If I don't get at least six letters from you I will be much disappointed. We are much amused over the Rebel

papers we get. All seem to take "gobs" of comfort from
Lee's declaration that "Tecumseh" can and must be whipped.
Several of them assert that our treatment of citizens is good.
Don't believe a word of it, though I wish it were so.

Twelve miles from Goldsboro, and six from railroad,

March 19, 1865.

Made 15 miles. Only two bad swamps. Very heavy artillery and musketry on our left (14th and 20th Corps) all day.
Hear this evening that our men suffered heavily. General Lee
is said to be here. Opinion is divided as to our having a battle
to-morrow. First rate country to-day and a good abundance
of forage. The farmers here have not many negroes. Rebel
cavalry demonstrated on our left to-day, quite lively and captured several foragers. Five foragers from our regiment who
had been out five days and whom we had about given up, returned to-night. They have been with the 17th A. C. All
quiet on our right.

One and one-half miles from Neuse River,

March 20, 1865.

We moved about a mile north and then west for five miles.
Pushed some Rebel cavalry before us all the time. Our
brigade was in advance and lost about 25 men. We are
about two miles east of where the battle was fought yesterday by the 14th and 20th corps, and right where the Rebel
hospital was. The Rebels are now due west of us, our
line running north and south, and I think there can be no
difficulty in communicating with Schofield. Goldsboro is
undoubtedly evacuated. In the fight yesterday one division of the 14th was worsted at first and driven some
distance, but rallied, repulsed the enemy, and the corps
getting into line, charged four to six times, and slaughtered
the Rebels awfully. Their loss was far greater than ours.

Ten p. m.—A Pennsylvania man, who was wounded in the
fight yesterday, and carried in by the Rebels who took off

his leg above the ankle, came in to us a few minutes ago. He crawled nearly half a mile, part of the way through a swamp. It seems that the Rebels had a hospital there they evacuated and left him and a half dozen other wounded, two of whom the man saw killed by the skirmish firing. We are on the skirmish line to-night. I suppose it is 400 yards to the Rebel skirmishers, and not a very dangerous line.

March 21, 1865.

We moved out this morning just before daylight and got within 50 yards of the Rebel skirmish line, but nothing going forward on our right or left, we returned to our original position. Had one man in Company H slightly wounded. We could have held our advanced line just as well as not. I think our right must rest on the river. Some 35,000 or 40,000 Rebels are reported here under Johnston.. Some prisoners report Lee. I would like to see them whaled, but would like to wait until we refit. You see that too much of a good thing gets *old,* and one don't enjoy even campaigning after 50 or 60 days of it together. I believe I am surfeited with oven bread—("death balls" our cook calls them), biscuit, and pork. I feel finely; wet from head to foot, has rained since noon hard most of the time. About 1 p. m. the main line moved out on our skirmish line, and as quick as they get their works up (about one-half hour), our regiment deployed as skirmishers on our brigade front, and our whole corps skirmish line moved forward. I think the 17th drove the enemy on our right at the same time. We took their skirmish pits along the whole front of our division, but they were very close to their main line and we did have a very interesting time holding them, I assure you. I don't think it was more than 75 yards to the main line of the Rebel works, and they in plain sight, only a straggling scrub oak undergrowth and a few large pines intervening. The Rebels came out of their works twice to retake their pits.

The first time the left of our regiment had to fall back, the brigade on our left giving way and exposing our flank, but we all rallied in a minute and made the Johnnies fairly fly back. The next time our brigade again broke, but our men held their pits, and the 26th Illinois, which was just coming out to relieve our regiment, faced its left wing for the pits occupied by the enemy, and went for them with a first-class yell. You should have seen the Rebels run. It did me a power of good. The other brigade then came back to their position, the 26th relieved me, and we are now ready for bed. We have been wonderfully fortunate to-day, only 10 wounded and none killed. The pride of the regiment, Frank Lermond, had his arm broken by a ball, but a resection operation will leave him a tolerably good arm. I think this has been as exciting and lively a p. m. as ever I saw. Terry's 24th Army Corps has come up, and lays about six miles back of us to-night.

Bentonville, N. C., March 22, 1865.

The enemy left about 2 a. m. Our brigade was ordered to follow them to Mill creek, about three miles, which we did almost on the double quick, the 26th Illinois in advance pushing their rear guard. The brigade went to Mill creek, but our skirmishers went a mile further, to Hannah's creek. The 26th had seven wounded. I saw in one place a dead Rebel and one of our men burned horribly. The woods have all been burned over here. In another place a dead Rebel and one of our men with his foot cut half off, one of his toes cut off, several more cuts on his body, and a bullet hole in his temple. Some of the boys saw one of our men with leg cut off in five places. Some surgeon had probably been practicing on the last two men.

They were 14th Corps men. Sherman again says the campaign is over, that he only came out here to show Johnston that he is ready to fight all the time. We start back for Goldsboro (24 miles), to-morrow. Hurrah for mail and clean clothes. Colonel and I occupy the outside of a house to-night, in the inside of which is a Chinese-eyed girl with a Creole mouth. She is as intelligent as a door post. You don't know how anxious I am to hear from you. I have had a reply to but one letter that I have written since last November (15th). Our little supper is now ready. Don't see how we will get along without Frank.

Goldsboro, N. C., March 25, 1865.

We were two days coming back from Bentonville. Have a nice camp ground and will enjoy ourselves, I think. Town don't amount to anything.

On picket, Raleigh road, three miles from Nahanta Station, on Weldon and Goldsboro railroad,

April 10, 1865.

Our division moved north to-day along the Weldon railroad to Nahanta, where we crossed and took a main Raleigh road. Our 1st brigade had the advance and had light skirmishing all day. Wheeler's cavalry is opposing us. Our regiment is on picket to-night, and the enemy shot a little at us before dark, but all is quiet just now. Passed through a very fine country to-day. It has rained all day. Some cannonading on our left. I think the whole army moved to-day. The 20th corps passed us near town this morning in exactly opposite direction to ours. The whole army, mules, wagons, bummers and generals have come out new from Goldsboro. The whole machine looks as nicely as an army can look. Our 1st brigade took a swamp crossing from the enemy to-day, that our brigade could hold against a corps. A bullet passed miserably near to me as I was arranging our picket line this evening.

Beulah, N. C., April 11, 1865, 12 m.

Our division is alone on this road I find, and the extreme right of the army. Our brigade ahead to-day. Dibbrell's division of Wheeler's men is ahead of us. We pushed them so closely that we saved all the bridges to this place. They destroyed the bridge here some way without burning it. Country to-day nearly all under cultivation, but no large farms. I reckon that the larger a farm a man has of this kind of land or sand the poorer he is. Our eyes were rested by seeing a little clay hill and a stony field, signs that we are again getting out of the coast flats. There was a house on our picket line last night with six women in it who were sights. They were the regular "clay-eaters." This Rebel cavalry ahead don't amount to a cent. They have not yet hurt a man on our road, and we don't know that more than two of them have been hit. They keep shooting all the time, but are afraid to wait until we get within range of them. They have not hindered our march a minute. Got me a new servant (a free boy) to-day. Both his grandmas were white women. He says the Rebel cavalry have been impressing all the able-bodied negroes for the army until within a few days. He understands they quit it because they found out in Richmond that they couldn't make "Cuffie" come up to the work.

Eight miles North of Smithfield, 4:30 p. m.

Crossed the river as quick as the bridge could be built and moved out three miles. The rest of our corps crossed two and one-half miles below. Country is quite rolling here. I hear that Johnston has left Smithfield, going towards Raleigh. Miserable set of citizens through here.

April 12, 1865, 10 a. m.

We hear this a. m. that Lee has surrendered to Grant the army of northern Virginia. It created a great deal of enthusiasm among us. It is hard to make our men believe anything, but Logan told us half an hour ago as he passed it is true as gospel. We have passed a large infantry camp that the Rebels left yesterday. Johnston is moving towards Raleigh. Our division has the advance to-day. We consolidated the regiment for the campaign into five companies.

Left bank of Neuse River, 20 miles East of Raleigh,

April 12, 1865, 4 p. m.

Twelve miles to-day. Our cavalry pushed ahead and drove
the Rebels past here at 8 a. m. Saw a barn and cotton press
in flames to-day. There has been no burning this trip worth
mentioning. This to-day was all I have seen and it was to
destroy the cotton. Poor country to-day, but one very nice
country place; the house 4th rate, but the grounds and shrubbery finer than any in our part of Illinois.

This is an army of skeptics, they won't believe in Lee's surrender. I do, and I tell you it makes this one of my brightest
days. His surrender makes sure beyond any chance that what
we have been fighting for for four years is sure. *Look for
me July 4th, 1865.* [This promise was kept. Ed.]

Four miles from Raleigh, April 13, 1865, 4 p. m.

The fourth anniversary of the fall of Fort Sumter. How
are you, chivalry? Made a nice little march of 16 miles and
could go on to town as well as not before dark if it was necessary. Our left wing occupied Raleigh this morning with
Kilpatrick and the 14th A. C. No fighting worth mentioning.
We crossed the Neuse six miles from Raleigh on the paper
mill bridge. This is the prettiest campaign we ever made. No
night marching, 60 miles in four days, and just what rations
we started with from Goldsboro in haversacks. Beautiful
country to-day, high and rolling. The bummers found whisky
to-day and I saw a number dead drunk by the roadside. They
found an ice house and to-night we have ice water. Picked
up a number of Rebel deserters to-day. The woods are full
of them.

Raleigh, N. C., April 14, 1865, 1 p. m.

We passed through town and were reviewed by Sherman,
who stood at the south gate of the State Capitol grounds.
Just as Colonel Wright saluted, his horse turned his heels towards Sherman and did some of the finest kicking that ever

was seen. It was most amusing. Raleigh is a fine old town. Many beautiful residences, and the gardens filled with the choicest shrubbery.

The 14th A. C. guards the place. Wheeler's men sacked it. Division hearquarters received orders to save their rations. What we have is to last 30 days and maybe 40 days. That means a long march, though it is hinted that we do not follow Johnston. Some think we are going into East Tennessee. The citizens of Raleigh generally come to their gates to look at us, but make no demonstrations that I have heard of. The 14th A. C. is protecting them in all their rights. Not a thing disturbed.

High rolling country and large farms. The town is fortified all around, but works were old. I never saw so few negroes in a Southern city. Our headquarter's foragers brought in five Rebel deserters to-night, and five dozen eggs which I think were the most valuable.

Raleigh, April 15, 1865.

To-day makes four years soldiering for me. It is a terrible waste of time for me who have to make a start in life yet, and I expect unfits me for civil life. I have almost a dread of being a citizen, of trying to be sharp, and trying to make money. I don't think I dread the work. I don't remember of shirking any work I ever attempted, but I am sure that civil life will go sorely against the grain for a time. Citizens are not like soldiers, and I like soldier ways much the best. We were to have moved out this morning but did not. Logan went out with our 4th division, report says, to confer with Johnston. Big rumors going that our campaign is over, and that Johnston's men are going home. We have been having heavy showers during the day, but the boys feel so good over the prospect ahead that they raise the most tremendous cheers right in the midst of the hardest rains. We think Johnston is in as tight a place as Lee was, and if he don't surrender we will go for him in a way that will astonish him. We consider our cause gained and are searching each other's records to see who was ever doubtful of success. I don't remember at any time of being despondent over the war or being doubtful of the issue. Was I? I did think the war might last for years yet, but take that back. I have not been in town since we came through, and think no one from the brigade has. Curiosity over captured cities is "old."

Raleigh, April 16, 1865.

Flags of truce are still flying between Sherman and Johnston. The latter is, I believe, some 30 miles west of Hillsboro. Some of Sherman's staff went out last night to offer the same terms that were offered to Lee, and are expected every hour with Johnston's answer. Everybody thinks Johnston will accept and many are offering to bet their all that we will be mustered out by July 4th, 1865.

I am trying to take the matter coolly and determined not to be very much disappointed if the result is different from what we all hope. We will be either ready to march to-morrow morning or to hang our swords on the wall. Hundreds of Johnston's men are coming into our lines. If he don't surrender his men will all desert. A lovely day. Disposes one to peace wonderfully. It is most difficult to realize that our war is over. I do from my heart thank God that I have lived to see the rebellion put down. Anyone who has been with us the last year and is alive *should* be thankful. The whole four years seems to me more like a dream than reality. How anxious I am to shake hands with you all once more. "How are you peace?"

Raleigh, April 17, 1865.

We have a brief dispatch this morning informing us of the assassination of President Lincoln, Secretary Seward and son. I have not the heart to write a word about it. The army is crazy for vengeance. If we make another campaign it will be an awful one. Sherman meets Johnston to-day. The delay in the negotiations was caused by some dispatches being missed. We hope Johnston will not surrender. God pity this country if he retreats or fights us.

24

Raleigh, April 18, 1865.

Sherman has gone out again to see Johnston. Johnston asked for another day in order to see Davis and get his permission to surrender the whole force in arms this side of the Mississippi. I was through the town to-day. Some very fine residences and asylums, but the town is no larger than Canton, and not as pretty except in shrubbery and shade trees.

I visited the Deaf and Dumb and Blind Asylums and the superintendent put a class in each through some exercises. It was very interesting. A *Herald* of the 10th gives us the particulars of Lee's surrender. Grant is the hero of the war. The papers all talk about Grant, Sherman and Sheridan, nothing said about Thomas. This whole army thinks that Thomas is slighted by the North. We have as much confidence in him as in Grant or Sherman, and then he never writes any letters or accepts valuable presents, or figures in any way for citizen approbation, or that of his army. The only objection that I ever heard against him is the size of his headquarters or "Thomasville" as it is called by the army. That comes from his West-Pointism.

Raleigh, April 19, 1865.

Joe Johnston surrendered the whole thing yesterday to Sherman. Our 4th division and a division of the 17th Corps receive the arms, etc. We go into a regular camp to-morrow to await developments. If any more Confederacy crops out, we, I suppose, will go for it, otherwise in a couple of months we'll muster out. That's all. Good bye, war.

Our last march. Near Rolesville, N. C.,

April 29, 1865.

Left Raleigh at 7 this morning on my way home, via Richmond and Washington. Made about 11 miles. Rather too warm for such fast marching as we always do. If we would just make 15 miles a day, say 10 of it between sunrise and 10 a. m., and the remainder after 2 p. m., it would not hurt a man or an animal, but we move when we *do* move at three or three and a half miles an hour, and not all even Sherman's men can stand it in as warm weather as this. I saw a number laid out this morning by the roadside looking as if they had been boiled. The 50 pounds of equipments is what uses them up. Well settled country, and it looks beautiful. The leaves are all out nearly full size; fine oak, elm and pine strips of woodland between farms is such an addition of comfort to citizens and cattle, and of beauty to scenery. The undergrowth is mostly dogwood and holly. We are on our good behavior this trip. No foraging, no bumming rails, or houses, and nothing naughty whatever. We have the best set of men in the world. When it is in order to raise h——they have no equals in destructiveness and ability to hate and worry, or superiors as to fighting Rebels, but now they have none, and they are perfect lambs. Not a hand laid on a rail this evening with intent to burn, not a motion toward a chicken or smoke-house, not a thing in their actions that even a Havelock would object to. They don't pretend to love our "erring brethren" yet, but no conquered foe could ask kinder treatment than all our men seem disposed to give these Rebels. We camped about 3 p. m. in a pretty piece of woods. Artillery has been booming all day at Raleigh.

Sunday, April 30, 1865.

Howardism (and it is a very good kind of ism), allows us to lay still to-day. It is a real Canton 1st of June Sabbath. It rained all night, but the effect is to improve these sandy roads. It will take a good deal more than a week to realize fully that the war is over. No more preparation for a coming campaign, dreaded at first, but soon looked for with feverish eagerness (human nature). No more finding the enemy driving in his skirmishers, developing his line, getting into position, and retiring every night, maybe for a month, after days spent in continuous skirmishing, expecting to be ordered to charge at daybreak. It is all over, thank God, but it seems impossible.

A Philadelphia paper of the 25th (first we have seen since the 21st) astonished us all. It gives us our first intimation of the hue and cry against Sherman, for the terms he offered Johnston, Breckenridge & Co. We did not before know anything he had done, only he told us in orders that he had, "subject to the approval of the powers at Washington, made peace from the Rio Grande to the Potomac, by an agreement with Johnston and other *high officials.*" We have only known that much, talked over the matter and were afraid that "Tecumseh" had made an attempt to do too much, and had compromised himself by having anything at all to do with other than military Rebels. I am very sorry for him, but we have thought for a year, and it has been common talk in the army, that he was ambitious for political honors, etc.

I have often heard it said that he was figuring for popularity in the South. He has written some very pretty letters to our erring Southerners. Instance, the one to the Mayor and citizens of Atlanta and one to Mrs. Bowen of Baltimore, and several more while at Savannah.

He also promised Governor Vance some kind of protection if he would return to Raleigh. "Pap" must be careful. We all think the world of him. I'd rather fight under him than Grant, and in fact if Sherman was Mahomet we'd be as devoted Musselmen as ever followed the former prophet, and if he has blundered here, as they say he has, we will feel it more at heart than we ever did the fall of our leaders before. I won't believe he has made a mistake until I know all about it. *It can't be.*

Near Davis' Cross Roads, five miles north of Tar river.

May 1, 1865, 4:30 p. m.

We are 35 miles from Raleigh to-night, which makes 24 miles to-day over Tar river, which is here about 50 yards wide and runs through a fine rolling, high country. The march was splendidly conducted, no straggling, and the peace orders were faithfully lived up to. It seems like the early days of my soldiering to see the citizens all at home, their horses and mules in the stables, and gardens full of vegetables passed untouched. When a man can pass an onion bed without going for them, and they did a number of them to-day, no one need talk to me of total depravity. The soldier goes more on onions than any other luxury. The citizens have all "war's over" news, and seem to feel good over it. At three different places there were groups of very healthy looking young ladies, well dressed, by the roadside, waving their handkerchiefs at us, and one told the boys she wished them to come back after they were mustered out, for "you have killed all our young men off." The virtuous indignation welled up in my bosom like a new strike of oil. I'll venture that these same women coaxed their beaux off to the war, and now that "Yank" is ahead, they shake their handkerchiefs at us and cry, "bully Yanks." The devil take them and he'll be sure to do it. You have heard of woodticks? The man who don't catch his pint a day is in awful luck. They have a tick picking twice a day in this country, regularly as eating. Saw a wild turnip in bloom to-day.

Two miles north of Shady Grove, N. C.,

May 2, 1865.

Twenty-six miles to-day, and everything in camp at sunset. That is No. 1 work with 300 sets of wheels to the division. We have reveille at 3 a. m. and start at 4 now.

We seem to have got pretty well out of the pine country. Hardly saw one the last three miles this p. m. Have also about left cotton behind us. Tobacco and wheat are *the* staples here. I saw as many as five large tobacco houses on one farm, built 25 logs high. Notice also some very fine wheat growing, now 12 inches high. Very large peach and apple orchards on almost every farm. The trees look thrifty, but show neglect. All kinds of fruit promises to be abundant this year.

The last five miles to-day was through beautiful country, fine houses, too. The people were all out to see us, but I am glad that I have no demonstration a la white handkerchief to chronicle. The men are full of the de'il to-day. Scaring negroes almost out of their wits. Our division is the right of the army. We have been side tracking so far, but to-morrow we get the main road and Corse takes the cow paths. I think that not more than one-fifth of the cleared land so far in this State is under cultivation this year, and that fully one-fourth of all has been turned over to nature for refertilization from four to forty years. On some of this turned out land the new growth is more than a foot in diameter. I saw a sassafras tree to-day that was 15 inches in diameter.

Right Bank Roanoke river, Robbin's Ferry, N. C.

May 3, 1865.

About 20 miles to-day and the latter fourth quite dusty. We did not get the main road, and have depended mainly on hog paths. The Roanoke is the largest stream we have crossed since leaving the Tennessee river, and is quite swift. The water is also colder than any we have found this march. We have not pontoons enough to reach across and will have to press ferryboats and skiffs, etc., to use as pontoons. Presume it will take all night to get up a bridge. We pontooned the Neuse when we crossed it the last time in one and one-half hours. As we crossed the Raleigh and Gorton Railroad to-day, saw a train of cars coming kiting along. Expect communication is open to Raleigh by this time. We are marching too hard. It is using up lots of men. Good country to-day. Many fine houses and every indication of wealth.

Thirteen miles south of Laurenceville, Va.,

May 4, 1865.

Our regiment in advance of the division crossed the Roanoke at 3:30 p. m. and went into camp here at sunset, making 13 miles. We crossed the N. C. and Va. line about three miles this side of the river. Good country, and people all out gazing.

Near Nottaway River, May 5, 1865.

Crossed the Meherrin river (a Copperas creek affair) this morning and pass through Laurenceburg, a 100-year old town, just as large as the top of a very small hill would hold. Such oceans of negroes; never saw half as many before in the same distance in Virginia. Sheridan was through this country ten days ago, but hearing that Johnston had surrendered he turned back. Kautz and Wilson were also raiding last summer, but there are no signs that war is known to the people by experience. We see Lee's and Johnston's men all along the road, taking a look at Sherman's army. All the soldiers and citizens we see seem to submit to the Government, and the war feeling is dead among them, but there is no love for us or ours, and they regard us only as subjugators. That is as warm a sentiment as I ask from them. I believe every family has lost a member by the war. I saw a member of Pickett's Rebel division this evening. He said that when his division surrendered to Grant, they stacked but 45 muskets. It was nearly 10,000 strong on the 24th of March, 1865.

This boy put in one of the 45 muskets. They all give Sheridan's cavalry the credit for doing the best fighting they ever knew "Yanks" to do.

They all speak highly of our 6th (Wright's) corps. The good conduct of our men continues even to the astonishment of the men themselves. I have heard of but one indiscretion, and that was only the carrying off of the table cutlery after dining with a citizen. We are traveling too fast, but our corps commanders are racing to see who will make Petersburg first. Heard of Booth being killed to-day. Also got a *Herald* of the 24th with Sherman and Johnston's peace propositions. We are very much shocked at Sherman's course. I have not heard an officer or soldier who had read them, sustain our general. It is hard on us and we regret his action as much as any calamity of the war, excepting the Washington horror. There isn't an element of man worship in this army, but we all had such confidence in Sherman, and thought it almost impossible for him to make a mistake. The army is very sore over the affair. We can't bear to have anybody say a word against Sherman, but he did act very strangely in this thing.

Left bank of Stony Creek, Va., 20 miles from
Pittsburg,

May 6, 1865.

About 20 good miles to-day. No sign of war yet. Have not had a very good road to-day. Crossed the Nottaway river this morning. Small affair. During Kautz and Wilson's disastrous raid last summer they threw their last piece of artillery into the Nottaway from the bridge on which we crossed. One of the officers says he noticed bullet marks on trees that indicated a pretty sharp skirmish having taken place where we stopped for dinner. We are fairly on classic ground. I hear that the 17th A. C. lost a number of men yesterday by a bridge falling.

Petersburg, Va., May 7, 1865.

Twenty miles to-day, and the longest kind of miles. Had some bad road in the morning. We struck the Weldon railroad two or three miles below Ream's Station, where the 6th Corps was whipped last June, and came right up to the city. Saw hardly any signs of fighting the whole way. Ours and the Rebel works where we came through are fully two and one half miles apart, and the skirmish line further from each other than we ever had ours when we pretended to be near the enemy. I think the whole army is up. Part of it got here last night. We lie here to-morrow. The 17th A. C. goes on to Richmond.

Petersburg, Va., May 8, 1865.

I'll take back all I ever said against the Potomac Army. I have been down to Fort Steadman to-day and troops who will work up to an enemy as they did there, will do anything if handled right. There were some sad sights along that part of the line. Right in front of Steadman 40 or 50 of our men are lying with only a few shovelfuls of dirt thrown over them, their heads and feet exposed. I passed through the Rebel burying ground, quite a large and thickly settled village. Poor fellows. I wish the leaders who led or rather pushed them into these little clay hills were all beside them. This is a nice town, not very pretty though. Good deal of business done. Hundreds of Rebel officers, Lieutenant General Gordon among them, walk the streets in full uniform.

Drury's Bluff, Va., May 9, 1865.

We were reviewed by Howard, Logan and Hartsuff this morning as we passed through Petersburg. We lie to-night along the outer line of Drury's Bluff defenses which Butler took a year ago this month. Signs of a good deal of fighting; good many roads, etc. The James river is about one mile to our right. I have been to some very fine forts. Fort Wagner and Fort Stevens (or Stephens) are the best, on the second and main line of Rebel works, which Butler was working against when the Rebels came out and whipped him. From one fort I saw the spires of Richmond, James river and Shipping, Fort Darling and Fort Harrison. Coming back toward camp we found one of our soldiers unburied in the bushes. His skull was brought in by our hospital steward.

Manchester, Va., May 10, 1865.

The rain yesterday made the road, which is a splendid one fifty yards wide, just right for traveling. We passed through three lines of Drury's Bluff and Fort Darling defenses, and are now at the second and inside line of works for the defense of Richmond. Hostile Yankees never saw either of these two lines at this point, or any other, I guess, *this side* of the James River. It is about

22 miles from Richmond to Petersburg. "Old Brains" (Halleck) issued his proclamation that no soldier or officer of this army should enter Richmond only when we pass through. Howard and Logan say they will pass around if they can. I hope they will.

We have a fine view of Richmond from here. It is situated much like Peoria and Columbia, S. C. The burned district shows very plainly from here and makes the resemblance to Columbia very striking. Several thousand men and officers of the corps made a raid on Logan last night and got a little talk from him. He was very careful not to say too much, all small talk. This got up a real elephant hunting mania, and I guess every regiment commanded in the corps was called out. Colonel Wright had to make a little talk. The 14th and 20th move out to-morrow.

May 11, 1865.

The 14th and 20th crossed the river and went as far as Hanover to-day.

May 12, 1865.

The 17th Corps has the road to-day. Heavy thunder storm last night with a great deal of rain. Four men of our division were killed by lightning about 200 yards from our tent. One of them, William Hall, belonged to Company D of our regiment. Two men were killed in a tent in which were 15, and of the four lying side by side, two were killed.

Can't hear yet for certain when we will be mustered out. We move towards Alexandria to-morrow.

North Bank of Chickahominy River,

May 13, 1865.

We crossed the James river this a. m. Our division, the rear of the corps, paraded a little around Richmond, saw Libby Prison, Castle Thunder, the bronze statue of Washington,

Lee's and Davis' residence, and a number of women. Some handkerchiefs flying. Two women told us they were Yankees and looked so sweet that I (in theory) lifted my hat to them. It always puts me out of humor to see Southern women cheer Yanks in public. We passed through the Rebel works where Kilpatrick made his bold dash in March, '64. We are six or seven miles above Mechanicsville, and McClellan's old battle ground.

Near Hanover, C. H., Va., May 14, 1865.

Only made nine miles to-day on account of the Pamunky river here being bad. We camp to-night in the Hanover "slashes," one mile east of the birthplace of Henry Clay, and about two miles from the residence of Patrick Henry. The court house is where the latter delivered his famous speech against the clergy. Henry's house is built of brick, imported, and was built in 1776. We passed the place where McClellan's famous seven days' fight commenced. The whole country is waste. I hear a country legend here that Clay was the illegitimate son of Patrick Henry. The court house was built in 1735.

South of Bowling Green, Va., May 15, 1865.

Crossed the Pamunky river this morning and the Mattapony this p. m. Beautiful country, but most desolate looking. Stopped at a house for the "cute and original" purpose of asking for a drink of water. While a servant went to the spring had a very interesting chat with the ladies, the first of the sex I have spoken to in Virginia. One of them was quite pleasant. She inquired if we Yankees were really all going to Mexico. Told her "such was the case," when she remarked, "Well, all our men are killed off, and if all you Northerners go to Mexico, we women will have our rights sure."

Heard of Davis' capture. Did not excite an emotion.

Five miles south of Fredericksburg, May 16, 1865.

Our division and brigade in advance of corps to-day. Made 24 miles by 2 p. m. Fences all gone on the road, but houses all standing. From a bluff three miles back had a beautiful view of about 15 miles of the Rappahannock valley and in all that did not see a fence or a cultivated field, or a specimen of either the kine, sheep, or swine families. This certainly does not largely rank the Sahara. Passed through a melancholy looking line of rifle pits, and mentally thanked Heaven for my poor prospect of ever using the like again. Passed through Bowling Green this a. m., only 11 miles from where Booth was killed.

Aquia Creek, Va., May 17, 1865.

We passed over the whole line of Burnside's battle ground this morning. (It was no fight, only a Yankee slaughter.) Through Fredericksburg, the most shelled town I ever saw; crossed the Rappahannock on a miserable shaky pontoon, and have been traveling ever since in the camps of the Potomac Army. Desolation reigns equal to the Sodom and Gomorrah country.

Country much more broken than I supposed; very hot part of the day. One man of the 48th Illinois fell dead while marching, and eight or ten in our regiment badly affected by heat.

Occoquan Creek, May 18, 1865.

Another day's march. Heavy rain and thunder storm commenced ten minutes before our wagons got in, and then the wind blew so hard that we could not get our tent up for an hour, and everybody got thoroughly soaked.

Near Alexandria, Va., May 19, 1865.

Rained all night. Reveille at 2 p. m., and started off before daylight. Men waded two or three creeks to their middles. March miserably conducted. Passed the church that Washington attended, built in 1783. It has nearly all, except roof and walls, been carried away by relic maniacs. Our division marched through Mt. Vernon by the vault and residence.

Thus closes this diary of one of the most memorable year's campaigns in the history of modern times.

We remained in camp between Alexandria and Arlington until the 23d, when we crossed the Potomac river, of which we had heard so much, and the next day (the 24th), participated in the Grand Review of the Grandest Army that ever was created.

FINALE

JOHN Y. SIMON, professor of history at Southern Illinois University at Carbondale, is the editor of *The Papers of Ulysses S. Grant* and a founder of the Association for Documentary Editing. He has published more than sixty articles in such journals as *Military Affairs, Journal of American History, Ohio History, Journal of the Abraham Lincoln Association,* and *Journal of the Illinois State Historical Society.* The editor of *The Personal Memoirs of Julia Dent Grant* and the coeditor of *Ulysses S. Grant: Essays and Documents* and *The Continuing Civil War: Essays in Honor of the Civil War Round Table of Chicago,* Simon has held office in national professional associations and has served as a consultant for federal and state agencies, university and commercial presses, and other editorial projects.